TROUBLED WATERS
THE GEOPOLITICS OF THE CASPIAN REGION

R. Hrair Dekmejian

and

Hovann H. Simonian

I.B.Tauris *Publishers*
LONDON • NEW YORK

Published in 2001 by I.B.Tauris & Co Ltd
6 Salem Road, London W2 4BU
175 Fifth Avenue, New York NY 10010
www.ibtauris.com

In the United States and Canada distributed by
St. Martin's Press, 175 Fifth Avenue, New York NY 10010

Copyright © R. Hrair Dekmejian and Hovann H. Simonian 2001

The right of R. Hrair Dekmejian and Hovann H. Simonian to be identified as the authors of this work has been asserted by the authors in accordance with the Copyright, Designs and Patents Act 1988.

All rights reserved. Except for brief quotations in a review, this book, or any part thereof, may not be reproduced, stored in or introduced into a retrieval system, or transmitted, in any form or by any means, electronic, mechanical, photocopying, recording or otherwise, without the prior written permission of the publisher.

ISBN 186064 6395

A full CIP record for this book is available from the British Library
A full CIP record for this book is available from the Library of Congress

Library of Congress catalog card: available

Typeset in Baskerville 11/12pt by The Midlands Book Typesetting Co, Loughborough
Printed and bound in Great Britain by MPG Books Ltd, Bodmin, Cornwall

Contents

Preface   v

Part One: The Caspian Basin: History, Politics and Resources

1. The Caspian in a Globalized World   3
2. The Caspian in History   10
3. Legal Status and Environmental Issues   19
4. Energy Estimates, Costs and Pipelines   28

Part Two: The Riparian States

5. The Riparian States: Politics and Interests   43
6. The Riparian States: Interstate Relations   74

Part Three: The External Actors

7. The Inner Circle   99
8. The Outer Circle   115
9. America, Europe, Japan and Asia   131
10. Non-State Actors in the Caspian Basin   150
11. The Caspian in the Global Marketplace   167

References   175

Bibliography   215

To our mothers Vahidé and Béatrice

Preface

The advent of a new administration in Washington in 2001 affords an opportunity to take stock of the nature and direction of American foreign policy toward the Caspian region in the light of post-Soviet developments, existing realities and changing circumstances. Without a doubt the basic configuration of the geopolitical, economic and cultural factors described in this book will pose difficult challenges to the Republican-controlled White House. Although it might be reasonable to assume significant continuities in foreign policy, particularly given the salience of the energy issue, the Bush administration may be more reticent than its predecessor in projecting US power into this unstable region. Indeed, the foreign policy team of Richard Cheney, Colin Powell and Condoleezza Rice may well pursue a somewhat different agenda in the Caspian littoral, perhaps one of strategic cooperation with Russia and even accommodation with Iran in the larger Caspian/Central Asian region. It is also possible that the Bush team will be guided by hard calculations of cost-benefit analysis, in which the interests of the oil companies are given precedence over ill-defined US geopolitical interests. Also difficult to gauge is the evolution of European policy toward the Caspian, in view of the diversity of voices within the European Union.

Whatever its contours, there can be no doubt that any changes in US/Western policy would have a lasting impact on the Caspian countries and the major and minor players in the region's affairs. As this book explains, the Caspian states and their immediate neighbours have become heavily dependent on the outside world, particularly the United States and Europe, in both political and economic spheres. Such dependency has left the region's oligarchic regimes at the mercy of Western policymakers.

The primary aim of this book is to depict the plethora of political, economic, legal, cultural and environmental factors shaping the dynamics of the Caspian milieu and its surrounding geopolitical space. The interaction of these factors is analysed in the context of the converging interests of state and non-state actors, seen through the prism of various theories of international relations. The facts, figures and analysis presented here are aimed at a general readership as well as a large coterie of professionals – scholars, policymakers, oil company executives, international bankers, diplomats, journalists and area specialists.

PREFACE

The authors gratefully acknowledge the help of friends and colleagues who directly or indirectly contributed to the completion of this opus. These include Robert Mosley, Irma Valencia, Gregory Dekmejian, Taline Simonian, Vartan Telian, Vartan Taikaldiranian, Marco Denes, Alfred Haft, Dr. Saud Alsati, Asbed Bedrossian, Juliet Ghazarian, Dr Sheldon Kamieniecki, chair of the University of Southern California's (USC) Department of Political Science, Professor Shirin Akiner of the School of Oriental and African Studies (SOAS), London, and Dr Jack Lewis, director of the IBEAR program at USC's Marshall School of Business.

Of course, the ultimate responsibility for the contents remains with the authors.

R. Hrair Dekmejian
Hovann H. Simonian
University of Southern California

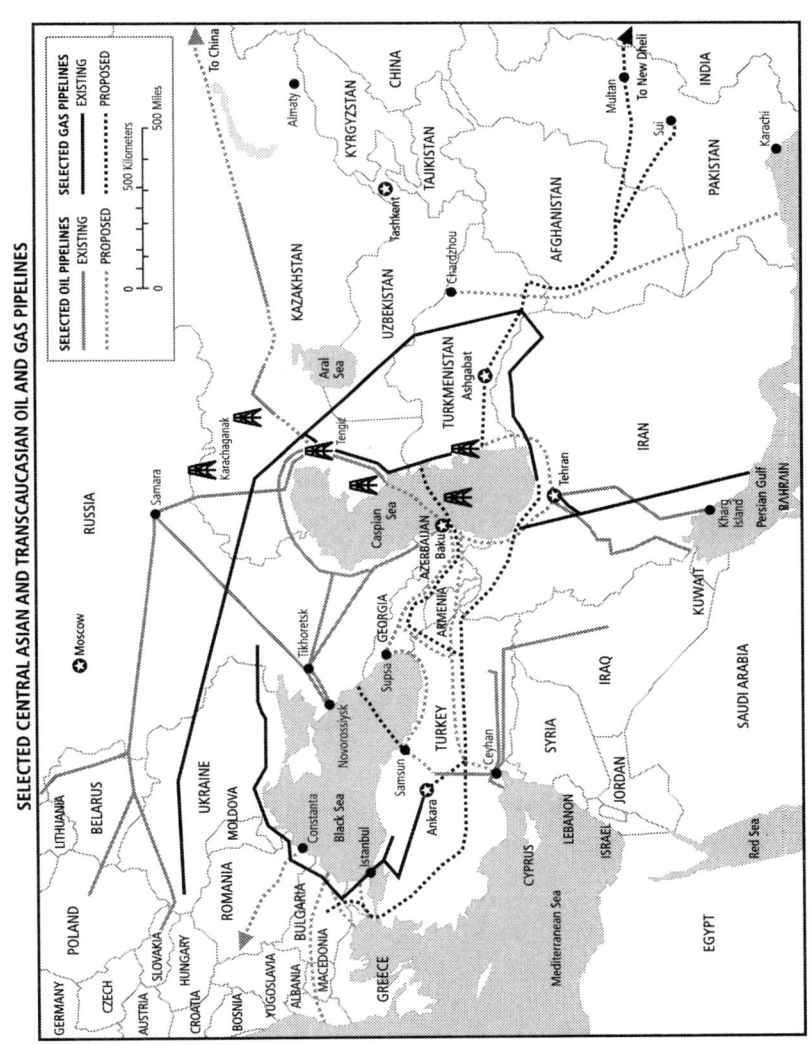

Part One: THE CASPIAN BASIN: HISTORY, POLITICS, AND RESOURCES

CHAPTER 1

The Caspian in a Globalized World

The world's largest inland sea, the Caspian, sits in a region that has been at the confluence of conflicting ethnic, national and international interests since the dismantling of the Soviet Union. This study seeks to identify and analyse the diverse political, economic and social forces converging on the Caspian region, which is broadly defined to include the five riparian states of Azerbaijan, Iran, Turkmenistan, Kazakhstan and Russia, and the adjacent countries of the Caucasus and Central Asia.

Caught in the throes of the restructuring of global power relations after the Soviet demise, the Caspian has emerged as a focus of world attention, reminiscent of the nineteenth century's Great Game between the clashing imperial ambitions of Great Britain and Russia. However, the new Great Game over the Caspian is far more complex than the old in its scope, determinants and implications. To explain the motivations and behavior of the many actors involved in the new Great Game, this study utilizes an eclectic set of theories of international relations. The resulting analysis of facts and figures provides answers to some recurring questions – why did the Caspian become a centre of international attention in the last decade of the twentieth century, and why was it accorded such a prominent position in the crowded policy agendas of the United States and the West? These answers may offer insights into the larger and more controversial discourse about the structure and evolution of the international political system since the Cold War.

In view of the interplay of many dynamic and constant factors in the politics of this oil-rich region, a comprehensive approach has been taken, including a variety of source materials reflecting the diverse perspectives of political actors and non-state interests. Part One details the components of the conceptual framework, the historical background of the Caspian rim, legal and environmental issues, and estimates of energy reserves, production costs and pipeline itineraries. Part Two focuses on the five states of the Caspian littoral, analysing their political systems, economies and interests, and the ten-fold relations among them. Part Three outlines the policies and interests of external actors which influence the politics of the Caspian littoral. These players include the states in the immediate vicinity and the larger periphery of the Caspian, as well as the United States, European countries, Japan and a plethora of non-state actors – ethnic movements, religious activists, criminal groups, entrepreneurs, multinational corporations, international institutions, non-governmental organizations and regional entities. The concluding chapter presents a comparative analysis of the Caspian region within the evolving milieu of globalization, through a risk assessment of its political future and its potential as a source of energy production.

Globalism, regionalism, and localism: an analytical framework

Grand strategists, policymakers and theorists of international relations were all caught unprepared by the Soviet demise and the Cold War's sudden end. Significantly, none of the dominant paradigms of international relations proved capable of predicting these events. In the post-Cold War era, the field of international relations has remained in flux and no dominant theory has emerged to cope with the new realities. Moreover, the task of new theory building has been complicated by the proliferation of ethnic conflicts, the clash of cultures, the growing role of regional associations, the impact of globalization and the communications revolution. Thus, a conceptual framework for the analysis of a region as complex as the Caspian would have to be both theoretically and methodologically eclectic, taking into account the interaction of a plethora of global, regional and local actors and interests.

The precipitous Soviet collapse, followed by the eroding Russian presence, left a power vacuum of major proportions in the Caucasus and Central Asia. Much of the history of the Caspian littoral in the last decade has been marked by the over-zealous and haphazard attempts of rival powers to fill the regional power vacuum amid proliferating ethnic conflicts. As a consequence, major and minor external actors – the United States, Western European states, regional powers, oil companies, international financial institutions and militant religious and nationalist movements – were sucked into the Caspian Basin's rivalries and disputes. In view of the multiplicity of the forces and interests operating in the Caspian region, any framework of analysis should necessarily include theories of geopolitics, balance of power, neorealism, interdependence and culture conflict, as these function within a globalized milieu. Given the growing involvement of external forces and movements in the region, this study will be cast into an overarching globalist framework.

Globalization

As an analytic construct, globalization can be conceptualized along four interacting dimensions, mostly activated by the epicentric role of the United States and other industrial powers. Thus, *political globalization* involves the projection of American power worldwide, as a consequence of the emergence of the United States as the sole global superpower in terms of military might and unrivalled political clout in international affairs. As such, the United States and its allies have sought to project their influence into the Caspian power vacuum in order to stabilize the region as a means of sustaining their political and economic interests. Reinforcing the Western-sponsored scheme of political globalization is *economic globalization*, representing the financial and technological capacity of the industrialized countries and multinational corporations to dominate world economies and markets. Political and economic globalization are accompanied by *cultural globalization*, where Western cultural norms and lifestyles have had a strong impact on the values and cultures of non-Western societies. A primary instrument propelling the dissemination of Western culture into the far reaches of the planet is the expanding networks of *globalized communication.*

Geopolitics

Since its appearance in the writings of Friedrich Ratzel (1844–1904) and Rudolf Kjellen (1864–1922), the importance of geopolitics has fluctuated in response to changing global forces and circumstances. As a subfield of political science and geography, geopolitics focuses on the relationship between territory and power, particularly the influence of geography on state behavior.[1]

The fundamental concern of geopolitics at the height of the imperial age was the struggle between sea and land power, as exemplified by the raging confrontations between Britain and Germany, and Britain and Russia. US Admiral Alfred Thayer Mahan believed in the superiority of sea power over land power, while the British geographer Sir Halford Mackinder saw land power as crucial to determining the outcome of the struggle.[2] Mackinder's geopolitical thought is particularly relevant to the Caspian/Central Asian region, which constituted an integral part of his 'Heartland' theory. He defined the Heartland as the core of the Eurasian landmass, inaccessible by sea, and considered it as the 'pivot' area of world politics. Around the Heartland was the 'inner crescent', consisting of China, India, Turkey and Germany, which was circumscribed by the 'outer crescent' of Britain, Japan and Southern Africa. Hence Mackinder's famous projection:

> Who rules East Europe commands the Heartland
> Who rules the Heartland commands the World Island (Eurasia)
> Who rules the World Island commands the World.[3]

Mackinder's hypothesis gained considerable relevance in the Second World War and the Cold War in the context of the German–Soviet struggle to control the Heartland, followed by the US containment policy toward the USSR. In a later revision of his theory, Mackinder saw the Atlantic Alliance as capable of countering Soviet land power. In a reformulation of Mackinder's theory, Nicholas Spykman (1893–1943) proposed a geopolitical model centered on the 'World Island', comprising the core of the Heartland and the inner crescent, and surrounded by a 'rimland' which coincided with Mackinder's outer crescent. As a realist thinker, Spykman viewed international politics as a struggle for power, in which American and British security necessitated control of the rimland as a means of blocking the expansion of the World Island.[4]

A century after the height of the Great Game between Russia and Britain, which centred on Mackinder's Heartland and inner crescent, a new contest was triggered in the far more complex milieu of the 1990s. Yet, in contrast to the territorial imperative of nineteenth century imperial rivalries, the new Great Game is ostensibly a power struggle for the Heartland's energy resources, which in reality constitute the signposts and stepping-stones of clashing hegemonic interests.

Balance of power and neorealism

Implicit in geopolitical thought are the related theories of balance of power and neorealism. As independent entities, the five states of the Caspian rim, as well as the regional and extraregional powers, can be assumed to pursue their individual self-interests defined in terms of power. In analysing the complex power aggregations and interrelations among the riparian states and the competing external powers, this book utilizes a balance of power approach in the context of neorealist theory. Under neorealism, the behavior of states is governed by the number of actors and the pattern of distribution of power among them – hegemony, bipolarity and multipolarity.[5] Changes at the state level will lead to a disruption of the system until a new equilibrium is established. In the present state of flux since the Soviet collapse, the Caspian region may be viewed as being in need of a new equilibrium of power.

Neoliberalism

In view of the realities of the Caspian and its periphery, theories of geopolitics and power need to be augmented by neoliberalism. The dramatic growth of transnational economic and social exchanges has had a significant impact on the power relations between states. Neoliberal theory underlines the complex interdependence that exists among nations in the flow of trade, finance and technology, as well as in the rise of supranational associations and multinational corporations. Thus, the higher the level of interdependence, the lower the likelihood of interstate conflict.[6] In the Caspian region, where energy resources are a principal object of international interest, neoliberal theory is particularly appropriate. This is because the exploitation of these resources requires close cooperation between the Caspian states and external state and non-state actors, such as banks and multinational companies. Consequently, increasing interdependence among these states, and between them and the outside world, is likely to promote regional harmony.

Irredentism and Kultur Kampf

The usefulness of any analytic framework to disentangle the Caspian knot will be limited if it does not take into account the destabilizing impact of the multiple irredentist claims, ethno-nationalist movements and civilizational conflicts which are endemic to the region. Significantly, every one of the riparian states and adjacent countries is beset by ongoing or potential ethnic conflicts, some of which possess an irredentist dimension involving territorial disputes with neighboring states. These micro-level ethnic conflicts are often exacerbated by what Samuel Huntington calls 'the clash of civilizations'. In Huntington's formulation, geopolitical fault lines coincide with the frontiers of clashing civilizations, i.e., Western, Confucian, Japanese, Islamic, Hindu, Slavic-Orthodox, Latin American and, possibly, African.[7] Viewed from this perspective, the Caspian landmass is located at the confluence of three competing civilizations – Islamic, Western and Slavic-Orthodox – a factor contributing to the region's instability.

Four levels of analysis

The foregoing conceptual framework may be applied to the Caspian context at four interrelated levels of analysis defined by the prevailing conditions in the region. At the micro-level, Caspian societies are a mosaic of heterogeneous communities divided by tribe, language, religion and historical memory. Such divisions often trigger conflicts at the subnational level, some of which have national and international implications. The second level of analysis focuses on state-to-state relations among the five core countries of the Caspian littoral. The third level encompasses the states located in the immediate and near periphery of the Caspian region and their relations with the Caspian riparian countries. The fourth level highlights the intrusion of extra-regional powers, multinational corporations and financial institutions, religious movements and non-governmental organizations.

These four foci of inquiry, reflecting four levels of political interaction among major and minor actors in the Caspian arena, are identified in Figure 1.

In order to understand the dynamic confluence of the actors in today's Caspian milieu, it is necessary to provide an overview of the region's history, an assessment of its energy resources, a brief analysis of the Sea's legal and environmental status, and a depiction of the network of existing and proposed pipelines to transport oil and gas from the area.

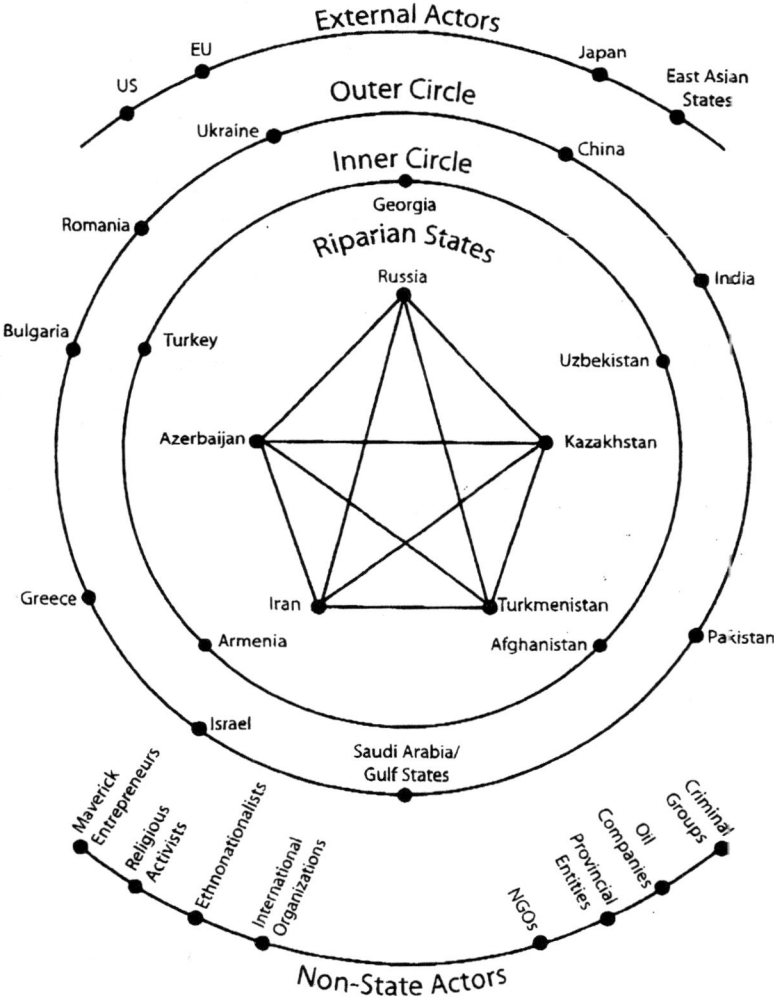

Figure 1. The Caspian Environment

CHAPTER 2

The Caspian in History

Since early times, the region surrounding the Caspian Sea has been a crossroads of cultures and civilizations and the focus of competing imperial ambitions. Throughout history, the region has had a high degree of tribal, religious, and ethnic heterogeneity. The lands at the northern and southern peripheries of the Caspian served as invasion routes for Central Asian nomadic empires expanding westward. After the Arab conquest, Persian Zoroastrianism was displaced by Islam; and in the sixteenth century the southern reaches of the Caspian were contested by the Shi'ite Persian and the Sunni Ottoman empires. The northern shores were dominated by numerous tribes and khanates, soon to be overcome by Russian power.

Russia and the Caspian

The Russian armies reached the northern shores of the Caspian following the conquest of Kazan in 1552. Astrakhan, located at the mouth of the Volga river, was occupied in 1556, followed by Russia's inexorable advance southward on both the western and eastern shores of the sea, culminating some three centuries later in the formation of the Trans–Caspian Oblast. The main victims of Russia's imperial ambitions were the region's indigenous peoples, their rulers, and the Persian empire, which dominated most of present-day Transcaucasia. With the exception of a small strip of Persian coastline in the south, the Caspian became a Russian, then Soviet, mare nostrum.

Russia's southward expansion was perceived as a threat to British control of India. Although British anxieties were first provoked by Peter the Great's moves into Central Asia, only in the nineteenth century did the Russo–British rivalry intensify, prompting Rudyard Kipling's famous reference to the conflict as the Great Game. The construction of a Russian railway network, the Trans–Caspian, alarmed the British, who had not built railways in their Indian dominions. It was the threat posed by the Russian rail network that inspired Sir Halford Mackinder's formulation of the Heartland theory.[1]

The vast expanse of territory occupied by Russia during the nineteenth century contained a highly diverse population of tribes and ethno-religious communities which had not been affected by European ideas of nationalism and modernity. While much of the conquered population was Muslim, there were differences in degree of attachment to Islamic orthodoxy. The Muslim population included both Sunnis and Shi'ites, as well as powerful Sufi movements. Within these groups tribal loyalties were paramount, along with dynastic allegiances to Gengiskhanid princes among the Kazakhs, and to the emirs and khans of Bukhara and Khiva.

Superimposed over this regional, tribal and sectarian mosaic were three emerging movements – Jadidism, Pan-Islamism and Pan-Turkism – which developed in response to the Russian conquest. Jadidism was a movement of societal renewal focused on educational and cultural reform, that later assumed a political dimension. Under the impact of external influences, the twin movements of Pan-Islamism and Pan-Turkism evolved out of Jadidism. Pan-Islamism represented an ideology of Islamic revival and political unity among Muslim peoples. In contrast, Pan-Turkism was a more secularist movement, seeking to unite all Turkic-speaking peoples around a rediscovered common cultural identity.

After the mid-nineteenth century, two ideologies imported from Europe made their appearance in the Caspian littoral – nationalism and socialism. The first nationalists were the Armenians and Georgians, who as Christians had had closer contact with Europe than the Muslims. Consequently, the consolidation of a sense of Armenian and Georgian national identity preceded that of their Muslim neighbors. The process of national identity formation among the Kazakhs and the Turkic peoples of the eastern Caucasus (present-day Azeris) remained nascent until the time of the Russian Revolution. Meanwhile, socialism appeared in the region, particularly among intellectuals and Baku's cosmopolitan oil proletariat. Two political manifestations of Muslim regional nationalism were the Turkestan unity scheme encouraged by the Emir of Bukhara, and the attempt to establish a North Caucasian confederation, which was crushed by General Denikin's White Russian forces and later the Red Army.

In the aftermath of the Russian Revolution, chaos prevailed in the Caspian region, marked by the Russian civil war, localized attempts at independence and interventionism by Ottoman Turkey,

Germany and Britain. In January 1918, a Transcaucasian Federation, the Seim, was constituted by the Armenians, Georgians and Turkic Muslims of the southern Caucasus, while a cadre of Bolsheviks established the Baku Commune, which held the city until its demise in late July 1918 at the hands of an anti-Bolshevik coalition supported by Britain. In mid-September, the city was taken by the combined forces of the Azeri Musavat regime and the Ottoman Turkish armies, pursuing Pan-Turanist aspirations and control over Baku oil. External pressures and internal bickering caused the breakup of the Transcaucasian Seim, resulting in the creation in May 1918 of the independent republics of Armenia, Azerbaijan and Georgia. Upon independence, Georgia was granted German protection, while Azerbaijan remained an ally of Turkey. German and Turkish troops withdrew at the end of the First World War, as British troops re-entered the region amid fighting between Armenia and Azerbaijan and Armenia and Georgia. After the consolidation of Bolshevik power in Russia, the Red Army occupied Azerbaijan in April–May 1920, while the resurgent Turkish Kemalist forces occupied the western part of the Armenian Republic in September–October of that year. A truncated Armenia was Sovietized in November 1920, followed by the Sovietization of Georgia in February–March 1921.

Unlike the situation in Transcaucasia, the Bolsheviks succeeded in retaining control over parts of Central Asia during the civil war years. The Red Army easily subdued nascent nationalist movements among Turkmen and Kazakhs and defeated the White Russian forces, prompting the withdrawal of the British expeditionary army in February 1919 from the Trans-Caspian region. Further east, the Bolsheviks took Khiva in February and Bukhara in September 1920, as a prelude to confronting the proliferating Basmachi guerilla bands. In November 1921, Enver Pasha, the former war minister of Ottoman Turkey, joined the Basmachi movement in a bid to mobilize a Pan-Turkist insurrection in the heart of Central Asia. This last challenge to Bolshevik power ended with Enver's defeat and death in April 1922 and the eradication of the Basmachi movement by the end of the decade.

With the creation of the Soviet Union, the territories inhabited by the non-Russian nationalities were divided into a series of union republics, autonomous republics and autonomous regions, within which indigenous cultures were permitted to prevail thereby reinforcing existing ethnic identities. The national territorial entities created by the Soviets became the crucibles of nation building in the

Muslim-populated rim of the Caspian, where such entities never existed. Because most of these republics were more the product of Soviet national engineering than of deeply rooted traditional identities, the process of nation building remained incomplete. Moreover, the existing multicultural mosaic, combined with Soviet territorial gerrymandering, left minorities in virtually every republic, setting the stage for divided political loyalties and ethno-territorial conflicts.

The oil fields of Baku became a magnet for the warring powers in the Second World War, when the German armies, which suffered chronically from petroleum shortages, sought to conquer the region. A tragic event was Stalin's deportation of several national minorities from the North Caucasus to Central Asia in 1944, for their alleged collaboration with the Germans who had briefly occupied the region. Unlike the Crimean Tatars or the Meskhetian Turks, the deported North Caucasian ethnic groups were later allowed to return to their homelands under Khrushchev, although some found their homes occupied by others, thus laying the basis for inter-ethnic conflicts after the Soviet demise. The resentment of the deported peoples because of their mistreatment became a fundamental part of their national consciousness, and determined much of their later attitude toward Moscow.

Iran and the Caspian

The Russian conquests of the first half of the nineteenth century left Iran with a reduced Caspian coastline. Moreover, Persia entered a long period of decline and owed its survival to the rivalry between Britain and Russia, which preferred to maintain it as an independent but weak buffer state separating their dominions. Attempts at military, political and economic reform either remained stillborn or ended in failure. Central authorities in Tehran had little control over the provinces, where power was concentrated in the hands of local governors and tribal chieftains. Both international and domestic contacts were impeded by the lack of modern means of transport and communication. Persia's northern territories enjoyed some economic progress, because the Caspian provinces of Gilan and Mazanderan were able to trade with Russia by sea, and Azerbaijan and Khorasan had some access to Russia's railway network.

However, Russia was not interested in the modernization of Persia, and dramatically increased its involvement in that country after the Constitutional Revolution of 1906 by occupying the province of Azerbaijan and other northern territories. Meanwhile, Britain introduced its own troops into southern Persia, which resulted in the effective partition of the country into British and Russian spheres of influence lasting until the First World War. A virtually powerless Persian government saw the country transformed into a battlefield during the war, with Ottoman troops invading Persian Azerbaijan and battling Russian forces stationed there. The Russian Revolution added to the chaos, as autonomist movements emerged in the provinces of Gilan and Azerbaijan following the withdrawal of Russian troops after the Bolshevik takeover.

The strategic importance of Persia received a powerful boost from the discovery of important oil reserves in the southern part of the country. Oil was destined to shape Iran's internal and external affairs, strengthening its strategic position and accelerating its transition into the twentieth century. In 1901, Muzaffar al-Din Shah had granted the British the first Persian oil concession for a 60-year period, covering most of the country with the exception of the provinces bordering Russia.[2] As early as 1888, it had been hoped that oil would strengthen Persia, as well as reduce world dependency on Russian oil.[3] Notably, a large number of the first workers in the Persian petroleum industry were brought in from the Baku oil fields.

After overthrowing the Qajar dynasty, Colonel Reza Khan proclaimed himself Reza Shah in 1925 and presided over the consolidation and modernization of the country, which he renamed Iran. In order to counter British and Russian pressures, Reza Shah effected a rapprochement with Nazi Germany, which he saw as a powerful model of nation building. His importation of several thousand German advisers constituted a threat to the Allies facing Hitler's victorious armies at the onset of the Second World War. The Allied forces invaded Iran in August 1941, forcing Reza Shah to abdicate in favour of his son Muhammad Reza, and dividing the country into two spheres of influence, reminiscent of 1908. The northern provinces were occupied by the Soviets, while Britain retained control of the south. In the Soviet zone of occupation, two ethno-secessionist entities were established – an autonomous government of Azerbaijan (December 1945) and the Kurdish Republic of Mahabad (January 1946). Strong pressure by the Truman administration prompted a Soviet withdrawal in May 1946 and the subsequent demise of the Azeri and Kurdish regimes in December 1946.

The onset of the Cold War brought an expansion of US influence in Iranian affairs, driven by the country's oil wealth and strategic position as an anchor of the containment policy toward the

USSR. On the domestic front, Iran was convulsed by the rise of powerful nationalist currents, along with the activism of Islamic groups and the Communist Tudeh party. The nationalist upsurge, primarily directed against Britain, culminated in the passing of a law by the Majlis in March 1951 to nationalize the oil industry. This was implemented by Prime Minister Muhammad Musaddiq, triggering deep concern in American and British government and business circles. Dr Musaddiq's aims were to take control of the British-run Anglo–Iranian Oil Company (AIOC) and to weaken the power of the pro-Western Shah. After two years of domestic conflict and confrontation with Britain, the Musaddiq regime was overthrown in a US–British sponsored coup with the help of the Iranian military.

Strengthened by his alliance with the United States and enriched by the exponential growth of oil revenues, the Shah presided over Iran's rapid economic development and rising military stature in the Middle East. His authoritarian rule, amid pervasive government corruption and mismanagement, and the unfulfilled aspirations of large segments of the population, led to mass unrest and revolutionary ferment. The monarchical regime collapsed after the Shah's departure on 16 January 1979, followed by the proclamation of an Islamic Republic in March 1979 by Ayatollah Ruhallah Khomeini, who emerged as the supreme leader of the revolutionary regime.

The oil boom

The full geopolitical implications of a new factor – petroleum – were not acknowledged by Great Game analysts of the nineteenth century. As an industry, oil production had started in the Baku area in 1848, and slowly developed in the following decades.[4] Until 1872, the oil industry of the Apsheron Peninsula functioned as a monopoly under which the Russian government leased to a single contractor, usually of Armenian origin (such as Ter-Gukasov and Mirzoev), all of the region's oil fields for four-year periods. This system was blamed for hindering oil production because the concessionaire had no incentive to invest large amounts of money, given the short period of the contract, and preferred to maximize production with minimum expense. The monopoly was finally abolished in 1873 and oil-bearing Crown properties were leased for a minimum duration of 24 years to the highest bidders. While production was thus stimulated, the refining industry became burdened by an excise tax, which was finally abolished in 1877, opening the way for the expansion of the oil industry. Oil production, which had increased from 3,500 tonnes per year in 1840 to 24,000 tonnes in 1871, had reached 2,500,000 tons by 1888.[5]

The Russian oil industry owed a great debt to the Nobel brothers from Sweden, Robert and Ludwig, who settled in Baku in 1873 and introduced new techniques of extraction, refining and transport, as well as modern methods of financing and management.[6] The Nobels soon came to dominate the Baku oil industry. In 1891, the prestigious French *Revue des Deux Mondes* published an article entitled 'La Péninsule d'Apchéron et le Pétrole Russe', which forecast Russian domination of world oil production.[7] This prediction would soon prove true, and its author, a 20-year old Istanbul Armenian by the name of Calouste Gulbenkian, would later make a fortune in the oil business and become famous as Mr Five Per Cent.

By the turn of the century, Baku oil production represented half of the world's oil output and dominated international markets. Oil became, after cereals and timber, the third largest Russian export and a major source of income for the Russian government. However, the high taxes that Russian authorities imposed on the oil industry proved to be the largest impediment to its development. In addition to these taxes, the industry was plagued by lack of modern drilling and refining techniques, poor storage facilities resulting in massive losses, rapid exhaustion of reserves due to anarchic exploitation, political instability and labor unrest which led to the Baku oil crisis of 1903, marked by a significant decline in production and loss of international market share.[8] The situation was further exacerbated by the Revolution of 1905 and ensuing communal clashes between Armenians and Tatars (present-day Azeris), resulting in widespread destruction of oil installations.

The development of the Caspian oil industry required foreign capital, mostly supplied by Great Britain, and the export of a significant share of production. Oil was exported from the Black Sea port of Batum, which was linked to Baku by a railway constructed in 1883 with funding from the French Rothschilds, and later by a pipeline built between 1897 and 1905. The prohibitive tariffs for the use of the pipeline, however, discouraged exports and pushed producers to sell on the internal Russian market.[9] In addition to the Apsheron Peninsula, oil was discovered in Grozny in 1893, as well as around Telavi in eastern Georgia, in the Kuban and Terek regions, near Batum and in other areas of the Caucasus.[10]

On the eastern side of the Caspian, oil production had started during the Tsarist regime, but on a more modest scale than in Baku. In the territory of present-day Kazakhstan, the Dossor and Makat fields, located in the Emba district of the Atyrau (formerly Guriev) Oblast, were developed in 1911 and 1915 respectively, while Turkmen oil production began in 1900 in the Cheleken field. In 1885, some small fields came into operation in the Ferghana valley, located in present-day Uzbekistan.[11]

After the Russian Revolution, the Baku petroleum industry kept its dominant position. Sixty percent of Soviet needs in 1931, and 80 percent in 1940 were supplied by the Baku fields. Gradually, however, a decline set in, perhaps due to the Soviet decision to invest in the strategically safer fields of the Urals-Volga and western Siberia.[12] In an effort to boost production, the Soviets built a 48-mile offshore platform in 1949. This massive engineering project to exploit the Neft Dashlary (Neftyaniye Kamni) field was a considerable technological feat.[13] Yet, this and other offshore projects could not stem the decline in Azeri oil production. Recently, a Western analyst has argued that 'the Soviet regime deliberately prevented the Caspian region's energy resources from being developed, and deprived Azerbaijan, Kazakhstan, and Turkmenistan of the opportunity to reach for substantially higher standards of living'.[14] More simply, the reduction of Azerbaijani oil production, despite the increase in offshore exploitation in the 1940s and 1950s,[15] could be attributed to lack of funding and adequate technology to exploit fields more difficult to access. Moreover, the decline in oil production was compensated by the development of a petrochemical industry and the manufacturing of drilling equipment, with Azerbaijan controlling 60 percent of the Soviet output by the 1980s. During that same period, oil from Azerbaijan accounted for only 3 percent of total Soviet oil production.[16]

While production was declining in Azerbaijan, especially in the 1970s, it was rising in Kazakhstan, another Soviet republic of the Caspian littoral. Kazakh oil production more than doubled between 1970 and 1990, while gas production quadrupled during the same period. Turkmen oil production was reduced by two thirds, but gas output increased almost sevenfold. Thus, in 1991, in the last year of the Soviet Union, Azerbaijan's oil production stood at 234,000 barrels per day (b/d) Kazakhstan's at 532,000 b/d, Turkmenistan's at 108,000 b/d, and Uzbekistan's at 57,000 b/d.[17] Russian production in the North Caucasus area, adjacent to the Caspian, was 134,000 b/d. These numbers, added up, represented some 10 percent of total Soviet oil production[18] and a modest 1.64 percent of world production.[19] Of a total Soviet gas production of 642 billion cubic metres (bcm) in 1991, 147.3 bcm came from the Caspian riparian and adjacent regions, with the following distribution: 84.3 bcm for Turkmenistan, 41.9 bcm for Uzbekistan, 8 bcm for Azerbaijan, 7.9 bcm for Kazakhstan and 5.2 bcm for the North Caucasus. The contribution of the Caspian area to world gas production was 7 percent, much higher than the Caspian share of total world oil output.[20]

The tumultuous historical legacy of the Caspian region would weigh heavily on the fate of the nascent independent states emerging from the ruins of the Soviet Union. The factors shaping the conflictual past – imperial rivalries, ethnic nationalisms, economic inequities, religious and civilizational antagonisms and competing ideologies – still plague the region and its unfortunate inhabitants, for whom oil wealth has proven to be a mixed blessing at best and a curse at worst.

CHAPTER 3

Legal Status and Environmental Issues

An S-shaped body of water, the Caspian Sea measures 1,200 km from north to south with an average width of 320 km. Covering an immense area of about 386,400 square km, the Caspian is the world's largest inland sea, located between the Caucasus Mountains and the vast flat lands of Central Asia. The northern, middle and southern sections of the Caspian vary in climate, salinity and physical features. The northern section is in a moderate continental climate, while the middle and southern areas are in a warmer climatic zone. As the repository of three major rivers – the Volga, Ural and Terek – the shallow waters of the northern Caspian have low levels of salinity, in contrast to the deeper and highly saline waters of the middle and southern sections. In terms of its rich biodiversity of animal and plant life and overall oceanographic characteristics, the Caspian is more of a sea than a lake.

Two distinct but interrelated issues affecting the politics of the Caspian states are the legal status of the Caspian as a body of water and the environmental problems of the sea and its littoral. Since the dissolution of the USSR, the five riparian states have engaged in ongoing controversies on the status of the Caspian under international law, concerning their respective control of the resources of the seabed, as well as sovereignty over the sea's surface and the waters below it. Although these controversies have included environmental issues, the riparian states have subsumed such concerns under their political and economic interests, despite the worsening ecological conditions in and around the beleaguered sea.

Legal Status

The international legal status of the Caspian has been left undetermined because of the peculiarity of its geographic location and the clashing geopolitical and economic interests of the riparian states. Indeed, the question of legal status was not a major issue during the Soviet period, because, with the exception of Iran, the Caspian was practically a Soviet lake. The situation became complicated after 1991, when four independent states and Iran began to contest control over the mineral wealth of the Caspian. Of lesser importance is the division of the Russian Federation's Caspian coastline between the Astrakhan Oblast, and the Daghestan and Kalmykia autonomous republics, the interests of which affect Russian policy.

The controversy over the Caspian's legal status was triggered when in January 1994 Russia protested Azeri and Turkmen attempts to unilaterally set sea boundaries, and contested the signing of the 'Contract of the Century' in September between Azerbaijan and a consortium of Western oil companies. There are principally two opposing views on sovereignty over the Caspian – division of the basin among the riparian states, or sharing the sea as their common property and, as such, making it subject to their joint sovereignty.

The 1729 Treaty of Rasht between the Persian and Russian empires was the first to deal with the sovereignty issues of the Caspian. Having defeated Persia in two successive wars, Russia received, by the treaties of Gulistan (1813) and Turkmenchai (1828), the exclusive right to maintain a military navy, while both Persian and Russian commercial fleets were guaranteed freedom of navigation and equal rights. None of these treaties traced a boundary in the Caspian. Both treaties were abolished following the Russian Revolution and replaced by a new set of treaties signed in 1921, 1935 and 1940, which established the legal regime governing the Caspian until the Soviet dissolution. These new agreements restored equality between the two sides by allowing Iran to maintain warships in the Caspian. The commercial and military vessels of third countries were forbidden; moreover, their nationals were not allowed employment in vessels or port installations. With the exception of an exclusive zone of ten nautical miles in coastal waters, freedom of fishing was granted to both countries. The treaties did not make mention of other resources found in the sea.[1]

The replacement of the Soviet Union by Azerbaijan, Kazakhstan, the Russian Federation and Turkmenistan created a quagmire of legal problems. Since the texts of the 1921 and 1940 treaties were concerned only with fishing issues and the exclusion of third parties from the Caspian, there has been no agreement as to whether the pre-1991 regime was equivalent to an Iranian–Soviet condominium over the Caspian.[2] In addition to the uncertainty about the nature of the former regime, there is also doubt as to whether Azerbaijan, Kazakhstan and Turkmenistan can be considered successor states of the Soviet Union under the terms of the 1978 Vienna Convention on Succession of States; thus far only the Russian Federation has been generally regarded as having the status of a successor state.[3] However, even if Azerbaijan, Kazakhstan and Turkmenistan are not considered successor states, they are still bound to the regime established by the 1921 and 1940 Soviet–Iranian treaties, in accordance with the Vienna Convention.[4]

A primary issue in establishing a new regime is whether the Caspian, as a body of water, should be considered a 'sea' or a 'lake' under international law. Indeed, the legal status of enclosed bodies of water, such as the Caspian or the Dead Sea, has been a subject of considerable debate among scholars of international law. While the 1982 Convention on the Law of the Sea (UNCLOS) provided a general definition of 'enclosed seas' in Articles 122 and 123, it failed to mention the Caspian.[5] Article 122 of UNCLOS states that

> enclosed or semi-enclosed sea means a gulf, basin or sea surrounded by two or more states and connected to another sea or the ocean by a narrow outlet or consisting entirely or primarily of the territorial seas and exclusive economic zones of two or more coastal states.

Article 123 is simply an invitation to states bordering such enclosed seas 'to cooperate with each other in the exercise of their rights and in the performance of their duties under this convention.' The vagueness of Articles 122 and 123 has fuelled the current controversy among Caspian riparian states and international legal scholars. Vinogradov and Wouters believe that the Caspian and Aral Seas cannot be classified as enclosed seas because they do not have any connection with other seas or with the ocean. While agreeing with the preceding formulation, Pratt and Schofield assert that the second half of Article 122 allows the Caspian to qualify as an enclosed sea.[6] In a strictly geographical sense, the Caspian is connected to other bodies of water – the Black Sea, the Baltic Sea and the White Sea. However, the Caspian's linkages with these bodies of water are through a complex and long network of lakes, rivers and man-made canals,[7] factors not covered in detail in Article 122. One has to agree with Allonsius that the poor formulation of Article 122 allows maritime states to interpret its provisions to fit their individual interests.[8]

Should the Caspian be considered a sea and become subject to the 1982 Convention on the Law of the Sea, its delimitation would follow the universal rules that apply to open seas, as the Convention did not establish any specific delimitation regime for enclosed seas. In accordance with these rules, the riparian states of the Caspian Basin would be entitled to extend their sovereignty over the *internal waters* and *territorial sea*, of a distance up to 12 nautical miles (nm) from the coast. Their rights beyond the 12 nm, known as the *contiguous zone*, which runs up to 24 nm from the coast, would be limited to police, customs, fiscal, immigration or sanitary functions, which would help them prevent or repress violations of their laws within their territory and territorial sea. They would then have sovereign rights – but not absolute sovereignty – over an area of up to 200 nm of the *continental shelf*, and even up to 350 nm depending on the physical configuration of the continental shelf, and over the *exclusive economic zone* of up to 200 nm as well. Given that the Caspian's width is far less than 400 nautical miles, no part of its expanse would be considered as *High Seas*, and the littoral states' exclusive economic zones and continental shelf will fall short of the 200 nautical miles limit. Instead, the Caspian states, in accordance with the Convention, will have to cooperate to achieve an equitable agreement. If the median line method is adopted, the border lines of the exclusive economic zones and of the portions of the continental shelf would be identical, but other delimitation rules could be applied, resulting in different boundary lines for each zone.[9]

Should the opposite view prevail, and the Caspian as a land-locked body of water be treated as a lake, its riparian states would not find specific guidance in positive international law, given the absence of a treaty or convention for lakes.[10] The riparian countries could turn to state practice, which in most cases has subjected frontier lakes to delimitation, but they would remain free to choose the status known as joint sovereignty or condominium, or to opt in favour of a sui generis status possibly combining national sectors with an area held in common. If the first choice prevails and the Caspian is divided into national sectors, then the respective states would be able to exercise greater control over their segments than if the Caspian was considered a sea and divided accordingly, because states enjoy absolute sovereignty over lakes, but only limited sovereign rights over most of their sea sectors.[11] Frontier lakes are usually divided along the median line, but in the case of special circumstances, other criteria might apply to reach more equitable results.[12]

A less consequential issue is the status of the Volga delta, involving Kazakhstan and Russia. Because the Akhtuba river is located at the Kazakh–Russian frontier and is connected laterally to the Volga, under international law the two rivers may be regarded as part of a single waterway complex. By extension, the whole Volga-Baltic system would receive international status, which would accord Kazakhstan and other states freedom of navigation up to the Baltic Sea and thereby diminish Russian sovereignty over the Volga and its control over access to the Caspian. However, it is unclear whether the international agreements regarding navigable rivers actually cover lateral canals such as the ones linking the Akhtuba and the Volga. Also, it must be noted that the Volga-Don and Volga-Baltic canals would become international waterways should the Caspian be considered a sea.[13]

Clearly, in view of the exceptional situation of the Caspian, the littoral states may agree upon a sui generis legal status, as was done in the past by Russia and Iran.[14] Naturally, all states use the issue of legal status as a weapon to maximize their political and economic objectives. Traditionally, Russia and Iran opposed sectoral division of the sea, as their respective areas were believed to contain limited energy reserves, while the other riparian states favoured such delimitation as would have allowed exploitation of their potentially rich resources.

The position of all five states, however, has varied over the years while numerous meetings have taken place to resolve the legal status issue, to no avail. At the November 1996 meeting of Caspian foreign ministers held in Ashghabad, each state came with a different proposal for the size of their exclusive economic zones. Iran suggested ten miles, Russia 20, Turkmenistan 60 and Kazakhstan 80, while Azerbaijan still insisted on a division of the whole sea into sectors. Although no final accord was reached, Iran, Kazakhstan, Russia and Turkmenistan seemed to agree on a compromise which could provide the basis for an ultimate settlement. The agreement established a working group to develop a convention on the status of the Caspian, and Russia displayed a willingness to recognize jurisdiction up to 45 miles, while the central part of the Caspian would be exploited in common by all riparian states. Russia even stated that it would recognize ownership of fields located in the central zone if drilling had already started or was about to start.[15] However, at the February 1997 Almaty Summit of Central Asian leaders, Kazakhstan and Turkmenistan supported the temporary division of the entire sea into national sectors and signed an agreement affirming the rights of riparian states to exploit the seabed.[16] More recently, there is a tendency to accept the division of the sea – or at least of its seabed – into national sectors, although the boundaries of each sector remain in dispute. A case in point was the July 1998 Russo–Kazakh accord dividing the northern part of the Caspian seabed and its resources.[17] In July 2000, a Russian special envoy toured the Caspian capitals with a proposal to divide the seabed into national sectors and split disputed oil fields between claimants, displaying a new flexibility dictated by the common need to solve legal issues with finality.[18]

Oil vs. caviar

The controversies over legal status, combined with political instability and economic decline experienced by the riparian states, have exacerbated the environmental degradation of the sea. Soviet policymakers were impervious to environmental concerns, and large expanses of their territory were affected by severe environmental problems. As a result, stretches on the eastern and western shores of the Caspian and vast areas of Central Asia became some of the most environmentally devastated regions of the Soviet Union.

To be fair to the Soviet legacy, it must be noted that Baku and the Apsheron Peninsula had started to suffer from serious pollution problems since the first days of oil development in the 1870s. In his book on Baku, J.D.Henry reports how huge quantities of oil and chemical products used in the refining process ended up either in the soil around the oilfields of the Apsheron Peninsula, destroying all vegetation there, or in the Caspian Sea. Acid or soda dregs from the oil installations formed pools in streets, while oil lakes appeared in places where the soil was unable to absorb additional quantities of oil.[19] Sanitary conditions were poor and life expectancy among oil workers was short.

Despite Soviet propaganda claiming improvement of sanitary conditions in Baku, urbanization and industrialization caused significant environmental degradation, especially since the 1950s. While existing cities continued to grow, new industrial urban centres were established along the Kazakh and Azerbaijani coastlines. Beginning in the 1930s, the sea level started to decline, dropping by 3.3 metres until 1977, when it reached its lowest point.[20] The lands exposed by the ebb of the sea were put to use for settlement or cultivation, thereby contributing to the Caspian's degradation. Indeed, during the Soviet era, the Caspian became a dump for the human, agricultural and industrial wastes of the sea's immediate littoral, and those of distant regions located along the rivers flowing to the sea, such as the Volga, the Ural and the Kura.

The statistics on the Caspian's environmental crisis are compelling.

The Volga, which supplies 80 percent of the sea's inflow, brought in the 1980s a yearly average of 367,000 tonnes of organic materials, 13,000 tonnes of petroleum waste, 45,000 tonnes of nitrogen and 20,000 tonnes of phosphorus.[21] In the same period, a yearly average of 3,500 tonnes of oil, 2 million tonnes of sulphates, and 580,000 tonnes of nitrates found their way to the sea. Beyond the spoilage caused by oil exploitation, the chemical industry in Sumgait has been a primary source of pollution.[22] Toxic waste storage has been a major problem; such wastes are either left in open air dumps, or placed in poorly constructed landfills risking leakage into the water table.[23] As a result, at the end of the Soviet period the average pesticide rate was 44 milligrams per liter, and in the sea coast around the Apsheron Peninsula fish and other forms of sea life had completely disappeared.[24] According to Mnatsakanian, pollution in the Caspian by petroleum and phenols exceeded maximum permissible concentrations by two to 43 times.[25] Although Russia and Azerbaijan are the Caspian's largest polluters, Kazakhstan also has contributed to the sea's contamination through seepage from its coastal industries and the Ural river.[26]

One of Caspian's most precious resources is sturgeon, which provides much of the world's caviar. There has been a significant decrease in the sturgeon population due to excessive fishing, reduction of spawning grounds and water pollution. Under Soviet rule, spawning grounds in the Volga region were reduced from 3600 to 430 hectares after the building of the Volga hydroelectric power plant.[27] Water pollution from the accumulation of copper, lead, zinc and pesticides has caused fish diseases in the sturgeon and other species.[28] The average yearly catch of sturgeon diminished from 36,000 metric tons in the 1900s to 14,500 metric tonnes in the late 1980s. More catastrophic was the drop of the sturgeon catch in the 1990s, because of increased poaching combined with pollution. Consequently, since the Soviet demise, the number of sturgeon in the sea has fallen from an estimated 200 million to 60 million; in the Astrakhan region alone, the total sturgeon catch decreased eight-fold between 1991 and 1994.[29] Since the late 1980s, Russian and Iranian caviar production declined by 90 percent and 20 percent respectively.[30] The situation may be reaching a point of desperation as poaching, overfishing and pollution threaten the very survival of the sturgeon population. In fact, the Convention on International Trade in Endangered Species (CITES) meeting in Harare, Zimbabwe in June 1997, placed sturgeon on its list of valuable fish requiring special protection measures. Yet, policing the rules established by

CITES could prove difficult because Azerbaijan, Kazakhstan, and Turkmenistan are not CITES members.[31]

A major concern of the littoral states is the continuing rise of the Caspian's water level and the resulting inundation of valuable territory and property. In the 1990s, among the states suffering significant financial losses from the inundation of land were Kazakhstan ($2 billion), Russia ($7 billion) and Iran (1,500 billion rials); Azerbaijan is expected to lose $4.1 billion by 2010.[32] In some areas of Kazakhstan and Turkmenistan where littoral areas are flat, floods provoked by wind-driven waves bring sea water inland up to 40 km.[33] The temporary or permanent inundation of various industrial structures, oil and gas fields, and agricultural lands treated with fertilizers and pesticides is adding to the pollution of the Caspian and the Volga delta. The sea has covered the ground levels of the nuclear power plant in Mangyshlak located on the Kazakh coast, and one can only imagine the possible catastrophic consequences of this event.[34] Despite a slight decrease in 1996 due to drought in Russia,[35] the rise of the sea level continued in 1997 and 1998; according to most experts, this trend is expected to persist at least until 2010, threatening to inundate such cities as Sumgait in Azerbaijan and Turkmenbashi (Krasnovodsk) in Turkmenistan.[36]

The rising sea level is attributed by most scientists to climatic causes rather than tectonic ones. In the 1930s, it was the decrease of the Volga river flow which provoked the fall in sea level, while a half century later, it is the increased Volga river flow and the decreased evaporation from the sea's surface which are believed to cause rising sea levels and strong winds that result in surging waves on the coast.[37] Scientists have also attempted to link the rise of the Caspian with the decline of the neighboring Aral Sea. According to one hypothesis, salt and dust clouds coming from the Aral's dried bottom have blocked the sun's rays over the Caspian, provoking increased rainfall and decreased evaporation.[38]

The ecological calamity visited upon the Aral Sea has had a parallel in the Kara-Bogaz-Gol Bay, located along the Turkmen coast, in the eastern part of the Caspian Sea. The bay, the waters of which have a very high salt content, was isolated from the rest of the Caspian by a dam built in 1980 to help stop the decline of the water level. As a result, its surface area diminished in two years from 10,000 to 2,000 km^2, exposing one of the world's largest salt deposits, which produced dust and salt clouds to the detriment of the region and its inhabitants.[39] The dam was destroyed in 1992, allowing water to flow into the gulf from the Caspian, thereby ameliorating its ecological condition. However, sanitary conditions around the Caspian, in particular along the Turkmen and Kazakh coasts, remain extremely serious, and are compounded by the lack of potable water and pollution of the water table. The death rates by infectious diseases or infant death rates in Atyrau, Kazakhstan, and Balkhan, Turkmenistan, are close to those of the Aral Sea region.[40]

The ecological future of the Caspian cannot be considered bright, given recent trends and the inability and unwillingness of the riparian states to take decisive action. One unintended consequence of the post-Soviet economic decline has been some decreases in pollution. However, the decline in pollution has not matched that of the decline in industrial production. For example, while Russian industrial production in 1994 decreased 21 percent, air pollution decreased only by 12.7 percent and water pollution by 9 percent. Among the reasons for this discrepancy are the reduction of expenditures on environmental protection and the failure of post-Soviet states to police their polluting industrial and agricultural enterprises.[41]

In the event that the ambitious plans of the Caspian states for oil and gas development become reality in the early 2000s, the ecological situation is bound to deteriorate significantly unless strict preventive and remedial policies are put in place. Even before the start of large-scale exploitation, the US Embassy in Baku reported the presence of an oily film on the sea's surface and air pollution resulting from 4.5 million cubic metres a day of flaring natural gas.[42] Aside from the growth of pollutants resulting from the planned quantum increases in oil and gas production, the newly constructed pipeline networks can be expected to further degrade the Caspian's ecology. A case in point is the potential of high environmental risk involving the planned sub-Caspian pipeline from Turkmenistan to Azerbaijan, in an earthquake-prone region. Despite the oil frenzy, it is surprising that local environmental groups have been active, especially in Russia and Kazakhstan. To counter official arguments about the financial benefits of expanded oil production, environmentalists have estimated the worth of Caspian biological resources at $500 billion, the loss of which would be economically and environmentally disastrous.[43] Should the region be more closely linked to the international community, pressures from Western environmental groups could be expected to produce a betterment of ecological conditions in and around the Caspian. With the passage of time, there could be a growing realization among the region's governments that economic and political interdependence also has social and ecological consequences.

CHAPTER 4

Energy Estimates, Costs and Pipelines

The primary factor that brought world attention to the Caspian Basin was the prospect of large energy resources found in the region. In the hyped atmosphere of the post-Soviet years, when major oil companies were lured to the Caspian shores, there were no reliable estimates of oil and gas reserves around and under the sea. What prompted the haphazard and precipitous involvement of the big oil firms and investors was the rumored promise of hidden wealth, rather than a sombre appraisal of the region's energy resources, costs of exploration and extraction and modalities of export. These considerations of political economy were also absent from the strategic calculations of the industrial countries which actively promoted large-scale participation by their oil companies in the region. Indeed, the power vacuum created by the Soviet collapse provided an inviting milieu for the West's political and economic intrusion into an uncharted territory.

As distinct from Western state interests, the oil companies' involvement in the Caspian was prompted by several factors peculiar to the petroleum industry of the early 1990s. North Sea production was declining and so were oil reserves in other regions. Also, the Persian Gulf countries were closed to foreign investment, while companies had a surplus of capital seeking new opportunities. After failing to make significant indents in Russia, oil companies shifted their attention to the Caspian region.[1]

Estimates of energy resources

The growth of significant foreign investment in the region's oil and gas projects in the 1990s has been accompanied by raging controversies over the amount of energy wealth and the problems associated with the economic feasibility of its development. This controversy, which involved a plethora of statesmen, oil executives, lobbyists, scholars and journalists, reached its zenith in 1997–98, in the midst of conflicting declarations and reports. The debate has been fuelled by technical difficulties inherent in the process of estimating oil and gas deposits, as well as by the geopolitical and economic motivations of regional and international actors.

The disagreement relating to estimates of Caspian reserves goes back to the Soviet era. In the mid-1970s, Soviet estimates were around 35 billion barrels,[2] although other estimates, a decade later, were substantially lower at around 10–11 bn, or 1 percent of total world reserves of 1000 bn barrels.[3] In the mid-1980s, the Soviets made grandiose claims of 200 bn barrels, presumably driven by political calculations. Yet the plausibility of such a grand claim could be questioned because of the Soviet lack of high-tech equipment to measure oil and gas deposits located at great depths under the sea, beyond their political need to flaunt such a figure at a time of economic stagnation. These exaggerated Soviet estimates may have been the source of similarly grandiose claims which started circulating in the 1990s.[4]

Indeed, at the signing of what was labelled the 'Contract of the Century' between Azerbaijan and a consortium of eight oil companies in September 1994, the energy resources of the Caspian states were said to be comparable to those of the emirate of Kuwait,[5] while other estimates placed the Caspian reserves on a par with the massive energy wealth of the Persian Gulf. The situation was well described by Matthew Sagers, an expert on Soviet energy:

> various figures on oil 'reserves' are now being touted by some government officials from the region as well. These reserve estimates largely reflect an effort to attract investment and Western interest ... Western companies also tend to announce deals or ongoing negotiations with a great deal of fanfare as well.[6]

As a result, within a few years estimates of Caspian oil and gas reserves grew exponentially. In 1993, Kazakh specialists claimed a combined 65.6 bn barrels of proven and possible oil reserves, the Turkmens 46 bn barrels, the Uzbeks 2.3 bn barrels, and the Azerbaijanis 10.3 bn barrels.[7] In 1996, a figure of 25 bn barrels of oil was given for the combined reserves of Kazakhstan, Turkmenistan and Uzbekistan.[8] Turkmen oil reserves to be transported through the future Afghan pipeline were said to be as high as 30 bn barrels.[9] Following a seismic survey which took place in the seabed near the Kazakh littoral, Kazakh officials claimed that their country's offshore reserves were at a level of 73 bn barrels of oil, while the Caspian Sea

Consortium (now OKIOC), the international group which carried out the survey, announced a more modest result of 29 bn barrels.[10] Kazakhstan's Tengiz field alone was reported to contain between 6 and 9 bn barrels.[11] Similarly, Turkmenistan's offshore reserves were estimated at 21.9 bn barrels of oil and 4.5 trillion cubic meters of gas (165 trillion cubic feet) by an American survey company which conducted the seismic tests off the Turkmen coast, while Turkmen officials claimed 47.5 bn barrels of oil and 5.5 trillion cubic meters of gas (194.15 tcf).[12] Meanwhile, Azerbaijani officials gave figures varying between 15 and 100 bn barrels, and even an astronomic 250 bn barrels.[13]

In early 1997, the US government stepped in and announced that the Caspian region possessed 15.6 bn proven, and 163 bn possible, barrels of oil. The distribution of the 163 bn barrels of possible reserves of the American estimate was as follows: 85 bn barrels for Kazakhstan, 32 bn for Turkmenistan, 27 bn for Azerbaijan, 12 bn for Iran, and 5 bn for Russia.[14] US Deputy Secretary of State Strobe Talbott declared that the fall of the Caspian region into the hands of religious and political extremists would 'matter profoundly to the US if that were to happen in an area that sits on as much as 200 bn barrels of oil.'[15] The highly optimistic American estimates triggered a new wave of sensationalized studies claiming equivalence between the Caspian and the Persian Gulf. To justify the scientifically unsound comparison between possible Caspian reserves with proven Gulf reserves, the argument was made that, while the Gulf had been thoroughly explored, very little research on the Caspian sea shelf had been conducted using ultra-modern Western methods.[16]

The heightened frenzy of speculation was suddenly moderated by the publication of three credible studies on Caspian energy. Published in rapid succession between October 1997 and April 1998, these studies injected a much needed dose of objectivity into the debate on energy reserves. The first study by Wood Mackenzie, a Scottish consulting company, revealed that the combined proven oil and gas reserves of Azerbaijan, Kazakhstan, Turkmenistan and Uzbekistan were 68 bn oil barrels equivalent. Of this amount, the total for oil was 25.2 bn barrels, 65 percent of which belonged to Kazakhstan (16.43 bn), and the rest to Azerbaijan (6.5), Turkmenistan (0.91) and Uzbekistan (1.34).[17] Two further studies published in April 1998 by Rice University's Baker Institute and the International Institute of Strategic Studies of London (IISS) confirmed Wood Mackenzie's figures.[18]

The general euphoria about the Caspian's energy potential was further dampened by the negative results of actual drilling in two Azerbaijani fields that had been expected to contain significant oil deposits. The first disappointment centered on the Karabakh field, where three drillings yielded insufficient amounts of oil and gas, forcing the Caspian International Petroleum Company (CIPCO), the international consortium which operated the field, to be dismantled in January 1999.[19] Equally abortive were the three attempts by the North Apsheron Operating Company (NAOC) to explore the Dan Ulduzu and Ashrafi fields, resulting in the dissolution of this consortium in April 1999.[20] The US–Russian Lukarco consortium, formed in 1998, was reported to be on the verge of abandoning the development of the Yalama field as preliminary surveys indicated insufficient oil quantities.[21] A fourth prospect focusing on the Shah Deniz field yielded mixed results; instead of oil, considerable gas deposits were discovered, which would necessitate the establishment of a costly Azerbaijani gas infrastructure.[22] The string of bad luck continued in 2000, when the well drilled at the Kurdashi exploration bloc by a consortium led by the Italian firm Agip was found to be 'almost completely dry'.[23] Even the legendary AIOC of 'Contract of the Century' fame was affected by misfortune, when drilling at the Azeri field produced oil with a high sulphur content, the handling of which would lead to production, storage and transport cost increases, thus raising the building costs of the Baku–Ceyhan pipeline.[24] Undeterred by these poor drilling results, SOCAR president Natiq Aliyev declared that the Azerbaijani sector of the Caspian contained 4 bn tonnes (30 bn barrels) of petroleum.[25]

Disappointments were not limited to offshore areas of Azerbaijan. In the North Caspian, drilling by the US company Oryx Energy found only a 'smidgeon of oil' off south-western Kazakhstan, leading the Texas firm to take a $15 million charge to cover its losses.[26] Five years earlier, the French Elf Aquitaine had experienced a similar misfortune while drilling in the Aktyubinsk area.[27] However, new drilling in the North Caspian yielded some promising results in Kazakhstan's Kashagan region (12 to 50 bn barrels) and Russia's Severny field (2.2 bn barrels).[28] Also significant was the Iranian discovery in August 2000 of new reserves in the South Caspian (2.5 to 3 bn barrels).[29] The Russian and the Iranian oil finds, if substantiated, would transform the Caspian oil map as these two riparian states would become involved in the geo-economics of the Caspian not only as transit countries, but also as producers.

In the wake of heightened expectations followed by disappointments, it is appropriate to analyse what appear to be the empirically realistic estimates offered by Wood Mackenzie, BP and the *Oil and Gas Journal*. According to the Wood Mackenzie study, Kazakhstan possesses the largest onshore and offshore proven and possible oil reserves, 15.01 and 47.78 bn barrels respectively; Azerbaijan is next with 7.39 bn proven and 8 to 14 bn possible barrels. More modest are the Turkmen and Uzbek deposits – 1.82 bn barrels of proven reserves for Turkmenistan and 1.79 of proven and 1.5 bn of possible barrels for Uzbekistan. Thus, the total Wood Mackenzie estimates for the Caspian region are 26.01 bn barrels of proven and 58 to 64 bn barrels of possible oil reserves.[30] This figure is significantly higher than the total estimate of 16.1 bn barrels advanced by BP in its authoritative *Statistical Review of World Energy*. In late 1999, BP's estimates of proven oil reserves were: Kazakhstan – 8 bn, Azerbaijan – 7 bn, Uzbekistan – 0.6 bn and Turkmenistan – 0.5 bn barrels, in all constituting 1.5 percent of world oil reserves.[31] A third credible source, the *Oil and Gas Journal*, estimates the total proven reserves of Caspian oil to be 8 bn barrels: 5.42 bn barrels for Kazakhstan, 1.18 bn barrels for Azerbaijan, 0.55 bn for Turkmenistan and 0.59 bn for Uzbekistan.[32]

The energy wealth of the Caspian countries also includes significant deposits of natural gas, the estimates of which remain in contention. According to Wood Mackenzie, Turkmenistan has 91.7 trillion cubic feet (2.58 trillion cubic meters) proven and 211.9 tcf (6.97 tcm) possible gas reserves; Kazakhstan has 68.64 tcf (1.94 tcm) proven and 200.81 tcf (5.69 tcm) possible reserves; Uzbekistan has 67.74 tcf (1.92 tcm) proven and 127.22 tcf (3.6 tcm) possible reserves; and Azerbaijan has 21.37 tcf (0.61 tcm) proven and 24.5 to 60.2 tcf (0.69 to 1.71 tcm) possible reserves. Wood Mackenzie's total estimates of Caspian proven gas reserves are 248.82 tcf (7.05 tcm), in addition to the recently discovered significant deposits in Azerbaijan's Shah Deniz field estimated at between 0.4 and 1 tcm (14.12 and 35.3 tcf).[33] BP's estimate of total proven Caspian gas reserves at the end of 1999 were 7.42 tcm (262.2 tcf), almost identical to the Wood Mackenzie estimate, although the BP figures attribute 2.86 tcm (101 tcf) to Turkmenistan, 1.84 tcm (65 tcf) to Kazakhstan, 1.87 tcm (66.2 tcf) to Uzbekistan, and 0.85 tcm (30 tcf) to Azerbaijan.[34] For the same period, the figures given by the *Oil and Gas Journal* are identical to BP's, except for Azerbaijan, which is credited with higher reserves of 44 tcf. Thus, total Caspian gas reserves stand at 5 percent of world gas reserves.[35]

It should be noted that the foregoing estimates of total Caspian oil and gas reserves are considerably higher than those provided in the early 1990s by the Congressional Research Service, as quoted by John Roberts in his study on Caspian pipelines. This source placed the total proven oil reserves at 6.8 bn barrels, with a further 23 bn barrels of possible reserves. Kazakhstan was placed first with 3.3 bn barrels of proven and 12 bn barrels of possible reserves, Azerbaijan second with 1.2 bn proven and 4 bn possible barrels, Turkmenistan third with 1.4 bn proven and 3 bn possible barrels, and Uzbekistan with 0.3 bn proven and 2 bn possible barrels. As to total estimates for gas, the figures given by the Congressional Research Service are somewhat higher than the estimates by Wood Mackenzie and BP: 189 tcf for Turkmenistan, 88 tcf for Uzbekistan, 19 tcf for Azerbaijan and 15 tcf for Kazakhstan, a total of 311 tcf (8.81 tcm).[36]

With the passage of time, one can expect more reliable estimates of Caspian energy resources as a result of new scientific studies and actual drilling in an admittedly large territorial expanse and sea surface. Until such credible research is available, oil companies, investors and policymakers are bound to be at the mercy of overly optimistic or pessimistic assessments, often prompted by the geopolitical calculations of political and economic elites, lobbyists and sensationalist media. Judging from the rich experience accumulated over the last century, one can safely agree with Igor Effimoff's truism that 'all the data will be known when all the wells have been drilled and when the last barrel has been drained. By that time, it is likely that nobody will care what the resource base was'.[37]

Costs of energy development

From a purely economic perspective, a major factor likely to shape the tempo and extent of the development of the Caspian energy fields is the costs associated with prospecting, exploration, extraction and transportation of oil and gas. Although there is a general lack of hard data, several factors are likely to increase the developmental costs of Caspian oil to place it among the most expensive in the world. A prime factor contributing to high cost is that the bulk of new exploration in Kazakhstan, Azerbaijan and Turkmenistan is focused on offshore fields. Thus, the development of oil deposits under the Caspian requires highly sophisticated and expensive infrastructures such as the newly ordered drilling unit to be used by a group of companies in Azerbaijan, with a projected cost of $180 million.[38] More specifically, the average cost of a single offshore exploratory well is estimated at $20 million, although in Azerbaijan the three unproductive wells drilled by CIPCO cost about $180 million.[39]

The development of Kazakhstan's Kashagan offshore field provides a prime illustration of the immense investments required for working in the Caspian environment. By late 1999, over $600 million had been spent without the actual onset of drilling operations. Of this amount, $300 million was spent in 1993–4 on seismic studies and $300 million in 1998 and 1999 on preparations for drilling. The cost of the rig and support systems during drilling operations is estimated at $250,000 per day. The full dimensions of this corporate gamble become explicit when 'participation' fees are added to the total cost of doing business. A case in point is the $500 million paid by Phillips and Inpex to the Kazakh government in 1998 for the privilege of joining the consortium of companies working in the Kashagan area.[40] After making these massive investments, the companies discovered in November 2000 that the presence of gas and sulphur would delay or cancel Kashagan's development unless technical problems were resolved.[41] Although production costs at existing fields are relatively low at around $5 per barrel, estimated costs for additional production place the Caspian countries at the high end of the spectrum. Thus, the capital cost per daily barrel of oil beyond peak production capacity is $10,700–$12,500 for Azerbaijan and $12,000–$14,300 for Kazakhstan. Although these figures are somewhat lower than North Sea production costs, they are much higher than those of Iraq ($1,000), Kuwait ($3,000), Saudi Arabia ($2,500–$4,000), Venezuela ($5,000), Gabon ($6,000) and Iran ($8,000).[42]

Cost calculations are further complicated by the large expenditures necessary for pipeline construction. Given the landlocked situation of the Caspian and the deterioration of existing networks, a new set of expensive pipelines is being built to take the energy to the marketplace. These include the pipeline joining the Kazakh Tengiz oil field to the Russian port of Novorossiisk which is expected to cost $2.2 bn,[43] and the repairs and extension of the Baku–Supsa pipeline costing $590 million.

Pipelines, more than any other form of transport of oil and gas, are a highly complex enterprise. According to Saule Omarova, the peculiar attributes of pipeline transportation are:

> high investments costs, a high degree of inflexibility, and significant economies of scale. Once the pipeline is built, its route cannot be changed – it is a fixed and highly product-specific investment ... Even refurbishing an oil pipeline for transporting natural gas is a very expensive undertaking.

Construction of compressors along the pipeline alone would incur high additional costs. Moreover, the specific design of a pipeline depends on the type and the quantities of oil to be shipped through it.[44]

Pipeline dilemmas

The transport of Caspian oil and gas to consumer countries is a central issue in the region's geopolitics. The pipeline issue involves a plethora of players – producing states, major oil companies, transit countries, ethno-nationalist groups and regional and international powers. Financial, technical and strategic considerations contribute to the issue's complexity. The inability to provide export routes has, until now, blocked the flow of oil and gas out of the region and has prevented Azerbaijan, Kazakhstan and Turkmenistan from enjoying the benefits of their energy wealth. Given the complexity of the transit problem, an overview of the major export options is offered here.

Unlike the situation in the Persian Gulf, where every oil-producing country has access to open seas, the landlocked nature of the Caspian makes three of its littoral states, Azerbaijan, Kazakhstan and Turkmenistan, dependent on adjacent countries for their trade and export of energy. The governments of these states and the multinational oil and gas companies have had to face the difficult task of choosing the most appropriate routes for both short-term 'early oil', and long-term shipment of large quantities of hydrocarbons.

The pipeline projects proposed to date can be classified into six geographical routing categories: the northern, the western, the north-western, the southern, the south-eastern, and the eastern. The northern or Russian route would take oil from Azerbaijan and Kazakhstan to the Russian Black Sea port of Novorossiisk. The Western route would transport Azerbaijani oil to a Georgian Black Sea port, or alternately to the Turkish port of Yumurtalik in the Gulf of Ceyhan via either Armenia, Georgia, Iran, or a combination of these three countries. This route would also transport Kazakh and/or Turkmen oil or gas in the event that a sub-Caspian pipeline is built to Azerbaijan. The north-western route envisages several alternatives across the Balkan states or the Ukraine in order to avoid passage through the congested Bosphorus and Dardanelles. Tankers from Novorossiisk or Georgia would take oil to Ukraine, Romania or Bulgaria for transshipment to Central and Western European customers. The southern or Iranian route would ship oil and gas through Iran for export to world markets from Persian Gulf ports.

Initially, the southern route would rely on swaps, by which Iran would place some of its oil or gas at the disposal of participating countries, in exchange for receiving from them an equivalent amount of oil and gas to supply its heavily populated northern provinces. Once pipelines are built through Iranian territory, Central Asian oil and gas would directly reach the Persian Gulf. The southeastern route would go to the Indian Ocean through Afghanistan and Pakistan and would concern principally Turkmen production, although the authors of the project hope to attract oil and gas from Azerbaijan and Kazakhstan as well.[45] The last and least likely option, due to the high construction cost, is the eastern route crossing all of China to supply consumer markets in East Asia, Japan, and Korea.[46]

After long and arduous negotiations, agreements were signed in March and April 1996 on a pipeline project that would solve Kazakhstan's export problems in the medium and long term. The project involved the construction of a 1600 kilometer-long pipeline linking Tengiz with Novorossiisk, using some existing and some uncompleted Kazakh and Russian pipelines. This pipeline, which was planned to be completed in three years at the estimated cost of some $1.2 to $2 bn, would have a capacity of some 500,000 b/d.[47] Its construction was only begun in May 1999, with a forecasted price tag of $2.2 bn and a completion date of October 2001.[48] In the meantime, Kazakhstan has had to rely on limited exports through the existing Russian pipeline network. Some of these exports include swap arrangements with Russia. As an alternate export route, Chevron, the main oil company involved in Tengiz, has sent oil by tanker to Azerbaijan to be transported by rail to a Georgian Black Sea port.[49] A future possibility is the Russian-built connection between the port of Makhachkala and the Baku–Novorossiisk pipeline. Swap arrangements with Iran, although scheduled since 1992, have been frequently interrupted for technical reasons, and sometimes because of US opposition.

In September 1997, Kazakhstan surprised all observers by concluding a $9.5 billion contract with the China National Petroleum Corporation (CNPC). The deal involved the construction of a 3,000 kilometer pipeline to western China with an estimated cost of $3.5 bn, and of a shorter 200 kilometer pipeline in Iran allowing swap deals between Iran and Kazakhstan. Also, the CNPC had plans to build a longer pipeline running south to the Persian Gulf through Turkmenistan.[50] Although these planned pipelines would have altered the geo-economic fundamentals of Caspian oil, by 1999 these projects had been indefinitely postponed. More remote is the implementation of the grandiose scheme to transport Caspian gas across the Asian continent to the Yellow Sea coast to supply Chinese, Japanese, and Korean markets.[51]

Export of oil from Azerbaijan has constituted a continuing dilemma since that country's independence. In October 1995, the Azerbaijan International Oil Company (AIOC) announced its decision to export short-term 'early oil' north to Novorossiisk and west to the Georgian port of Supsa. The cost of this northern route was relatively modest, because it was only necessary to reverse the direction of flow of an existing pipeline and to conduct repairs, particularly in the section going through Chechnya. The line was initially expected to handle 100,000 b/d and, once operating at full capacity, 180,000 b/d in the section from Baku to Grozny and 340,000 from Grozny to Tikhoretsk. The second branch going to Supsa was expected to cost $250 million, as more work was necessary particularly in the construction of a 117 km pipeline between Kazakh in Azerbaijan and the Georgian village of Gachiani, from where an existing pipeline began.[52] However, both lines experienced considerable delay. The long-expected Baku–Novorossiisk branch became operative on 25 October 1997, when Azerbaijani oil at last reached the Black Sea, although oil flow was frequently interrupted by the conflict in Chechnya.[53] The Baku–Supsa branch was opened on 16 April 1999, costing about $600 million, twice the amount of earlier estimates.[54]

The most consequential route from a geopolitical perspective is the planned pipeline to transport Azerbaijani 'main oil' from Baku to the Turkish port of Ceyhan on the Mediterranean. After years of politicking and deliberation, on 18 November 1999 several agreements were signed at the OSCE summit in Istanbul, creating the political framework to construct the Baku–Ceyhan pipeline. Estimated to cost $2.4 bn, the 1730 kilometer long pipeline will traverse Azerbaijan, Georgia and Turkey; it is expected to be completed in 2007.[55] It is important to note that the realization of this project would depend on the decision of the oil companies to fund it, which is itself dependent on the availability of substantial oil reserves to justify the pipeline.

The preferred route of the Turkmens to export oil, and more so gas, was through a major pipeline to be built across Iran and Turkey to reach the Balkans and Western Europe. A first agreement was signed in January 1994 between Iran and Turkmenistan,[56] followed by several others involving Turkey as well. American opposition to

Iran, however, has delayed the project by making it impossible to finance. Nevertheless, a small stretch of 140 km, linking the Turkmen and Iranian networks, was completed in December 1997. A major diplomatic roadblock appeared to be removed in July 1997 when the United States announced that the projected pipeline did not violate the American embargo against Iran, although subsequent American opposition dashed hopes for early implementation. Once built, this pipeline would transport 30 bn cubic meters per year over a 30-year period. The cost of the pipeline was estimated by John Roberts at $9 billion, with some $3.5 billion for the 1,400 km long Iranian section alone.[57] Another reason for the postponement of the project has been Turkmenistan's commitment, under US pressure, to exporting gas through the planned sub-Caspian pipeline to Baku and thence to Turkey. According to a feasibility study conducted by an American company, the sub-Caspian pipeline connecting the gas fields of eastern Turkmenistan and Erzerum in Turkey will have a total length of 2,000 km and an initial capacity of 10 bn cubic meters per year to be increased to 30 bn at a cost of approximately US$2.5 to $3bn. A contract was signed between Turkmenistan and various companies involved in the project on 19 February 1999,[58] only to be shelved a year later.

A second possibility on which the Turkmens have placed much hope is the south-eastern route that would reach the Indian Ocean through Afghanistan and Pakistan, with a possible extension to India. For this route, both gas and oil pipelines are contemplated.[59] Due to the anarchic situation in Afghanistan, the project does not appear to be realistic, even if protocols and contracts are concluded. A preliminary agreement was signed in July 1997 between Turkmenistan, Pakistan, the American Unocal company and the Saudi Delta,[60] leading to a $2 billion contract concluded on 25 October 1997. Turkmenistan claimed to have obtained the support of all Afghan factions for the construction of the 750-kilometer stretch running through Afghanistan.[61] Because of continued Afghan instability under the Taliban regime and the vicissitudes of Pakistani politics, Unocal decided in August 1998 to place its projects on hold, and then in December 1998 to withdraw from the region, bringing to naught Turkmen efforts to find an outlet to the Arabian Sea.[62] Finally, plans for an eastward mega-pipeline of 6,700 km across China appeared to be postponed because of the immense cost and size of the project.[63]

In a creative move to counter American attempts to exclude it from Caspian deals, the Iranian government announced a three-stage plan involving swaps and direct exports to develop a trans-Iranian route for Kazakh, Azeri and Turkmen oil. In the first stage, a 392 kilometers-long pipeline with a 370,000 b/d capacity would link Neka, an Iranian town near the Caspian, with Tehran. In a second stage, 450,000 b/d would reach Isfahan and Arak through the flow of existing pipelines. In the third stage, Caspian oil would directly reach the Persian Gulf through the flow reversal of existing pipelines and the construction of missing links, allowing the direct export of up to 800,000 b/d.[64] Following the announcement of the discovery of substantial oil quantities in Kashagan in May 2000, the Iranian authorities proposed a 1,500 km-long pipeline with a capacity of 1 million b/d and a cost estimate of $1.2 bn. Added to the amounts carried by the smaller pipelines facilitating swaps, Iran would be able to transit up to 1.8 billion b/d of oil.[65]

The three interrelated topics analysed in this chapter – energy reserves, production costs, and projected pipelines – are likely to remain in flux in the foreseeable future. Clearly, the costs of oil and gas development and pipeline options depend on the amount and location of recoverable supplies. Thus, it would be safe to assume that only a handful of the many proposed pipeline routes outlined above will come into reality. Ultimately, however, the choice of pipeline routes would be determined by both economic and political considerations. It would be foolhardy to make the immense investments to build pipelines before the actual discovery of significant recoverable energy reserves.

Part Two: THE RIPARIAN STATES

CHAPTER 5

The Riparian States: Politics and Interests

In order to achieve a comprehensive understanding of Caspian geopolitics, it is first necessary to analyse the dynamic forces within the five littoral states, their governmental systems and national interests, which form the basis of their interaction with one another and with the outside world. The shoreline of the Caspian Sea is shared by five states – Russia, Iran, Kazakhstan, Azerbaijan and Turkmenistan. With the exception of Iran in the south, all the riparian states are former Soviet republics. As Iran struggles with internal and external conflicts brought about by the consequences of its revolutionary order, all of the four ex-Communist states are in the throes of state building and of the political and economic transition from Soviet rule. Consequently, all five riparian states suffer from various degrees of political uncertainty, which has had a direct impact on the geopolitics of the Caspian.

Russia

As the main successor state to the Soviet Union, the Russian Federation is the repository of most of the latter's geopolitical status, military might and economic resources. In addition, Russia has over half of the Soviet Union's population and controls two thirds of its territory, including the north-western shores of the Caspian Sea.

The appointment of Mikhail Gorbachev as general secretary of the Communist Party in March 1985 initiated a half-decade of reforms which culminated in the dismemberment of the USSR. Gorbachev's reformist agenda, centring on the twin processes of glasnost (openness) and perestroika (restructuring), were based on the premise that political liberalization of the Soviet Union would be a prelude to dynamic economic development. However, the net effect of the intended reforms was economic chaos and the rise of separatism among some non-Russian nationalities. While the turmoil resulted in factionalism and indecisiveness in the Kremlin, there was a growing sentiment among Russians that a Russia freed from the burdens of the other Soviet republics would fare better in political and economic terms. The abortive coup against Gorbachev in August 1991 sealed the fate of the Union and ushered in the rise of Boris Yeltsin as president of the Russian Federation. On 7–8 December 1991, the leaders of Russia, Ukraine and Belarus decided to dissolve the Soviet Union and replace it with the Commonwealth of Independent States (CIS), which was expanded to include eleven former Soviet republics at a meeting in Alma-Ata three weeks later.

Political evolution (1991–2001)

Yeltsin's eight-year presidency was marked by multiple internal and external challenges which sapped the country's economy and weakened its status as a great power. The first difficult task was to define the federation's identity in view of its multi-ethnic populace, in which the Russian element was politically and demographically dominant. In March 1992, the Federation Treaty was signed by all 89 territorial components of the Russian Federation, with the exception of Tatarstan and Chechnya. These components included 21 autonomous republics, one autonomous region and ten autonomous districts. Other challenges were to rebuild a viable state structure capable of preserving the federation's unity and to institute a market economy. Even more serious was the confrontation between the president and the legislative branch. The struggle for power culminated in Yeltsin's dissolution of the Congress of People's Deputies and the Supreme Soviet on 21 September 1993, which was rejected by the parliamentarians and the Constitutional Court. In the midst of clashes around the parliament building (White House) on 4 October 1993, Yeltsin declared a state of emergency as army troops stormed the White House, leaving 100 dead and many wounded.

The country's situation gradually stabilized after the legislative elections of 12 December 1993 and the referendum for a new constitution, which was approved by 58 percent of voters. A total of eight parties won representation in the 450-seat State Duma, but none commanded a majority. However, Russia reverted to crisis conditions when Yeltsin moved troops into the breakaway republic of Chechnya in December 1994, setting the stage for a costly military and political disaster. Russian forces were withdrawn after an armistice was concluded in September 1996, leaving unresolved the determination of Chechnya's final status.

In the parliamentary elections of 1995, the Communists won the largest share of the votes (22.3 percent), and in June 1996, Yeltsin narrowly defeated the Communist candidate for president, Gennady Zyuganov. An important hallmark of Yeltsin's rule was the rapid succession of prime ministers and top-ranking officials, reflecting the instability within the ruling elite as well as the president's fear of emerging rivals. Meanwhile, the country's economy continued a downward trend, highlighted by the devaluations of the rouble in October 1994 and August 1998. Russian society was again thrown into turmoil in August 1999, after attacks in Daghestan by Islamist militants from Chechnya and bombings of apartment buildings in several Russian cities which were blamed on the Chechens. In response, Russian troops were sent to Chechnya for a second time, in a determined offensive against the secessionist republic.

Beset by the Chechen attacks in Daghestan and a declining economy, Yeltsin once again changed prime ministers in October 1999 by appointing Vladimir Putin, a former KGB official. Putin's emergence signalled the beginning of a hardline policy in Chechnya and the ascendence of the security services and the military within the regime. The full-scale invasion of Chechnya, ostensibly triggered by the government's determination to crush Islamist terrorism, set the stage for a repetition of the 1994–6 war. However, unlike the earlier conflict, the new Russian campaign had considerable popular support. Putin's tough stance and the initial battlefield successes of Russian arms brought great popularity to the new prime minister, assuring his accession to the presidency. In a surprise move at the year's end, Yeltsin resigned the Russian presidency, making Putin acting president and a successful candidate for the March 2000 presidential election.

Political system

The 1993 Constitution established a federal system of government, with a strong president, a weak legislature and an independent judiciary, ruling over a vast country divided into 89 provincial units. Elected for a four-year term, the president heads the armed forces and appoints members of the executive branch; and with parliamentary approval he appoints the prime minister, the Central Bank governor, and Constitutional Court chairman. He may dissolve the State Duma if it passes two no-confidence motions within three months, or if it repeatedly rejects the president's nominee for prime minister. Moreover, the president can rule by decree without Duma approval.

The Russian parliament consists of a 450-member State Duma

and 178-member Federation Council. Because of its division into many parties and blocs, the popularly elected Duma was unable to marshal a two-thirds majority to mount an effective challenge to Yeltsin. As the upper house of parliament, the Federation Council consists of two representatives from each of Russia's territorial units, who are the locally elected governors and legislative chairmen. Centre-periphery relations between Moscow and the provincial authorities have been in flux in a situation of asymmetric federalism, because several autonomous republics have been given greater self-government than the smaller provinces.[1] The continuing decline of federal power under Yeltsin weakened central control over the provinces, some of which assumed considerable independence in political and economic affairs.

The Russian political parties are usually organized around prominent individuals and lack institutionalized structure and cohesion. The sole exception is the Communist Party, the successor to the Communist Party of the Soviet Union. The Duma elections of December 1999, held at the height of Putin's popularity, created a fragmented legislature dominated by seven political parties. The largest bloc of seats was won by the Communist Party (113), followed by Unity (72), Fatherland-All Russia (66), Union of Rightist Forces (29), Yabloko (21), Liberal-Democratic Party (17), Our Home is Russia (7), and a large coterie of independent members (106).

Since its establishment in February 1993, the Communist Party led by Zyuganov has been Russia's largest, with half-a-million members and a nationwide organizational structure. Despite its Communist label, the party's ideological commitment has declined, because it includes many nationalists and social democrats. Because of Putin's popularity, the Communist Party experienced a significant loss of seats in the December 1999 elections. Unlike the Communist Party, the Unity bloc is a recent creation with no institutionalized structure except the support of Yeltsin's 'Family'. Unity's sole distinction is its association with Russia's ruling elite, led by Putin. The Fatherland-All Russia bloc was a short-lived alliance between Moscow mayor Yuri Luzhkov, former prime minister Yevgeny Primakov, and some regional governors. After its poor showing in the last election, it split into two factions in the Duma. The Union of Rightist Forces and Yabloko are liberal, pro-business groups led respectively by former prime minister Sergei Kiriyenko and Gregory Yavlinsky. At the far right of the political spectrum is Vladimir Zhirinovsky's Liberal-Democratic Party; once considered a threat to Russian democracy after its strong showing in the December 1993 elections, the party's strength progressively declined in the 1995 and 1999 elections, due to its leader's ultra-nationalist rhetoric. Our Home is Russia, founded in 1995 by Prime Minister Viktor Chernomyrdin, has lost much of its strength since its founder's dismissal from the government in 1998.

Economic system

After the Soviet demise, the state apparatus continued to weaken. Consequently, the central authorities failed to fill the power vacuum created by the collapse of the powerful Soviet party-state apparatus, thereby reducing the government's ability to steer the country's economy, particularly in collecting taxes and reducing corruption. The result was the increase of the power and economic influence of regional governors and business oligarchs, which detracted from market reforms.

In today's Russia, much of the Soviet command economy has been dismantled. Yet the emerging market system has been unable to reverse the progressive contraction of the economy since 1990, although Russia has fared better than most other Soviet republics. The financial collapse of August 1998 caused great turmoil and dissipated illusions about a Russian economic miracle. Since then an economic recovery has begun, triggered by the rouble's devaluation and rising oil prices. However, a full range of issues awaited the new president – restructuring the banking system, reducing business subsidies, cracking down on corruption, limiting the power of billionaire 'oligarchs', and offering better protection to foreign investors.

Energy sector

The oil and gas sector is a major component of Russia's industrial base. In proven oil reserves Russia ranks eighth, with an estimated 50 bn barrels; it also contains the world's largest natural gas reserves.[2] Since its peak of 570 metric tonnes in 1987, total crude oil production declined to 304.8 metric tonnes in 1999 because of financial problems, late payments by consumers, lack of new exploration, shortage of investment and deterioration of transport infrastructure.[3] Oil and gas exports are Russia's largest currency-earning commodities, bringing in $22.8bn in 1998.[4] Income from oil and gas price increases made up 40 percent of Russia's trade surplus in the first quarter of 2000.[5]

As a result of market reforms, Russia's monopolistic oil industry was divided into eleven major oil companies, the largest of which are Sidanco, Lukoil, Yukos, Surgutneftegas, Tyumenoil and Rosneft.[6]

Lukoil, one of the world's largest oil companies, has aggressively entered the global energy market. A single company, Transneft, controls the transport of oil throughout the Russian Federation, with extensions into former Soviet republics. Another global player is Gazprom, a huge privatized monopoly which controls every aspect of gas production, distribution and export. Despite Russia's well-endowed energy resources, foreign investment has been limited because of corruption, political instability, and weaknesses in the legal system. A case in point was BP–Amoco's costly misadventure with Tyumenoil, which was settled in December 1999, leaving a bitter aftertaste.[7]

Trends and prospects

In the near future, the fate of Russian democracy and market economy is likely to be determined by the configuration of the Putin government and the degree of its commitment to reform. In his first year, Putin strengthened the power of the central government in order to assert control over Russia's unruly provinces and to limit the influence of the oligarchs. However, the new regime still needs to reduce the flight of capital and to normalize relations with the multilateral funding agencies and private foreign investors. These difficult tasks, combined with the continuing challenges in Chechnya and the issue of human rights, present Putin and a new generation of Russian elites with a complicated agenda. Their ability to overcome these challenges can be expected to have a direct influence on Russia's role in the politics of the Caspian Basin.

Iran

Occupying the southern coast of the Caspian, Iran is the second most powerful riparian actor in the geopolitics of the region after Russia. Iran has had a distinct political and cultural identity for three millennia, unlike its Muslim Caspian neighbors, whose national identity is in its formative stage. Iranians are overwhelmingly Shi'ite Muslims, a faith they share with neighboring Azerbaijan. The country's body politic is quite diverse, consisting of Azeris, Kurds, Baluch, Arabs, Turkmen, Lurs, Armenians, Jews, Assyrians, Zoroastrians, Baha'is and several tribal confederations.

Today's Iran is the product of the 1979 Revolution, which overthrew the Pahlavi dynasty and replaced it with an Islamic theocracy. As the charismatic embodiment of the revolution, Ayatollah Ruhallah Khomeini established a political system led by Shi'a clerical experts in Islamic law. Khomeini assumed sweeping powers under the 1979 Constitution as the leading Islamic jurisprudent (*vali-e faqih*), with power to control the armed forces, appoint top judicial functionaries and veto the selection of presidential candidates. Executive authority was vested in a president elected by universal suffrage, but subservient to the supreme authority of the vali-e faqih. The constitution also provides for a popularly chosen legislative branch – the Majlis – of 207 members elected for four-year terms. A 12-member Council of Guardians supervises elections and determines the Islamicity of all laws passed by the Majlis. The judicial branch, consisting of a Supreme Court and lower courts, is led by Shi'a jurists who rely on Islamic law as the guiding framework for deciding cases.

After the death of Ayatollah Khomeini in June 1989, President Ali Khamenei was chosen as the leading faqih, and Majlis Speaker, Ali Akbar Hashemi Rafsanjani, was elected president. Rafsanjani's tasks included the moderation of Iran's Islamic revolutionary zeal and reconstruction of the economy after the ravages of the eight-year war with Iraq. Also, Rafsanjani sought to normalize Iran's external relations and break out of its political and economic isolation. However, Iranian–American relations remained antagonistic, because of past US interventionism in Iranian affairs, the 1979 embassy hostage crisis and charges of Iranian support for international terrorism.

Political evolution (1990–2001)

President Rafsanjani's efforts to turn Iran away from Islamist extremism culminated in the victory of moderate pragmatists in the 1992 Majlis elections. The trend toward pragmatism gained momentum in the mid-1990s, leading to the election of Muhammad Khatami in the May 1997 presidential election. A moderate middle-ranking cleric, Khatami was elected with 70 percent of the vote, representing a powerful groundswell for change among young Iranians, professionals and women. However, many of Khatami's liberalizing reforms were blocked by Iran's conservative clerical establishment, although he did succeed in promoting greater freedom of expression and diplomatic normalization with regional and European powers such as Germany, Great Britain and Saudi Arabia.

The conflict between the pro-Khatami progressive forces and the Islamic conservatives culminated in the student-led demonstrations of summer 1999, which were suppressed. These events, coupled with popular dissatisfaction with the stultifying economic and cultural policies of the Islamic establishment, fuelled a grass-roots protest movement which resulted in a massive victory for the progressive forces in the February 2000 Majlis elections. Despite the broad-based electoral support for his policies, Khatami failed to promote political and economic reforms because of determined opposition from the Islamic conservative leadership. However, his re-election in June 2001 with 76 percent of the vote was a reaffirmation of the popular sentiment for reform.

Economic system

In the two decades since the 1979 Revolution, the Iranian economy has been in decline because of the confluence of internal and external destabilizing factors. These included a high rate of population growth, the calamitous impact of the Iran–Iraq war, falling oil prices, bureaucratic corruption and mismanagement and the US-imposed embargo. The Iranian economy is heavily influenced by its reliance on oil, as it has been for the last half-century. Both under the Shah and the Islamic Republic, the state has played a central role in economic development, thereby stifling private enterprise. A large sector of the economy remains in the hands of the politically powerful Bonyad-e Mostazafin – the Foundation of the Oppressed. Originally founded as charitable institutions and led by Islamist hardliners, the Bonyads are monopolies which were given the Shah's holdings after the revolution. The break-up of the Bonyads, the liberalization of the economy and privatization of inefficient public sector companies and banks were priority items in President Khatami's economic agenda, which he could not implement because of strong resistance from conservative circles.

Energy sector

Iran is one of the world's leading oil producers, with a daily output of 3,515,000 barrels in 1999.[8] According to OPEC, oil revenues in 1998 and 1999 were $10.5bn and $13.0bn, over three times Iran's non-oil earnings. In 1999, oil production was reduced in line with the OPEC decision to cut production to push up prices. A year later, Iran reluctantly raised production in keeping with OPEC's decision to moderate rising prices. In the next five years the National Iranian Oil Company plans to add 800,000 to 900,000 b/d capacity,[9] although because of lack of capital such expansion would have to be funded by foreign firms. Despite constraints imposed by the United States, several European oil companies have become major players in Iran's oil and gas sector.

With enormous gas reserves, Iran is a major producer and an

emerging exporter. Much of Iran's gas is used domestically, and in order to realize its ambitious plans to export gas, the government would need to find funding to build extensive pipelines. When these projects come to fruition, Iran will emerge as a significant competitor to neighboring gas producers such as Qatar, Russia, Kazakhstan and Turkmenistan.[10] However, Iran's gas industry is not likely to develop its full potential unless the regime undertakes major reforms in restructuring and privatization.

Trends and prospects

The victory of the progressive forces in the February 2000 legislative elections positioned Iran at the brink of an era of accelerated change in the political, economic and socio-cultural spheres. Although emboldened by the dominance of reformist allies in the Majlis, President Khatami adopted a cautious path designed to effect gradual change, while hoping to minimize a backlash from conservative and radical elements. More conservative in orientation, Ayatollah Khamenei, Iran's spiritual leader (rahbar), sought to play a mediator's role between the ultra-conservatives and Khatami's reformist constituency. None of these initiatives, however, dampened the escalating confrontationist fervour of the opposing reformist and conservative factions, raising the specter of internecine violence. The political and economic liberalization of Iran is likely to be a gradual process, given the continued hold of conservative clerics over the country's military, security apparatus and judicial structure. Iran's policies in the Caspian sphere will be shaped by the success or failure of the reformist agenda and the nature of its evolving relationship with the West and Russia.

Kazakhstan

As the largest of the former Soviet republics after Russia, Kazakhstan controls the northern and north-eastern shores of the Caspian. Despite an expanse of 2,717,000 km^2, Kazakhstan has a population of only 16 million, concentrated in the north along the Russian border, and in the south close to Uzbekistan and Kyrgyzstan. As a result of the Russian conquest and the Soviet policy of encouraging migration to Central Asia, there is a large Russian and Slavic element in Kazakhstan's population. The native Kazakhs, representing approximately 45 percent of the population, are nominally affiliated with Sunni Islam, although strong shamanistic influences persist.

Outside perceptions of Kazakhstan since independence have evolved from admiration for its success in preventing ethnic strife and partition, to disappointment over the shift toward authoritarianism in recent years. The existence of the overwhelming Russian majority in the north had evoked widespread fears of partition along a north-south divide. This catastrophic scenario has been averted so far, thanks to the enlightened policies adopted by both Russia and Kazakhstan. However, the young Central Asian republic still faces the daunting challenges of nation building and of creating an overarching 'Kazakhstani' identity that will appeal to both Kazakhs and non-Kazakhs alike.

In Kazakhstan, 'political leadership' might be considered a euphemism for President Nursultan Nazarbayev, in whose hands all political power is concentrated. The hope that Nazarbayev would promote democracy has eroded over the years, reaching a nadir with the controversial presidential elections of January 1999. The failure of some of the president's economic policies, and the resulting economic malaise, have further tarnished Nazarbayev's image at home and abroad. Moreover, like all former Soviet republics, the country suffers from an all-pervasive and endemic corruption, which distorts the economy and deters foreign investment.

Political evolution (1991–2001)

The sudden dissolution of the Soviet Union caught Kazakhstan unprepared for independence. The situation in the republic had been calm during the perestroika years, except for the violent repression of the December 1986 demonstrations by young Kazakh nationalists protesting the nomination of an ethnic Russian to lead their country. After becoming secretary general of the Communist Party of Kazakhstan in 1989, Nazarbayev worked with Soviet leader Mikhael Gorbachev in attempting to preserve a restructured Soviet Union. Kazakhstan was the last republic to proclaim independence in December 1991, and has since been one of the most enthusiastic proponents of associative schemes among former Soviet republics, such as the Commonwealth of Independent States.

In April 1990, Nazarbayev exchanged his title of Communist Party secretary general for that of President of Kazakhstan, when the Supreme Soviet of the republic elected him to that position. His assumption of the presidency was confirmed by an election held in December 1991, which he won with 98 percent of the vote, running without opposition. In subsequent years, Nazarbayev orchestrated a series of political manoeuvres that eliminated all possible challenges to his power. These included two dissolutions of parliament in 1993 and 1995; a referendum in April 1995 cancelling the scheduled 1996 presidential election and extending Nazarbayev's term until December 2000; and another referendum in August 1995 for a new constitution, further strengthening the substantial presidential powers that had been granted by the 1993 constitution.[11] A new bicameral legislature, completely subservient to Nazarbayev, was elected in December 1995 to replace the parliament dissolved in March 1995.

Nazarbayev's authoritarian policies have evoked little popular protest because of general apathy and cynicism toward the political elite. Indeed, the members of the dissolved parliament and the judges of the Constitutional Court had discredited themselves in the eyes of the public by their financial profligacy, lack of effectiveness, and dedication to the advancement of their personal interests. The only field in which parliament had been active until 1995 was in opposing the economic reforms of the president, including privatization. Nazarbayev has been forthright in justifying his monopolization of power by citing the special circumstances of his presidency, in particular 'the transitional character of our epoch, the complexities of the lengthy socio-economic transformation, the huge territory of our state and its ethnic composition'.[12]

Unlike the mixed record of his economic initiatives, Nazarbayev's ethnic policies have been more effective. Under the policy of 'Kazakhization', the president has strengthened the position of native Kazakhs within the political, economic and demographic structure of the newly independent state. This policy has included encouraging immigration of ethnic Kazakhs from China and Mongolia, replacing Russians with Kazakh officials, and requiring a knowledge of the Kazakh language to gain access to higher education and employment. However, out-migration of skilled Russians and pressure from Russia forced Nazarbayev to slow the process of 'Kazakhization' by reducing pressure on adult Russians to learn Kazakh and giving the Russian language an official role in the constitution. The Russian language was defined as 'the social language between peoples' and has been used officially as equal to the Kazakh language.[13] During a meeting with Putin in June 2000, Nazarbayev proposed the creation of a foundation for the protection of the Russian language in the CIS, declaring that 'Kazakhs need the Russian language like bread, every day'.[14] Tension over legalization of dual citizenship, which Nazarbayev refused to accept, was mitigated after the conclusion of a treaty with Russia in 1995 easing changes of citizenship and choice of country for military service. Most ethnic Russians have come to accept their diminished status as citizens of Kazakhstan or chosen to migrate from the country.

In a move to neutralize the threat of separatism by ethnic Russians, the Kazakh parliament, at Nazarbayev's request, voted in July 1994 to move the capital from Almaty (former Alma-Ata) to Akmola (Tselinograd). Located in the north, Akmola is situated in an agricultural region originally developed in the late 1950s as a part of Khrushchev's 'virgin lands' program. By moving the capital to Akmola, Nazarbayev has sought to reinforce the Kazakh identity of this Russian-populated region. This decision was severely criticized, especially because of the high cost of the transfer – estimated at a minimum of $1 billion, including a $50 million presidential palace – at a time of scarce financial resources. A first inauguration ceremony was held in December 1997 to mark the move of the government. At a second celebration in July 1998, the name of the new capital city was changed from Akmola, meaning 'white grave', to Astana, a more auspicious – but less original – word meaning 'capital'. While government officials have reluctantly accepted the transfer and moved to the new capital city, the central bank and the diplomatic community have been slow to follow.

As the end of his second term approached, there were clear indications that Nazarbayev wished to remain in office. In October 1998, the government announced its decision to hold the presidential election on 10 January 1999, instead of waiting for the year 2000. Also, a series of measures were passed by parliament which allowed Nazarbayev to become president for life. Protests by the opposition and international human rights organizations that the early elections would not allow other candidates to mount effective electoral campaigns did not alter Nazarbayev's decision. The only candidate capable of presenting a serious threat to Nazarbayev, former prime minister Akezhan Kazhegeldin, was barred from participation under the pretext that he had attended an illegal meeting, while two other candidates were briefly detained for the same reason. These moves were accompanied by harassment of the independent media, to the extent that Holly Carter, executive director of Human Rights Watch's Europe and Central Asia division, declared that 'these presidential elections have been blatantly unfair', and characterized by 'coercion, threats, and the repression of opposition activists'.[15] The OSCE made similar protests and sent only a limited assessment mission, instead of the usual teams of observers. What surprised some analysts is that despite the conditions under which the election took place, Nazarbayev received only 80 percent of the vote, instead of his traditional score of 98.99 percent. While Nazarbayev used the 80 percent vote to make a point about the democratic nature of the election, he admitted that poverty among some sections of the population had motivated the 20 percent of the electorate to vote against him.[16]

Political system

The constitution defines Kazakhstan as a unitary state with a presidential form of government. The 1995 Constitution transformed the legislative branch into a bicameral parliament, with a lower house, the Majlis, composed of 67 members, and a Senate of 47 members. Both senators and Majlis members serve for four years. The judicial branch is headed by a Constitutional Council of six members, two appointed by the president, two by the Senate and two by the lower house. Other important institutions are the National Bank and the Committee for National Security, which succeeded the KGB. The constitutional changes of October 1998 further reinforced the power of the president, eliminating the restrictions that stood in his way to rule for life. Term limits for the presidency were similarly removed, while the president's term of office was extended to seven years. The article barring candidates over 65 years of age was abolished, thus allowing Nazarbayev's candidacy in 2006, when he becomes 66 years old. Members of Parliament extended their own terms of office to five years for the Majlis and six for the Senate. Finally, the Majlis membership was increased to 77,[17] 67 elected by single seat constituencies and 10 by proportional representation.

The role of Kazakh political parties is limited, as most decisions are taken by the president and his entourage. Political parties can be divided into two groups, those supporting the regime, most of which have been set up by the president, and four main opposition groups which include Kazakh nationalist, Russian nationalist, and extremist and moderate leftist parties. In the October 1999 parliamentary elections, which were criticized by OSCE observers, two pro-government parties, the Republican Party Otan and the Civic Party, won 23 and 13 seats respectively. Otan was created in March 1999 to replace the People's Unity Party as a mainstay of regime support. Four opposition parties won eight seats and the rest of the seats went to independent candidates, most of whom were likely supporters of the regime.[18]

At the forefront of the opposition is the Communist Party which brings together those who are nostalgic for the Soviet era. Serikbolsyn

Abildin, the party's leader, ran a campaign focused on economic hardships in the presidential elections of January 1999, and obtained some 11.7 percent of the vote. In the Majlis elections of October 1999, the party received 18 percent of the vote, winning three seats. A Communist fringe group, the Workers' Movement, is led by Madel Ismailov, who has been repeatedly arrested for his oppositional activities. Other opposition parties include the Agrarian Party, with three seats, and the National Cooperative Party with one seat.

As a result of government manipulation and coercion, several opposition groups have been denied Majlis representation. The center-left Azamat, once Kazakhstan's most popular opposition party, failed to win a single seat in 1999. Similarly, former prime minister Akezhan Kazhegeldin's Republican People's Party won only one seat, due to obstacles preventing its registration in all electoral districts and the exile of its leader, who faced an arrest warrant for alleged corruption.[19] The Kazakh nationalist movement is rather small, and split into a radical Islamist and Pan-Turkist faction called Alash, which was outlawed by Nazarbayev, and the more moderate Azat group. Lad (Harmony) is the largest of the parties which appeal to the Russians and other Slavic minorities, although it is weak and poorly organized. More radical Russian and Cossack nationalist groups, such as the Society for Assistance to the Cossacks in Semirechye, have been crushed by the police while moderate Cossack movements are allowed to operate. Lastly, one should note the existence of Tagibat, an ecological and environmental movement, which has expressed opposition to oil projects in the ecologically sensitive areas in the Caspian.

The role of clans

Clans play an important role in the life of Kazakhstan. The Kazakh people traditionally have been divided into Hordes, or zhus, which dominated their historic territories – the Lesser Horde in the west, the Middle Horde in the north and east, and the Greater Horde in the south. Hordes are divided into tribal groups which, in turn, are divided into clans.

In response to their early incorporation into the Russian Empire, the Lesser and Middle Hordes produced most of the Kazakh nationalists, and suffered most from Stalin's repression. In contrast, the presence of socialists in the Greater Horde made its members dominant in the government of Soviet Kazakhstan. This dominance was accentuated by the choice of Almaty as capital, a city located in Greater Horde territory. Both Dinmukhamed Kunaev, who ruled

Kazakhstan from 1964 to 1986, and Nazarbayev, belong to the Greater Horde.

Since the demise of the Communist Party and its patronage system, clan and tribal consciousness have played an increasingly important role in both the economics and politics of the country, thereby alienating non-Kazakh minorities which do not belong to any Horde. According to Kazakh analyst Nurbulat Masanov, clan membership is an essential factor in the selection and career paths of public officials. President Nazarbayev's exploitation of clan identities enables him 'to manipulate personnel policy in his personal interest and to exclude competition, corporate consolidation, or the appearance of political opponents within the government'.[20]

Economic system

Kazakhstan's economic development has followed the general pattern of all former Soviet republics, with the collapse of industrial production, a sharp decline in GDP, and growth of inflation and unemployment. The GDP, at purchasing power parity, fell continuously between 1990 and 1995, with the largest fall in 1994.[21] As a result, at the beginning of 1996 GDP stood at less than half of its 1990 level. An improvement took place in 1996 when the GDP rose by 0.5 percent, and in 1997 by 2 percent. GDP per head stood at $2,587 at the end of 1997, or $1,370 at real value (without PPP), only to drop by 2.5 percent in 1998 as a result of the Russian economic crisis and low oil prices. The oil price increases of 1999 helped the GDP recover by 1.7 percent.[22]

It was only in 1994, after two years of strong recession, that Kazakhstan introduced a reform and stabilization policy with IMF support. Despite the hyperinflation of 1994, provoked by Nazarbayev's cancellation of repayment of agricultural loans until 2000, production growth was restored and inflation reduced. The Kazakh currency, the tenge, introduced in November 1993 following the expulsion of Kazakhstan from the rouble zone, was made convertible in July 1996. Growth, however, was concentrated in a few sectors, such as oil, gas, metal industries and agriculture, while other sectors continued to decline. Budget deficit has been a constant problem, standing at about 3.5 percent of GDP in recent years. These deficits would have been significantly higher had it not been for the income from privatization.

Budget deficits have been accentuated by falling tax revenues due to loopholes in taxation policy, the existence of economic zones which are not subject to import duties, and special tax benefits to foreign investors. The situation has been worsened by the privatization of most of the profitable companies, leaving the unprofitable ones in the public sector. Assessments of the privatization process have been mixed. While a significant part of state-owned companies and farms have been privatized, the restructuring has been insufficient to allow these enterprises to operate without government help in the form of subsidies, protection, and tax and debt deferral. The entire program of privatization has been unpopular, due to public perceptions of a rigged process that transfers the country's wealth into the hands of a small class of nouveaux riches, while the living standards of the rest of the population are in decline.

The GDP growth in 1996 and 1997 was helped by foreign investment, most of which went to the energy sector, which attracted US$3.2 billion. Encouraged by these results, Nazarbayev gave an address in Autumn 1997 entitled 'Kazakhstan 2030', in which he announced his desire to crack down on corruption, to maintain political stability, to remain committed to a market economy and to bring Kazakhstan to a high level of development and prosperity by the year 2030. In a reference to the flourishing economies of the 'Asian Tigers', Nazarbayev compared Kazakhstan to a 'Snow Leopard'. The fall in oil prices in 1998 and the crisis in the East Asian and Russian economies had negative consequences for the Kazakh Snow Leopard, which shared the misfortunes of the Asian Tigers and the Russian Bear.[23] A poor grain harvest did not improve the pessimistic atmosphere. Kazakhstan was saved from economic collapse by the rising oil prices of 1999.

The positive achievements of Kazakhstan's economy have included macroeconomic restructuring, the establishment of a legal framework for a private economy, the adoption of a tradeable currency, liberalized prices and the influx of large amounts of foreign investment into the oil and gas sector. On the negative side, there is widespread corruption and growing income maldistribution between a small minority, which has appropriated a large share of the state's wealth, and the rest of the population, which finds it increasingly hard to survive. Other negative factors include the lack of diversification and overemphasis on the oil and gas sector, as well as the government's inability to pay pensions and wages on time.

As in other post-Soviet regimes, nepotism and corruption have plagued Kazakh political and economic life. Several members of the president's family have occupied key bureaucratic and economic positions. Top officials have been involved in diverting signature bonuses into their personal accounts and taking millions in bribes from oil companies. Recent investigations in Switzerland and the United States have triggered a widening scandal implicating former Prime Ministers Kazhegeldin and Balgimbayev and Nazarbayev himself.[24]

Energy sector

Among the former Soviet republics, Kazakhstan is the second largest oil producer, with 30 million metric tonnes in 1999, while its natural gas production was 9.8 bn cubic meters. Energy exports play a dominant role in the Kazakh economy and, given the country's significant reserves, this role is expected to increase dramatically in the coming years. As a result of Soviet policies and the configuration of existing pipeline networks, Kazakhstan exports most of its oil and gas production, while importing oil from Russia and gas from Uzbekistan and Turkmenistan for domestic needs. The country has three major refineries in Atyrau, Shimkent and Pavlodar, all of which require technological renovation.

The Kazakh oil and gas sector experienced several changes since independence. In March 1997, a major restructuring took place when three ministries were consolidated into a single ministry of energy, industry and trade. Moreover, the state-owned Munaygaz holding company was disbanded and most shares of its subsidiaries were absorbed by Kazakoil – the new state oil company. In 1996, the state began privatizing the oil and gas sector in order to increase efficiency and revenues. However, this program faltered in 1997 and was halted in 1998 because of opposition from Kazakoil executives. Instead, the government began a search for a 'strategic partner' for Kazakoil, without success. Following major financial losses in 1998, Kazakoil sold its 14.28 percent stake in the Offshore Kazakhstan International Operating Company (OKIOC). Meanwhile, the government developed a new legal framework in order to create an attractive climate for foreign investors.

Trends and prospects

The political evolution of Kazakhstan since the constitutional amendments of October 1998 has altered the political landscape. Clearly, the liberal experiment has waned and basic political freedoms have become constrained.[25] The opposition has become progressively weakened, while there has been an unprecedented increase in presidential power that culminated in the granting of 'special powers for life' to secure Nazarbayev's future position, even in retirement.[26]

It can be reasonably argued that the country's future is likely to depend on the regime's willingness to reform itself, reduce corruption and avoid inter-ethnic conflict, as well as its ability to bring increasing amounts of Kazakh oil to international markets. Given the centrality of the oil factor to the Kazakh economy, the future dynamics of oil prices can be expected to determine the future viability of the Kazakh regime and economy.

Azerbaijan

In the last decade, the Republic of Azerbaijan has been a focus of international interest, having been propelled from obscurity into the limelight because of the reported presence of large offshore hydrocarbon reserves. In addition, the country has strategic significance due to its location on the western shores of the Caspian, and as a potential bridge between Central Asia and the outside world.

At the time of the Soviet dissolution, the Soviet Republic of Azerbaijan was in the midst of successive sociopolitical convulsions. These included the Nagorno-Karabakh conflict, the rise of the anti-Soviet Azerbaijan Popular Front (APF), and the intervention of Soviet troops in January 1990 to quell the anti-Armenian pogroms of Baku – all of which have weighed heavily on the country's development to this day.

These political factors, combined with the severe post-Soviet economic decline, destabilized the young state until 1995, when Haidar Aliyev's hold on power was consolidated. Other factors, intrinsic to Azeri society, also contributed to the difficulties of the country. Among these is the formation of an Azeri national identity, which began at the onset of the twentieth century, and is still in the process of consolidation and redefinition.[27] Even the name 'Azerbaijan' has been a subject of controversy. Until 1918, when the Musavat regime decided to name the newly independent state Azerbaijan, this designation had been used exclusively to identify the Iranian province of Azerbaijan.[28] The country's alphabet has been changed several times, from Arabic to Latin, Latin to Cyrillic, and from Cyrillic back to Latin. Azeris are linked to the Turkic world by their language, to Iran by their Shi'a religion, and to the Caucasus region by geography.

Political evolution (1991–2001)

Since its onset in 1988, the conflict over the Nagorno-Karabakh Autonomous Oblast has dominated Azerbaijani politics. The conflict was triggered when the ethnic Armenian majority of the province petitioned the Soviet authorities to reverse Stalin's 1921 edict placing the area within Soviet Azerbaijan, and voted to unite with neighboring Armenia. The dispute took a violent turn following the pogroms by Azeri mobs against the Armenian population in the Azerbaijani city of Sumgait in February 1988, triggering the first ethnic conflict in the Soviet Union. What had been a low-scale armed conflict was transformed into a full-scale war after the Soviet dissolution in late 1991. The shifts in the fortunes of war made and unmade the first leaders of independent Azerbaijan. It was suspected that anti-government factions often orchestrated military defeats on the Karabakh front in order to discredit and topple those in power.

The first president of independent Azerbaijan, the neo-Communist Ayaz Mutalibov, was removed from power in February 1992 after Armenian separatists took the town of Khojaly in Karabakh. In May, Mutalibov attempted, in vain, to regain power after the fall of the Azeri stronghold of Shusha. Mutalibov was overthrown by the Azerbaijan Popular Front (APF), a nationalist movement led by Abulfaz Elchibey, who was formally elected president in June 1992, after an electoral campaign in which his control of the state apparatus assured his victory.[29]

Upon election, Elchibey launched an offensive against Karabakh Armenians, which brought under Azeri control 40 percent of the province's territory. An Armenian counter-offensive in February 1993 recovered some of the lost territories and captured Kelbajar, an Azeri district wedged between Armenia and Karabakh. This reverse was followed by a rebellion in June 1993 led by Surat Husseinov, a businessman and military commander from Ganja. Husseinov's troops marched on Baku, ousting Elchibey and the APF from power.

In order to strengthen his control, Husseinov appealed to Haidar Aliyev to join the new government. A veteran of Soviet politics, Aliyev had transformed his home province of Nakhichevan into a personal fiefdom in 1991–3, waiting for an opportunity to assume power in Baku. In August 1993, a referendum legitimized Elchibey's ouster, followed by presidential elections in October which Aliyev won with 98.9 percent of votes.[30] Meanwhile, the military situation had dramatically deteriorated on the Karabakh front, leaving some 14 to 15 percent of Azerbaijani territory, including the Karabakh province, in the hands of ethnic Armenian forces. In June 1993, there was a short-lived separatist attempt led by Akram Himmatov, who sought to establish an independent Talysh-Mughan republic in the south-eastern part of the country.[31]

In the two years following his election, Aliyev consolidated his grasp on power. In October 1994, Husseinov, who had briefly served as Aliyev's prime minister, was forced to flee to Russia after a failed coup attempt. In March 1995, Aliyev thwarted another coup by Rovshan Javadov, a former deputy minister. While some analysts saw in the attempted coups the hand of Moscow, which was dissatisfied with Aliyev's foreign and oil policies, those familiar with his Machiavellian tactics were inclined to believe that Javadov's coup had been masterminded by Aliyev himself in order to get rid of rivals.[32] Legislative elections were organized in November 1995, giving Aliyev's supporters the overwhelming majority of seats. Both the opposition and international observers agreed that the government had rigged the election and violated most electoral procedures.[33] Aliyev was accused of choosing the members of parliament before the election, and his choices were published by mistake in the press two months before the elections. The list even included the four percent of seats allocated to the opposition.[34] This pattern of electoral impropriety was repeated in the October 1998 presidential elections, as Aliyev was elected with 76.1 percent of votes in the first round amid charges of widespread fraud. Similar improprieties marked the November 2000 legislative elections, characterized by an OSCE official as 'a crash course in the different methodologies of manipulation'.[35]

Political system

According to the constitution that was adopted by referendum in November 1995, Azerbaijan is a presidential republic, with sweeping powers in the hands of the president. The constitution describes the state as democratic, secular and unitary, with special mention of the autonomous status of Nakhichevan. The legislative branch is monocameral, with a 125-member parliament, the Milli Majlis. The judiciary is composed of several courts, including the Constitutional Court and the Supreme Court.

The ruling elite is composed mainly of members of Aliyev's personal family and clan from Nakhichevan. His son, son-in-law and one of his brothers became members of parliament in 1995. His son Ilham is also the vice-president of SOCAR, the Azerbaijani oil company. Indeed, kinship has traditionally played a crucial role in Azeri society and politics. Aliyev belongs to the group of families which relocated from Armenia to Nakhichevan, and hence are derisively called 'Yerazeris' (Yerevan Azeris).[36] Nakhichevan has been the breeding ground of many opposition leaders as well, such as Elchibey, who hails from the Ordubad district.[37] Former Parliamentary Speaker Rasul Gouliev and National Independence Party leader Etibar Mamedov, himself a Yerazeri, are also Nakhichevan natives.[38] According to a study by Kechichian and Karasik, 'Azeri families and clans chose geographical locations to launch their various platforms independent of, and sometimes counter to, each other'.[39] Another opposition figure, Surat Husseinov, was well entrenched in the Ganja region, where he was director of a textile factory prior to launching himself into military and political activities. Some clans have an ethnic base which they can use when they fail to accomplish their ambitions in Baku. For example, Akram Himmatov played the separatist card in the Talysh region when he failed to take power in Baku. Membership in political parties is similarly affected by family and clan links.

There are a large number of political parties in Azerbaijan, but less than an dozen can claim a substantial membership. These parties can be divided into three categories: supporters of the president, centrists who occasionally collaborate with the president, and the opposition. Aliyev has outlawed several political groupings, including the Azerbaijan Islamic Party, and some factions of the Communist party.[40]

The Yeni Azerbaijan Party (New Azerbaijan Party) was created in 1992 by Aliyev's supporters. Its leadership mostly consists of Nakhichevanis and former Communist apparatchiks. This party lacks any particular ideology; its program is to promote Haidar Aliyev as 'the guiding light of the Azeri nation'.[41] The opposition includes the Azerbaijan Popular Front (APF), which ruled the country in 1992–3. As a movement opposing Soviet rule, the APF became an umbrella organization over groups with divergent ideological positions. However, APF's overarching ideology was clearly 'nationalist, pro-Turkish, and even pan-Turkist'.[42] Forced into the opposition after Elchibey's fall, the APF won three seats in the 1995 election.[43] After Elchibey's death in August 2000, APF split into two groupings, weakening its leading role within the opposition. A rival of the APF, the Yeni Musavat Party led by Isa Gambar, has attracted Azeri intellectuals and former ministers and diplomats of the Elchibey era. In keeping with the legacy of the Musavat ruling party of independent Azerbaijan (1918–20), the Yeni Musavat's ideology is based on nationalism, Pan-Turkism and Islamism. Because of restrictions imposed by the regime, the Musavat won only one seat during the 1996 run-off election, and in February 2000 its headquarters were ransacked by a hostile crowd.[44] Persecution by the regime and APF's decline made Isa Gambar's Musavat the leading opposition party. Sharing the nationalist ideology of the APF and Musavat is the left-wing Milli Istiqlal (National Independence) Party, founded in 1991 by Etibar Mamedov. In the October 1998 presidential elections, Mamedov won second place with 11.6 percent of the votes – a surprising outcome in a contest rigged in favour of Aliyev. The party held four seats in the parliament elected in 1995. These three opposition parties have strongly opposed Aliyev's attempts to achieve a peaceful resolution of the Karabakh conflict and advocate the use of force to recover the province.

In March 2000, a cooperation agreement was announced between Mamedov's Milli Istiqlal Party and the Democratic Party of Azerbaijan, which represents the interests of former Parliamentary Speaker Rasul Gouliev. Reported to be one of the richest people in the former Soviet Union, thanks to a fortune built during his years as head of a large oil refinery, Gouliev went into exile in the United States in 1996 after falling out with Aliyev. Gouliev is often presented as one of the most plausible alternatives to Aliyev, although absence from the country has impeded his active participation in political affairs.[45]

To the right of the political spectrum is the extremist Azerbaijan National Democratic Party, also known as Bozkurt Dunyasi (World of the Grey Wolf), which advocates ultra-nationalist and Pan-Turkist policies. Led by Iskendar Hamidov, the party fielded a substantial military force which fought in Karabakh. 'Grey Wolf' refers to a totem of the Turkic peoples in Central Asia and is also the symbol of an ultra-nationalist Turkish party to which the Azeri Bozkurt is linked. In 1995, Hamidov was arrested for his role in an alleged coup against Aliyev, and the party was banned.[46]

In sharp contrast is the Azerbaijan Social Democratic Party, led by Zardusht Alizadeh, former leader of APF's moderate wing. This is a centrist party critical of both the nationalist opposition parties and Aliyev's authoritarian rule. The party favors cultural autonomy for national minorities, including for the Armenians of Karabakh, and cooperates with international human rights organizations; it is believed to have a pro-Russian orientation.[47] Another moderate grouping is the Mustaqil Azerbaijan Party (Independence Party), led by Nizami Suleimanov, a former Aliyev ally who ran against Elchibey in 1992 and won 38 percent of the ballots. In a second try for the presidency in October 1998, Suleimanov came third with 8.6 percent of the votes.

The authoritarian nature of Aliyev's regime has prompted his opponents to warn that Azerbaijan is becoming an Oriental Khanate.[48] Yet his regime has had two significant achievements – bringing stability and attracting large amounts of foreign investment in the oil sector. These successes can be attributed to Aliyev's personal qualities, which even his enemies acknowledge. Often called 'the fox', Aliyev is a master strategist and tactician, with a highly developed capacity to adapt to new situations. Indeed, these were the qualities which helped him to rise in the KGB apparatus, to assume the leadership of Soviet Azerbaijan (1969–82), and later to become a member of the Politburo of the Soviet Communist Party. In 1987, Aliyev fell from power when Gorbachev purged him for his lack of enthusiasm for the perestroika reforms.[49]

However, as leader of independent Azerbaijan, Aliyev has failed to deliver on his two main promises: to resolve the Karabakh conflict to Azerbaijan's advantage and to improve the living standards of the population. A primary factor responsible for his retention of power is a general consensus that a diplomatic solution is the only possible option to regain Karabakh, given the dangers inherent in a renewed military campaign.[50] Hence, the preference for Aliyev the diplomatist over the hot-headed nationalists of the opposition who could push the country into new disasters. Another factor in Aliyev's resilience is that, unlike Elchibey, he has succeeded in monopolizing all the means of coercion and the economic resources of the country. This allows him to distribute lucrative, income-generating government positions and contracts. According to one observer, 'Azerbaijani politics has more and more come to resemble a form of court politics where different politicians and interest groups seek to obtain the ear of Aliyev in order to promote their careers.'[51] The government's policies have benefited a parasitic class of nouveaux riches which supports Aliyev lest it lose its privileges under another regime. A third factor contributing to Aliyev's longevity is the political and financial support accorded to him by the Western powers, Turkey, international financial institutions and oil companies.

The weakness of the opposition, stemming from its structure, has given Aliyev considerable freedom to pursue his policies. Most parties are based on personalities and clans rather than on political programs; as such they lack a popular base and legitimacy among the population. The adherence of some opposition parties to radical ideas of nationalism and Pan-Turkism evoke little popular support. Fear of the harmful consequences of extremist ideologies should the APF or the Musavat come to power explains the estrangement of a large portion of the electorate from the opposition. The first declaration of Elchibey on his return to Baku in November 1997 was to call for a military reconquest of Karabakh. This was particularly ironic, given the disastrous military record of the Azerbaijani army during Elchibey's presidency.

The Achilles' heel of Aliyev's ruling order is Aliyev himself. Serious questions about his health were raised in January 1999, when he was taken to Turkey for an emergency heart operation. There are rumours that Aliyev is grooming his son to succeed him, although the leadership capabilities of Ilham Aliyev have not been tested. The stability which Aliyev brought might not outlast him, and Azerbaijan might plunge again into turmoil.

Economic system

The Azerbaijani economy, like those of other former Soviet republics, went through a sharp decline that was compounded by the Karabakh war. The GDP in 1996 was only 42 percent of its 1990 level, although it has dramatically improved in recent years.[52] The pace of structural reforms has been lagging and progress toward a market economy has been quite slow. However, a number of economic and legal reforms have being implemented, especially in fiscal policy and taxation laws.

The partial recovery of the economy has been primarily driven by foreign investment in the oil sector. Between 1994 and June 1998 these investments brought in $1.8 billion, out of a total of about $40 billion pledged by the oil companies. However, foreign investors avoided non-oil industries because of high political risk, high levels of corruption and distrust toward the bureaucracies in charge of privatization and foreign investment. The 1998 fall in oil prices heightened the vulnerability of an economy lacking diversification. Despite the regime's promise to reduce dependency on oil, experts remained sceptical about the capacity of the authorities to alter the situation.[53]

Energy sector

Oil and gas production constitute the most significant factor in Azerbaijan's economy. After the Soviet dissolution, oil production declined significantly until 1996, when the trend was reversed. In 1999, oil production, with 14.7 million tonnes, exceeded the 1990 level of 12.5 million tonnes. Azerbaijan also produces gas, most of which is consumed locally. Three refineries process all of the country's production.[54]

Azerbaijan lacks a coordinating body on energy issues, and policy is set by the president's office and state-owned monopolies. The State Oil Corporation of the Azerbaijan Republic (SOCAR) was created in 1992 by combining companies controlling onshore and offshore operations. SOCAR oversees most of the oil and gas sector, including the negotiation of deals with foreign investors. Azerigaz, founded in 1992, is charged with the storage, transportation and sales of natural gas.[55] Except in small-scale enterprises such as gas stations, privatization has been impeded by government design. Energy companies were excluded from the 1997 mass privatization program. In recent years, Azerbaijan has attracted considerable foreign investment to renew its energy infrastructure and develop new offshore fields. The state has concluded Production Sharing Agreements (PSA) with foreign firms, each of which requires parliamentary ratification due to the lack of a general legislative framework covering the energy sector.[56]

Trends and prospects
President Aliyev has managed to take advantage of the West's prioritization of political and economic interests over democracy and human rights concerns in the Caspian region.[57] When under international pressure to improve his country's dismal human rights situation, Aliyev has implemented cosmetic changes, such as officially abolishing media censorship, although the office in charge of censorship has continued to operate.[58] Barring health problems, Aliyev is likely to continue in power and manage to develop the oil industry. He might even, with the help of the United States and other Western powers, negotiate a favorable settlement on Karabakh. However, low levels of oil production, combined with high costs of extraction and widespread corruption, are likely to prevent a substantial improvement in the living standards of the population. Growing maldistribution of income and the accompanying frustration may trigger the rise of radical revolutionary movements. The price that the West would then pay for its indifference to democracy and human rights in Azerbaijan would be quite high, given the billions invested in the development of the country's energy resources.

Turkmenistan

The pattern of authoritarian rule characteristic of former Soviet republics also defines the political system of Turkmenistan. What distinguishes Turkmenistan from its neighbors is its singularly autocratic nature, with President Saparmurad Niyazov controlling a polity devoid of opposition parties and constraints to his rule. An autocrat with a personality cult, Niyazov has been the dominant figure in the Turkmen landscape since Communist times.

In 1986 Niyazov was named the head of the Communist Party of Turkmenistan, when Gorbachev fired the Brezhnev-era leader, Muhammednazar Gapurov. Gorbachev's glasnost and perestroika had little effect on Turkmenistan, as Niyazov opposed their implementation ostensibly because these policies had triggered ethnic conflicts in other parts of the Soviet Union. Significantly, Niyazov was among those leaders who strongly opposed the dissolution of the Soviet Union. Indeed, Turkmenistan voted overwhelmingly in the March 1991 referendum to preserve the Soviet Union, and Niyazov supported the abortive August 1991 putsch against Gorbachev. In October 1991, however, Niyazov followed the other Soviet republics in organizing a referendum in favour of independence. The poverty of Turkmenistan, one of the least developed Soviet republics, and its consequent dependence on Moscow, was the major cause of the Turkmen desire to preserve the Union. Yet the prospect of income generated by the country's gas reserves did evoke some support for the proclamation of independence.

Political evolution (1991–2001)

The Soviet demise allowed Niyazov to do away with the timid democratization efforts that had taken place in Turkmenistan during the Gorbachev era. Instead, Niyazov established a political system almost identical to the pre-Gorbachev Soviet polity, except in its substitution of Turkmen patriotism for Communist ideology. Since independence, Niyazov has emphasized the need for stability and gradual reform, and opposed the introduction of democratic practices and multi-party politics into Turkmen political life.

Niyazov was twice elected president, in October 1990 and in June 1992, running unopposed and garnering over 98 percent of the votes. A referendum held in January 1994 extended Niyazov's term of office until 2002, thereby cancelling the scheduled 1997 election. In late 1994, the first Majlis of 50 members was elected. All the candidates ran unopposed, and all belonged to the Democratic Party, the new name of the re-baptized Communist Party. Typically, the Turkmen practice is to claim overwhelming electoral victories (99 percent), reflecting Niyazov's belief that Turkmen psychology requires such displays of unanimity.[59] This pattern was repeated in the October 1999 Majlis elections, where political parties were disallowed, and when the Halk Maskhalaty – the People's Council –

took the unprecedented decision to proclaim Niyazov president for life in December 1999.

The late 1980s saw the emergence of several political movements that were outlawed after independence, and their leaders sent to prison, labour camps, psychiatric hospitals or into exile. Thus, the regime's opponents, both at home and abroad, have had a negligible impact on the life of the republic. A rare manifestation of popular discontent occurred in the July 1995 demonstrations against shortages, resulting in arrests and incarceration.[60]

Niyazov's dominant role is best shown by his adoption of the name Turkmenbashi – the head of all Turkmen – a title made official in October 1993 by parliament, which also declared his birthday a public holiday.[61] Turkmenbashi has become a prized name given to schools, farms, streets, institutions, districts and the city-port of Krasnovodsk on the Caspian. One of parliament's preoccupations has been to decide where to build the next statue of Niyazov, or which avenue to name after him. Although in several instances Niyazov has publicly requested a halt to the honorific usage of his name, the cult of personality has persisted. Aside from satisfying the needs of the president's psyche, the political utility of his personality cult is its role to promote unity in a population divided along tribal lines. Niyazov's background as an orphan, lacking firm family or tribal ties, places him in a unique position to become a symbol unifying all Turkmen, irrespective of clan differences.

Political system

According to the constitution adopted in 1992, Turkmenistan is a democratic and secular republic, with a presidential system. The constitution contains clauses on human rights, political freedoms, elections and representation, although these provisions are rarely put into practice. Above the 50-member Majlis is the Halk Maskhalaty, the country's supreme representative body, which brings together all cabinet ministers, local officials, provincial governors, Majlis members, Supreme Court judges and the procurator general. Niyazov uses the Halk Maskhalaty as a national forum of elites to legitimize his policies. The legitimizing function in a symbolic sense is reinforced by a Council of Elders, which harks back to the pre-Soviet Turkmen tradition of consultation with respected elder citizens and tribal leaders.

The constitution assigns a pre-eminent role to the executive branch, headed by the president. His wide-ranging powers include the appointment, without parliamentary approval, of the cabinet, regional governors and judges, and the dissolution of parliament. He also is empowered to appoint the Chairman of the Supreme Court and the General Procurator, with parliament's approval. In addition, Niyazov heads the Council of Defence and National Security, a cultural association called the National Revival Movement, and the Humanitarian Association of Turkmen of the World, which promotes relations with the Turkmen diaspora.

The President's Democratic Party is the only legally registered political organization. As the successor to the Communist Party, the Democratic Party inherited its membership and Leninist party structure, with cells in factories, enterprises and institutions. Its membership is estimated to be between 60,000 and 112,000, and it is chaired by the Turkmenbashi. The Peasants' Party of Turkmenistan, founded in early 1992, was part of the regime's short-lived attempt at creating an 'official' opposition to improve the country's international image. In December 1993, the party was allowed to register without the minimum membership of 1,000 required by the constitution. As the economy declined dramatically in 1994, the Peasants' Party was neutralized by Niyazov, who feared that it could gain popularity at the expense of his Democratic Party.[62]

The political movements that emerged in the perestroika years met their demise during Niyazov's stewardship. The Agzybirlik, founded in 1989 as the Society for the Preservation of the Turkmen Language, advocated independence, revival of Turkmen language and history, and reversal of the ecological degradation caused by Soviet central planning and prolonged cotton monoculture. Its membership consisted mainly of urban intellectuals. The party was banned in January 1990, and its members became victims of harassment, dismissal from work, imprisonment and occasionally death. In 1992, after serving two years in jail, Agzybirlik's leader, Shiraly Nurmyradov, went into exile in Moscow. Another opposition grouping is the Democratic Party of Turkmenistan, which broke away from Agzybirlik in late 1990. The party's leader, Durdymurat Khoja-Mukhamedov, was incarcerated in a mental hospital for two years, only to be released in April 1998 during Niyazov's first official visit to the United States. The party shares with Agzybirlik a newsletter, *Dayanch*, published in Moscow. The opposition also included the Movement for Political Reforms, which had two deputies in Turkmenistan's Supreme Soviet, the legislative body that was replaced by the Majlis.

Tribes and clans

Traditionally, Turkmen have been organized along a tribal structure. The Tekke is the largest tribe, divided into two groups, the Tekke of Ahal province and the Tekke of Mary province. Other large tribes include the Yomuts and Ersary, while the Salyr, Sarik and Choudour are smaller tribes. Tribal identity remains strong, as reflected in the practice of endogamy and differences in dialect and dress. Opinions differ as to whether tribal loyalty was as strong in Soviet times as it is today, as some argue that Turkmenistan has experienced a revival of tribalism since independence.[63] Niyazov plays a careful balancing act among the tribes in the distribution of official positions. The potential threat of inter-tribal conflict has been his main justification in rejecting a more democratic mode of government.

Economic system

The Turkmen economy is based on agriculture, mostly cotton, and the export of gas. The quantity of cotton harvested since independence has declined from 1341 thousand tonnes in 1993 to 437 thousand tonnes in 1996, after which it registered substantial increases, returning to its previous high point in 1999.[64] The production of gas fell from 65.2 billion cubic meters in 1993 to 13.25 billion in 1998, but rose to 22.9 billion in 1999. The economy was harmed by the failure of several CIS republics to pay for Turkmen gas deliveries, and Gazprom's blockage of gas exports through its pipeline network. The GDP for 1997, which was expected to register its first positive growth of about 10 percent since independence, fell by 25.9 percent.[65] As Niyazov could not afford to cut subsidies for utilities, rent and public transport, or to reform the pension system, any improvement in the economy depended on the development of new gas export routes or a new arrangement with Gazprom, rather than on Niyazov's unrealistic grand economic plans. Thus, the resumption of gas deliveries to Russia and rising energy prices resulted in GDP growth rates of 9 percent and 17 percent in 1999 and 2000 respectively.

Although Turkmenistan has often been called the Kuwait of the Caspian, it has yet to benefit from the export of its oil and gas resources. Meanwhile, Niyazov and a small circle of officials and relatives have developed a lifestyle comparable to that of Persian Gulf elites. The country's meager resources are wasted on useless projects, such as presidential palaces and numerous hotels, which remain unoccupied as tourists rarely come to visit Turkmenistan. Executives of major international oil companies know that unofficial payments are part of the rules of doing business in Turkmenistan, although such handouts do not guarantee protection against sudden cancellation of verbal or written contracts, as experienced by Bridas, an Argentine company.

Like Nazarbayev, Niyazov has the habit of periodically sacking government officials to deflect attention from his policy failures. A wave of dismissals took place in summer 1998 and included district governors, cabinet ministers and prosecutors, for reasons ranging from corruption and nepotism to incompetence. The secrecy that surrounds Turkmenistan's politics makes it almost impossible to determine the reasons for each purge, which could be motivated by tribal politics or fear of the rise of potential rivals.

Energy sector

With proven gas reserves at around 2.28 trillion cubic meters, the country has the capacity to become one of the world's foremost gas producers. In 1993, a presidential decree consolidated all energy-related companies under a single ministry, although they were decentralized three years later. Major components of the Turkmen oil and gas sector are Turkmenneft, Turkmengaz, Turkmenneftegaz and Turkmenneftegazstroi.[66] Turkmenistan has two refineries, a small network of crude oil pipelines and an extensive gas pipeline grid.[67] In keeping with the Soviet precedent, the state remains in control of the energy sector, which is excluded from privatization projects. In view of the centrality of the energy sector, all oil and gas decisions are made by Saparmurad Niyazov, the Turkmenbashi.

Trends and prospects

The short-term prospects for Turkmenistan's development are not encouraging, despite progress on the economic front in 1999 and 2000. This is all the more disappointing as the country did not experience civil war, like Azerbaijan, or inter-ethnic tension, like Kazakhstan. While Niyazov shares much of the responsibility for the economic and political failures of the young state, he is not completely at fault, because other factors such as low commodity prices and landlocked location have played a significant role. The tacit contract between Niyazov and the Turkmen people might be severely tested in that the regime is increasingly unable to provide for basic needs, making more intolerable the president's authoritarian rule. While no revolution is likely to happen, given the control exerted by the state, any event altering the present status quo, such as health problems affecting Niyazov who has had two heart surgeries, might trigger a period of trouble and chaos in Turkmenistan.

CHAPTER 6

The Riparian States: Interstate Relations

At the crux of Caspian geopolitics is the network of relations among the five riparian states. Each of these states possesses a set of interests and foreign policies which are shaped by a combination of domestic, regional and global determinants. The actual formation of foreign policy in all five states is heavily influenced by domestic factors, and especially by the ruling elites. Indeed, foreign policymaking is the exclusive domain of the presidents of Azerbaijan, Kazakhstan and Turkmenistan, while in Russia and Iran interest groups and popular sentiment also play a significant role.

As newly independent states, Azerbaijan, Kazakhstan and Turkmenistan had to forge foreign policies consonant with the views and perceptions of their leaders, all of whom lacked diplomatic experience. All three states share foreign policy priorities – to secure their independence and territorial integrity, and to develop strong links with the outside world in order to counterbalance the influence of Russia and other regional hegemons. Another shared factor is their use of energy resources in order to maximize their political roles in the regional and international spheres.

In the case of Azerbaijan, the dispute over the Nagorno-Karabakh enclave has been a focal foreign policy concern and has even shaped the government's energy strategy. By seeking a large number of politically influential countries to invest in its oil and gas sector, the Aliyev regime has sought to marshal international support in its struggle to recover Nagorno-Karabakh. An additional priority is the development of peaceful relations with neighboring states in order to secure oil and gas export venues.

The foreign policy priorities of Kazakhstan are shaped by the country's large size, proximity to Russia and demographic balance between its Kazakh and Slavic citizens. Two additional foci of Kazakh foreign policy are the expanding influence of China and Uzbekistan's irredentist tendencies. Also, as a landlocked energy exporter, Kazakhstan tends to support initiatives to achieve regional harmony. Similar concerns define the foreign policy of Turkmenistan, which needs to export its gas production. Moreover, the country's geographical position dictates the need to maintain a balance between two powerful neighbors – Iran and Uzbekistan.

As the largest and most powerful riparian state, Russia's foreign policy interests require particular attention. The four major goals of Russian foreign policy are to preserve the federation's territorial integrity, to maintain Russia's status as a great power, to revive its struggling economy, and to reassert Russian influence in the former Soviet republics. In this context, the Central Asian and Caucasian republics represent a special challenge to Russian foreign policy, in view of the expansion of American and Western influence in those countries. Russia's internal problems and economic decline in the 1990s resulted in differences of views among policymakers and a lack of clarity of policy objectives. Consequently, Russian regional policy assumed an *ad hoc* character, evolving according to the needs of the day.

In the early post-Soviet period, Russia was beset by internal problems and showed little interest in the affairs of Central Asia and Transcaucasia. It was not until April 1992 that Foreign Minister Andrei Kozyrev first visited the region.[1] The next phase witnessed a more activist Russian role in the affairs of the 'Near Abroad', as the former Soviet republics came to be known. Russia began to push for integration in the Commonwealth of Independent States (CIS), and intervened directly or indirectly in the conflicts besetting Azerbaijan, Georgia and Tajikistan.[2] This renewed Russian involvement drew heavy criticism from Western circles, which referred to it as the 'return of the Empire'.[3]

Despite recent vicissitudes in Russian policy, there is a consensus that Russia has strategic security interests in the southern former Soviet republics, and that it cannot remain indifferent to events in the area or be superseded as the region's dominant power. In its security dimension, this policy has resulted in the establishment of Russian military bases along the external borders of CIS members and the deployment of troops in conflict zones. Politically, the emphasis was placed on integration within the CIS and the conclusion of various bilateral and multilateral agreements, in which the fate of Russians living in Central Asia and the Caucasus played a prominent role. As to the economic dimension of Russian policy in the Near Abroad, the energy sector has assumed a dominant position in recent years.[4] Indeed, energy issues have gained prominence in the relations between Russia and the former Soviet republics, as the energy sector has assumed a leading role in the Russian economy, providing 40 percent of the budget and over half of export earnings. The growing clout of the energy industry was seen in the rise of oil barons, such as Viktor Chernomyrdin, to top positions in the state apparatus.[5]

Russia's interests in the Caspian stem from its riparian location and strategic goals, as well as the region's energy wealth. Control over production and transport of the oil and gas resources of the newly independent republics is a primary instrument to maintain Russian influence in these states. In the Yeltsin period, Caspian policies were often fuzzy amid policy differences among political and business elites. 'Pragmatists', mostly associated with the oil and gas industry, favored cooperation with Western oil companies and the energy-producing states of the Caspian rim, while hardliners, or 'post-imperialists', preferred to use forceful means to accomplish Russian foreign policy objectives.[6] However, such pragmatism did not prevent the oil and gas interests from restraining the transit of Kazakh oil and Turkmen gas through the Russian pipeline network. It was only following the departure from power of Viktor Chernomyrdin that a more accommodative policy toward Kazakhstan emerged with the signing of the July 1998 accord on the division of the seabed and increases in the volume of Kazakh oil transiting Russia.[7]

Under President Putin, the Caspian region has witnessed a more assertive brand of Russian policy. Criticizing past Russian passivity, Putin stated in April 2000 Russia's determination to compete in all aspects of Caspian development, while avoiding confrontation. As a part of his new Caspian initiative, Putin appointed Viktor Kalyuzhny as Russia's special representative in the region, and pressured Gazprom to join Lukoil and Yukos in forming the Caspian Oil Company to strengthen the Russian presence in the Caspian.[8]

As the second most powerful Caspian state, Iran is a major player in the region's political arena. The four main objectives of Iranian foreign policy are to preserve the country's security against threats from Iraq, the Afghan Taliban, Turkey, Israel and the United States; to break out of the political and economic isolation imposed by the United States; to create a Persian Gulf security system without the interference of outside powers; and to forge a regional alliance system in order to defend its territorial integrity and play an expanding role as an energy supplier.

In the Caspian setting, Iran has sought to come to grips with the radical changes that have taken place along its northern borders since the USSR's dissolution. The new configuration of power around the Caspian after 1991 presented the Islamic Republic with both opportunities and challenges. Iran was concerned about the spillover of instability from its northern neighbors which could foment domestic unrest, although it also wished to develop amicable relations with these republics.[9]

Hence, Iran's Caspian policies revolve around five main objectives: the development of bilateral links with all riparian states; the limitation of Western and other outside influences in the region; the creation of regional cooperative associations; the promotion of its role as a transit venue for energy resources; and upholding the 1940 Iranian–Soviet Treaty until the littoral countries agree on a new legal status for the Caspian that would give Iran an 'equitable' (20 percent) share of the sea's resources.[10] On the cultural front, Iran has disappointed most observers who expected the Islamic Republic to export its revolutionary ideology to its northern neighbors. Although it shares a common faith with the Muslim republics of the Caspian, Iran has accorded a higher priority to its relations with Russia.[11]

It is against the backdrop of these determinants of state policy that the dynamics of the Caspian should be considered. At the epicenter of the region's geopolitics are the ten-fold relationships among the five riparian states which are determined by their respective national interests, the influence of an inner circle of regional actors and of an external ring of state and non-state actors, as depicted in Figure 1.

Iran and Russia

Observed from a historical perspective, the excellent relations that Russia and Iran share nowadays might appear ironic. In addition to nineteenth century Iranian territorial losses to Russia around the Caspian, Iran has had to confront Soviet-backed separatist movements in Gilan in the 1920s,[12] and in its Azeri- and Kurdish-populated areas in the mid-1940s. In the years preceding the collapse of the Soviet Union, some influential clerics had publicly declared that Tajikistan, Turkmenistan, Uzbekistan and part of Georgia, which Russia had usurped in the nineteenth century, should be restored to Iran.[13] Meanwhile, in a missionary mode, Ayatollah Khomeini advised Soviet leader Gorbachev in 1989 to study Islam as a substitute to Communism as the Soviet Union's dominant ideology.[14]

In the post-Soviet period, ideology and rhetoric were replaced by pragmatism and realism in Iranian foreign policy. Isolated by the West, Iran recognized the benefits of amicable relations with Russia, most notably in securing arms and nuclear reactors, and abstained from antagonizing its northern neighbor, even sacrificing Islamist causes it would have been expected to support.[15] According to Shireen Hunter, 'Iran's Central Asia policy has been so devoid of ideological influence or sentimentalism as to be nearly cynical.'[16] This policy can best be exemplified by Iran's moderate attitude during the Tajik crisis, as Iranians preferred to limit themselves to mediation among the warring parties rather than providing material support to the so-called Islamist opposition.[17]

Russia became more responsive to Iranian interests in 1992, as it shifted its foreign policy from a pro-Western or Atlantist emphasis, to a more eastern and southern-oriented Eurasianist position. Moreover, Russia abandoned its initial preference for Turkey over Iran for an expanded role in the former Soviet South. By April 1993, the Russian position had been reversed in favour of Iran. In the words of Foreign Minister Andrei Kozyrev, spoken during an official visit to Tehran, 'a strategic parity had to be established between Iran and Russia to ensure stability in Transcaucasia and Central Asia'.[18] Andranik Mihranian, an adviser to Yeltsin, countered American objections to the Iranian–Russian rapprochement by declaring: 'We will not let the West dictate to Russia how far it can go in its relations [with Iran]'.[19] Russia considered Western accusations of Iranian-sponsored terrorism as exaggerated, and saw Iran's isolation by the United States as counter-productive.[20] The closeness between the two countries could be mostly credited to Iran's success in dissipating Russian concerns about Iranian intentions in Central Asia and the Caucasus.

Iran and Russia share a number of mutual interests beyond their commercial ties in the defence sector and the civilian nuclear power industry. Unlike the United States, Russia does not oppose the building of a trans-Iranian pipeline to export Turkmen gas.[21] Continued access to the Iranian ports on the Persian Gulf is important for Russia. The two states view with suspicion the growth of American and Turkish influences in the former Soviet South, which in the Caspian context is expressed by their opposition to the building of the Baku–Ceyhan and the trans-Caspian pipelines. The emergence of a US–Turkish–Azerbaijani axis has made close Russian–Iranian ties a geopolitical imperative. Furthermore, Iran and Russia support the factions opposing the Pakistani-backed Taliban in Afghanistan.

Iran fears unrest on its northern borders and appreciates the presence of Russian military units in the Caucasus and Central Asia.[22]

Despite the generally friendly tenor of Iranian–Russian relations, it should not be forgotten that the two countries remain competitors for the transit of Caspian oil and gas. In addition, several conflictual issues have emerged in recent years. In July 1998, Iran opposed the Kazakh–Russian agreement on the division of the Caspian seabed, emphasizing the necessity of equal sharing of undersea wealth by the littoral states.[23] Iranian officials were irritated by the proposals to resolve the sea's legal status, which were advanced during Russian special envoy Viktor Kalyuzhny's visit to Caspian capitals in July 2000.[24] Another point of contention is Iran's displeasure with the human rights violations of the Russian military in the second Chechen war, despite Moscow's assurances that its campaign does not have an anti-Islamic objective.[25]

It would be tendentious to describe the amicable state of relations between Iran and Russia as merely the rapprochement of 'two authoritarian states conducting policies that have isolated them to some degree from the international community'.[26] It is not authoritarianism that brings Iran and Russia together, and there is little that the two countries share ideologically. Clearly, the new Russia–Iran axis is the result of common interests; one such in the geopolitical realm being to contain US and Turkish expansionism, in conformity with balance of power and neorealist theories.

Iran and Kazakhstan

Among the Central Asian peoples, the Kazakhs and the Kyrgyz have been least influenced by Iran due to their Turkic–Mongol nomadic origins and their lack of strong attachment to Islam. In addition to cultural and religious differences, the relations between Kazakhstan and Iran are hindered by physical distance, as they do not share common borders, although they are connected by the Caspian. The two states established their first contacts in November 1991, in the aftermath of the Soviet collapse.[27]

Iranian–Kazakh relations were initially slow to develop, as Kazakhstan did not want to antagonize the United States, feared Iranian proselytism and was unimpressed by the Iranian model of Islamic government.[28] However, once Kazakhstan realized that Iranian priorities were mostly of an economic nature, relations developed with fewer constraints. After the mid-1990s, US opposition to Kazakh–Iranian ties became a lesser concern because

Kazakhstan was replaced by Uzbekistan as America's most favoured Central Asian partner.[29] Some 45 Iranian companies were operating in Kazakhstan by spring 1995, and the figure had increased to 250 by mid-1997.[30] Due to its geographic location, Iran represents for landlocked Kazakhstan the most economically sensible route to the outside world; the two countries are now connected by land after the inauguration, in April 1996, of the link between the Turkmen and Iranian railway networks. In a statement made during his visit to Washington in November 1997, Nazarbayev did not exclude the construction of a Kazakhstan–Turkmenistan–Iran pipeline.[31] Agreements have been signed concerning long-term pipeline projects and immediate oil swaps deals, although technical problems and disagreements have led to interruptions of oil deliveries. Contacts have been established at the sub-national level as well, between Iranian and Kazakh provinces of the Caspian littoral.[32]

Relations were harmed by the arrest of three Iranian citizens in February 1998, who were charged for spying in Kazakhstan.[33] Yet this was only a temporary setback, as reflected in President Nazarbayev's friendly visit to Tehran in October 1999, which resulted in agreements on railway transportation, grain sales, cultural exchanges, counter-terrorism and counter-narcotics. However, no final agreement was reached on tariffs and conditions for oil swaps.[34] After the discovery of substantial deposits in the Kashagan sector off the Kazakh coast in May 2000, Iran revived its proposal to build a trans-Iranian export route for Kazakh oil.[35]

The legal status of the Caspian is the sole issue of importance on which the two countries disagree, as Kazakhstan has expressed a preference for a division of the sea into national sectors. Having previously advocated the joint development of Caspian resources by the riparian states, Iran proposed in November 1999 to split the seabed into equal sectors, a position repeated by President Khatami in June 2000. Kazakh foreign minister Erlan Idrisov welcomed Iran's new stance, although he rejected the principle of division of the seabed into equal sectors.[36]

Iran and Turkmenistan

It is with Niyazov's Turkmenistan that Iran has found its most flourishing Central Asian relationship. Niyazov has always shown little enthusiasm for regional or international multilateral cooperation schemes, instead favoring bilateral and trilateral contacts. Since 1992, he has resolutely engaged his country in a close relationship with Iran. The independent-minded Niyazov has remained deaf both to American warnings against the threat of Islamism from Iran, and to Iranian discontent at his dealings with the Taliban, Pakistan and Israel. Turkmenistan desperately needs to export its gas and oil to international markets, because its CIS clients have been unable to pay for their gas supplies. Iran provides Turkmenistan with one of its most realizable options to reach the outside world. This possibility explains Niyazov's persistent pursuit of the trans-Iranian gas pipeline project, and the construction of a link between the Iranian and Turkmen railway networks, even at the risk of alienating the United States.[37] Thus, Turkmenistan would welcome any improvement in US–Iranian relations which would help resolve its pipeline dilemma.

Furthermore, given Turkmenistan's small population, it cannot afford to antagonize Iran, with which it shares a 1,500 km long border; it also regards Iran as a counterweight to Uzbek expansionism. Finally, Turkmenistan has periodically sided with Iran and Russia on the question of the legal status of the Caspian, criticizing Azerbaijan's 'unilateral' decisions on that issue. While Turkmenistan has not opposed the demarcation of national sectors, it favors consultation among riparian states in all domains related to the sea.[38] In an expression of solidarity, in July 2000 the Turkmen foreign minister told the Russian special envoy on the Caspian that his country would not take part in any discussion on legal status without Iran's participation.[39]

Because of Turkmenistan's multifaceted vulnerabilities, its relations with Iran are affected by the interests of third parties such as Azerbaijan, Turkey, Russia and the United States. Hence Niyazov's frequent policy reversals on the trans-Afghan, trans-Iranian, and trans-Caspian pipeline projects. Also, Iran has shown irritation over Niyazov's changing stance on the Caspian's legal status. Thus, Iran–Turkmenistan relations have gone through ups and downs despite their overall amicability. In October 1999, agreements were concluded to build the Druzhba dam on the Tejan river and expand the highway system between the two countries.[40] Yet, Turkmen gas exports through the newly built pipeline have dropped considerably, causing Iranian displeasure. Iran has blamed Turkmenistan for delays in expanding gas production as well as for charging prices higher than its Ukrainian and Russian customers.[41] The long term prospects of mutual cooperation may be clouded by the potential rivalry of the two countries as major gas exporters to such markets as Pakistan. Despite this rivalry, Iran sees Turkmenistan as a potential partner in a scheme to establish a natural gas consortium bringing together all major producers, including Russia. Such an effort could evolve into a natural gas equivalent to OPEC, which could fix price levels or market share.[42]

Azerbaijan and Iran

The relationship between Iran and Azerbaijan may be qualified as problematic. The territory that is now the Republic of Azerbaijan used to belong to the Persian Empire, until its annexation by the Russians in the early nineteenth century. The Azerbaijanis are Shi'a like the Persians, but speak a Turkic dialect. In addition, there is a sizeable Azeri minority in north-western Iran, with estimates ranging from 10 to 20 million.[43] Consequently, Baku and Tehran have been wary of each other, the Iranians fearing Azeri nationalist plans for a 'Greater Azerbaijan', and the Azerbaijanis fearing the expansion of Iranian influence in their country, especially through the medium of the Shi'a faith that is shared by both states.

Relations deteriorated in 1992–3 during the tenure of Abulfaz Elchibey, leader of the Azerbaijani Popular Front. Elchibey's pro-Turkish policies and his frequent allusions to 'the oppressed brothers of Southern Azerbaijan' deeply alienated Iran. Azerbaijan was critical of Iran's neutral position in the Armenia–Azerbaijan conflict over the province of Nagorno-Karabakh; it even accused Iran of siding with the Armenians.[44] Relations between the two countries improved somewhat after Elchibey's overthrow in 1993 and the accession of Haidar Aliyev. However, despite some progress on the development of economic links and projects in transport infrastructure,[45] it soon became apparent to the Iranians that they came second to the West and Turkey on Aliyev's foreign policy list. Aliyev's attitude was best exemplified by his cancellation of Iranian participation in the 'Contract of the Century' as a result of American pressure, including a phone call from President Clinton.[46] In retaliation, Iran joined Russia in opposing the division of the sea, and has adhered to that position consistently. Despite Azerbaijani offers to include Iran in other oil development contracts, relations remained far from amicable.

Among the critical issues troubling Azeri–Iranian relations are Azerbaijan's close ties with the United States, Turkey and Israel; Azerbaijan's refusal to consider a trans-Iranian oil export route; Iran's insistence on the equal division of the resources of the Caspian; and problems relating to Iran's Azeri population. Azerbaijan's expressed desire to establish a NATO base on its territory have triggered strong Iranian protests. Oil contracts signed by the two sides have brought mutual recrimination regarding the encroachment by each side into the other's seabed sector. After an incident in July 2000 involving Iran's removal of a buoy placed in the Caspian by Azerbaijan to demarcate its sector, Ayatollah Khamenei declared that his country would defend its historic rights and borders on land and on sea. Yet, the subsequent conclusion of a preliminary accord to conduct joint research in border areas was interpreted as a sign of possible Iranian flexibility on issues of the Caspian's legal status.[47] More serious were Iranian concerns about Azerbaijani complicity in provoking the January 2000 demonstrations of ethnic Azeris in the Iranian city of Tabriz, which led to a government crackdown.[48] In an apparent response, while visiting Tehran in March 2000, Foreign Minister Velayat Guliev complained about restrictions on the linguistic rights of ethnic Azeris in Iran.[49] The rift between the two neighbors was widened by the severing of Iranian electricity supplies to Nakhichevan province in late October 2000 due to Azeri debt arrears, which evoked an attack on the Iranian consulate.[50] The multiplicity of issues between the two countries – Caspian boundaries, energy transit, foreign policy and ethnic tensions – do not bode well for the improvement of bilateral relations in the near future.

Kazakhstan and Russia

Under Soviet rule Kazakhstan constituted a region of its own, distinct from the four other Central Asian republics, which were grouped together as 'Middle Asia'. From a Russian foreign policy perspective this distinction remains, because Kazakhstan is held to be more important than the rest of the Central Asian republics combined. The border between the two countries is 6,846 kilometers long, one of the longest in the world. Despite the withdrawal of nuclear weapons from its territory and the shut-down of the Semipalatinsk nuclear test site, Kazakhstan still hosts military-industrial installations essential to Russia, such as the Baikonur space launch complex and the early-warning radar centre at Sari-Shaghan.[51] The economic interdependence between the two countries, the richness of Kazakhstan's natural resources, its size and strategic location, are key elements placing Kazakhstan in the highest category of Russian foreign policy priorities.

Analysts agree that the large Russian community in Kazakhstan is by far the most consequential factor in Kazakh–Russian relations.

Once co-equal to the Kazakhs, the estimated 5.6 million Russians still represent some 34 percent of Kazakhstan's total population.[52] Thus, a primary objective of the Kazakh leadership has been to reduce the threat of partition by pursuing a policy of alliance and cooperation with Russia and by championing bilateral and multilateral integration efforts, even at the risk of limiting Kazakhstan's sovereignty and thereby alienating its nationalist youth.[53] This policy of accommodation toward its powerful neighbor is likely to continue until Nazarbayev's skilfully pursued 'Kazakhization' policies produce tangible results that would allow Kazakhstan to loosen the Russian hold on its destiny. It should also be noted that a strong Russian presence in the area is seen as protection against possible threats from China and Uzbekistan, as the Kazakhs are acutely conscious of the geopolitical consequences of having a large territory and a small population. Hence the existence of multifaceted security and defence agreements both at the bilateral level and with other neighboring states within the CIS framework.[54] Yet, despite the necessity for Russian protection, Nazarbayev has remained firm on the rejection of dual citizenship for ethnic Russians living in Kazakhstan.[55]

Nazarbayev, an admirer of the European Union, proposed in 1994 the formation of a 'Eurasian Union', which would limit the sovereignty of member states while containing Russian supremacy within a majority vote structure. In response to the lack of enthusiasm among CIS members for such a scheme, in 1995 Kazakhstan formed a tripartite customs union with Belarus and Russia, which expanded to include Kyrgyzstan and Tajikistan.[56] The Customs Union was superseded by the creation of the Eurasian Economic Community in October 2000.[57]

On the legal status of the Caspian, to the admiration of Western observers, Kazakhstan has resisted Russian and Iranian pressure to abandon its support for the division of the sea into national sectors. However, it has shown greater flexibility than Azerbaijan and has refrained from exploiting offshore fields too distant from its coastline.[58] In an interesting twist of the legal status question, in August 1997 Kazakhstan protested Russian plans to organize a tender for offshore fields located in an area it considered as Kazakh territory.[59] This stance prompted a rebuff by a Russian foreign ministry official: 'the sovereignty of littoral countries ends on the coast and does not extend to the seabed or the surface. In line with the existing status ... all of the Caspian Sea is open for use by all littoral states'.[60] Kazakhstan's position ultimately prevailed when, in a further twist, the two countries agreed to divide the seabed in July 1998, although the demarcation of the sectors and the joint exploitation of contested fields remain to be determined.

In the economic domain, particularly in the energy sector, Russian influence has translated into a number of concessions, or rather 'gifts', that Kazakhstan has been forced to grant, including shares given to Russian companies in the Tengiz oilfield, the Karachaganak oil and gas field, and the Caspian Pipeline Consortium.[61] Acknowledging Russia's regional authority, a senior executive at Chevron, the first major oil company involved in Kazakhstan, stated:

> so much of what happens in the Caspian area is derived from Russia. Much of the technology we use is Russian and we want to use Russian pipelines to get oil out of there. We just feel that if there is a Russian content, then all these things may work better. I guess it's our view that having a strategic Russian partner would be awfully good for the project.[62]

The withdrawal from Chechnya in 1996 signified the limits of Russian power and provided Kazakhstan with more room to maneuver in its relationship with its neighbor. America's growing involvement in the Caspian area also contributed to diminished Russian influence. Moreover, the Kazakhs appeared to be exasperated by Russia's failure to reciprocate their goodwill. In August 1997, Gazprom announced that it would 'never' authorize the export of Kazakh gas from the Karachaganak field to international markets through the Russian network.[63] Kazakh resentment came to the surface during the October 1997 CIS Summit in Chisinau, when Nazarbayev joined other CIS leaders in a 'revolt' against Russia's heavy-handedness. In response, Russia promised to take into account the complaints of its CIS partners and moderate its regional policies.

Since the 1997 summit, some progress has been made in resolving the outstanding issues. Progressive expansion of quotas on the transit of Kazakh oil has reduced Kazakh concerns, although excessive fees and the need for yearly renewals of transit contracts continue to be sources of contention.[64] Delays in Russian payments for the Baikonur space centre remain a persistent problem. More compelling could be the long-term situation of the Russian minority in Kazakhstan. In November 1999, 22 ethnic Russians were arrested for separatist activities in Ust-Kamenogorsk, although Russia pointedly refrained from lending support to their cause.[65] Yet, in a possible counter-move by the Kremlin harking back to the ethnic realpolitik of Soviet times, several congresses were held by Kazakhs inhabiting Russia's Saratov and Orenburg regions to deliberate the establishment of an autonomous Kazakh region within the Russian Federation. The creation of a Kazakh entity on the Russian side of the border could be a prelude to demanding autonomy for the Russian-populated regions of northern Kazakhstan.[66]

These problems, however, have not outweighed the multi-dimensional ties that link Kazakhstan to Russia. On the positive side, the construction of the CPC pipeline from Atyrau to Novorossiisk has proceeded apace, in the context of improving Russo–Kazakh relations. Kazakhstan refrained from criticizing Russia's 1999 military campaign in Chechnya and refused haven to Chechen refugees,[67] because of a reluctance to alienate Russia, fears of separatism within Kazakhstan and misgivings about the spread of Islamist extremism. Putin's accession to the presidency has added impetus to the strengthening of mutual ties, based on greater sensitivity of each other's interests and priorities.

Russia and Turkmenistan

Unlike Kazakhstan, Turkmenistan's policies toward Russia are shaped by President Niyazov's determination to remain maximally independent from Moscow and to refrain from joining any regional alliance that would limit Turkmen independence and alienate southern neighbors, especially Iran.[68] Declaring its neutrality, Turkmenistan joined the non-aligned movement in October 1995, and in December the United Nations officially recognized Turkmenistan as a neutral state.[69]

Turkmenistan has tried to compensate for its refusal to sign various CIS and Central Asian regional accords by developing bilateral links with Russia. In its first years of independence, attention was given to military cooperation, as Turkmenistan relied heavily on Russia to handle its security concerns. The Turkmen–Russian treaty of friendship and cooperation signed in July 1992 placed the defence of Turkmenistan under Russia's military umbrella.[70] President Yeltsin described the relationship between the two countries as a strategic partnership.[71]

Geographical remoteness from Russia, along with a small Russian minority, allowed Turkmenistan to work closely with Russia without feeling too concerned about jeopardizing its independence. Unlike Kazakhstan and other CIS republics, Turkmenistan accorded the right of dual citizenship to resident Russians, in an effort to accommodate Russia and stem the flow of Russian emigration.[72] Russia derived obvious benefits from its alliance with Turkmenistan. By maintaining forces on the old Soviet border, a strategic area linking Central Asia to the outside world, Russia was spared the cost of building a new defence line further north.

Soon however, the Turkmen–Russian military alliance became a victim of disagreements in the gas sector. In 1995, the treaty of alliance was annulled and Turkmenistan demanded the withdrawal of Russian anti-aircraft and air forces from its territory. After the Taliban takeover in Kabul, the Turkmens sought to reduce the Russian military presence at the Afghan border, as a prelude to developing working relations with the Taliban regime. In May 1999, Turkmenistan ended its border protection treaty with Russia and requested that Russian border troops withdraw from the country by the year's end.[73]

It is in the economic domain, especially the energy sector, that Turkmenistan has felt suffocated by the embrace of the Russian bear. After permitting the flow of Turkmen gas to non-CIS markets until 1993, Gazprom denied access to its gas pipeline network to Europe. This reduced Turkmenistan's client base to the cash-poor CIS republics, depriving it of sorely needed revenues. To remedy the situation, Niyazov attempted to coax the Russians by giving Gazprom a 45 percent share in Turkmenrosgaz, a joint venture set up in November 1995 to handle Turkmen gas exports to the CIS. In March 1997, however, Niyazov terminated gas exports in response to Ukraine's accumulation of unpaid debt and Gazprom's decision to hike transit fees. He then dissolved Turkmenrosgas in June 1997, sparking a crisis with Russia and Gazprom.

This crisis did not turn to Turkmenistan's advantage, because Niyazov was soon forced to conclude an agreement to create a new joint venture which featured a main condition: Turkmen gas would flow exclusively to the CIS. A bitter Niyazov publicly complained about Russia's heavy-handedness, which, he declared, reminded him of 'old Soviet ambitions'.[74] This unfair agreement was stillborn, and gas did not flow through Russian pipelines until the signing of a new accord in December 1999 for the delivery in 2000 of 20 bn cubic meters of natural gas.[75] During President Putin's visit in May 2000, Niyazov agreed in principle to supply Russia with an additional 10 bn cubic meters; another 30 bn cubic meters was promised for the year 2001.[76] Meanwhile, Gazprom had replaced Turkmenistan as the main gas supplier to Ukraine, Georgia and Armenia. Two interrelated factors have clouded Russo–Turkmen dealings in the gas sector. The first is Gazprom's reluctance to permit Turkmen use of its pipeline network for exports to the West, because, as a major gas producer, it considers Turkmenistan a competitor. Hence the Russian insistence to buy Turkmen gas at low prices and to charge excessive transit fees.

The ebb and flow of Russo–Turkmen relations demonstrates the disproportionate power relationship between the two countries. Niazov's preference for bilateral links over collective arrangements might not have been the appropriate strategy, as Russia was given a free hand to dictate terms to an isolated Turkmenistan. Another consequence of the crisis over gas deliveries was Niyazov's decision to seek new outlets to international markets through Iran, Turkey and Afghanistan.[77] From a Russian perspective, the relationship with Turkmenistan is generally held to be satisfactory, despite a perceptible irritation at Niyazov's somewhat erratic personality. The frequent changes in the Turkmen position on the legal status of the Caspian have not been well received in Moscow. A case in point was the Russian protest challenging Niyazov's decree of September 1999, which proclaimed Turkmen control over not only a sector of the Caspian seabed, but of the waters above it.[78] As a consequence, in the Azeri–Turkmen dispute over three offshore fields, Russia backed Turkmenistan's claims to Kyapaz/Serdar alone, instructing Russian oil companies to withdraw from the Azerbaijani project to develop that field.[79] More irritating to the Turkmens was Russian special envoy Kalyuzhny's mention only of Kyapaz/Serdar in his proposal for the joint development of contested fields by the disputing sides, implying that the other two fields claimed by Niyazov belonged to Azerbaijan.[80] Aside from this irritant, the year 2000 marked the beginning of a more amicable relationship with Russia, prompted by Turkmen disappointment with the lack of progress on Western-sponsored pipeline projects, disagreements with Iran over gas trade, and the need for Russian military protection against perceived Islamist threats in the Central Asian region.

Azerbaijan and Russia

The Azerbaijan–Russia relationship is one of the most conflictual among the Caspian littoral states. Azerbaijanis blame Moscow for the ethnic conflict and instability that has devastated their country since 1988, while the Russians accuse Azerbaijan for attempting to eliminate Russian influence from Transcaucasia. Russia has deeply resented Azerbaijan's breakaway from its sphere of influence and its close alignment with Turkey and the United States. Baku's pro-Turkish inclinations are a particular irritant to Moscow, which fears Azerbaijan's emergence as a Western-backed bridgehead for the spread of Turkey's political and economic influence in the Caucasus and Central Asia.

Although Azerbaijani–Russian relations reached their nadir during the rule of Abulfaz Elchibey,[81] there was no significant improvement under the successor regime of Haidar Aliyev. Despite the political debt owed to the Russians for their support of Elchibey's overthrow in 1993, Aliyev has, especially since 1995, led a policy of independence from Moscow which has often bordered on hostility.

To be sure, in the first years of his rule, Aliyev attempted to placate Russia through several concessions, such as the reintegration of Azerbaijan into the CIS, granting Russian companies participation in oil contracts, and choice of the Baku–Novorossiisk pipeline as one of two routes to export 'early oil'. Yet Aliyev, unlike his Armenian and Georgian neighbors, was categorically opposed to allowing Russian bases in his country and handing over control of borders to Russia. Also, Azerbaijan is a most vocal critic of the CIS, especially in regard to Russian hegemony over that organization.[82] Furthermore, regional experts have suspected that Azerbaijan lent support to the Chechen rebels in the 1994–6 war;[83] similar accusations were made by Russia during the second Chechen war.

Contracts concluded by Azerbaijan with Western oil companies and its insistence on the division of the Caspian into national sectors have been major sources of Russian discontent. Indeed, the Russian Foreign Ministry contested the validity of the Contract of the Century, regarding it a unilateral move violating the legal status of the Caspian. It was significant that the initial Russian letter of protest was not sent to the government of Azerbaijan, but to the United Kingdom, and to the respective governments of the companies involved in the deal. This action may have reflected Russian contempt for the sovereignty of Azerbaijan and other former Soviet republics.[84] Russia was suspected of masterminding a coup attempt in Baku on 4–5 October 1994, two weeks after the signing of the Contract of the Century.[85]

It soon became apparent to Russia that Aliyev's policies could not be altered by extreme measures or by policies of accommodation – extradition of Azerbaijani opposition figures from Russia or the expression of Russian support for keeping Nagorno-Karabakh under Azerbaijani sovereignty.[86] Indeed, after 1995, Russia found in Aliyev a straightforward antagonist driven by a self-confidence reinforced by Russia's misfortunes in Chechnya, his new-found popularity in the United States, and the flow of substantial Western investment into the oil sector. The Russian proposal of November 1996 on the status of the Caspian, which accepted the principle of national sectors, could be interpreted as a significant Azerbaijani victory, even if such division was to be limited to 72 km from the coast. Relations reached a new low when Aliyev's foreign affairs adviser, Vafa Guluzade, called upon Turkey and the United States to establish a NATO base on Azerbaijani soil.[87] In November 1999, Russia joined Iran in vehemently protesting the signing of the Baku–Ceyhan pipeline agreement in Istanbul.

Another source of contention is the Baku–Novorossiisk pipeline. Since its opening in October 1997, the operation of the pipeline was impeded by the anarchic situation in Chechnya, Transneft's managerial shortcomings and, subsequently, by the Azeri failure to make oil deliveries.[88] Despite a limited rapprochement under Putin, any long-term improvement in Russo–Azeri relations would be conditional on the conclusion of an agreement on the legal status of the Caspian, a greater Russian role in Azeri oil projects, diminished Western and Turkish influence in Azerbaijan, and a change in Russian policy to favour Baku in the conflict with Armenia over Nagorno-Karabakh.

Azerbaijan and Kazakhstan

Relations between these two riparian states have been amicable because of a degree of complementarity in their interests and the absence of serious points of tension. Upon independence, Kazakh–Azeri ties began on a positive note when Azerbaijan was invited to join the Coordinating Council of Central Asian Leaders, which had been created a year earlier at the initiative of Nazarbayev.[89] The two countries share membership in CIS, the Caspian Sea Cooperation Organization and the Economic Cooperation Organization. Along with some commonality in ethnic and religious background, Azerbaijan and Kazakhstan are linked as energy producers. Skilled Azerbaijani and other workers from the Caucasus were instrumental in developing the Kazakh oil industry during the 1960s and 1970s, although most left after the riots against migrants from the Caucasus in June 1989 centered in Novy-Uzen in western Kazakhstan.[90] The two countries face a number of common issues related to their energy resources, foreign policy choices – particularly toward Russia – and problems with ethnic minorities.

Kazakhstan might be somewhat envious of Azerbaijan's relative freedom from Russia and its higher profile in the West regarding oil contracts. Although their potential rivalry to supply Western energy markets cannot be excluded, the emphasis has been on mutual cooperation.[91] Bilateral accords have been signed since independence, culminating in a declaration of 'strategic partnership', and a memorandum to transport Kazakh oil across the Caspian via Azerbaijan, signed in June 1997 during Aliyev's visit to Almaty. This ambitious $2.5 billion plan, if realized, would consist of a 2,500 km pipeline running onshore from western Kazakhstan to Turkmenbashi, and from there offshore to Azerbaijan.[92] In the meantime, limited quantities of Kazakh oil are being exported by tanker to Baku and thence by rail to the Georgian port of Batum. The upgrading and expansion of the port of Baku should allow substantial increases in the amount of oil so transported.[93]

Kazakhstan and Azerbaijan agree on the legal status of the Caspian and favour a division of the sea into national sectors. However, under pressure from Russia during the November 1996 meeting of littoral states, Kazakhstan blamed Azerbaijan for blocking a new convention by its insistence on the division of the entire sea, and not only of the mineral resources of the seabed.[94] Instead, the Kazakhs want the sea's surface and water resources to be used jointly, a position which they reiterated at a foreign ministers' meeting in October 1999 in Astana.[95]

The preponderant issue that would define future relations is the long-awaited Kazakh decision regarding the trans-Caspian pipeline link feeding the prospective Baku–Ceyhan route. Nazarbayev's willingness to support the Baku–Ceyhan project during the November 1999 OSCE Istanbul summit was tempered a few days later by his statement that Kazakhstan could not guarantee to export significant volumes of crude to Azerbaijan unless future discoveries warranted it.[96]

Kazakhstan and Turkmenistan

The transport of oil and gas also plays a prominent role in Kazakh–Turkmen relations. At a meeting in Almaty in February 1997, Nazarbayev and Niyazov emphasized the necessity for mutual cooperation in order to develop export routes for their energy resources.[97] Despite the tone of official communiques, Nazarbayev has found it difficult to cooperate with the eccentric Niyazov, who has snubbed most Kazakh proposals aimed at developing regional institutions in the CIS or in Central Asia. The two countries, however, share misgivings about Uzbek aspirations for regional hegemony. Consequently, Nazarbayev and Niyazov have set up a joint political council charged with common security and economic issues.

During the Soviet era Turkmenistan supplied gas to Kazakhstan. In 1992, Turkmenistan announced prematurely that it would interrupt gas supplies to Kazakhstan in 1994, by which date pipelines carrying Turkmen gas to non-CIS markets were expected to be in operation.[98] With its extravagant hopes dashed, Turkmenistan had to negotiate bilateral trade agreements with Kazakhstan, based on the exchange of Turkmen gas for Kazakh processed goods and food products.[99] Also, under the terms of a swap deal, Turkmenistan was to deliver 3 bn cubic meters of gas to southern Kazakhstan, in exchange for which the latter would supply the same amount to Russia on Turkmenistan's behalf. Apprehensive of dependence on transit routes across Uzbekistan, Kazakhstan is developing a transport infrastructure, involving railways and gas pipelines, linking it directly with Turkmenistan.[100]

Niyazov's numerous changes of position on the legal status of the Caspian are known to have irritated Nazarbayev. Niyazov first agreed to the Russian proposal of November 1996, then was persuaded by Nazarbayev to change sides and push for a temporary division of the sea. By August 1997, Niyazov had reverted to the Russian point of view.[101] Personality differences between the two leaders aside, the potential for friction between the two countries is limited. Except for a minor territorial dispute over the Mangyshlak peninsula, there are no known land or maritime border problems or ethnic issues. Although both countries adhered to trans-Caspian pipeline projects in Istanbul in November 1999, subsequent developments have dampened their enthusiasm.

Azerbaijan and Turkmenistan

Despite some cultural links and complementarity of interests, Turkmen–Azerbaijani relations are beset by disputes regarding sea boundaries and pipeline projects. In the first years of independence, a friendlier relationship was anticipated. The two countries provide a link between Transcaucasia and Central Asia, thanks to the ferryboat system connecting Baku and Turkmenbashi.[102] Both Azeris and Turkmen are Oguz Turks and their languages are more closely related than to the other Turkic languages of Central Asia. Also, since Soviet times, Turkmenistan has been Azerbaijan's main gas supplier. Azerbaijan's inability to pay for the gas supplies has resulted in interruption of the gas flow.[103]

Azerbaijan began to develop offshore oil much earlier than Turkmenistan, which was busy operating its onshore gas fields. By the time Turkmenistan turned its attention to the Caspian, Azerbaijan had already signed contracts with major oil companies for the exploitation of several fields which Turkmenistan considered a part of its own sector. The controversy was made public during a press conference in January 1997, when Niyazov claimed ownership of the Azeri field (formerly the 26 Baku Commissars) and part of the Chirag field (Kaverochkin). The Turkmen leader requested Azerbaijan to stop exploitation of the contested fields, and to respect the Soviet–Iranian agreements on the Caspian until the resolution of the dispute. In a dramatic move, he pointed a finger at a map of the Caspian and with a pen scratched out the name of one of the contested fields, declaring 'I'll put my own name on it so there can be no mistake about who it belongs to'.[104] Azerbaijan contended that it had claimed the fields since 1970, as proven by maps of the Soviet period.[105] Russia took an ambivalent position, declaring that Azeri and Chirag were within the Azerbaijani sector, but found inadmissible Azerbaijan's unilateral actions. The controversy deepened in March 1997, when the Turkmen oil and gas minister threatened to appeal to the United Nations if the two countries failed to reach agreement.[106]

As early as 1994, Western analysts had noted the problems that could be created by Azerbaijan's development of offshore fields lying at a greater distance from its shores than from the Turkmen coast, and the shaky legal grounding of some Azerbaijani arguments. According to these claims, the fields belong to Azerbaijan, either because they were managed from Baku in imperial Russian and Soviet times, or because they were discovered by Soviet geologists based in Baku.[107] Russian support for Azerbaijan's sovereignty over the Azeri and Chirag fields could have been based on two factors: the simple reality that Azerbaijan had already begun developing these oil fields and Moscow's irritation at Turkmenistan's disputation over maritime boundaries, which implied recognition of national sectors within the Caspian. The Russian position remained unclear due to contradictory statements made by foreign ministry officials. While a Russian diplomat pointed out in February 1997 'that the Azeri and Chirag structures belong to the Azerbaijani sector of the Caspian Sea',[108] the foreign ministry spokesman rejected both the Turkmen and Azerbaijani claims, because it regarded the Caspian as the common property of the littoral states.[109] Although Turkmenistan is believed to favor a division of the Caspian into national sectors, having backed Azerbaijan's right to exploit its sector of the sea in 1994, it later supported Russia out of a desire not to alienate her, as well as out of resentment toward Azerbaijan.[110]

A new Azerbaijani–Turkmen dispute erupted after the signing of a contract between the Azerbaijani SOCAR company and the Russian Rosneft and Lukoil companies on 4 July 1997 to develop an offshore field located 145 kilometers east of Baku, called Kyapaz by the Azerbaijanis and Serdar by the Turkmens. This time Niyazov succeeded in enlisting Russian support and the deal was cancelled by Yeltsin in August 1997. Azerbaijan regretted Russia's withdrawal, and argued that Kyapaz/Serdar was discovered in 1959 by Azerbaijani geologists. Nevertheless, it recognized that the field belonged partly to Turkmenistan and offered to develop it in common.[111]

In order to resolve their differences, a joint commission was established, co-chaired by the two foreign ministers. A positive outcome of the commission's work was an agreement to divide the Caspian into national sectors along the median line. Thus, Niyazov's obvious preference for sectoral division placed his country in the same camp as Azerbaijan, Kazakhstan and the United States, and in opposition to Russia and Iran.[112] The trend toward mutual rapprochement received a boost in November 1999, when Niyazov adhered to the trans-Caspian gas pipeline agreement. This era of good feeling ended abruptly when Azerbaijan laid claim to half the capacity of the projected gas pipeline through Turkey because of its newly discovered offshore reserves, while Turkmenistan was prepared to cede only one sixth. The result was the cancellation of the trans-Caspian project, thereby intensifying their rivalry as producers of natural gas.[113]

The foregoing analysis of the relations among the five riparian states underlines the complexity of national interests at the core of the region's geopolitics. These involve conflicting sovereign rights over the Caspian, choice of energy export routes, differing foreign policy orientations, ethnic tensions and defence and security issues. These questions have persisted since the Soviet demise, although there has been a shift in their relative importance over the years. In the early 1990s, a major concern for Azerbaijan, Kazakhstan and Turkmenistan was how to strengthen their independence vis-à-vis Russia's political and military influence. With the partial erosion of

Russian power after 1995, and the rise of energy development, the foci of interstate relations has shifted to controversies over the Caspian Sea's legal status, transit routes and relations with external powers.

Part Three: THE EXTERNAL ACTORS

CHAPTER 7

The Inner Circle

The ten-fold relationships among the Caspian's five riparian states and the larger geopolitics of the region are shaped, to a considerable degree, by the influence of three sets of external state actors. The first set consists of an inner circle of the five countries in immediate proximity to the Caspian Basin. Because of their location, these countries not only affect developments in the riparian states, but are also affected by events within and relations among them. Beyond the interstate realm, the landlocked position of the Caspian Basin places added importance on the countries of the inner circle – Afghanistan, Armenia, Georgia, Turkey and Uzbekistan. All five assume crucial importance in the transhipment of hydrocarbon resources to international markets. Moreover, all of these states, except Uzbekistan, are potential consumers of Caspian oil and gas.

Afghanistan
Russian and subsequent Soviet rule did not completely cut off the Caspian/Central Asia region from Afghanistan. Contacts persisted through trade and migration of people. The northern part of Afghanistan, known as Afghan Turkestan, is populated by Turkmens, Uzbeks and Tajiks, whose kinsmen also populate the bordering Central Asian republics. Part of this population fled to Afghanistan during the Bolshevization of the 1920s. Soldiers from both the Caucasus and Central Asia served in the Soviet forces that occupied Afghanistan from 1979 to 1989. Also, Afghanistan maintained a consulate in Tashkent during the Soviet period.[1]

Since independence, the countries of the former Soviet South have feared the spread of Islamist militancy and instability from Afghanistan. The fear of Islamist extremism was intensified after the emergence of the Pakistani-supported Taliban movement in 1994, which soon swept most of Afghanistan. In parallel with the rise of the Taliban, a new element affecting Afghan–Central

Asian relations emerged – the possibility of trans-shipping Turkmen, Kazakh and Uzbek oil and gas through Afghanistan.

It was ironic that the Taliban movement was also supported by the United States, which would later suffer the consequences of Islamist violence perpetrated by Usama Bin Ladin, the Saudi extremist based in Afghanistan. US covert aid to the Taliban partly stemmed from the hope that they would bring the stability needed for the construction and operation of pipelines running south to the Arabian Sea across Afghanistan and Pakistan. A case in point was the October 1994 visit of the US Ambassador in Pakistan to Taliban-controlled areas of western Afghanistan, without the authorization of the Afghan government and in violation of international diplomatic standards. The panic provoked by the fall of Kabul to the Taliban in September resulted in an emergency meeting on 4 October 1996, attended by Russia and all Central Asian states except Turkmenistan. Niyazov, desperate to secure export routes for Turkmen gas, made no mystery of his contacts with the Taliban and his lack of concern for the feared fundamentalist contagion from Afghanistan. Meanwhile, the United States and Pakistan attempted to gain Uzbekistan's approval of a Taliban regime by encouraging an alliance, which did not materialize, between the Afghan Uzbek warlord, General Dostum, and the mostly Pashtun Taliban fighters.[2]

The ongoing Afghan civil war did not deter the development of trans-Afghan pipeline plans. The optimism of Turkmenistan and the oil companies remained high until 1998, mostly rooted in the cynical realization that Afghan warlords needed the funds generated by the pipelines for the purchase of armaments.[3] However, the Taliban soon revealed themselves to be less manipulable than their different sponsors had believed. Niyazov, who once claimed he had received the support of all Afghan factions for the agreement signed on 25 October 1997 to construct a trans–Afghan pipeline, was publicly contradicted by the Taliban, who criticized both the Turkmen government and the international oil companies for not consulting them.[4] After lengthy negotiations, in January 1998, the Taliban formally agreed to the pipeline project and pledged to provide full security for it.[5]

Meanwhile, the Taliban had alienated public opinion in the West for their gross violation of human rights, particularly their mistreatment of women, which had enraged the American feminist movement.[6] What doomed the pipeline project was the August 1998 bombing of US embassies in Kenya and Tanzania, which were blamed on Bin Ladin's Islamist network based in Taliban territory.

The retaliatory missile strikes on suspected Bin Ladin bases worsened US–Taliban relations, leading to Unocal's withdrawal from the pipeline project.[7] Yet, none of these calamities was to dampen Niyazov's hopes to build the pipeline. In May 1999, Turkmen and Taliban officials sought to revive the pipeline project amid Niyazov's continued efforts to mediate between the warring Afghan factions.[8] The trans-Afghan pipeline project was also discussed at the May 2000 meeting between Niyazov and Pakistani ruler General Parvez Musharraf, although there is little likelihood that any Western company will participate in its construction in the near future.[9]

Two other Caspian countries, Iran and Russia, have been affected by Taliban extremism, prompting them to join efforts to support the anti-Taliban Northern Alliance. Soon after the Taliban's massacre of Shi'ite Hazaras in Mazar-i-Sharif and Bamyan, and killing of ten Iranian diplomats in August 1998, Iran militarized its border and threatened war against the Taliban regime. Doctrinal differences between Iran's Shi'ite ideology and Taliban's Sunni extremism are a key factor in their confrontation, as is the export of drugs and the influx of refugees into Iran fleeing Taliban despotism. Russian concerns regarding the Taliban involve the dispatch of Islamist guerillas into Chechnya and Daghestan. In January 2000, the Taliban leader, Mullah Omar, met former Chechen President Zelimkhan Yandarbiev in Afghanistan and officially announced his recognition of Chechnya's independence. In response to Taliban military support to the Chechens, Russia threatened to bomb Afghan targets.[10] However, faced with the likely permanence of Taliban rule, most Central Asian republics could be expected to follow Niyazov's lead and seek a modus vivendi with Afghanistan's Islamist regime.

Uzbekistan

The role of Uzbekistan in the geopolitics of the Caspian should not to be underestimated, even though the country does not border the sea. The decline of the Uzbek economy in the mid-1990s was less pronounced than that of neighboring republics. Uzbekistan even managed to increase its oil and gas production after independence, although by the decade's end, its economic situation remained precarious. In terms of population, Uzbekistan is the largest Central Asian state. It is also unique in sharing borders with all four Central Asian republics, as well as with Afghanistan, its only non-CIS neighbor. Because of the country's geographic centrality, its leaders possess the leverage to mobilize irredentist movements among Uzbek minorities concentrated in the bordering states. This demographic factor is a constant source of concern for the Kyrgyz, Tajik and Turkmen governments, especially because the Uzbek-populated regions constitute the richest and most industrialized parts of these countries. The southern provinces of Kazakhstan, which contain an Uzbek minority, could be similarly threatened should Kazakhstan be weakened by a secession of the Russian-populated north.

The policies of the Uzbek president, Islam Karimov, have not helped to assuage these anxieties. What is feared is a repetition of the Tajik situation of the early 1990s, with the Uzbek army, the most powerful in Central Asia, intervening in one of the neighboring countries experiencing civil unrest and transforming it into an Uzbek protectorate.[11] Karimov's frequent statements that his country, which contains the capital cities of former Central Asian empires, is destined to dominate the region, have caused tension with his neighbors. The choice of the fourteenth-century conqueror Tamerlane as the Uzbek national hero, is perceived to be a symbol of Uzbekistan's imperial ambitions.[12] To complicate matters, personal relations between Karimov and other Central Asian leaders have been strained. Karimov has publicly displayed disdain for Nazarbayev and Niyazov on numerous occasions, and has humiliated the Kyrgyz leader, Askar Akaev.[13] In addition, these leaders, in particular Niyazov, have been the target of criticism by the Uzbek media.

According to neorealist theory, two options are available to states facing a regional bully. The first is to neutralize the more powerful state through multilateral arrangements or regional integration, thus 'bandwagoning with a bigger power by locking the larger state into a structure that can contain it',[14] while the second is to balance the source of the threat. Turkmenistan's avoidance of involvement in multilateral cooperative projects schemes where Uzbekistan would play a leading role, and Tajikistan's inability to participate due to internal problems, meant that only Kazakhstan, the Kyrgyz Republic and Uzbekistan could be active participants in regional integration efforts.[15] The failure of these schemes left the balancing option as the only remaining choice. Thus, fear of Uzbek expansionism has become a key factor driving the foreign policy choices of Central Asian states. Such choices include close links with Russia and, in the case of Turkmenistan, close ties with Iran. The two most powerful Caspian states, Iran and Russia, resented Uzbekistan's newfound role in the mid-1990s as America's favourite Central Asian partner.

Also, tensions with Uzbekistan have affected the stance of Kazakhstan and Turkmenistan toward Afghanistan. Indeed, Niyazov's hope of a Taliban victory that would allow the construction of pipelines across Afghanistan was not the only reason why he supported the Taliban. Both he and Nazarbayev were pleased with the setbacks of General Dostum, Karimov's Afghan protege, at the hands of the Taliban in May 1997.[16] Finally, Uzbekistan, which suffers from a landlocked geography, is particularly interested in pipelines going across its territory that would carry Uzbek oil and gas. The Mitsubishi-planned mega-pipeline between Turkmenistan and the Yellow Sea is one such project that would include a stretch through Uzbekistan.[17]

From the early days of independence, Karimov has ruled Uzbekistan by autocratic methods, a factor contributing to the rise of an Islamist opposition. Since 1997, the growing Islamist threat has affected Uzbek relations with the states of the Caspian rim. In August 1997, fears of extremist indoctrination led to the withdrawal of 2000 Uzbek students from Turkish universities. After a series of bomb attacks in Tashkent in February 1999, Karimov initiated a rapprochement with Russia, despite his earlier withdrawal from the CIS Collective Security Treaty. The growing Russian–Uzbek rapprochement was consecrated during President Putin's May 2000 visit to Tashkent.[18] Yet, four months later, following the withdrawal of the Islamist insurgents, Karimov denounced Russia for using the Islamist threat as a pretext to dominate the region.[19] Meanwhile, Uzbekistan's relations with Kazakhstan deteriorated, due to Kazakh non-payment for Uzbek gas shipments, a protracted trade war, border disputes resulting in armed clashes in January 2000, and a Kazakh ban on Uzbek train traffic in October, purportedly to stop illegal migration, drugs and terrorists.[20] By all indications, Islamist insurgency constitutes a long-term problem for the Uzbek government both internally and in shaping relations with other states. Possibly in response to Karimov's pro-Western attitude, Uzbek Sunni Islamists have found a measure of sympathy in Shi'a Iran as the Tehran government has allowed the Islamic Movement of Uzbekistan to make radio broadcasts from Mashad in eastern Iran.[21]

Armenia

Of all the countries affected by developments in the Caspian Basin, Armenia is the most vulnerable, standing to lose the most from the growing importance of oil in the region's international politics. Since

1988, Armenia has been locked in a bitter conflict with Azerbaijan over Nagorno-Karabakh, a region placed in Soviet Azerbaijan by Stalin in 1921, despite its Armenian identity attested by history and demography. The conflict escalated into a full-scale war following the collapse of the Soviet Union. While Karabakh Armenians and the Azerbaijanis were the main protagonists, Armenia itself was involved in the war by providing material, moral and military support to the Karabakh separatists, including volunteers who took part in the fighting. When a Russian-sponsored ceasefire in May 1994 ended the fighting, Azerbaijani forces had been expelled from most of Karabakh and some surrounding territories in the west, east and south of the enclave. About 14 percent of Azerbaijan's territory, including Karabakh, remained under the control of Karabakh Armenians. However, despite their battlefield victories, there was little reason to rejoice for the Armenian side. Armenia had been economically ruined by the combined effects of the devastating 1988 earthquake, the blockade imposed by Azerbaijan and Turkey,[22] the civil war in Georgia and the difficulties of transition from a Communist to a market economy.

In order to preserve the survival of the small landlocked republic, the Armenian leadership adopted a pragmatic foreign policy by seeking friendly relations with all its neighbors. In addition, Armenia established strong ties with countries containing large Armenian communities, such as Argentina, France, the United States, Lebanon, Syria, Egypt, Canada and Greece.[23] However, the initial successes of Armenian foreign policy and military prowess remained at the risk of being jeopardized by Azerbaijan's growing oil-based profile on the international scene. Armenia found itself gradually isolated in 1996-8 for its continued support of Nagorno-Karabakh. In addition to the strain imposed by the reluctance of the international community to recognize changes in boundaries inherited from Soviet times, Armenia has been placed under tremendous pressure by the increased Western interest in Azerbaijan's energy resources. The activities of the oil lobby in Washington have threatened the amicable relations between Armenia and the United States, which had flourished with the help of the American-Armenian community.[24]

In some Western circles, the close relations between Armenia and Russia, culminating in the friendship treaty of August 1997, are unfavorably contrasted with Azerbaijan's refusal to allow the presence of Russian military bases on its territory. The alleged delivery of $1bn worth of Russian weapons to Armenia between 1994 and

1996, triggered the 'Armeniagate' scandal in Russia, while being criticized in the American media.[25] Russia considers Armenia its only reliable Transcaucasian partner, without which Russian influence would be eliminated from the area and replaced by Turkey as the dominant regional power. Iran also values the role of Armenia as a wedge between its two Turkic neighbors, Azerbaijan and Turkey. The flourishing Armenian–Iranian relationship has been another potential source of friction between Armenia and the United States.[26] In recent years, Iran has been Armenia's only outlet to the world, and significant work has been done to improve the transport infrastructure between the two countries. Although the establishment of diplomatic relations between Armenia and Israel evoked Iranian displeasure, the Islamic Republic has continued to maintain close ties with Armenia. Among current projects is the construction of a gas pipeline and a highway linking the two countries.[27]

Armenia's relations with Georgia have significantly improved since the accession of Eduard Shevardnadze, as the Armenian leadership has persistently avoided raising issues that would antagonize Georgia. The Armenian authorities have been instrumental in reducing tensions between the Armenian population of the Javakhk province of southern Georgia and the Shevardnadze government. Even the deplorable human rights situation of the Armenian community, the confiscation of dozens of Armenian churches and the forced Georgianization of the surnames and ethnoreligious status of an estimated 70,000 Armenians have not provoked complaints from the Armenian government. The transit of goods through Georgia is of critical importance to Armenia, given its landlocked position and blockaded status.[28] Georgia also constitutes the only land corridor joining Armenia to Russia. In this context, the progressive nurturing of Georgia's ties with Turkey and Azerbaijan has generated considerable Armenian concern.

With respect to Turkey, the Armenian government has made repeated overtures to establish diplomatic relations, without setting any preconditions linked to the 1915 Armenian Genocide, at the risk of alienating the Armenian population at home and in the diaspora. However, Armenia's policy of rapprochement with Turkey has come to naught. Although Turkey did not intervene directly in the Azerbaijani–Armenian conflict, its policy has had a clear pro-Azeri bias, which has prevented Ankara from playing the role of honest broker.[29] In addition to cooperation in the military sector, including the training of Azerbaijan's army and supply of weapons,[30] Turkey has made the evacuation of occupied Azerbaijani territories a sine qua non to opening its borders and establishing diplomatic relations with Armenia. Only in April 1995, in response to American pressure, did Turkey reopen its airspace to planes traveling to and from Armenia.[31] The presence of Turkish troops in the Azerbaijani enclave of Nakhichevan is another cause of Armenian concern, as memories of the Genocide and the Turkish invasions of 1918 and 1920 are still fresh. As a consequence, Turkey is held to be the primary security threat to the Armenian Republic.[32]

In recent years, the fate of Karabakh has been linked to pipeline projects. Proposals put forward by the USA, Turkey and Azerbaijan have suggested a pipeline for land deal: Armenian withdrawal from the occupied territories and recognition of Azerbaijan's sovereignty over Nagorno-Karabakh in exchange for the passage of the Baku–Ceyhan pipeline through Armenia. This possibility, mentioned in June 1995 by Turkish President Demirel and in May 1997 by Aliyev, was rejected by the Armenian foreign ministry on the grounds that the two issues should not be linked.[33] In December 1997, Ilham Aliyev, the vice-president of SOCAR, brushed aside the option by declaring that it would never be considered, even in the case of Armenian concessions.[34]

Armenia fears that Azerbaijan, emboldened by support from Western governments and oil companies and its growing wealth from oil wells, will be able to finance a Krajina-style reconquest of Karabakh. It is reported that Azerbaijan has bought massive quantities of armaments from the Ukraine and Russia.[35] In a future armed conflict, Azerbaijan would need an overwhelming military advantage allowing it a quick and decisive victory, because it cannot afford a lengthy war that would scare away foreign investments. A possible Armenian counter-strategy would be to move into the Azerbaijani districts contiguous to north-eastern Armenia and sever the pipeline going west to Georgia, thereby depriving Azerbaijan of its main source of income.[36]

Armenia has watched with some satisfaction the lack of Azerbaijani success in mobilizing Central Asian support in the Karabakh conflict. Baku has obtained only symbolic declarations from some Central Asian leaders, such as Karimov, in favor of Azerbaijan's territorial integrity.[37] Relations between Armenia and the Central Asian states have not been affected by the Karabakh conflict. During the Karabakh war, Baku was irritated by Niyazov's refusal to interrupt Turkmen gas exports to Armenia, a major buyer of Turkmen gas until 1997. Armenian–Turkmen and Armenian–Iranian–Turkmen agreements in the gas sector may have played a role in the failure of Azeri–Turkmen pipeline projects in the mid-1990s, and exacerbated tension between the two countries prior to their dispute over Caspian maritime boundaries.[38]

Since 1998, a flurry of diplomatic activity led by the US and OSCE has sought to resolve the Karabakh conflict, but to no avail. Solutions have ranged from an autonomous Karabakh within Azerbaijan, to the innovative concept of a 'common state' between Azerbaijan and Karabakh, to a territorial swap handing over Meghri, Armenia's southernmost district, to Azerbaijan in exchange for Karabakh. The proposed swap deal over Meghri faced opposition from Russia, Iran and the Armenian diaspora. The launching in 1999 of a new US peace initiative led by Ambassador Carey Cavanaugh may well lead to a breakthrough in settling the Nagorno-Karabakh conflict, thereby removing a major threat to the development of Caspian energy resources.[39]

Turkey

In the last decade, Turkey has sought to play a formative role in the politics of the Transcaucasus, Central Asia and the Caspian Basin. Unlike the apprehensive attitude of China and Iran, the independence of the republics of the former Soviet South was welcomed by Turkey. Indeed, the breakup of the Soviet Union provided Turkey with an auspicious and timely opportunity to obtain a new role enhancing its status in the eyes of the West. The end of the Cold War had left Turkey, which had presented itself as staunch defender of NATO's south-eastern flank, with diminished importance in the new European geopolitical context. In 1989 the Turkish proposal to join the European Union was rejected. In addition, Turkey was unpopular in the EU Parliament, which frequently denounced the country's poor human rights record, continued occupation of Cyprus, repression of the Kurds and refusal to recognize the 1915 Armenian Genocide. The Iraqi invasion of Kuwait improved the situation by demonstrating that Turkey remained an important regional actor because of its geostrategic location. The restoration of Turkey's international position was also due to the expectation that it could develop privileged links with the five republics of the former Soviet Union with which it shared a common Turkic cultural heritage.

There was no general agreement in Turkey on how the relationship with the newly created Turkic states would be shaped. Proposals ranged from the establishment of economic and cultural bonds to the creation of a union or federation based on Pan-Turkist ideology. What these proposals had in common was that Turkey would play an epicentric role in the regional politics and economics of the newly independent Transcaucasian and Central Asian states. After having spent years as the last country of Europe, Turkey aspired to occupy a dominant position in the new regional setting created by the Soviet demise. Also at issue was how Turkey's new Central Asian focus would affect the other priorities in Turkish foreign policy, such as relations with Western Europe and the Middle East. This issue found its partial solution in the formulation that Turkey would be the 'bridge' between the West and the former Soviet South, and would offer its own Western-oriented model of economic and political development to these countries.[40]

In retrospect, Turkish foreign policy toward the former Soviet South in the last decade went through three successive phases. The initial phase can be described as one of idealistic enthusiasm driven by emotions and Pan-Turkist myths and dreams, harking back to the Ittihadist (Young Turk) ideology of the last days of the Ottoman Empire. However, it soon became clear that the results of Turkey's involvement in the former Soviet South fell far short of its original expectations, which had been set too high and with little knowledge of local conditions. The capacity of Russia to retain influence in the area had been neglected by early Turkish analysts, who saw only Iran as an obstacle to the expansion of Turkish influence. Also, Turkey proved incapable of directly challenging Russia in the region. In the Transcaucasus, Turkey was unable to prevent Azerbaijani defeats by the Armenians and the removal from power of the Turcophile leader, Abulfaz Elchibey. In Central Asia, a feeling of 'mutual disenchantment' followed the initial optimism when it became apparent that Turkey lacked the financial capability needed to revive the moribund Central Asian economies. Turkish initiatives at the regional level, such as the Black Sea Economic Cooperation, or sponsorship of conferences of Turkic states, failed to produce concrete results.

Despite the rhetoric on shared ethnicity and identity, there was also a cultural gap separating the Turks of Turkey and the Turkic peoples of Azerbaijan and Central Asia. This gap was not only the consequence of Russian/Soviet hegemony, but of centuries of separation during which Central Asia and the Ottoman Empire had been cut off from each other by Shi'a Persia. Consequently, the Balkans, the Black Sea littoral and the Near East had been the foci of Ottoman expansion. In addition, Turkey's paternalistic attitude was resented in Central Asia, whose leaders did not want to exchange Soviet domination for a Turkish one. Finally, Pan-Turkism did not have a strong appeal in Central Asia, and in the rare cases when it did, such as in Uzbekistan, it took a form different from the model propounded in Turkey. Karimov, the Uzbek leader, does not oppose Pan-Turkism, as long as its epicenter is Tashkent and not Ankara. His position is similar to that of his distant predecessor, the Emir of Bukhara, who, at the turn of the century, expressed interest in the nascent Pan-Turkist movement only if it would be led by him, and not by the Sultan in Istanbul.[41]

However, the Turkish experience in the first years of the newly independent states should not be discarded as a mere failure. The level of Turkish activity in the area, in view of the limited capacity of the Turkish economy, was quite remarkable. The audacity of Turkish entrepreneurs contributed perhaps more than government policies to making Turkey a major trade partner of these countries.[42] Abandoning its initial illusions while maintaining its ambitions, the Turkish government developed more realistic policies that emphasized country-to-country relations over grand regional schemes.[43]

The second phase of Turkish policy toward Central Asia and the Caucasus was one of relative indifference, prompted by the limited successes of the first phase as well as changes in Turkey's internal politics. The rise of the Islamist current culminating in the accession of the Welfare (Refah) Party leader Necmettin Erbakan to the prime ministership in June 1996, resulted in a temporary refocusing of Turkish foreign policy away from the Turkic east and closer to the Muslim/Arab orbit. Also, there was considerable indifference toward Turkish concerns in Central Asia. A case in point was Kyrgyz President Akaev's defiance of Turkish sensibilities when he accused Turkey of responsibility for the 1915 Armenian Genocide and for its continued occupation of Cyprus.[44]

In the years since Erbakan's ousting by the Turkish military in late June 1997, a more activist phase of Turkish foreign policy has become discernable. In this phase, the hydrocarbon resources of the Caspian have come to play a central role in Turkish policy. The centerpiece of this policy is the building of the Baku–Ceyhan pipeline through Turkish territory. Turkey's geopolitical and economic benefits from this pipeline would include:

(1) transit fees and other economic benefits;
(2) a reduction of energy dependence on Arab suppliers;
(3) increased utility and prestige in the eyes of the West; and

(4) a strengthening of its economic and political position in the Caucasus and Central Asia.

Indeed, Turkey's interest in providing transit for Caspian oil goes back to the early 1990s. Ankara came close to success in March 1993, when an outline agreement was reached on the construction of a pipeline between Baku and the oil terminal of Yumurtalik, located in the Gulf of Ceyhan on Turkey's Mediterranean coast.[45] These hopes were dashed a few months later when Elchibey's exclusion of Russian companies from oil contracts may have contributed to his overthrow by a Moscow-backed coup in June 1993;[46] his successor, Haidar Aliyev, cancelled all contracts signed by the Elchibey government. This setback was deeply resented in Turkey, where the Baku–Ceyhan pipeline would soon become a national obsession. In July 1994, Turkey retaliated by restricting oil tanker transit through the Bosphorus and the Straits, arguing that, should the main export route for Azerbaijani and Kazakh oil go through Novorossiisk, the increased traffic could cause accidents with catastrophic consequences for Istanbul.[47] This was accompanied by an intense campaign in which officials, journalists and academics were enlisted to promote the indispensability of a Turkish route for Caspian oil and gas exports. The political and strategic advantages of having a pipeline running through Turkey, rather than Iran and Russia, were presented as incentives to encourage Western countries to invest in the costly project, which Turkey could not afford to finance. The pipeline campaign intensified in 1997 and included emotional appeals directed at the Azeris and Central Asians, culminating in a boycott of BP and Amoco in November 1998, for their reticence to endorse the project.[48] However, despite American support and an improvement in Turkish–Azerbaijani relations after Turkey's initial displeasure with Aliyev's accession, it took Azerbaijan five years to commit itself to the Baku–Ceyhan line as the main export route for its oil. The signing of the Baku–Ceyhan agreement in November 1999 was the culmination of a long tortuous process marked by numerous summit meetings and intense controversies regarding the political and economic viability of the pipeline.

The Turkish quest to play an active role in the Caspian region, culminating in the Baku–Ceyhan scheme, necessitated the marshalling of a coalition of allies by the Ankara government. Aside from strengthening its relations with Azerbaijan, it was imperative that close ties be developed with Georgia as a connecting link to Baku and as a substitute for a shorter pipeline route through Armenia, an unrealizable option given the unsettled state of Turkish–Armenian and Azerbaijani–Armenian relations. To solidify the Turkish–Azerbaijani–Georgian alignment, the Turks sought the aid of Israel, a potent player in regional and international affairs. In view of Israel's own developing interest in the former Soviet South, it was not difficult for Turkey to transpose its only Middle Eastern ally into the Caspian milieu.[49] Yet, in view of its geopolitical complexity, progress on the Baku–Ceyhan scheme would have been impossible without the blessing of the United States. The growing American involvement in the Caspian area, while enhancing the chances of building the Baku–Ceyhan pipeline, underlines Turkey's inability to play a decisive role in the region. Russia's ability to confront the Turkish challenge to its regional leadership prompted the necessity of direct American intervention in an attempt to loosen the Russian hold on the Caspian and its energy resources.

To be sure, the extent to which Turkey intended, or could afford to antagonize Russia, remains an open question. Despite the multiple flashpoints in Turkish–Russian relations, the two sides have sought to maintain a working relationship based on certain shared interests. Faced by similar types of secessionist insurgencies, Russia and Turkey have refrained from intervening too directly into each other's internal conflicts, despite mutual accusations by Moscow and Ankara of help provided to the Chechen and Kurdish separatists respectively.[50] Notwithstanding the rhetoric of Turkish–Central Asian solidarity, the volume of Turkish trade with Russia is higher than that of the combined Turkish trade with the Central Asian, Azerbaijani and Georgian republics.[51] In December 1997, Russia and Turkey signed a $20bn contract for the delivery of Russian gas to Turkey.[52] The construction of this pipeline project, known as Blue Stream, has been underway since May 2000, while new funding from international investors during the same months has reinforced its viability, in contrast to the declining fortunes of the trans-Caspian pipeline to transport Turkmen gas. Hence, Niyazov's rage at the visiting Turkish energy minister in October 1999, and the ensuing controversy in the Turkish press about the ostensible betrayal of Turkic solidarity by the making of a deal with Turkey's Russian rival.[53]

One consequence of Turkey's determination to play a leading role in the last decade has been the emerging polarization of the Caspian Basin into two rival blocs. Thus, the formation of the Turkey–Israel–Azerbaijan–Georgia bloc, sponsored by the United States, has triggered a rival alignment bringing together Russia,

Iran, Armenia and, to a lesser extent, Greece. Notably however, the two coalitions are far from being monolithic. The relations among many of the members of the rival camps remain quite amicable and conducive to forging mutually beneficial ties based on pragmatic considerations of self-interest. One exception to the pragmatic imperative is Turkey's refusal to establish diplomatic ties with Armenia.

Georgia

Georgia perceives itself as a bridgehead between East and West. In pursuit of this strategic vision, Georgia has actively supported the various Euro–Asian corridor projects,[54] which aim at resuscitating the Silk Road of the past, in particular, the Transport Corridor Europe–Caucasus–Asia project (TRACECA), sponsored by the European Union. A central aspect of this east–west corridor is the transport of hydrocarbon resources. Thus, Georgia is considered as one of the main transit countries for Caspian oil and gas. Pipeline projects across Georgia would mainly involve the trans-shipment of energy from neighboring Azerbaijan, although oil and gas from Kazakhstan and Turkmenistan may also pass through the country. The Georgians consider the presence of pipelines running through their land to be the most effective way of stimulating Western interest in their country, which would help its economy and preserve its independence and territorial integrity.

Georgia's pre-eminent problems since independence have been the maintenance of political stability and the preservation of territorial integrity. Since the final years of the Soviet Union, Georgia has been confronted with secessionist movements among two of its ethnic minorities, the Abkhazians and the Ossetians. The ensuing armed conflicts ended in Georgian military defeats, resulting in loss of central control over the two contested provinces. In addition, the Georgian government has had little sway over the affairs of Ajaria, a third autonomous unit inherited from Soviet times with an ethnically Georgian, but religiously Muslim, population. Furthermore, there have been tensions in the Armenian-populated south (Javakhk) and the Azerbaijani-populated south-east (Marneuli). Secessionist sentiment has been manifested even among the once loyal Mingrelians of western Georgia.

In addition to multiple ethnic conflicts, Georgia was ravaged by civil wars in January 1992 and autumn 1993, which ended after Russian military intervention in support of the government of

Eduard Shevardnadze.[55] Russian help came at a heavy price. Independent-minded Georgia was constrained to join the CIS, to allow Russian military bases on its territory, and to agree to Russian control of its external, that is, non-CIS, borders. Throughout their difficulties, the Georgians have pointed an accusing finger at Russia, whom they blame for having fomented and supported the separatist rebellions that have threatened the survival of their country. The ultimate goal of Russia, according to Georgian and some Western analysts, is to keep Georgia under Russian domination by encouraging unrest among its minorities. While the Abkhaz and the Ossetians did receive material support from Russia or from elements within the Russian military,[56] their desire for separation from Georgia was more attributable to historical reasons and resentment of Georgian domination than to Russian manipulation. Russia did not create minority discontent, although it exploited it. To be sure, maintaining Georgia within the Russian sphere of influence is given a high degree of priority in Moscow's foreign policy, in view of the country's geostrategic location astride the Black Sea.

Since the rebellion which brought him to power in January 1992, President Shevardnadze has achieved a large measure of internal stability and a loosening of Russia's hold on the country. At the risk of Russian displeasure, Shevardnadze has forged links with the United States, Western Europe and the former Soviet republics opposing Russia's 'imperial return' – the Ukraine, Uzbekistan, Azerbaijan and Moldova.[57] In this vein, these republics were joined by Georgia to form the GUUAM (originally GUAM) grouping.[58] In addition, Georgia, Azerbaijan and Ukraine have discussed the formation of a battalion of troops to protect the planned Azerbaijani and Georgian sections of the Baku–Ceyhan pipeline.[59] Relations with Turkey have been on the upswing; in defiance of Russia, Turkey has provided Georgia with military assistance and training of officers.[60] Some tensions remain due to the presence of Turkish citizens of Abkhaz origin among Abkhazian forces and implicit Turkish support for Ajarian autonomy.[61] Georgians have also displayed some irritation and concern about the environmental hazards of a joint project to build a series of 11 dams on a border river and of the Blue Stream gas pipeline scheme between Turkey and Russia.[62] These points of friction, however, are insignificant in comparison with the important commonalities in Turkish and Georgian strategic and economic interests.

Utilizing his well-known diplomatic skills, Shevardnadze garnered the support of the international community for Georgia's territorial integrity with regard to the Abkhaz and Ossetian conflicts. However, Shevardnadze refrained from attempting a military reconquest of the secessionist areas, and until late 1997 avoided antagonizing Russia too openly, even if the Russian media were critical of his foreign policy conduct.[63] The Russian defeat in the first Chechen war and the embarrassment of the Yeltsin administration in the Armeniagate affair allowed him to step up his criticism of Russian policies in the CIS and the Caucasus.[64] Yet, the success of his policies would depend, in Shevardnadze's words, on 'turning [the Eurasian bridge] from an idea into a reality', and thus achieving 'the restoration of Georgia's geopolitical role'.[65]

These are ambitious goals which might be difficult to realize in the prevailing milieu of insecurity, marked by repeated attempts to assassinate the president and several abortive military coups against his régime, in which some have seen a Russian hand. Angered by Russia's alleged machinations and emboldened by Western support, Shevardnadze declined to renew Georgia's membership in the CIS Collective Security Treaty in May 1999, asked for the withdrawal of Russian troops guarding Georgia's external borders, and negotiated the closing down of Russian military bases.[66] These bold steps however, are likely neither to solve Georgia's ethnic conflicts, nor to reduce the endemic corruption or improve the depressed economic status of its people, three essential factors in determining the future role of Georgia in Caspian affairs.

CHAPTER 8

The Outer Circle

Beyond the five states of the inner circle, about a dozen large and small countries play geopolitically significant roles because of their location and different interests in the Caspian Basin. These countries range from major powers like China and India, to regional players such as the Ukraine, Pakistan, Israel and Saudi Arabia, as well as several lesser states. All these nations expect to be influenced by developments in the Caspian Basin and, in turn, seek to influence the future geo-economic configuration of the region. In terms of their national interests, the countries of the outer circle are motivated by one or more of several factors:

(1) the need to import energy for their growing economies;
(2) the benefits to be derived from the transit of pipelines through their territory;
(3) the prospect of competition from Caspian oil and gas in world energy markets; and
(4) the fear of power configurations around the Caspian which could affect their strategic interests.

China

As an emerging superpower with a rapidly expanding economy, China constitutes one of the potentially most important actors in Caspian affairs. Its interests include strategic considerations, the need to import Caspian energy and trade relations outside the energy sector. The spectacular growth of the Chinese economy in the 1990s has made China a net importer of energy. The country's hopes of expanding domestic production have not kept up with its escalating energy needs, because of the lag in oil investment and technology and disappointing results in discovering sufficient reserves on Chinese soil.

The growth of Chinese influence in the Caspian region and Central Asia has been a source of concern to both Russia and the

West. This concern was heightened by the signing of a $9.5bn agreement by China and Kazakhstan on 24 September 1997. The contract confirmed the award to the Chinese National Petroleum Corporation of two important projects. The first involved the development of the Aktyubinsk structure, which contains two major oil fields, Zhanazhol and Kenkayak, and the rehabilitation and exploitation of the Uzen oil field, as previously announced in June and August 1997 respectively. The aim of the second project was the construction of a 3,000 kilometer pipeline linking Kazakh oilfields to the western Chinese province of Xinjiang, and a 250 km pipeline connecting the Kazakh and Iranian networks through Turkmenistan.[1] This agreement was the largest oil deal thus far concluded between a former Soviet republic and a foreign investor. Indeed, this accord would have been more deservedly called the Contract of the Century than the $7.2bn contract signed in 1994 by Azerbaijan and Western companies, had its implementation not been delayed because of China's lack of capital. Shortages of capital could have been also responsible for the Chinese abandonment of the pipeline project linking the Iranian town of Neka, near the Caspian, with Tehran, intended to facilitate swaps of Kazakh and Turkmen oil.[2] Meanwhile, limited quantities of Kazakh oil have been shipped to China by rail.[3] In March 2000, China approved the construction of a 4,200 kilometer pipeline linking gas fields in Xinjiang to the Yellow Sea.[4] This line could be extended to receive Kazakh, Uzbek or Turkmen gas.

These oil and gas agreements reflected a Chinese foreign policy of proactiveness in confronting the new challenges on China's western borders raised by the collapse of the Soviet Union. Indeed, China has had serious strategic concerns about developments in the former Soviet South, particularly regarding inter-ethnic tensions. Initially, China feared that the independence of Central Asian nations across its border might encourage nationalist or Islamist elements among the Uyghur and Kazakh minorities of Xinjiang province. Since the establishment of permanent Chinese control over Xinjiang (Eastern Turkestan) in 1949, there has been strong separatist sentiment in the region. The 1980s and 1990s witnessed a series of riots and the emergence of a small-scale Uyghur secessionist guerilla movement.[5] Beijing's responses have consisted of heavy-handed repression, strengthened control over the borders of the autonomous region, and increasing resettlement of Han Chinese in the area. In the decade since the Soviet demise, Chinese fears of cross-border ethno-religious agitation have not been realized, partly because of the strong determination of the bordering republics of Kazakhstan, Kyrgyzstan and Tajikistan not to encourage irredentist movements among Xinjiang's Muslim minorities.

As a result, there has been a notable change in Chinese attitudes toward the newly independent Central Asian states, based on the Chinese leadership's realization that Central Asians had no interest either in adopting Pan-Turkism or Muslim fundamentalism at home, or in exporting these ideologies to Xinjiang.[6] In addition, China concluded that the development of exchanges between Central Asia and Xinjiang would improve the economy of the area, and thus alleviate some of the sources of regional discontent. The conditions were therefore set for China to cast its growing economic and political shadow over its western neighbors.

China's policy of openness toward Central Asia has had positive consequences. Trade surged between Xinjiang and Central Asia following the opening of a dozen border posts; by 1995, the dollar value had reached $570 million.[7] In 1994, Kazakhstan, Uzbekistan and the Kyrgyz Republic had a larger volume of trade with China than with any of the regional powers competing for influence in the area, such as Iran or Turkey. Significant efforts were made to improve the communication and transport infrastructure between China and Central Asia. The construction of the railway line between Almaty and Urumqi, begun in 1956 and interrupted by the deterioration of Chinese–Soviet relations, was completed in 1992.[8]

The silencing of ethnonationalist movements among Uyghur exiles in Central Asia has been the political price exacted by China from its new partners. The main objective of Prime Minister Li Peng's visit to Central Asian capitals in April 1994 was to secure promises of cooperation against Uyghur separatists. The subsequent crackdown on Uyghur activism in Kazakhstan and the Kyrgyz Republic demonstrated that Beijing had achieved its objective. In July 1998, China and Kazakhstan concluded an agreement that resolved boundary issues inherited from the imperial Russian and Soviet eras.[9] Chinese immigration, particularly into the Kyrgyz Republic, remains an important concern for Central Asians.[10] Finally, both China and Kazakhstan have encouraged the migration of ethnic Kazakhs from Xinjiang to Kazakhstan; China was understandably only too happy to see a decrease in the proportion of Xianjiang's non-Han minority, while the increase of the proportion of ethnic Kazakhs was desired by Kazakhstan.

Despite the flowering of Chinese–Central Asian relations, certain obstacles remain that are likely to limit the growth of Chinese influence around the Caspian. China is not very competitive as an exporter of advanced technology, for which the Central Asian states will have to turn to Europe, America or Japan. China and the Central Asian republics are also concerned not to alienate Russia. Following the conclusion of the contract with China, Kazakh officials hurried to emphasize how much Russia stood to gain from the agreement.[11] Western analysts, however, regard Russia as the potential loser from China's increased role in Central Asia.[12] While partly true, this conclusion cannot hide a certain frustration at the fact that China, rather than Turkey, the United States or Western Europe, might be benefiting from the decline in Russia's regional influence, forecast so long ago and awaited so impatiently in Western circles.

Instead of the anticipated conflict between Chinese and Russian interests in the Caspian/Central Asian region, there has been a progressive strengthening of Chinese–Russian cooperation, based on their mutual economic interests and shared security concerns regarding terrorism, separatist movements, drug trafficking and illegal migration. In order to tackle these security issues within a regional framework, Russia, China, Kazakhstan, the Kyrgyz Republic and Tajikistan reconstituted the agenda of the Shanghai Five group in August 1999, which had been established in 1996 to resolve boundary issues between China and its neighboring former Soviet republics.[13] On another front, manifestations of growing American power have evoked resentment and irritation among Asia's three great powers, Russia, China and India, which have fuelled speculation about the formation of an anti-NATO Asian axis.[14] Should such a tripartite alliance emerge, it would certainly alter the correlation of forces in the Caspian Basin.

Pakistan

Pakistan's relevance to Caspian geopolitics is defined along three dimensions. As a geographically contiguous country, Pakistan provides access to India and the Arabian Sea. Moreover, Pakistanis share a community of faith in Islam with many inhabitants of Central Asia and the Caspian Basin. In addition, Pakistan could be a potential importer of Caspian oil and gas, considering its large population and lack of energy resources. Lastly, Pakistan possesses sufficient military and ideological capabilities to play the role of spoiler in Caspian regional schemes.

The collapse of the Soviet Union provided Pakistan with a new regional set of opportunities. Pakistan hoped to compensate for its strategic weakness vis-a-vis India by establishing control over Afghanistan and forging alliances with the Muslim states of the Caucasus and Central Asia. In pursuit of this strategic vision, there was heightened Pakistani activity in the region during the Gorbachev era and soon after the Soviet demise.[15] To Pakistan's disappointment, the Caspian/Central Asian states were interested neither in the Islamic imperative behind Pakistani activism, nor in forming alliances based on Islamic solidarity or anti-Indian objectives. The cultural gaps between Pakistanis and the mostly Turkic peoples of the former Soviet South were too substantial to be subsumed under Islamic ideological rhetoric, particularly in view of the 70 years of secularization imposed by the Soviet regime. As a result, relations soon came to be based on economic issues.

The inherent weaknesses of Pakistan's economy and the numerous problems faced by Pakistani business ventures in Central Asia had a dampening effect on ambitious initiatives. The absence of direct communication and transport links was a major obstacle to the development of Central Asian relations with Pakistan. The necessity to overcome such obstacles, coupled with the potential benefits of becoming the main access point between Central Asia and the outside world, prompted the Pakistani leadership to push for the construction of a transport infrastructure across Afghanistan. As stated by Michael Dunn, 'Pakistani planners have recognized that the shortest distances between Central Asia and the Indian Ocean lie through their territory. They could become not merely the pipeline outlet but the major port for Central Asian goods.'[16] This geo-economic factor provides partial explanation for Pakistan's patronage of the Afghan Taliban. This patronage, however, and the Taliban's own extremist policies, have had an alienating impact on virtually most of the region's governments who fear the spread of Islamist militancy across their borders. Moreover, the persistence of instability in Taliban-ruled Afghanistan has caused the failure of the trans-Afghan pipeline project, although both Turkmen President Niyazov and Pakistani leader General Musharraf sought to revive it during their May 2000 meeting in Ashghabad. The two leaders also committed themselves to improving the transport infrastructure across Afghanistan.

The only instance where Islamic solidarity has played a role is in Pakistan's relations with Azerbaijan, where, in the absence of substantial economic interests, Pakistan has given strong support to Baku in the conflict over Nagorno-Karabakh. At the June 2000 meeting of the Economic Cooperation Organization in Tehran,

General Musharraf went as far as to place Pakistani military units at Azerbaijan's disposal whenever it opted for the use of force to regain control over Nagorno-Karabakh. In return, Aliyev expressed support for Pakistan's militant stand on Kashmir, which brought an instant protest from India. Despite subsequent denial of Musharraf's offer of military assistance, Pakistani diplomatic sources acknowledged the existence of military cooperation between the two countries.[17]

India

India's three main interests in the Caspian Basin are related to strategic developments, oil and gas imports and increasing exports to the region. As an emerging world power with a large population and economic potential, India has displayed a keen interest in the future course of strategic alignments around the Caspian. Its rapidly expanding economy, combined with its near total dependence on energy imports makes India a potential consumer of Caspian oil and gas. In addition, India would be interested in developing export markets in Central Asia for both its inexpensive consumer goods and its high-tech products.

India's close ties with the Soviet Union provided it with an established presence in Central Asia and the Caucasus. The large Indian consulate in Tashkent was upgraded to embassy status following Uzbek independence. In addition, Indian culture was highly regarded, and Indian cinema was popular throughout the area.[18] In the early years of independence, Pakistani initiatives in Central Asia gave rise to heightened Indian concerns about the development of an Islamic bloc, which Indian diplomacy aimed to counter by an all-out offensive. Another Indian preoccupation is the growth of China's influence east of the Caspian, although the weakening of the Chinese–Pakistani alliance and the improvement of Chinese–Indian relations have partly alleviated these fears.

In India's Central Asian policy, economic issues have come second to strategic ones. Indeed, Central Asia could represent a market for Indian products, especially consumer goods. The leaders of the two largest Central Asian states, Kazakhstan and Uzbekistan, have complained about Indian timidity in investing in their countries.[19] Several factors explain the relatively modest Indian economic involvement in Central Asia. First, India does not have at its disposal the necessary capital to increase the scale of its participation. Second, the Indian leadership, having realized that Central Asia may be immune to Pakistani messianic and strategic initiatives, has given the region secondary priority. Finally, because the most direct routes linking India to Central Asia go through Pakistan, India is reluctant to improve the transport infrastructure and develop a large volume of trade which would be dependent on, and highly vulnerable to, its neighbor's goodwill. As a result, India has not given much attention to the possible extension into India of the projected pipeline carrying Turkmen gas across Afghanistan and Pakistan.[20] Instead, India prefers the opening of road and rail connections between Iran and Central Asia. In the Indian perception, Iran 'will remain a favored route to the Central Asian republics, since it is shorter, economical and thoroughly reliable, and passes as it does through a state, Iran, with which India has the warmest of relations'.[21]

Consequently, cooperation with Iran, as well as with Russia, has characterized India's policy toward the former Soviet South and Afghanistan. In terms of strategic priority, India shares with Russia, Iran and most Central Asian states a common imperative in containing the spread of Sunni Islamist militancy. All these countries vehemently oppose the Taliban and have granted support to their opponents. Also, Russia and India view with disfavor the growth of Turkish influence in Central Asia. A 1993 joint study by Indian and Russian scholars concluded that the Turkish model of political development could not be applied in Central Asia because

> in Turkey, the secular nation state that is tolerant of the religious practices of the Sunni majority without endorsing them, came about after the massacre of Armenian and Greek minorities and the suppression of the Kurds ... such a solution in Central Asia's ethnic mix is inconceivable.[22]

Finally, there have been no significant developments in relations between India and the Transcaucasian republics, although some have suggested that India and Armenia could increase their ties to counter the good relations between their respective rivals, Pakistan and Azerbaijan.

Saudi Arabia and the Gulf States

The emergence of the Caspian/Central Asian sphere as a focus of international attention has presented the Arab monarchies of the Gulf with an ironic paradox. Saudi Arabia and her partners in the Gulf Cooperation Council (GCC) rightfully greeted the liberation of the six mostly Muslim states of the Soviet South from the Communist yoke. However, the importance accorded to these countries by the United States and its allies, because of their geostrategic position and potential as energy exporters, confronted the GCC countries with the prospect of an emerging rival in the world marketplace.[23] At present, Saudi–GCC interests in the former Soviet South center on energy, strategic issues, the Islamic factor, trade and investments.

As custodian of the holy sanctuaries of Mecca and Medina, the Saudi Kingdom has played a leading role in sustaining the Islamic ethos in the former Soviet South. In Soviet times, the Saudis initiated a campaign against Communist ideology through Islamic propagation. The liberalizing atmosphere of Gorbachev's perestroika provided Saudi Arabia with a welcome opportunity to build mosques in the Muslim republics and to dispatch one million copies of the Qur'an offered by King Fahd.[24] Other fields of Saudi activity included funding pilgrimages and opening religious schools. These efforts were accelerated with the coming of independence, as the Saudis led a campaign of extensive proselytization guided by the tenets of the Sunni Muwahhidun (Wahhabi) movement. Beyond its purely religious motives, Saudi involvement in the region was prompted by geopolitical considerations vis-a-vis Iran and other potential hegemons. Prompted by the traditional doctrinal rivalry between Sunni and Shi'a Islam, the Saudi propagation of Sunnism could be seen as a pre-emptive move against the perceived threat of growing Iranian Shi'a influence. In the late 1990s, the success of the Afghan Taliban movement, which appeared to share some puritanical Wahhabi maxims, represented a challenge not only to Iran but to Russia and the secularist regimes of the Caucasus and Central Asia.

With the rise of Islamist militancy in Taliban-ruled Afghanistan and in some regions of Central Asia and the Caucasus, there was a significant cutback in Saudi support of Islamist groups. It had become obvious to the kingdom that the term 'Wahhabism' was being misused both by Islamist militants and the secular governments they opposed, and that the original meaning of Wahhabi puritanism as a non-political creed had become perverted in the Caspian/Central Asian context. Moreover, the rise of Islamist extremism was as much a threat to conservative Arab regimes as to secular post-Soviet governments. Indeed, missionary outreach from the GCC area has been denounced by Central Asian governments and media, and has had a deleterious impact on their relations with some Arab countries.[25] A case in point was an article in the Kazakh press accusing Arab states of condoning religious extremism and terrorism, which drew an immediate protest from the ambassadors of Egypt, Libya, Palestine and Saudi Arabia.[26] As distinct from the non-involvement of GCC governments, it is widely believed that non-governmental groups and individuals continue to fund the cause of political Islamism around the Caspian.

In recent years, there has been a reduction of Saudi concern regarding the spread of Iranian ideological and political influences. Initial Saudi–GCC fears of Iranian expansionism were unfounded, as Iran refocused its policies on the pursuit of economic relations with its northern neighbors. Also, the growing rapprochement between Iran and Saudi Arabia and most of its GCC partners has had a dampening effect on their rivalry in the former Soviet South. Yet the religious factor continues to find resonance among the GCC states in the context of Islamic solidarity. The repeated protests against Russian military intervention in Chechnya, and the significant financial support given to Chechen fighters by GCC and other Arab states, represent manifestations of an Islamic bond with coreligionists suffering persecution. Such support has evoked Russian warnings to several Arab and Muslim countries and has harmed their traditionally amicable relations with Russia.

A salient issue for the Arab countries is the individual orientation of the Caspian Basin states toward the Arab–Israeli conflict. Although most Caspian/Central Asian countries gave rhetorical support to the Palestinian cause, they were also eager to establish diplomatic relations with Israel soon after independence. Such links have had an alienating impact on Arab public opinion and angered the Islamist constituency. Despite some early Saudi successes in limiting Israeli influence in the region,[27] Azerbaijan and the Central Asian states have remained impervious to Arab and Islamist opposition to the development of ties with Israel.

In the economic sector, the initial optimism regarding large-scale GCC investments has proven unfounded. Although some progress was made in trade and investment, the relatively modest results reflected the non-complementarity of the GCC and Central Asian economies. In addition, the immense costs of the 1991 war against Iraq depleted GCC treasuries, leaving little to invest abroad. Repeated reciprocal visits by high-ranking officials and the signing of numerous trade agreements have yet to produce significant results.[28] A partial exception is the involvement of some Arab investors in the region's energy projects.[29] Oman was a founding member of the Caspian Pipeline Consortium (CPC) project, and the Saudi Delta company is a participant in various Azerbaijani oil deals and the failed trans-Afghan pipeline scheme. In Turkmenistan, the Dragon oil company of the United Arab Emirates signed a production-sharing agreement in November 1999 to develop offshore oil deposits and to restore the Hazar (former Cheleken) port.[30]

The Caspian energy factor is the foremost issue of interest for Saudi Arabia and its GCC partners. In view of the epicentric position of the kingdom, Kuwait, Qatar, Oman and the United Arab Emirates in the global oil and gas marketplace, the possible emergence of the Caspian Basin as a new energy source is a cause of serious concern to these states. To Arab producers and Iran, the US/Western determination to develop Caspian hydrocarbon resources is perceived as part of a persistent campaign to find alternative sources of oil and gas in order to lessen dependence on Gulf supplies. Consequently, GCC producers view with disfavor the hype about the Caspian, the flow of foreign investment, and the Baku–Ceyhan and trans-Afghan projects circumventing the Persian Gulf region. Of course, the Saudis possess the ability to hinder the development of the Caspian hydrocarbon industry by reducing oil prices through overproduction, combined with the reopening of their oil industry to large-scale Western investment, which could divert potential investors from the Caspian region.[31] According to former Saudi oil minister Ahmad Zaki al-Yamani, Gulf Arab states should open up their upstream sectors to foreign investors to resist future competition from the Caspian.[32]

Israel

In sharp contrast to the Arab countries, Israel has been more successful in establishing extensive diplomatic, economic and security ties with many of the Central Asian/Caspian states. In the early 1990s, Israeli diplomacy moved decisively into the vacuum created by the Soviet collapse. Although the benefits of its ambitious multifaceted involvement may be long in coming, there can be no doubt that Israel has established a notable presence to exploit economic opportunities and to counter Arab, Islamist, Iranian and Russian influences.

Israeli interest in the Caucasus and Central Asia is shaped by strategic concerns, the development of export markets, investment opportunities and energy imports. As a country not at peace with the Arab world, Israel has long sought to forge ties with non-Arab Muslim countries. This strategy in the Central Asian/Caspian context has aimed at projecting a favorable image of Israel, while checking Arab, Islamist and Iranian inroads and preempting

Palestinian efforts to mobilize support for their cause. Notably, Israel's ambitious outreach fell in line with the general thrust of US post-Cold War policy in the former Soviet South and Turkey's own eastern strategy. This alignment of interests resulted in the projection of the US-sponsored Israeli–Turkish alliance into the Caspian/Central Asian arena.

The earliest links between Israel and the republics of the former Soviet South can be traced to Jewish communities residing in that region. Although the growth of Jewish national consciousness in the 1970s resulted in emigration to Israel, small communities still remain in these republics. This ethnic link provided Israel with a bridgehead to advance its political and commercial interests. Soon after their independence, Israel established diplomatic relations with all Transcaucasian and Central Asian republics,[33] which perceived such relations as enhancing their sovereignty and economic development. To be sure, Israel could provide these states with a useful link to the West, technical assistance in desert agriculture and foreign investment.[34]

Azerbaijan has been a primary focus of Israeli attention. In addition to commercial links, Israel has given strong backing to Azerbaijan in its conflict with Armenia over Nagorno-Karabakh, which reportedly has included military assistance.[35] Even more significant has been the Israeli role in marshalling US political support for three issues of major importance to Azerbaijan – its claim to Nagorno-Karabakh, the passage of the Silk Road Strategy Act by Congress, and the Baku–Ceyhan pipeline project. Hence the grateful acknowledgment of former Azerbaijani Foreign Minister Hassan Hassanov: 'We don't conceal that we rely on the Israeli lobby in the US.'[36] Israel's efforts on behalf of Azerbaijan were part of its larger strategy of alignment with Turkey since 1995, which involved lobbying by a coalition of Jewish–American organizations on behalf of both Turkish and Azerbaijani interests.[37] The importance attached to Azerbaijan was underlined by Prime Minister Binyamin Netanyahu's brief stopover in Baku in August 1997, where he underlined the importance of cooperation between Israel, Turkey and Azerbaijan against Iranian Islamism, and expressed interest in importing Azerbaijani oil through the Baku–Ceyhan pipeline.[38] The new Israel–Azerbaijan–Turkey alignment has generated deep concern among Iranian, Russian, Arab and Armenian diplomatic circles.[39] Yet Israel's eagerness to please Azerbaijan did not prevent President Aliyev from declaring at the 1997 Tehran summit of the Organization of the Islamic Conference that 'the Azerbaijani people consider

Zionists dangerous for all Muslims and believe they are common enemies of Muslims'.[40]

In parallel to the strengthening of its relations with Azerbaijan, Israel has developed close ties with Georgia. Shevardnadze's role as Soviet foreign minister in lifting restrictions on Jewish emigration from the Soviet Union and his pro-Western policies have laid the basis for a solid relationship. Another contributing factor is Georgia's strategic location as a land bridge between Turkey and Azerbaijan. The importance attached to Georgia was underlined by the award of the Israeli Democratic Institute's prestigious prize to President Shevardnadze in January 1998, and Prime Minister Netanyahu's visit to Tbilisi in March 1999.[41]

In contrast to Azerbaijan and Georgia, Armenia has not been a target of priority attention by the Israeli government. The factors dampening the Armenian–Israeli relationship have included divergent state interests, Israel's alliance with Turkey and Azerbaijan, the Jewish lobby's support for all Turkish and Azerbaijani causes in Washington, and Armenia's good relations with Syria and Iran.[42] However, since 1998 relations have improved, with Armenian President Robert Kocharian's visit to Israel in January 2000 and the frank acknowledgment of the 1915 Armenian Genocide by Israeli ministers Yossi Sarid and Yossi Beilin, which provoked Turkish ire.[43]

Since the establishment of diplomatic ties in 1993, Israeli–Turkmen relations have grown dramatically both in the political and economic realms. In 1994, there was an exchange of visits by the Turkmen deputy prime minister and Israeli Foreign Minister Shimon Peres, as a prelude to Turkmenbashi Niyazov's trip to Jerusalem in May 1995. The two sides have concluded numerous agreements on economic cooperation, including healthcare, financial services, agriculture and education. Despite Iranian displeasure, in August 1996 Niyazov signed a US $500 million contract with an Israeli company, Merhav, to upgrade the Turkmenbashi refinery. Merhav's owner, Yossi Maiman, became a key adviser to Niyazov and was charged with Turkmenistan's negotiations with Western oil companies, including setting up a consortium to build the trans-Caspian gas pipeline.[44] In March 1997, high-ranking Turkmen and Israeli officials discussed a proposal to ship Turkmen gas via Turkey to Israel through a pipeline to be built under the Mediterranean.[45]

Another major target of Israeli diplomacy is Kazakhstan, where strategic and economic concerns have played a formative role. An early Israeli preoccupation has been the fear that atomic weapons based in Kazakhstan since Soviet times would fall into the hands of extremist groups or countries hostile to Israel, such as Iran or Libya.[46] This concern has gradually subsided as a result of an American-sponsored program to withdraw such weapons to Russia. In the economic sphere, Israel has been active in agricultural projects and various other sectors, such as banking and telecommunications. Eager to develop relations with both Israel and the Arabs, the Kazakhs have welcomed any progress in the Israeli–Palestinian peace process. The growing Israeli–Kazakh links culminated in Nazarbayev's visit to Israel in December 1995, where he obliged his hosts by a pledge to prevent the spread of Iranian influence in Kazakhstan.[47]

Israel's relations with the two other littoral states of the Caspian – Russia and Iran – date back to the founding of the Jewish state in 1948. After the vicissitudes of Israeli–Soviet relations, there was an improvement in ties with the new Russian state. However, Israel's 'special relationship' with the United States and alliances with Turkey and Azerbaijan have placed Israel and Russia in opposing camps within the framework of the Caspian Great Game. As to Israel's relations with Iran, a condition of antagonism has persisted since the 1979 Iranian Revolution. Despite their covert cooperation against Iraq in the 1980s, Iran and Israel have treated each other as primary adversaries and bitter rivals for influence in the Caspian/Central Asian arena.

Greece

Despite its relative remoteness from the region, Greece's strategic relations with Turkey, Russia, Iran and Armenia make it a notable actor in the geopolitics of the Caspian. Given its geographical position, Greece may also provide a venue of transit for Caspian oil. In response to its conflictual relations with Turkey regarding Cyprus and the Aegean, Greece has established strategic and economic ties with Iran and Armenia, with which it shares concerns regarding Turkish expansionism. Formed in 1997, ostensibly to promote economic cooperation, this trilateral framework also possesses strategic and military components that remain unstated.[48] More explicit however, are Armenian–Greek military ties including exchanges of military intelligence and training of Armenian cadets in Greece.[49] Yet, Greece's close ties to Armenia did not prevent its stated recognition of Azerbaijan's territorial integrity and sovereignty over Nagorno-Karabakh, in order to become a participant in the Caspian

Great Game.[50] Another factor influencing Greece's position is the recent thaw in its relations with Turkey, although this may not last or be sufficient to give Greece a greater role in Caspian affairs.

The Turkish threat and Christian Orthodox solidarity have been responsible for the rather friendly relations between Greece and Russia. Following Turkey's decision to limit oil tanker traffic through the Straits, Russia, Greece and Bulgaria signed a tripartite agreement in September 1994 to build a pipeline from Burgas on Bulgaria's Black Sea Coast to Alexandroupolis on the Aegean. This pipeline would allow Caspian oil shipped by tankers from Novorossiisk to Burgas to reach international markets by bypassing the Turkish Straits.[51] After completion of a feasibility study, the Trans-Balkan Pipeline Co. was established for the construction and operation of the project.[52]

Bulgaria

Bulgaria's connection to the Caspian Basin is primarily based on its geographical position for the transit of oil and gas to European markets. Beyond its interest in the proposed Burgas–Alexandroupolis pipeline, Bulgaria has welcomed US support for a trans-Balkan pipeline to transport Kazakh oil from the Black Sea to the Adriatic across Bulgaria, Macedonia and Albania.[53] The US offer to fund a feasibility study raised Turkish suspicions that Washington might prefer shipping Caspian oil across the Balkans rather than through the Baku–Ceyhan.[54] After a government change in April 1997, Bulgaria moved away from its traditional pro-Russian orientation to one of rapprochement with the USA and Turkey. In order to achieve its goal of becoming a key transit country for Caspian hydrocarbons, Bulgaria has established friendly ties with Kazakhstan and Azerbaijan, in addition to its traditionally close relations with Armenia. To pursue this goal, Bulgarian President Peter Stoyanov visited Azerbaijan and Armenia, where he also sought to play the role of mediator in the Nagorno-Karabakh conflict.[55]

Romania

Romania's interests in the Caspian Basin are mainly economic, involving oil transit, trade and refining. As a former major oil producer, Romania possesses considerable expertise in the energy industry. Under Ceaucescu, its processing capacity was expanded to include ten refineries which are currently under-utilized because of low reserves and economic stagnation. Hence Romania's desire to import Caspian oil for its refineries as well as to provide oil transit through its territory.[56] The focus of Romanian hopes is a pipeline linking its port of Constanza on the Black Sea to Trieste on the Adriatic, passing through Serbia, Croatia and Slovenia. To this end, Romania held an international conference in Bucharest in September 1998, and entered into discussions with Azerbaijan. In 1999, the Romanian oil company SNP Petrom bought a 51 percent stake in the Kazakh Tasbulat oil field.[57] Aside from energy, Romania aspires to become a part of the 'New Silk Road' linking Central Asia to European markets.[58]

Ukraine

Among the countries of the outer circle, Ukraine is the largest and the most influential in Caspian affairs. Its multifaceted involvement is driven by strategic and economic interests, as well as by its aspiration to become a transit venue for Caspian oil and gas. Since 1991, Ukraine has sought to assert its identity as an independent nation, often pursuing confrontational policies toward Russia. These have included Ukraine's rapprochement with NATO and the United States, and its reluctance to become active in the CIS because of Russia's dominant position. Another complicating factor in Russo–Ukrainian relations is Ukraine's dependence on Russian and Turkmen gas, and its inability to pay for it. To compensate for Ukraine's huge debt, Russia has proposed to take over several Ukrainian energy companies and pipelines.[59] Russian irritation over large-scale siphoning of Russian gas transiting Ukraine to European markets and fear of a Ukrainian stranglehold over gas exports have prompted plans to build an alternate pipeline across Belarus to bypass Ukraine.[60] Because of Ukraine's non-payment of its energy debt, Turkmen gas deliveries were halted after March 1997, except for a brief period in early 1999.[61] A new agreement signed in October 2000 set the terms for the resumption of gas deliveries – 35 bn cubic meters – through 2001 in exchange for a mix of hard currency and goods and services.[62]

In the Caspian context, Ukraine is a founding member of GUAM (now GUUAM, with the addition of Uzbekistan), a grouping of CIS countries seeking to counter Russian influence and provide a route for Caspian energy outside Russia's control. Also, Ukraine has actively promoted the development of a route across its territory for the export of Caspian oil. In pursuit of this goal, President

Leonid Kuchma courted Azerbaijan and Kazakhstan about shipping oil from the Georgian port of Supsa to Odessa. The Ukrainian plan envisages an oil export venue connecting Baku on the Caspian to Gdansk on the Baltic – a project fully supported by the Polish government.[63] If realized, this grand vision would satisfy Ukraine's energy needs, reduce its dependence on Russia and revive its sagging economy. During US Secretary of State Albright's visit in April 2000, President Kuchma pleaded for American support for the Odessa–Gdansk pipeline.[64]

To emphasize Ukraine's interest in Caspian energy, the government has termed the building of the Baku–Gdansk route a 'national priority'.[65] In April 1999, Kuchma joined his Azeri and Georgian counterparts for the inauguration of the Baku–Supsa pipeline; on a return visit to the region in March 2000 he reiterated Ukraine's determination to develop its transit corridor, made all the more urgent by Russia's interruption of oil supplies. Although Azerbaijan showed little enthusiasm for Kuchma's pipeline project, it did agree to provide 50,000 tonnes of oil products to relieve the oil shortage in Ukraine.[66] A tripartite agreement signed by Ukraine, Georgia and Azerbaijan included the formation of a joint battalion to protect the Baku–Supsa pipeline.

CHAPTER 9

America, Europe, Japan and Asia

Within the Caspian arena, the interests of the advanced industrial democracies – the United States, Japan and Western Europe – are both complementary and competitive. These countries share an interest in the political stability of the Caspian region because of its strategic importance and hydrocarbon wealth. From the perspective of these industrialized countries, the Caspian/Central Asian states are perceived as energy exporters, as importers of Western products, and as targets of investment. Indeed, since the retreat of Soviet power, the Western countries have gradually increased their involvement both in the economic and political realms. This increase in Western presence, combined with Russia's military and economic decline, has resulted in a significant diminution of Russian influence in the region.

The United States
Any assessment of the growing American role in the Caspian Basin would have to proceed from the uniqueness of the United States as the world's only superpower. This attribute has shaped US foreign policy goals, which are an eclectic application of the theories of balance of power, geopolitical realism and neoliberalism/globalization. In specific terms, US interests in the Caspian Basin include a strategic dimension, reinforced by economic considerations centring on energy resources, trade and investment opportunities.

The year 1997 was a turning point in America's policy toward the Caspian Basin, signified by the dramatic rise in the importance given to the region by US policymakers. Indeed, Central Asia/Caspian was not considered strategically vital to the USA in the first years following the Soviet collapse, and was treated as an accessory to American interests in Russia and the Middle East. In a sharp twist, the priority given to the Caspian since 1997 has affected American policy toward Russia and the countries of the Middle East's northern tier, in particular Iran and Afghanistan.

American relations with the republics of the Caucasus and Central Asia went through three phases. In the immediate post-Soviet period, the United States sought to conciliate the emerging leadership of Russia under Yeltsin. Thus, until mid-1994, it abstained from taking any steps that could be perceived as threatening to Russia. Official American declarations emphasized coordination with Russia in the former Soviet South. The declared US objectives were to:

(1) consolidate the independence and the sovereignty of the republics of the Caucasus and Central Asia;
(2) strengthen stability by working toward conflict resolution;
(3) promote democracy;
(4) encourage a transition to a market economy and free trade;
(5) achieve the denuclearization of Kazakhstan;
(6) seek the adoption and application of human rights principles;
(7) prevent the spread of radical Islamist tendencies, especially from Iran.[1]

Given the somewhat limited American interest in the area, the United States relied on its regional allies, Israel, Pakistan and especially Turkey, to counter Iranian influence. The United States expected the new republics to emulate the Turkish state-building model, and Turkey was regarded as a potential regional leader, in partial contradiction of America's Russocentric policy.

During this period, the United States displayed less concern for the independence of the republics of the Caucasus and Central Asia than it did for that of the Baltic republics and the Ukraine.[2] Calls for help from Transcaucasian and Central Asian leaders against perceived Russian infringement of their countries' newly established independence went generally unanswered.[3] After a meeting with Yeltsin in January 1994, President Clinton lauded the stabilizing role of Russia in the Georgian crisis, and told the Russians that, 'You will be more likely to be involved in some of these areas near you, just like the United States has been involved in the last several years in Panama and Grenada near our area.'[4] One month later, Nazarbayev, who had come to Washington to request American support for a pipeline carrying Kazakh oil through Turkey, was advised by American officials to choose a route through Russia.[5]

Moreover, American policy differed from country to country. In Transcaucasia, special attention was given to Armenia, because of the presence of a large American–Armenian community, and to Georgia, following the accession to power of Eduard Shevardnadze, who enjoyed strong sympathy in the West for his role during the last years of the Soviet Union. There was concern that its ethnic mix might threaten the stability of Kazakhstan because nuclear weapons were stationed there. The observance of international human rights standards in the Kyrgyz Republic was particularly appreciated, while Azerbaijan was penalized for its blockade of Armenia. The authoritarian regime imposed by Aliyev, following the June 1993 coup that overthrew his democratically elected predecessor Elchibey, did not help American–Azerbaijani relations. The onset of authoritarian régimes with poor human rights records contributed to America's lukewarm relations with Turkmenistan and Uzbekistan.[6]

The second phase of American policy in the Caucasus and Central Asia lasted about three years, from mid-1994 to mid-1997, although signs of policy change could be detected earlier. In October 1993, Strobe Talbott, then US Ambassador-at-large to the new states of the former Soviet Union, declared that the United States, while understanding Russian security concerns, would not 'support actions that violate the independence, sovereignty, or territorial integrity of other states'.[7] After the October 1993 attack on the Russian parliament, the United States grew increasingly concerned with the possible evolution of Russia toward authoritarianism. The elections of December 1993, which saw the surge of the ultra-nationalists under Vladimir Zhirinovsky, compounded American anxieties. US policymakers began to lend an ear to voices denouncing Russian policies which threatened the survival of states such as Azerbaijan and Georgia. During a summit held in September 1994, Clinton modified his January 1994 stance and asked the Russians to respect the independence of the former Soviet republics.[8]

This new phase of American policy witnessed an increase in US aid to the Central Asian countries.[9] After initially favoring Kazakhstan, during 1995 the USA switched to Uzbekistan as its preferred Central Asian partner. US interest in Kazakhstan waned after the removal of nuclear weapons from its territory and the realization that the Kazakhs could not afford to dissociate themselves from Moscow. The emergence of Uzbekistan as a favored partner was due not only to that country's political and economic importance, but also to Karimov's anti-Russian, pro-Israeli, and anti-Iranian rhetoric – including a temporary compliance with the American embargo against Iran. The Uzbek régime's violations of human rights were conveniently downplayed in State Department reports, partly prompted by the newly appointed US Ambassador, Stanley Escudero, who regarded strategic interests as more important than humanitarian concerns. Presumably because it maintained good relations with Iran, Turkmenistan was treated more harshly in the State Department's human rights reports, despite the comparable level of Turkmen and Uzbek human rights violations.[10] The relativism in US human rights policies also applied to neighboring Afghanistan, where the Islamist Taliban were achieving military dominance through Pakistani sponsorship. US determination to isolate Iran and the plans to build a pipeline through Afghanistan may have contributed to the State Department's tendentious statement that the Taliban victory in 1996 was a 'positive' development.[11]

In the Caucasus the first steps of a US rapprochement with Azerbaijan were taken, once it became clear that Aliyev was intent on limiting Russian influence in his country. As Aliyev quickly consolidated power, he was perceived as a man one could do business with. Oil was crucial in this rapprochement, as American oil companies complained that unless the American government played a greater role in Azerbaijan, they risked being left out of highly profitable energy contracts. Moreover, the first Chechen war diminished Russia's stature as a military power and reinforced the view that Russian influence could be easily contained in the former Soviet South. After the conclusion of the Contract of the Century in September 1994, the heightened American interest was demonstrated by President Clinton's order to set up a Caspian task force headed by Deputy Secretary of State Strobe Talbott, and composed of individuals from the energy and commerce departments, the National Security Council and the CIA. In addition to the protection of the interests of American oil companies, one of the main objectives of the task force was to prevent the building of pipelines through Iran.[12]

In 1995 American intervention was decisive in Iran's exclusion from the Contract of the Century, and in the choice of two pipeline routes through Georgia and Turkey for the export of 'early' Azerbaijani oil, which reflected the US preference for multiple pipelines out of the Caspian.[13] On the issue of the legal status of the Caspian, the United States expressed support for the Azerbaijani position, arguing that the sea had to be divided into national sectors.[14] Meanwhile, Washington intensified efforts to find a solution to the region's ethnic conflicts, such as Karabakh and Abkhazia, which could promote instability and disrupt oil exports.[15] However, at a time when the US was challenging Russia with NATO's eastern expansion, it had no desire to confront Russia too openly in the Caspian.

Such restraint was criticized by American policy analysts and oil companies, which had recruited former high-ranking officials such as Zbigniew Brzezinski, John Sununu, Richard Cheney and James Baker to lobby for their cause.[16]

In the first half of 1997, pressure for a change in US policy intensified, with a lobbying campaign in Washington, in the media and in academic and policy journals.[17] In the perception of influential policy analysts, the Caspian region had become extremely crucial for American interests, necessitating a larger and more dynamic US role. In a reversal of the situation from the early 1990s, US policy toward Iran and Russia had to be adapted to suit the new Caspian realities. Consequently, it was suggested that the US embargo against Iran be lifted in order to offer Caspian oil-producing states an alternative to the Russian route.[18] Another target of criticism was Section 907 of the 'Freedom Support Act', which denied US aid to Azerbaijan until the lifting of its blockade of Armenia. Adopted in 1992 at the urging of the American–Armenian lobby, Section 907 has been seen by Azerbaijan's supporters as a hindrance to the betterment of US relations with that state.[19]

The third phase of American policy toward the Caucasus and Central Asia began on 21 July 1997, when the region became, for the first time, the focus of a policy address by a top US official. In a speech delivered at the Central Asia Institute, Talbott described the former Soviet South as a 'strategically vital region' and part of the 'Euro–Atlantic community', which the United States could not afford to neglect.[20] Despite Talbott's affirmation that politics in the Caspian rim was not, and should not become, a modern replay of the Great Game, and that the Clinton administration wanted all players to be winners, there was little doubt left among policy analysts that the United States had joined the new Great Game in force, without modifying its rules. This was confirmed by Sheila Heslin, a former National Security Council aide, who declared during a Senate hearing in September 1997, that the aim of the US administration was 'to promote the independence of these oil-rich republics, to in essence break Russia's monopoly control over the transportation of oil from that region.'[21]

In pursuit of heightened US interest in the Caspian, First Lady Hillary Clinton visited Kazakhstan, Kyrgyzstan and Uzbekistan in November 1997, while US Energy Secretary Federico Peña was attending the inauguration ceremony of Azerbaijan's first 'early oil' in Baku. For its part, the White House extended the welcome mat during summer and autumn 1997 to Presidents Akaev of

Kyrgyzstan, Shevardnadze of Georgia, Aliyev of Azerbaijan, Nazarbayev of Kazakhstan and Prime Minister Utkur Sultanov of Uzbekistan. Washington officialdom reserved particularly warm receptions for Aliyev and Shevardnadze during their highly publicized visits in July and August 1997. These diplomatic moves were supplemented in September 1997 by a modest but symbolic US military outreach – the dispatch to Kazakhstan of 500 paratroopers from the 82nd Airborne Division, along with small contingents of Kazakh, Kirghiz and Uzbek troops for peacekeeping exercises with soldiers from Russia, Turkey, Latvia and Georgia.[22]

The Clinton administration's campaign in support of Baku–Ceyhan continued throughout 1998, despite declining oil prices and the publication of several credible reports questioning the exaggerated estimates of Caspian energy reserves.[23] These reports were contested by US officials, who persisted to claim potential Caspian reserves of up to 200 bn barrels.[24] At a conference in Istanbul in May 1998, US Energy Secretary Peña announced a new Caspian Sea Initiative that would coordinate the efforts of the Export-Import Bank, the Overseas Private Investment Corporation (OPIC), and the Trade Development Agency (TDA), which were expected to commit $6bn to Caspian projects.[25] To implement this initiative, the United States established the Caspian Finance Centre in Ankara, under the umbrella of the US Embassy, to channel funding to energy and non-energy projects.[26] In October 1998, a further step was taken by his successor, Bill Richardson, who signed, along with the presidents of Azerbaijan, Georgia, Kazakhstan, Turkey and Uzbekistan, the 'Ankara Declaration' to provide financing and incentives to build Baku–Ceyhan.[27] US diplomacy was also active in attempting to mediate the sectoral dispute between Azerbaijan and Turkmenistan, whose president, Saparmurad Niyazov, was belatedly received in Washington in April 1998 with a lower level of enthusiasm than was displayed during his neighbors' earlier visits.[28] At the risk of offending his American hosts, Niyazov refused to abandon the trans-Iranian gas pipeline project, and later declined to become a signatory to the Ankara Declaration.[29]

A persisting feature of US policy toward the Caspian was the isolation of Iran and Russia. The repeated insistence of US policymakers about the desirability of multiple pipelines represented mere rhetoric, behind which was the determination to avoid passage through Russian and Iranian territory. Preliminary indications in mid-1997 that the United States would not oppose building the trans-Iranian pipeline to ship Turkmen gas to Turkey were refuted a few months later. As an alternative, the United States promoted the trans-Caspian gas pipeline project, along with a promise to finance it and insure it against political risk.[30] Furthermore, US companies were denied authorization to export oil from their Kazakh and Turkmen operations across Iran in swap deals.[31] As to Russia, the US position pretended to show a higher degree of flexibility than with Iran. This was demonstrated by US backing for the Caspian Pipeline Consortium (CPC) linking Kazakh oil fields to Novorossiisk – the sole instance of American forbearance for a trans-Russian route, beyond the Baku–Novorossiisk pipeline for 'early' Azeri oil which had come into operation in late 1997.

Despite the singular determination of the White House to implement Brzezinski's concept of 'creating a geopolitical belt around Russia',[32] the prospects for Baku–Ceyhan appeared bleak, due to opposition from the oil companies. In the midst of an intense lobbying effort, Richard Morningstar, presidential advisor on Caspian energy, stated the four goals of US strategy:

- Strengthen the independence, sovereignty and prosperity of the new Caspian states and encourage political and economic reform
- Ease the likelihood of regional conflicts by building economic linkages between the new states, which have little or no history of cooperating with one another
- Bolster the energy security of the United States and its allies and the energy independence of the Caspian region by ensuring the free flow of oil and gas to world markets
- Enhance commercial opportunities for American companies[33]

The phalanx of the administration's supporters included none other than Henry Kissinger, who after meeting with Aliyev in November 1998, expressed his admiration for the Azeri leader, underlined Azerbaijan's strategic importance, voiced support for Baku–Ceyhan and pledged to do his best to eliminate Section 907.[34] For its part, in a surprise move, Azerbaijan offered in January 1999 to base US/NATO troops in the Apsheron Peninsula. Having been ruled for centuries by their Russian and Persian neighbors, the Azeris wanted the United States and the West to guarantee their independence, even if this meant accepting a degree of neocolonialism.[35] Although the United States was not prepared to accept Azerbaijan's proposal to extend NATO to the Caspian shores,[36] it was anxious to conclude an agreement on the Baku–Ceyhan pipeline, which was finally signed in November 1999 at the Istanbul OSCE conference.[37] This document provided the political framework on the basis of which the oil companies would proceed to fund the building of the pipeline.

The eight-year evolution of American policy toward the Caspian Basin, from one of relative disinterest to a major component of national interest, was striking. What Graham Fuller had described as an area devoid of American interest[38] had been transformed by the Clinton administration into a panacea to resolve a variety of foreign policy issues:

(1) to contain Russia;
(2) to isolate Iran;
(3) to reward allies old and new (Turkey, Georgia, Azerbaijan);
(4) to pacify the Caucasus (Nagorno-Karabakh and Abkhazia);
(5) to develop alternative energy sources to reduce reliance on the Arabs and Iran;
(6) to project US influence into a regional power vacuum, ostensibly to maintain stability.

The administration's obsession with 'pipeline politics' was a far cry from its earlier interest to promote democracy, human rights and socially beneficial economic development.[39] In view of the US record of support for a plethora of authoritarian and corrupt rulers, the sacrifice of human rights and democratic values was not surprising. However, the burden of long-term US military and economic commitments in the Caspian region could prove too costly and possibly unbearable even for a superpower.

It may well be that, more than any other factor, the pre-eminent aim of the United States is geostrategic – to project power into the Caspian/Central Asian arena in order to check Russian, Chinese and Islamist influences. If this is indeed the case, the pursuit of such a Pax Americana, despite the exertions of the Clinton administration, is still at a nascent phase. Multiple obstacles are likely to impede the establishment of an American hegemonic presence.

Iran, Russia and various ethnic groups involved in separatist struggles are the likely losers as a result of America's entrance into the Game, and as such constitute primary opponents of US penetration.[40] Against all expectations, Russian reaction to American inroads in the Caspian was limited to expressions of anger and protest in the Yeltsin years.[41] Since the second Chechen war and Putin's rise to power, a more activist Russian policy has been manifested. As to Iran, it has successfully resisted US attempts to isolate it from new-found partners in the Caucasus and Central Asia. The leaders of these states, who are highly conscious that Iran offers their countries the shortest and least expensive routes to the outside world, have been unwilling to break with Tehran. Denouncing American policies in the region, the Iranians pointed to the obvious contradiction between US opposition to Islamic fundamentalism and support for the Taliban.[42] In the words of Iranian Supreme leader Khamenei, the presence of US oil companies in the Caspian will pave the way for US military presence.[43] US backing for the territorial integrity of post-Soviet states, and close relations with Azerbaijan, Georgia and Turkey, are likely to alienate such ethnic groups as the Abkhaz in Georgia, the Armenians of Nagorno-Karabakh, the Kurds of Turkey, the Chechens, and the Lezgins of the Russian–Azerbaijani borderlands, to name a few. The unfulfilled national aspirations of these groups could destabilize the region and threaten the safety of pipelines.[44]

At this early stage, it is impossible to prognosticate with any assurance the outcomes of America's new strategy. Aside from the Baku–Ceyhan agreement and the cooperative relationships with the region's rulers, there has been little in the form of tangible success. In the face of Islamist opposition, and irritated by US criticism of their human rights policies, the Central Asian countries turned to Russia, after Putin's rise, to enhance their external and internal security. The US sponsored trans-Caspian scheme was shelved, while the construction of Russia's Blue Stream gas pipeline project to Turkey was proceeding apace. Finally, US and Western mediation efforts remained stalled in Nagorno-Karabakh, South Ossetia and Abkhazia.

Europe

The interests of the European democracies in the Caspian/Central Asian sphere are both strategic and economic. To the European members of NATO, the strategic importance of the larger Caspian complex is determined by its proximity to and the involvement of Turkey, a NATO member, in the region. However, it would be a mistake to suppose the existence of a unified NATO strategy, because its member states have different national interests. Thus, the West European members of NATO, except Britain, may be reluctant to share the strategic priorities of the United States. Moreover, as members of the emerging European Union, the policies of Europe's democracies are bound to be influenced by their collective interests as members of that organization. The same logic of individual versus collective interest also applies to the economic sphere.

As advanced industrial countries which lack energy resources, these states share a desire to promote open economies in the Caspian/Central Asian region, a stable environment for their trade and investment, and a secure source of energy supplies.

Clearly, at this stage there is no unified European policy, except four complementary EU initiatives toward the newly independent states: EU Partnership and Cooperation Agreements (PCA); EU Technical Assistance Programs (TACIS); European Energy Charter and Treaty; and Interstate Oil and Gas Transport to Europe (INOGATE). PCA agreements with each of the former Soviet states provide comprehensive frameworks covering economic issues, political dialogue and democratic institutional development. The TACIS programs, involving technical assistance, are the largest such financial contribution to the Newly Independent States, with grants of €2.3 billion in 1991–8, a significant share of which was committed to the Caucasus and Central Asia. The Energy Charter and its Treaty, signed by 49 states in December 1994, provides binding guidelines and principles for the protection of investments. The INOGATE program was designed to create opportunities to exploit and export energy which would promote economic development and political independence. Under this program, €50 million was allocated for 1996–9 to implement the following projects:

- The rehabilitation, expansion and modernization of regional gas transmission systems and of supply systems for oil and oil products
- The assessment of the prospects for enhancing the transport of hydrocarbons from the Caspian Basin and Central Asia to European markets
- The transfer of 'know-how' needed to ensure conformity with international standards
- The feasibility of alternative routes, notably, new routes across the Caspian Sea[45]

As the European Union's four-pronged outreach to the former Soviet South, these initiatives represent a policy of creating a regional balance of power that would prevent the establishment of hegemonic control by any outside or local state. A corollary to this strategy is the quest to promote the progressive democratization of these countries in coordination with the Organization for Security and Cooperation in Europe (OSCE), NATO's Partnership for Peace, and the Council of Europe.[46]

Within the foregoing framework the EU has undertaken a number of specific projects, such as combatting narcotics trafficking and opening of a Eurasian transport corridor. In February 1998, the EU began a drive against opium and heroin smuggling from Afghanistan. This campaign sought to help the authorities in Kazakhstan, Uzbekistan, Tajikistan, Turkmenistan, Kyrgyzstan and Iran to stop the flow of drugs through their countries to European consumers. In particular, this campaign would target drug mafias and gangs whose activities have threatened the internal stability and governmental authority in Caucasian and Central Asian states.[47]

A more ambitious EU undertaking is the revival of the historic Silk Road as a corridor linking Europe and Asia. Under the umbrella of TRACECA (Transport Corridor Europe Caucasus Asia) launched in 1993, the project envisages a Eurasian transport route consisting of highways, railroads, fibre optic cables, oil and gas pipelines and expansion of seaports. In December 1998, a high profile conference was held in Baku, bringing together leaders and representatives of 12 international organizations and 34 countries, including Georgia, Azerbaijan, Moldova, Romania, Bulgaria, Uzbekistan, Kyrgyzstan, Ukraine, Turkey, Armenia, China, Iran and Kazakhstan.[48] The participants signed what was called a 'historic' agreement, despite opposition from Russia and Iran.[49] By 1998, the EU had already spent $75 million on TRACECA projects, and was soliciting another $300 million in loans. Additional funds were pledged by the European Bank for Reconstruction and Development (EBRD).[50] In July 1999, the EU convened a conference in Kiev attended by 50 delegations from the countries of the former Soviet Union, Central and Eastern Europe and the Black Sea region, and from international financial institutions, to initiate the INOGATE Umbrella Agreement. This accord would provide a single legal and administrative framework to facilitate cooperation among the INOGATE member countries, under a secretariat to be established in Kiev. In a further step to extend its outreach, in December 1999, the EU approved a new seven-year TACIS program with a price-tag of €3,138.39 million.[51]

Beyond its economic interests, the European Union has sought to extend humanitarian aid and economic assistance to the states of the Southern Caucasus and provide impetus to the resolution of conflicts in the area – the Georgian–Abkhazian conflict, Nagorno-Karabakh, and the Georgian–Ossetian dispute. To that end, the EU Council of Ministers signed a joint declaration with the presidents of Armenia, Azerbaijan and Georgia in June 1999 at a special EU–Caucasus summit in Luxembourg. However, by October 1999, it had become apparent that this attempt at conflict resolution had failed, at least in the case of Nagorno-Karabakh. In response to the European Commission's suggestion that Azerbaijan soften its stance and lift the embargo on Armenian participation in TRACECA, an Azeri deputy foreign minister stated that the EU, as an economic body, should not interfere in political issues, and that economic cooperation with Armenia on the basis of EU proposals was not possible until resolution of the Nagorno-Karabakh conflict.[52]

The EU's increasingly activist pursuit of an economic and energy agenda, and its strategic implications, evoked not only Russian concerns but also American misgivings. Clearly, the INOGATE and TRACECA projects represented the quest for routes circumventing Russia, and even an attempt to drive a wedge between Russia and other CIS members.[53] Indeed, the EU's strong backing for the revitalization of Romania's Black Sea port of Constanza, its partial funding of the Baku–Supsa pipeline and financial assistance for a new ferry service between the Georgian Black Sea port of Poti and Ilyichevsk in the Ukraine, could be perceived as attempts to bypass Russia.[54] Yet, these initiatives also constituted a clear challenge to American–Turkish strategic priorities in the Caspian. According to Vittorio Jucker, a senior EBRD official, the European Union does not want Caspian oil to reach the Mediterranean, and as such is opposed to the Baku–Ceyhan pipeline.[55] To be sure, some European officials are not prepared to relinquish to Washington the entire responsibility to set security policy in the Caspian region.[56] The European attitude could be best summarized in the words of Ernst Muehlemann, vice-president of the Council of Europe's Parliamentary Assembly, to an Azeri audience: 'There are no more Russian military bases in Azerbaijan and this is a great achievement. But your country has gained a new "big brother" in the person of the USA and that is apprehended with caution in Europe.'[57] A related problem is the fear among NATO's European members that the United States and Turkey would commit the alliance to involvements which are not consistent with NATO's collective interests in the Caspian.[58]

The policy differences between the United States and EU are the natural consequence of the mostly geostrategic priorities of a superpower and the predominantly economic interests of a regional organization. The diverging positions of the two sides could be detected by a careful analysis of a common statement on the Caspian issued at the US/EU summit conference held in Washington, DC, in May 1998. In the development of energy projects and export routes, this statement emphasized the primacy of commercial considerations and the necessity of private sector investment, factors which bear the EU's imprint and its determination to uphold the principle of economic viability over America's geopolitical priorities, exemplified in its support for Baku–Ceyhan.[59] These disagreements over Caspian policy came in the context of the European challenge to continued US sanctions on Iran.

The EU's initiatives in the former Soviet South have been criticized for diplomatic bumbling, poor performance and programmatic overlaps, as well as for wasteful spending on consultants.[60] The benefits of these programs have not trickled down to the peoples of the region, dampening their heightened expectations from Europe. This is unfortunate, because the European nations are seen by many people in the former Soviet South as models to emulate, more than Turkey, Iran or even the United States. Indeed, some of these countries, particularly in the Caucasus, would like to consider themselves as Europeans and even aspire to membership in the European Union.

Aside from the activities of the EU as a collective body, several European countries have been individually involved in the Caspian region. Among the most prominent is Great Britain, with significant commercial interests as well as some strategic concerns. Britain was among the first countries to establish close ties with Azerbaijan, chiefly prompted by the ambitious objectives of British oil companies, such as Ramco and BP. In September 1992, the two sides signed a joint declaration to expand relations.[61] Ties were further solidified in February 1994 with the signing of a declaration of friendship and cooperation during Aliyev's visit to London. This included a package of agreements on economic partnership, in particular the exploration by BP of the hydrocarbon reserves of the Caspian shelf. Aliyev emphasized Britain's recognition of his country's territorial integrity and hoped for British assistance in settling the Nagorno-Karabakh conflict.[62] The high point of British–Azeri relations was the signing of the Contract of the Century in September 1994, with BP taking a leading role in the AIOC consortium. Another visit by Aliyev to London in July 1998 resulted in three additional oil contracts, signifying Britain's growing commercial presence in Azerbaijan.[63] To a lesser degree, Britain maintains an economic presence in Turkmenistan. Monument Oil and Gas, a British company now part of Lasmo, has been developing the Burun field near Nebit Dag.[64] British–Kazakh relations had an early start when Nazarbayev travelled to London in November 1991,[65] with several return visits throughout the 1990s. By 1999, Britain had become

Kazakhstan's biggest trading partner after Russia, as well as its largest European investor.[66]

Unlike her European partners, France has long striven to play a foreign policy role independent of the United States. This has been exemplified in the Caspian context by France's clash with the United States on the routing of pipelines. French opposition to the USA was dramatically manifested at the Baku Oil Industry Conference of June 1998, where Industry Minister Christian Pierret stated: 'The French point of view is that the nations of this region are themselves able to find the route with which they can export their oil and gas'.[67] Hence, the French reluctance to endorse the Baku–Ceyhan option, perceived as being primarily motivated by US plans to isolate Iran.

Not to be outdone by Britain and other European countries, France has sought to establish a presence in Azerbaijan, Kazakhstan, Turkmenistan and Uzbekistan. Although an agreement of friendship and cooperation was concluded during Aliyev's visit to Paris in December 1993, there was a lag in the development of French–Azeri economic relations,[68] perhaps due to the Azeri perception that France was pro-Armenian. Thus, no French oil company was included in AIOC, and only a small share was given to Elf Aquitaine a year later. Economic relations improved somewhat after Foreign Minister Hervé de Charette's October 1996 visit to Baku.[69] Aliyev's return visit to France in January 1997 resulted in the signing of a $2bn contract with Elf and Total to develop two Azeri offshore fields. Yet Aliyev remained adamant in finding French policy biassed in favour of Armenia, which led to his opposition to France's co-chairmanship of OSCE's Minsk group, charged with mediation in the Karabakh conflict.[70] By April 1998, Aliyev's attitude had softened considerably, when he requested French support to resolve the conflict over Nagorno-Karabakh and gain membership in the Council of Europe.[71]

Two other targets of French investment are Kazakhstan and Russia. In December 1993, France's Total took a leading role to explore Kazakhstan's Caspian shelf, as part of an international consortium later renamed OKIOC.[72] After a lull, French–Kazakh relations were jump-started with President Nazarbayev's visit to France in June 2000, resulting in several economic agreements, such as the opening of a generous credit line and contracts of $240 million with Bouygues to build oil and gas facilities in Atyrau and Mangistau.[73] France also extended a credit line of $70 million to Russia, in order to build a second oil terminal at Novorossiisk.[74]

German objectives in the Caspian Basin involve both economic and strategic issues. Germany's emergence as the leading European power has led to the realization that the Transcaucasus is a geostrategic 'bridge and crossroads' which should remain free of hegemonic designs by regional powers.[75] Thus, Germany's strategic objectives are closely aligned with its partners in the European Union in bolstering the political and economic stability of the Newly Independent States and establishing a balance of interests in the region that would include Turkey, Iran and Russia.[76] Yet Germany's lack of regional political ambitions, and its avoidance of combining business activities with strategic concerns, are perceived positively in Central Asia and the Caucasus and facilitate the expansion of German trade and investment.[77]

Germany has considerable economic interests in the region. Fifty German companies are engaged in trade with Azerbaijan. German firms working in Azerbaijan's oil sector include Deminex, Grunewald, Deutag, Gabeg and BASF Wintershall.[78] The Azeri authorities have encouraged greater German involvement in their economy and have sought German assistance in resolving the Karabakh dispute. On the question of pipeline routes, Germany supports the EU position. Other foci of German interest are Georgia, Kazakhstan and Turkmenistan. Germany is the largest European aid donor to Georgia, amounting to DM650 million since 1993. Such generosity is prompted by German gratitude to Shevardnadze for his role when Soviet foreign minister in facilitating German unity, as well as the desire to promote the stability of a strategically located country. In March 2000, Chancellor Gerhard Schroeder joined a long line of world leaders to visit Georgia in order to endorse Shevardnadze's re-election;[79] and in an exceptional move, Germany has sponsored a small program of military training and assistance to the Georgian army.[80] With respect to Kazakhstan, trade interests have been preponderant since the departure of most of the German community exiled by Stalin. Germany is one of Kazakhstan's major trade partners, with annual trade estimated at $650 million.[81] In Turkmenistan, the German company Mannesmann has been involved in building the Turkmenbashi refinery; in February 1999, Mannesmann and Siemens signed an agreement to build a large compressor station for the gas pipeline to Iran.[82]

Italy's interests in the region are mainly economic, focusing on hydrocarbon resources. The oil company ENI has been at the forefront of Italian penetration of the region. ENI is a partner in Kazakhstan's Karachaganak gas field, the CPC consortium and the

OKIOC, and holds a 25 percent stake in Azerbaijan's Kurdashi contract.[83] Italy is one of Russia's main trade partners, and ENI accounts for 30 percent of total trade between the two countries.[84] ENI has also had a major role in the development, with Gazprom, of the Blue Stream project to bring Russian gas to Turkey, which has irritated some American observers.[85]

Several smaller European countries have been active in the Caspian states. The Belgian Prime Minister Jean-Luc Dehaene was the first EU leader to visit Azerbaijan, followed by stops in Kazakhstan and Uzbekistan. The Belgian firm Petrolina owns stakes in two Azerbaijani production sharing agreements (PSA), and Tractebel was charged in 1998 with the operation of Kazakhstan's power grid.[86] Norway's Statoil was an early investor in Azerbaijan's oil industry. All too frequently, Azerbaijan has used the promise of oil and pipeline deals as leverage to garner support from West European countries in the Nagorno-Karabakh dispute. As a result of this policy, numerous European countries have been rewarded with stakes in Azerbaijani PSAs.

Japan

In keeping with Japan's policy of political non-involvement since the Second World War, its interest in the Caspian region has been mainly economic, consisting of energy-related investments and trade. As an advanced industrial power and a major energy importer, Japan has had a keen interest in the hydrocarbon resources of the region. Japanese activity has mostly focused on Azerbaijan and Turkmenistan, and to a lesser degree on Kazakhstan and Uzbekistan.

Azerbaijan stands as the largest beneficiary of Japanese investment. In March–April 1996, the Itochu Corporation joined the Contract of the Century by buying part of McDermott and Pennzoil's share in the AIOC consortium.[87] In 1997 Itochu made two additional deals, acquiring a 20 percent stake in the consortium developing the Dan Ulduzu and Ashrafi offshore fields and forming, together with the Japan National Oil Company and two other Japanese companies, a consortium to develop three offshore fields in the South Caspian.[88] To solidify and expand the budding ties with Japan, Aliyev visited Tokyo in February 1998, which resulted in a contract with Mitsui for participation in developing the Kurdashi and neighboring oil fields and in low-interest Japanese loans.[89] Aliyev's trip was reciprocated by the visit of Foreign

Minister Masahiko Komura, who underlined Japan's expanding interest in Azeri energy and the new Silk Road project.[90]

An early manifestation of Japanese interest in Turkmenistan was Mitsubishi's grand proposal in June 1995 to construct a massive pipeline to Japan across Central Asia and China.[91] Although this fantastic project was shelved, Japan's Chioda and Nichimen Petrochemical companies joined a Turkish firm in 1996 to modernize a catalytic plant in Turkmenbashi at a cost of $125 million.[92] A few months later, the Turkmens asked the Japanese to develop eight oil and gas fields in common.[93] In February 1996, Japanese companies joined firms from Germany, France and Turkey to sign a $500 million contract to build several refineries and other installations.[94] In addition, a consortium of Japanese companies was awarded a $414 million contract to build a polypropylene plant.[95] Also, Japan's Itochu held a stake in the trans-Afghan pipeline consortium, which was disbanded due to instability in Afghanistan.

The great bulk of Japanese financing for Turkmen projects has been in the form of loans through the Export–Import Bank, which is also the case for Kazakhstan. In September 1995, Japan made two loans to support Kazakh economic reforms and modernize telecommunication networks.[96] The largest Japanese commitment to the Kazakh economy came in September 1998, with the signing of four contracts totalling $2 billion by the Marubeni and Mitsubishi companies for work in the oil processing, petrochemical, aluminum and drilling equipment industries. Another contract involving a partnership with Phillips Petroleum gave Japan's Inpex Nord rights to develop a ten-block oil field on the Caspian shelf – the equivalent of a 7 percent share in the OKIOC. Inpex is owned by the Japan National Oil Corporation (50 percent), the government-affiliated Indonesian Petroleum Ltd. (45 percent), Japan Petroleum Exploitation Co. (2.5 percent) and Mitsubishi Corporation (2.5 percent). In addition, a low-interest credit line of $1 billion was opened to develop infrastructure and social services.[97]

At a more modest level, Japan has extended major credits to Uzbekistan and Georgia. A package of loans in 1995–6 to Uzbekistan, worth $600 million, targeted modernizing the Ferghana oil refinery, upgrading communications, investments in the energy sector, developing foreign trade and expanding three airports.[98] Meanwhile, in September 1997, the Itochu corporation signed a memorandum to build a $300 million oil refinery at the Georgian port of Supsa on the Black Sea.[99]

Although primarily centered on energy and trade, in 1997

Japanese policy began to assume a proactive character, not only to expand investment and economic cooperation but also to encourage democratization and non-proliferation. This policy of comprehensive engagement was propounded by former prime minister Ryutaro Hashimoto, who sought to promote greater Japanese involvement in the former Soviet South as part of a more ambitious role in international affairs.[100] Such a role would involve greater Japanese independence from the United States in the pursuit of national interests, particularly the securing of new energy sources for its industrial complex.

Other Asian countries

Three Asian countries have developed interests in the Caspian/Central Asian region in a display of entrepreneurship and dynamism which have surprised their Western competitors. South Korea is a major oil importer, while Malaysia and Indonesia are oil producers with considerable expertise in the petroleum industry. The initial optimism of these countries was tempered by the 'Asian Flu' which forced them to scale down their involvement in Central Asia. Nevertheless, their economic presence in the region is far from negligible.

As an Asian Tiger with a highly developed industrial base, South Korea's interests in the Central Asian region require a stable environment for trade, investment opportunities and energy imports in the event that projected pipelines become reality. The two primary targets of South Korean economic activity are Kazakhstan and Uzbekistan. Since 1991, South Korea has been the second cumulative investor in Kazakhstan, mainly in the car manufacturing, mining, electronics and tea processing industries. Korean contractors are also involved in building Astana, the country's new capital city. An important factor in South Korean–Kazakh relations is the large Korean community, one of the first victims of Stalin's deportation policies. In Uzbekistan, South Korea is the largest foreign investor, mainly in the manufacture of automobiles and textiles.[101]

The relations of Indonesia and Malaysia with the Central Asian states are mainly focused on the energy sector, although cultural ties based on Islam also play a role. The Indonesian Central Asia Petroleum holds a 60 percent stake in a joint company for the development of the Mangistau oil fields in Kazakhstan.[102] Malaysia's national oil company, Petronas, has developed a significant presence in Turkmenistan's oil industry. Petronas has been the first foreign company to establish a PSA with the Turkmen government to develop Block 1 in the Caspian shelf, where it struck oil in March 1999.[103] Petronas works closely with the Iranians, in swaps of Turkmen oil and as a partner in the South Pars development consortium, which formerly had been opposed by the United States.

CHAPTER 10

Non-State Actors in the Caspian Basin

Explanations based on realpolitik, highlighting the central role of states, are necessary but not sufficient for a comprehensive understanding of Caspian geopolitics. In today's milieu of globalization, the Caspian countries find themselves at the convergence of multiple cross-currents emanating both from state actors and non-state entities or movements. Although non-state actors are sometimes employed by states as instruments of their policies, all too often clashes of interests divide them. Eight categories of non-state actors have had an impact on Caspian geopolitics and geoeconomics – ethnonationalists, religious militants, provincial entities, maverick entrepreneurs, criminal groups, multinational corporations, international organizations and non-governmental organizations.

Ethnonationalists

Movements of ethnic separatism or autonomism are endemic in the Caucasus and Central Asia. This is not surprising, because the region is a mosaic of ethnocultural diversity divided along linguistic, racial, tribal, religious and regional dimensions. Another reason for the frequent upsurge of ethnic instability in these countries is the recency of their emergence as independent states, with national boundaries often determined by political considerations with little regard to ethnic realities. The great heterogeneity of the region contributes to instability, especially because of the authoritarian character of virtually all the regimes in place. Such instability is anathema to energy development and security of pipelines.

Southern Russia has long been an epicenter of ethnic conflict, with the war in Chechnya being the most destabilizing factor. After a history of resistance to Russian imperial rule, the Muslim Chechens were exiled to Central Asia by Stalin, who accused them of collaboration with the Germans. Under Khrushchev's destalinization policy, the Chechens were allowed to return to their homeland. At the end of Soviet rule, led by Dzhokhar Dudayev, the Chechens declared independence from the Russian Federation. After a three-year stalemate, Russian forces invaded Chechnya to restore the federation's sovereignty, and presumably to secure the pipeline route from Baku to Novorossiisk.[1] After two years of intense fighting, the defeated Russian forces were withdrawn under an agreement that left the final status of Chechnya to future negotiations. Although unable to consolidate control over the various warlords and mafiosi, President Aslan Maskhadov did succeed in rebuilding, with Russian help, the portion of the pipeline within Chechen territory. However, he was unable to ensure the smooth operation of the pipeline, because of endemic siphoning and disputes over transit tariffs between Azeris, Russians and Chechens. By July 1999, the Russians had stopped using the pipeline, and later built a new one circumventing Chechnya. In September 1999, following attacks by Chechen Islamists in Daghestan, the Russians returned in force to subdue Chechnya. The second Chechen war triggered a protracted conflict, which could destabilize neighboring areas of the Russian Federation and even threaten the security of the newly built bypass pipeline.

Chechnya's eastern neighbor is Daghestan, a territorial unit of the Russian Federation. One of the most ethnically diverse regions of the world, Daghestan is the mountainous homeland of about 30 distinct Muslim ethnic groups, speaking as many languages. In the post-Soviet period, Daghestan was beset by lawlessness, poverty, corruption and overpopulation, amid rivalry among the largest ethnic groups for leadership positions. To Russia, Daghestan's strategic importance stems from its location along the Caspian's western shores and its position as a gateway to the Transcaucasus. It is surprising that Daghestan's ethnic tensions have not exploded into bloody conflicts, in view of Moscow's inattention to the area's economic plight and poor administration. Ethnic rivalries have been sharpened as a result of Russia's provision of weapons to regional leaders, ostensibly to defend Daghestan from Chechen incursions.[2] This policy has upset the balance of power among ethnic groups, setting the stage for future conflicts.

One disaffected group are the Lezgins, populating the borderlands between Daghestan and Azerbaijan. In Daghestan, the Lezgins feel politically marginalized, but in Azerbaijan they face forceful cultural and linguistic assimilation. A Lezgin nationalist movement, Savdal, was charged with the 1994 Baku metro bombing and other separatist activities. Some Lezgin groups want to establish a united homeland, while others seek cultural autonomy in Azerbaijan and removal of border controls that impede ties between northern and southern Lezgins. In June 1997, Sadval called for the mandatory transport of Azeri oil via Russia, i.e. Daghestan, and a share of oil transit fees for the Lezgins.[3]

To the west of Chechnya is Ingushetia, which was detached in 1991 from the former Soviet Chechen–Ingush Autonomous Republic when Chechnya proclaimed independence. Ingushetia's territorial claims to the Prigorodny Raion of North Ossetia led to an armed conflict in 1992 and the expulsion of thousands of Ingush. Prigorodny had been Ingush territory until Stalin's deportation of the Ingush to Central Asia in 1944. Although two thirds of the Ingush did return to North Ossetia in the late 1990s, tensions between the North Ossetian and Ingush autonomous republics of the Russian Federation did not abate.[4] Aside from the Prigorodny conflict and the economic deprivations suffered in the last decade, Ingushetia has been destabilized by the upheavals in Chechnya and the influx of refugees from there. Similar conflicts have become endemic in the western republics of the North Caucasus – Kabardino–Balkaria, Karachaevo–Cherkessia and, to a lesser degree, Adygea. The region has been rife with simmering ethnic and tribal tensions, pitting Kabardians against Balkars, and Karachais against Cherkessians and Abazas. These tensions are exacerbated by economic hardship, government corruption and regional mafias. The situation is further complicated by the presence of Cossacks throughout the Northern Caucasus, who seek to revive their pre-Soviet traditions and privileges.

The Southern Caucasus, even more than the North, has been riven by inter-ethnic strife. Described as an essential component of the Eurasian Corridor, Georgia has been its weakest link because of ethnic problems. One of the most serious of Georgia's six major and minor ethnic flashpoints is South Ossetia, an autonomous region in Soviet times which sought to unite with North Ossetia in the last years of Gorbachev's rule. The ensuing armed conflict ended in 1992, leaving the north and the regional capital in Ossetian hands and the rest under Georgian control. A tripartite Russo–Georgian–Ossetian force has been charged with enforcing the ceasefire. An even bloodier conflict was that of Abkhazia, in western Georgia. The Abkhaz separatist movement defeated the Georgian army in a two-year war that resulted in the expulsion of ethnic Georgians from Abkhazia, which has been in a state of precarious autonomy and economic devastation. Since the 1994 ceasefire, there have been periodic clashes between Abkhaz forces and Georgian militias.

To the south of Abkhazia is the region of Mingrelia, the home base of the late Zviad Gamsakhurdia, Georgia's first elected president. After he was ousted in January 1992, considerable suffering was inflicted upon the Mingrelians by the unruly militiamen of the central authorities seeking to quell rebellions by Gamsakhurdia's supporters. Georgian refugees from Abkhazia, mostly Mingrelians, were another source of resentment toward Tbilisi. Any future unrest in this poverty-stricken province would threaten the Baku–Supsa pipeline which passes through the region.[5] Further south, on the Black Sea coast, is the autonomous republic of Ajaria. This strategic province, adjoining Turkey, is populated by Ajars, who are Georgian-speaking Muslims. Since independence, Ajaria has retained its autonomy under the rule of Aslan Abashidze, who has managed to maintain stability. While expressing fealty to Georgia's sovereignty and territorial integrity, Abashidze has skillfully managed to exclude Georgian influence in Ajarian affairs by forging close ties with Turkey and Russia. Hence his opposition to the removal of the Russian base at the Ajarian capital Batumi, which could have become the terminal, instead of Supsa, for the westbound pipeline from Baku, had it not been for Georgian reluctance to have the pipeline under Abashidze's control.

Contiguous to Ajaria in the south-east is the Georgian province of Samtskhe–Javakhetia (or Meskhet–Javakhetia), the southern half of which, bordering Armenia, is mostly populated by Armenians. The rise of Georgian nationalism under Gamsakhurdia, followed by a Georgianization campaign, had a detrimental impact upon Georgia's minorities, particularly the Armenians scattered across Georgia, resulting in forced assimilation, takeover of church properties and a large-scale exodus. Protected by their own militia, Javakhetia Armenians were spared such persecution, although the region remains a flashpoint of tension.[6] Another complicating factor is the possible return of the Meskhetian Turks, who had been exiled by Stalin in 1944. Even though this would affect mostly Meskhetia, where Georgians predominate, rather than the Armenian-populated Javakhetia, the Georgian authorities have refused to repatriate the Meskhetians, arguing that their return would provoke tensions with local Armenians. Instability in Samtskhe–Javakhetia would directly threaten the projected Baku–Ceyhan pipeline, which is routed through this region.[7] Less consequential for pipeline politics is the Azeri-populated Marneuli district, contiguous to Azerbaijan, which is likely to remain quiescent as long as Georgian–Azerbaijani relations remain amicable.

After Chechnya, the conflict over Nagorno-Karabakh between Armenia and Azerbaijan was the most perilous in terms of loss of life, destruction and displacement of populations, including 400,000 Armenians expelled from Azerbaijan and 800,000 Azeris from Armenia, Nagorno-Karabakh and adjoining territories. Since the cessation of hostilities in 1994 this dispute has proved intractable, despite repeated attempts at resolution by OSCE, the United States and other European powers. Any renewal of fighting would destabilize a crucial link in the projected Eurasian Corridor and scare off investors. Thus, a negotiated solution to the Nagorno-Karabakh conflict is essential for Azerbaijan's oil industry and the security of westbound pipelines located in close proximity to the northern borders of Armenia and Nagorno-Karabakh.

The most serious ethnic threat to the proposed Baku–Ceyhan pipeline is the restive Kurdish minority concentrated in Turkey's eastern provinces.[8] Constituting about one-fourth of Turkey's population, the Kurds have been persecuted since the founding of the Turkish Republic. Turkey's assimilationist policies and its denial of Kurdish identity, combined with the economic backwardness of the Kurdish regions, have fuelled repeated insurrections which have been brutally suppressed. The latest of these uprisings, led by Abdullah Ocalan's PKK, was finally contained by the Turkish army in 1999, at the cost of the devastation of large sections of Kurdish-populated areas. Yet the core issues of Kurdish dissatisfaction remain unresolved, representing the most consequential long-term menace to trans-Turkish pipelines.

A host of mostly dormant ethnic problems can be considered potential sources of instability in Iran and Central Asia. Nascent manifestations of nationalist unrest in the Azeri-populated areas of north-western Iran could spread, if President Khatami's policies of political liberalization and economic development do not succeed. Future instability in Iranian Azerbaijan could lead to a larger inter-state conflict, drawing in Azerbaijan, Turkey and Russia, and disrupting the production and flow of oil in the whole southern Caspian region. Of lesser significance are the ethnic factors east of the Caspian. In the foreseeable future, Kazakhstan's Slavic minorities are a potential source of conflict, although the problem has been contained by Nazarbayev, with the assistance of Moscow. Another potential ethnic flashpoint that could impact Caspian fortunes is the presence of Uzbeks in Kazakhstan and Turkmenistan, who could become instruments of leverage by the government of Uzbekistan.

Religious activists

An emerging non-state actor in Caspian affairs is Islamic activism. After 70-odd years of Soviet atheism in these mostly Muslim countries, Islam has made a comeback as a religion, and in some cases as a mobilizing ideology for militancy. The nature of Islamic revival in each country is determined by local traditions and conditions, as well as the impact of external forces. Thus, indigenous currents of religious resurgence have been influenced by Islamist movements from outside the region, to create new blends of Islamism with implications for national and cross-national politics.

Upon independence, the ex-Communist leaders of the Soviet South used Islam as a medium of self-legitimization and national identity. As in Soviet times, the Islamic clerical establishment forged an alliance with the ruling elites to support the status quo, which was soon challenged by both indigenous and external Islamist movements seeking to proselytize at the mass level. In the context of the economic crisis besetting these countries after the Soviet collapse, combined with growing maldistribution of wealth, several activist variants of political Islamism found fertile soil in the region. In the Russian territories of the Northern Caucasus – Chechnya, Ingushetia and Daghestan – the nativist brand of esoteric Sufi Islam assumed a militant character as an anti-Russian ideology. In the crucible of the Chechen wars, this movement was further radicalized by the arrival of Islamist militants and funding from the Arab world, Pakistan and Afghanistan.

A common reference to the Islamist groups of Russia and the former Soviet South is 'Wahhabi', denoting an affiliation with the Hanbali tradition of Islam practiced in Saudi Arabia. This term, however, is not always appropriate to describe the diverse Islamist groups fighting in the name of Islamic puritanism to establish theocratic rule in the region. Moreover, most of these groups are not linked to Saudi Arabia. Despite some successes, Islamists have not always been welcome, particularly those from foreign countries. Thus, proponents of 'Wahhabism' have faced rejection from Daghestani Sufis, while finding a degree of acceptance in next-door Chechnya. So-called Wahhabi missionaries have also appeared in Kabardino–Balkaria, despite the region's mild religious credo tempered with pagan traditions.[9] In Azerbaijan, as in neighboring countries, the Islamic religious establishment is involved in large-scale commercial activities which have corrupted its religious mission and alienated the faithful, 90 percent of whom live below the poverty line.[10] Because Azerbaijan belongs to the Shi'a branch of Islam, it has been relatively immune to Sunni Islamist propaganda, and Shi'a Iran has generally refrained from exporting its own brand of Islamic fundamentalism.

On the Caspian's eastern rim, Islamism has made some inroads in Kazakhstan but little progress in Turkmenistan. However, the régimes of the Central Asian countries as a whole view militant Islamism exported from Afghanistan, Pakistan and the Middle East as a serious security threat. A center of Islamist militancy is Uzbekistan's Ferghana valley, and several areas of Tajikistan which have served as springboards for Islamist infiltration into the rest of Central Asia. Islamist activity also has been noted in southern Kazakhstan and Atyrau, the oil-producing region on the Caspian Sea.[11] In addition to the so-called Wahhabis, the group known as Hizb al-Tahrir, of Palestinian origin,[12] has been involved in aggressive proselytization and violence in and around the Ferghana valley. One great concern among Central Asian leaders is the possibility of spillover of militancy from the Ferghana valley. Because Islamist extremism is viewed as a common threat, the Central Asian states, Russia and China have drawn together to undertake joint political and military action against it. A related source of threat is the export of Islamism from Afghanistan, particularly after the Taliban military successes in the north-eastern part of the country. To confront these challenges, in October 2000, a six-nation summit met in the Kyrgyz capital, Bishkek, to renew the 1992 CIS Collective Security Treaty for the next five years. The six leaders agreed to a plan for a joint military force to defend their countries from external aggression and internal insurgency. The participation of President Putin signified an expansion of Russia's security role in the region, which was denounced by the Taliban régime.[13]

Criminal groups

As non-state actors, mafia-style criminal organizations have been a pervasive feature in the Caspian/Central Asian landscape. The meltdown of state authority in the wake of the Soviet Union created a power vacuum which was propitious for the rise of criminal gangs. All too often, these groups were linked with state officials and business interests. The overall impact of these mafias was the spread of insecurity and corruption throughout the region. Some of these groups are tied into transnational networks, including the Russian and Turkish mafias.

The activities of the criminal networks involve drug trafficking, money laundering, arms trade, caviar, alcohol, prostitution and kidnapping for ransom. Five major drug routes from Afghanistan pass through Tajikistan, Kyrgyzstan, Kazakhstan, Turkmenistan, Azerbaijan, Georgia, Iran and the Northern Caucasus, on their way to Russia, Turkey and Western consumers.[14] In addition, significant amounts of drugs are produced in Kyrgyzstan, Tajikistan, Uzbekistan and Kazakhstan, supervised by local drug barons. Only recently have state authorities begun to make efforts at drug interdiction, except Iran's determined long-term campaign against narcotics producers and traffickers. The drug mafias include Russians, Kyrgyz, Georgians, Azeris and Chechens.[15] These criminal organizations are often connected to security agencies, political parties, the military and ethnic groups, making it difficult to identify the real culprits. For example, Turkish authorities have been accused of drug trafficking and use of mafia connections to aid the Chechens against Russia, while Kyrgyz Islamists have acted as a cover for drug traffickers.[16] This pattern of linkage between Islamist militants and drug traffickers was highlighted at an international conference held in Tashkent in October 2000, that brought together representatives from 70 countries and 40 international organizations under the sponsorship of the OSCE and the United Nations.[17]

Other areas of criminal activity having a bearing on regional stability are the arms trade, kidnapping and murder. Since the Soviet demise, there have been numerous reports of attempts by rogue states and terrorist groups to buy sophisticated weaponry and nuclear materials from former Soviet republics, in particular Kazakhstan. Also, there have been hundreds of unsolved murders and hostage-taking for ransom, the latter mostly in Chechnya.[18] Clearly, the freewheeling operations of criminal organizations in the Caspian/Central Asian region are a detriment to the long-term stability of régimes and the security of oil production and pipelines.

Maverick entrepreneurs

The fabled oil wealth of the Caspian region and the opportunity to strike it rich attracted a plethora of ambitious entrepreneurs, maverick businessmen and carpetbagging adventurers. In emulation of the oil barons of yesteryear, like the Nobel brothers and Calouste

Gulbenkian, these men sought to make fortunes as solo players in the new Great Game. Among the most notable were Johann Deuss, James Giffen, Viktor Kozeny, Yossi Maiman, Igor Makarov, Stephen Remp and Roger Tamraz.

One of the earliest solo players was Johann Deuss, a Bermuda-based Dutch oil trader who sought to fill the role of 'oil statesman' with mixed success. Reportedly a confidant of Sultan Qabus of Oman, Deuss brokered, in May 1992, a multi-billion dollar deal with Chevron for a pipeline between Tengiz and Novorossiisk. The deal collapsed after a four-year stalemate, when Chevron rejected Deuss's demand to finance the whole project without any funding from Oman or Deuss himself. A new consortium (CPC) formed in 1996 excluded Deuss and left Oman with a small share.[19]

Johann Deuss found a nemesis in James Giffen, whose entrepreneurial role was only revealed in July 2000, in a US Justice Department investigation of $60 million in payments from oil companies to Kazakh officials.[20] A friend of the Kazakh leader since the last days of the Soviet Union, Giffen was involved in bringing Chevron to develop the Tengiz field in negotiations with Gorbachev and Nazarbayev, which made him a very rich man. By 1995 Giffen had become a key advisor to Nazarbayev, and was instrumental in the ousting of Johann Deuss from the CPC. His next coup was selling concessions in the Kashagan oil fields of the Caspian. Now the head of Mercator Corp, a private New York merchant bank, Giffen's future as a major player in the oil business could depend on the outcome of the ongoing investigation under the Foreign Corrupt Practices Act.

A former Israeli intelligence agent, Yossi Maiman is both an entrepreneur and a geopolitical strategist. An early investor and builder of greenhouses in Turkmenistan, Maiman soon became Niyazov's trusted advisor and dealmaker by arranging the funding to upgrade the Turkmenbashi refinery. Maiman was also involved as an intermediary in negotiations for the trans-Caspian pipeline project, which would bypass Russia and Iran in keeping with US–Turkish–Israeli objectives.[21] This project was shelved in mid-2000, although it might be revived given the vicissitudes of the Caspian environment.

As one of the youngest of the Caspian entrepreneurs, Igor Makarov is a Russian born in Turkmenistan. A former cycling champion, Makarov has played an influential role in Turkmenistan, Russia and other CIS countries. After starting a business to trade food for Turkmen oil in the early 1990s, Makarov founded Itera, a worldwide conglomerate with close ties to the Russian giant Gazprom. In 1994 Itera opened an office in Jacksonville, Florida, and began lobbying US officials, including OPIC (Overseas Private Investment Corporation), to secure guarantees to cover political risk for its operations in Turkmenistan and Ukraine.[22] Although Makarov's foray into US politics failed, his Itera company continued to prosper in joint ventures with Gazprom to supply gas to Ukraine, Armenia, Georgia and Moldova. Itera's phenomenal growth and Makarov's relationship to Gazprom remain mysteries, amid suspicions that Itera is nothing but a front for Gazprom executives.[23]

Another buccaneer of the murky geopolitics of the Caspian is Viktor Kozeny, a young Czech promoter based in the Bahamas. After graduating from Harvard, Kozeny settled in Prague as a 'business consultant', launching a Ponzi scheme involving the sale of privatization vouchers which made him a fortune. Under the threat of an official investigation, Kozeny left his homeland never to return, having won the title of 'Pirate of Prague'. Kozeny's next target was Azerbaijan, where the Aliyev government was offering its citizens privatization vouchers. Soon Kozeny set up a massive investment venture to gain control of SOCAR by buying vouchers. Kozeny's victims included former Senate majority leader George Mitchell, financier Leon Cooperman, and a slew of big-name investors hoping to get a slice of SOCAR's wealth upon Aliyev's 'imminent decision' to privatize the national oil company. Despite repeated assurances from Azerbaijani officials, the privatization of SOCAR never took place, leading to massive financial losses for the investors. Aliyev refused to hear the pleas of Kozeny and Wall Street investors, although some of his advisors profited immensely from the collapsed venture.[24] Under the threat of major lawsuits, Kozeny accused the Azeris of double-crossing him and threatened to sue the Azeri government.

One of most controversial figures in the Caspian firmament is Lebanese financier Roger Tamraz, another Harvard graduate. Charged with mishandling funds in Lebanon's second largest bank, Tamraz fled to Paris in 1989. In 1994 he emerged as a major dealmaker in the Caspian, a self-styled 'financial commando' who sought lucrative contracts in Turkmenistan and attempted to raise $2 billion for the Baku–Ceyhan pipeline. To realize this ambitious goal, Tamraz made an unsuccessful bid at peacemaking between Armenia and Azerbaijan, and sought to buy influence at the White House which got him involved in the 1996 fundraising scandal. As a star witness in the 1998 Congressional investigations, Tamraz claimed to have had dealings with the CIA and Yeltsin's advisors seeking campaign money; he also confirmed his $300,000 contribution to the Democratic National Committee. The campaign scandal had a dimming effect on Tamraz's grand schemes in the Caspian Basin. It was ironic that the Baku–Ceyhan project which Tamraz had promoted in 1994–5 was soon adopted as a policy priority by the Clinton administration, which disavowed its past dealings with Tamraz.[25]

Stephen Remp, founder and chairman of Ramco Energy plc., has been instrumental in the revival of Azerbaijan's hydrocarbon industry. Born into a family of American oilmen, Remp went to Aberdeen, Scotland, in the 1970s to participate in the North Sea oil boom. After an unsuccessful foray into the Siberian oil industry in 1986, Remp moved on to Azerbaijan in 1989 to establish a long-term presence as a trusted advisor of the Azeri leadership. To reward his key role in bringing major Western oil companies to Azerbaijan, Ramco Energy was given a 2 percent equity stake in the consortium that concluded the 1994 Contract of the Century. In recent years, Ramco has expanded its activities to Georgia and Eastern Europe, while selling its stake in the AIOC to Amerada Hess for $150 million.[26] Stephen Remp has achieved remarkable success in transforming his small company into an important player in the oil business.[27]

Multinational companies

In the Caspian as elsewhere, multinational corporations constitute a primary nexus where politics and economics interact in a dynamic manner to have a profound impact on society. Clearly, more than any other non-state actor, the MNCs play a powerful role in Caspian affairs, second only to that of the great powers. Because of their global outreach and immense financial and technical resources, MNCs have an enduring impact on the politics, economics and culture of host country societies.

As transnational organizations mostly based in the major industrialized countries, MNCs operate in a triangular relationship with their home and host countries. Within this configuration, all too often, MNCs and their home and host countries face the classic dilemma of power versus profit. Indeed, the mostly political interests of nation states and the profit motive of multinational firms are inherently divergent, although the mutual need for complementarity provides incentives for cooperation. Thus, the primary needs of

MNCs from their home country are political support to gain access into host countries and guarantees to protect their investments. With respect to host countries, MNCs look for a stable environment and accommodating political leaders in order to maximize their profits. In theory, MNCs prefer to remain uninvolved in home or host country politics, although in practice they are often dragged into the political arena, with sometimes costly consequences. These complex dynamics of multinational enterprise are in the process of being tested in the Caspian arena, revealing some preliminary patterns of evolving relationships.

The history of MNC-home country relations reveals many instances where powerful companies successfully lobbied their governments to take political action when the two sides were pursuing common or complementary objectives in a host country. Thus, in Iran (1953) and in Chile (1973), the US government was instrumental in overthrowing régimes perceived as detrimental to the national interest and to MNC operations. With respect to American oil companies, US policies at home and abroad have historically been supportive, in view of the strategic and economic importance of oil and the immense political clout of the oil companies. Indeed, the relationship between the US government and the oil companies can best be described as one of interdependence or even symbiosis, a situation which also applies to the Caspian context. In their drive to penetrate the newly independent Caspian countries, the oil companies sought and received backing from both the Bush and Clinton administrations, as did French and British companies from their governments. In fact, French President François Mitterrand was reported to have refused to sign any agreement with Russia until the conclusion of an oil agreement with Elf Aquitaine.[28]

However, after the mid-1990s, the old pattern of oil company-government relations began to change. Soon after President Clinton's re-election in 1996, the White House adopted a proactive policy toward the Caspian rim, characterized by a greater degree of involvement in the region's political and economic affairs. Driven by its own calculations of US strategic and economic interests and pressures from Turkey, the White House took the lead in pushing for greater MNC investment and activity, instead of reacting to the needs of the US companies. A notable example of this policy was the Baku–Ceyhan saga.

After their initial exuberance, the oil companies began to reassess their Caspian operations in light of lower than expected reserves, falling oil prices, political instability and corruption and the high cost of production and transport. This reassessment resulted in the preference of the companies for an Iranian export route for Azeri oil, because it was economically the most sensible choice. Based on geostrategic considerations to isolate Iran and reward Turkey, the White House vetoed the Iranian route and pressured the companies to choose Baku–Ceyhan. The confrontation came to a head at a meeting between US National Security Council officials and senior oil company executives, who emphasized that the Baku–Ceyhan project was not commercially viable.[29] In the ensuing year, intense pressure was applied by the American and Turkish governments, culminating in BP–Amoco's half-hearted declaration of support for the Baku–Ceyhan project in October 1999.[30] Against the history of business-government relations, characterized by deference shown to company interests, the bullying experienced by the captains of the oil industry was unprecedented. In the event that Baku–Ceyhan is built, and proves commercially unprofitable, it would be a clear-cut example of the victory of state power over company profits. The intense displeasure of the oil companies was best described in an editorial of the *Oil and Gas Journal*:

> Investors, not governments, decide what's commercial and what's not. Investors, not governments, will decide whether to place at risk the $4 billion that the Baku–Ceyhan project might require ... Under Clinton, the US government intrudes too frequently in foreign commerce to pursue policy goals too often flawed. The Baku–Ceyhan pipeline should be built only if – and only when – investors decide it makes commercial sense. Because the US has no proper say in that decision, it should quit saying anything at all.[31]

Another case illustrating the clash between perceived state interests and company priorities is found in the vicissitudes of Russia's Caspian policy. The post-Soviet meltdown of the Russian state apparatus and the dramatic rise in importance of the oil and gas complex for Russia's economy set the stage for a contentious state-company relationship. Given its ties to government leaders, the powerful oil company Lukoil openly defied positions expounded by the Russian foreign ministry by participating in various Azerbaijani PSAs, including the Contract of the Century. Another conflict of interests involved Gazprom's exclusion of Turkmen gas from its pipeline network, which went against Russia's national interest by alienating Turkmenistan and forcing it to seek non-Russian export routes.[32] In addition, Gazprom's disinterest in the Burgas–Alexandroupolis project may be seen as the company's reluctance to serve as a conduit of Russian strategic interests.[33] Under Putin's leadership, there are indications that the Russian government would assume a stronger position vis-a-vis the oil companies.

Relations between MNCs and host countries include a set of complex issues, such as corrupt officialdom, involvement in political disputes, culturally undesirable practices and promotion of income inequalities. A few of these problems have become apparent at this early stage of MNC involvement in the Caspian countries. Corruption and bribery are endemic features in all of the states of the Caspian rim and the neighboring countries. Of course, oil companies have had years of experience in dealing with corrupt officials in host countries around the globe. The Caspian is no exception, although paying bribes to corrupt officials is illegal under US law. Another problem is how to deal with host country political realities in order to secure a hospitable environment for company operations. The usual practice of oil companies has been to support those in authority. One possible exception was the reported involvement of BP and Amoco in aiding the 1993 overthrow of the Elchibey régime.[34] Other aspects of MNC-host society relations, such as Western cultural influences imported by the oil companies, have yet to generate serious opposition in the Caspian context. More pressing is the growing maldistribution of wealth, partly a consequence of large-scale foreign investment, which in the long term might become a source of resentment and opposition to Caspian governments, oil companies and their home countries.

Any assessment of the aggregate presence of oil MNCs in the Caspian region would have to be based on such measures as the total number of joint ventures, the number of foreign firms involved in them and the total amount of their investment. All these figures are in constant flux due to the ongoing movement of foreign companies in and out of joint ventures, termination of joint ventures, and creation of new ones. As of 2000, there was an approximate total of 75 joint ventures and other types of foreign investments of various sizes in the region: Kazakhstan claimed the largest number (45), followed by Azerbaijan (24), Turkmenistan (6) and Iran (1). Over 80 foreign firms were directly involved in the oil business in various capacities. Companies from 28 different countries were represented, the largest contingent being American firms, followed by the United Kingdom, Japan, Germany, Canada and other countries. These figures are a reflection both of the extensive foreign interest in Caspian resources and the conscious policy decision of Azerbaijan and Kazakhstan to maximize international support by involving as many countries as possible in their energy sector. Collectively, these companies have signed contracts to invest up to $100bn over several decades, although the actual amounts disbursed until 2001 have been relatively modest. This could mean that the companies have sought to secure a foothold in the region, but are not prepared to make large investments in the near term. Among the 80-odd companies involved in the Caspian region are oil giants such as Chevron, BP–Amoco, Royal Dutch Shell, Exxon–Mobil, Lukoil, Texaco, Totalfina and Agip.

International organizations

A plethora of international organizations played important roles in the Caspian geopolitical and economic milieux. These include various UN agencies, regional security organizations, special interest groupings and global financial institutions. At the supranational level, several UN agencies have been involved in the region's development. These include the Office of the Coordinator for Humanitarian Assistance (OCHA), the High Commissioner for Refugees (UNHCR) and the UN Development Program (UNDP), which collectively have sought to care for displaced populations and the poor. Also, the UN sent an observer mission to manage the Abkhaz conflict in Georgia, as well as monitoring human rights practices in Central Asian and Transcaucasian states.

At the political level, the régimes in power have sought the involvement of international organizations to secure their independence vis-a-vis Moscow, as well as to strengthen their own survival against secessionist movements. A case in point is the key role of OSCE in mediating the South Ossetia–Georgia and the Nagorno-Karabakh conflicts.[35] Although OSCE was instrumental in reducing Russia's role in these conflicts, it was unable to resolve them. In the same vein, the Council of Europe has begun to take an active interest, admitting Georgia, Armenia and Azerbaijan into its membership.

Perhaps more successful has been the role of global financial organizations in terms of long-lasting impact. The IMF has provided Russia with billions of dollars in order to balance its budget, pay pensions and support the rouble. Similar programmes have been implemented in other CIS states. On the developmental side, the World Bank has lent large sums to energy projects in Azerbaijan and Kazakhstan. These countries, along with Russia and Turkmenistan, have received additional funding from the European Bank for Reconstruction and Development.[36] Two other lending institutions active in the region are the Asian Development Bank and the Islamic Bank of Development.[37]

Non-governmental organizations (NGOs)

As an outgrowth of globalization, the proliferation and multinational outreach of non-governmental organizations (NGOs) has been phenomenal. Among the best-known NGOs are Amnesty International, Human Rights Watch, the Eurasia Foundation, the Open Society Institute, Médecins Sans Frontières, the Harvard Negotiation Project, International Alert, Vertic and Caucasian Links. While some of these NGOs focus on the monitoring and promotion of human rights, others seek to prevent and resolve conflicts or extend humanitarian assistance. Not all NGOs have been welcomed to the region, particularly those committed to human rights. Given their generally authoritarian nature, Caspian governments have often obstructed NGO operations.[38] Consequently, the protracted efforts of NGOs and other intergovernmental organizations to build civil society in the Caspian/Central Asian countries have produced limited results.

Provincial entities

In three states of the Caspian littoral, sub-national or provincial units have emerged as political actors. These include Russia's three Caspian provinces – Astrakhan Oblast, Daghestan and Kalmykia – as well as Iranian and Kazakh provinces contiguous to the sea. As a federation, Russia's provincial units enjoy significant independence from the center, and consequently, Russia does not always behave as a unitary actor in Caspian geopolitics. In the ensuing center-periphery relationship, the interests of the Astrakhan Oblast have shaped Russia's Caspian policies in such fields as fishing, ship-building, ecology and hydrocarbon resources.[39] Because of its importance, Astrakhan has had the ability to affect Russia's geopolitical designs in the Caspian. A case in point was the oblast's influence on Moscow to oppose the division of the Caspian.[40] The autonomous republics of Daghestan and Kalmykia have less clout in Moscow than Astrakhan, because they lack the resources that the Astrakhan Oblast possesses. However, Daghestan and Kalmykia have taken some initiatives in developing economic and commercial ties with other Caspian states and their provinces. For example, Kalmykia contracted two Iranian companies for construction of a port to facilitate transit with Iran.[41] This Kalmyk–Iranian project follows various other trade and cooperation agreements involving Azerbaijani Nakhichevan, Iranian Gilan, Mazanderan, Khorasan and East Azerbaijan, Kazakh Mangistau and Russian Astrakhan.[42] All these indicate an emerging trend whereby provinces are taking the initiative, particularly in the economic sphere, to establish cross-Caspian enterprises.

CHAPTER 11

The Caspian in the Global Marketplace

In the guiding logic of this book, the Caspian's future will be determined by the correlation of conflicting and reinforcing forces converging on the region, and their interaction with local realities. Inasmuch as indigenous rulers try to limit the impact of external forces, to a large extent they are bound to remain at the mercy of the powerful currents of globalization sweeping the region. Yet today's milieu of globalization, far more than the olden days of the Great Game, is one of encompassing and multifaceted influences − political, economic, cultural and technological. Indeed, for the Caspian states there is no escape from the global marketplace, precisely because of their strategic location and energy wealth. Thus, the Caspian states would have to learn to survive within a globalized marketplace not only of energy, but also of ideas, institutions and socio-economic currents.

Aside from the political consequences of the region's strategic location, the future of the Caspian will be determined to a large extent by the dynamics of the energy market. After all, the primary commodity of value that the Caspian is able to offer the world economy is energy. Hence the question − how competitive is Caspian energy likely to be in global markets?

Parameters of competitiveness and scenarios
The analysis presented in the preceding chapter suggests that, in the next two decades, at least six interrelated determinants are likely to shape the region's development as an energy source. These are magnitude of reserves, transport issues, global demand and price trends, new discoveries, policies of the Gulf states and intrinsic political risks.

Magnitude of reserves
The determination of the actual extent of Caspian oil and gas

reserves, both proven and potential, will remain a contentious issue because of technical difficulties as well as the political gamesmanship of politicians and lobbyists. As discussed in chapter 4, after a decade of exploration, estimates of the combined proven oil reserves of Azerbaijan, Kazakhstan, Turkmenistan and Uzbekistan are about 16 bn barrels – 1.5 percent of world reserves.[1] Their combined proven gas reserves are placed at 250 trillion cubic feet – less than 5 percent of world reserves. These are not compelling statistics, particularly relative to the massive oil reserves of the Persian Gulf and the large gas reserves of Russia and Iran, although future exploration could well raise the estimates of Caspian energy wealth.

Production costs

The costs of Caspian oil/gas exploration and extraction are comparatively high because of geological and technological factors, particularly in offshore fields. Given the likelihood of high marginal production costs relative to the Persian Gulf countries, Caspian oil will become competitive only in high price/high demand markets.

Transport issues

As a landlocked region, far from major consuming nations, the export of Caspian energy is mostly dependent on long pipelines routed through difficult terrain. The cumulative cost of pipeline construction and transit fees would add up to $5 a barrel, not including tanker transportation charges from pipeline terminals to consumer markets. Such high transport costs, added to the high costs of production, would render Caspian oil uncompetitive except in high-price and high-demand markets.

Global demand and price trends

Caspian oil would be a hard sell in times of low demand brought on by economic downturns in one or more major energy consuming regions, combined with over-production by OPEC and non-OPEC countries. A case in point was the cheap oil markets of the 1990s, caused by overproduction and the 1997 Asian meltdown, until production cuts by Saudi Arabia and other majors in 1999 resulted in sharp price increases. Moreover, future oil prices will be affected by the extent to which the newly developing economies of such populous countries as China, India, Indonesia and Brazil put pressure on demand.

New discoveries

The discovery and development of new core oil fields that are geographically closer to consuming countries or have better access to the open sea are also likely to influence negatively the Caspian future. Potential core areas include the Russian Far East and the African states of Sudan, Chad, Angola and Namibia.

Gulf States policies

The single most consequential factor likely to affect the Caspian energy future is the changing political economy of the Gulf states. With their commanding position in global oil markets, backed by possession of 65 percent of the world's proven reserves and excess production capacity, the Gulf countries, led by Saudi Arabia, possess unrivalled power to affect world supplies and prices in the foreseeable future, which could prove detrimental to lesser producers such as those of the Caspian. Supremely confident in their wealth and pre-eminence in energy markets, only recently have the Gulf's Arab producers begun to view the Caspian Basin as an emerging rival. Having nationalized their energy sector in the 1970s, and excluded participation by multinationals, the Gulf régimes have watched with displeasure the flow of investments to the Caspian region – a repeat of the pattern leading to the development of North Sea oil. However, the hydrocarbon policies of the Gulf states may be changing, albeit incrementally, as new leaders have come to reassess old patterns and priorities. Crown Prince Abdallah's 1998 invitation to oil majors to negotiate new projects may be a precursor to opening up the kingdom's vast untapped resources for foreign investment. Should this happen, the oil giants would return to the Persian Gulf in full force, leaving the Caspian short of new investments and shorn of its claim to world attention.

The future policies of other major Gulf producers – Iran, Iraq, Kuwait, Qatar and the United Arab Emirates – will also impact the Caspian countries. Should President Khatami's reformist forces prevail over the conservative clerical establishment, a whole new set of regional relations would emerge that could have a bearing on pipeline routes and investment flows. More difficult to prognosticate is the political evolution of Iraq and the market consequences of its return to full-scale production, and possible investment opportunities to tap its vast hydrocarbon deposits.

Political risk

Beyond these economic parameters, the future of the Caspian and its energy resources will be shaped by the tenor of political developments within the area and its larger periphery. Thus, any prognosis of the Caspian's viability as an energy supplier requires the systematic analysis of political risks emanating from sub-national, national and extra-regional actors and events, as these interact within a globalized environment.[2] The role of political risk analysis is particularly salient in the energy sector, because of the extreme vulnerability of oil and gas production and exportation to instability.

Sub-national risks:
As discussed in the preceding chapter, a half-dozen unresolved ethnic conflicts have plagued the region and its immediate periphery during the last decade. These conflicts have had a withering impact on governmental authority and even triggered interstate strife. In addition to its threat to pipeline routes, the Chechen conflict has destabilized the North Caucasus, in particular the coastal province of Daghestan. The ethnic conflicts of South Ossetia and Abkhazia have sapped the power of the central Georgian authorities and constitute a threat to pipeline routes to the Black Sea. A renewed outbreak of war over Nagorno-Karabakh would not only jeopardize the security of westbound pipelines, but would also ruin the investment climate in the Azerbaijani oil industry. Even more risky is the proposed construction of the Baku–Ceyhan pipeline across Turkish Kurdistan, in view of the protracted conflict between the Turkish military and Kurdish nationalists.

National level risks:
These arise from the relative political inefficacy of governing elites and institutions and the socio-economic impact of resulting policies. Without exception, the Caspian states and their neighbors are ruled by authoritarian oligarchies characterized by suppression of opposition elements, gross corruption and cumbersome bureaucracies, in a pattern common to all the successor states of the Soviet Union. Although authoritarian regimes have provided extended periods of relative stability for oil company activities in the Middle East and elsewhere, the Caspian oligarchies may not prove to be as durable. The classic developmental pattern in oligarchic régimes flooded with oil wealth is the phenomenon known as relative deprivation, characterized by gross income inequality amid conspicuous

consumption by superficially Westernized elites. The persistence of such conditions could result in widespread social unrest and long-term political instability, and even revolution.

Extra-regional political risks:
The primary sources of extra-regional political risk derive from the policies of foreign powers and the machinations of transnational extremist movements and criminal organizations. In their quest to develop a strategic east-west corridor, the United States and the European powers have sought to strengthen their regional allies to the detriment of the human rights of more than a dozen minority groups. The east-west strategy of the West is directly challenged by a north-south axis being promoted by Russia and Iran, in a clash of interests that has heightened political risk throughout the region. The lessening of such political risk would have to await the betterment of Russian relations with the West and the normalization of American relations with Iran. Equally destabilizing is the impact of transnational actors such as Islamist militants and criminal groups, which have moved into the region since the Soviet demise.

Why the Caspian: the geopolitical imperative

This study has sought to identify and analyze the diverse political, economic and ideological forces converging upon the Caspian countries which are caught in the throes of nation building as newly independent states. To explain the motivations and behavior of the many actors involved in the new Great Game, a variety of theories of international relations have been utilized, ranging from balance of power and neorealism to neoliberalism and globalization. The resulting analysis of facts and figures has helped to illuminate some recurring questions: why did the Caspian become a center of international attention in the last decade of the twentieth century, and why was the Caspian accorded such a prominent position in the crowded policy agendas of the United States and the West? The answers to these questions could provide insights into a larger and more controversial discourse about the structure and evolution of the international political system since the Cold War.

This study suggests that the West's decade-long involvement in the larger Caspian region was motivated by interrelated political and economic interests, which were both mutually conflicting and complementary. Thus, the 'great oil rush' of the early 1990s was driven mainly by the oil companies in their scramble to secure participation in a potentially energy-rich region. It was only natural for Western governments to lend support to oil companies in their quest for new sources of energy and pursuit of profitable ventures. In a sense, the companies were leading the way, letting the 'flag' follow in their wake. By the late 1990s, however, the situation was dramatically reversed, with governments taking the lead in setting the agenda for the companies.

The reason for this reversal of roles is rooted in the dialectic between power and profit. A half-decade after their headlong rush into the Caspian's troubled waters, the initial enthusiasm of the companies had begun to wane in the face of limited energy finds, pipeline dilemmas and political uncertainties. Having jumped into the Caspian fray without the benefit of reliable data on reserves and a sober analysis of political risk, the oil majors began to re-evaluate their stakes in order to limit their economic risks. Yet the declining momentum of the companies was not shared by their governments, especially the United States, which continued to push for high levels of investment. The high point of 'power over profits' policy was the campaign orchestrated by the White House and a slew of lobbyists to promote building the Baku–Ceyhan pipeline over the objections of the oil companies. Indeed, the Caspian episode has defied the near-sacrosanct logic of economic determinism, both in its Marxist and capitalist variants. Given their declared faith in the virtues of the market, how could governments justify large-scale investments in the Caspian, in view of its relatively limited energy reserves, high production costs, difficulties of transport, high levels of political risk and its likelihood of being dwarfed by the vast reserves of Saudi Arabia, the Persian Gulf and untapped resources elsewhere? The obvious answer is that the United States, and to a degree its European allies, regard Caspian energy investments as a convenient raison d'être to project their power into the region, presumably to check competing hegemonic moves by Russia, Iran, China or Islamist militants. This strategy of US-led political globalization should not surprise anyone except the most dedicated idealists. The tendency toward the pursuit of geopolitical interests flows from America's unrivaled superpower status since 1991, the deep-rooted patterns of international politics and the ingrained behavioral habits of policymakers. To be sure, the geopolitical imperative that motivates the United States and its rivals is not too different from that of the Great Game, when Britain and Russia acted according to the time-tested rules of balance of power, by expanding their spheres of influence not only through military might, but also by riding piggyback upon their pre-established economic interests.

However, in contrast to nineteenth century imperialism, the modalities of Western penetration into the Caspian are more subtle and, thus far, mostly benign. The initial method of Western involvement through energy deals was supplemented by efforts to propagate Western values and practices – democratization, marketization and promotion of human rights – which have been largely ignored by most regional governments and even by their American and European sponsors, when these practices conflicted with their perceived national interests. Simultaneously came the employment of instrumentalities such as diplomatic exchanges, peacemaking missions, economic aid and military assistance, with the declared aim of promoting the stability and political independence of these countries.

If the primary determinant of US/Western policy is that of geopolitics, then it would be appropriate to ask whether the Caspian region's strategic importance rises to the level of significance attached to it by some American thinkers. Moreover, the pursuit of purely strategic objectives contradicts to some degree the vision of constructing a global community of peace and comity. If the future of humankind is to be one of growing interdependence, integration and interpenetration of ideas, economies and markets, does it make any sense for statesmen to be guided by theories and practices harking back to the most tumultuous periods of the nineteenth and twentieth centuries? The experience of history is replete with examples of pre-emptive expansion into power vacuums in remote regions which have had disastrous consequences for the competing states as well as for the indigenous population.

Not all the foregoing Western initiatives should be viewed as self-serving or detrimental to the general good of the Caspian region. Clearly, the implantation of Western-inspired democratic values and human rights practices, while unwelcome by local governments, could benefit the people although Western consumerism has had a far greater impact. Equally salutary are Western attempts to enhance state independence and regional stability in the Caspian's anarchic environment. These efforts, combined with multilateral peacemaking initiatives, have had a dampening effect on the region's conflictual milieu. Yet, the main thrust of US/Western policy has been to strengthen the hold of about a half-dozen, mostly ex-Communist, autocrats, to the detriment of their impoverished citizenry and ethnic minorities. If the ultimate objective of the West's geopolitical and economic reach into the larger Caspian arena is to promote regional stability and social well-being based on energy wealth, this aim would have to be pursued through a 'concert' of the competing powers, and in a manner designed to produce tangible socio-economic benefits for the common people.

References

Chapter 1
1. Patrick O'Sullivan, *Geopolitics* (New York: St Martin's Press, 1986).
2. Alfred Thayan Mayer, *The Influence of Sea Power upon History, 1660-1783* (Boston: Little, Brown, 1897).
3. Halford Mackinder, *Democratic Ideals and Reality* (New York: Norton, 1962), p. 150.
4. Nicholas Spykman, *The Geography of Peace* (New York: Harcourt, Brace, 1944), pp. 39-44.
5. Kenneth M. Waltz, *Theory of International Politics* (Reading, MA: Addison-Wesley Publishing, 1979), pp. 60-7 and 93-101.
6. Robert O. Keohane and Joseph Nye, *Power and Interdependence: World Politics in Transition* (Boston: Little, Brown, 1977).
7. Samuel P. Huntington, *The Clash of Civilizations and the Remaking of World Order* (New York: Simon & Schuster, 1996).

Chapter 2
1. Geoffrey Kemp and Robert E. Harkavy, *Strategic Geography and the Changing Middle East* (Washington, DC: Carnegie Endowment for International Peace, 1997), pp. 34-7.
2. Daniel Yergin, *The Prize: The Epic Quest for Oil, Money and Power* (New York: Touchstone/Simon & Schuster, 1990), p. 137.
3. P. de Tchihatchef, 'Le Pétrole aux Etats-Unis et en Russie', *Revue des Deux Mondes*, 89, no. 5, 1888, p. 634.
4. Some minor exploitation of oil had taken place in past centuries. During antiquity and the Middle Ages, oil was used, among other things, as fuel, medicine and in construction. Marco Polo reported that oil from Baku was exported as far away as Baghdad. The 'eternal fires' of the Apsheron peninsula, on which Baku stands, were considered manifestations of pagan gods, and Zoroastrians from India maintained a temple in the village of Surakhani, not far from Baku, until 1879. Finally, in the seventeenth and eighteenth centuries, the Baku Khans

drew a significant part of their income from the sale of oil. J.D. Henry, *Baku: A Eventful History* (London: Archibald Constable & Co., 1905), pp. 17–28.

5. Henry, pp. 29–38; A. Beeby Thompson, *The Oil Fields of Russia and the Russian Petroleum Industry*, 2nd ed. (London: Crosby Lockwood and Son, 1908), pp. 3–4.

6. Robert W. Tolf, *The Russian Rockefellers; The Saga of the Nobel Family and the Russian Oil Industry* (Stanford, CA: Hoover Institution Press/Stanford University, 1976).

7. Calouste S. Gulbenkian, 'La Péninsule d'Apchéron et le Pétrole Russe', *Revue des Deux Mondes*, 105, no. 3, May–June 1891, p. 397.

8. CRES/ACI, *Le Pétrole et le Gaz Russes: Histoire et Perspectives* (Geneva: CRES, 1995), p. 36.

9. Pinar Batur-VanderLippe and Stephen Simmons, 'Oil and Regional Relations in the Caucasus and Central Asia in the Post-Soviet Period', in *Oil in the New World Order*, Kate Gillespie and Clement Moore Henry (eds), (Gainesville, FL: University Press of Florida, 1995), p. 164; Robert E. Ebel, *Energy Choices in the Near Abroad: The Haves and Have-Nots Face the Future* (Washington, DC: Center for Strategic and International Studies, 1997), p. 9.

10. Henry, p. ix; Rasul Gouliev, *Oil and Politics* (New York: Liberty Publishing House, 1997), p. 30.

11. Matthew J. Sagers, 'The Oil Industry in the Southern-Tier Former Soviet Republics', *Post-Soviet Geography*, 35, no. 5, May 1994a, pp. 274, 291, 296. This study is principally concerned with the five riparian states of the Caspian basin. However, whenever relevant and available, references will be provided for adjacent countries and regions.

12. Ebel 1997, p. 38.

13. Rasim Agayev and Valeri Grigoryev, *Azerbaijan* (Moscow: Novosti Press Agency Publishing House, 1981), pp. 24–5; Ara Sanjian, *The Negotiation of "the Contract of the Century" and the Political Background to the Revival of Azerbaijan's Oil Industry* (Yerevan: Armenian Center for National and International Studies, 1997), p. 7; Steve LeVine, 'Neftyanyye Journal: Caspian Sun on the Rise, Chasing Russian Shadow', *New York Times*, 27 October 1995, p. A10.

14. Robert V. Barylski, 'Russia, the West, and the Caspian Energy Hub', *Middle East Journal*, 49, no. 2, Spring 1995, p. 218.

15. Sagers, 1994a, p. 284.

16. Batur-VanderLippe and Simmons, p. 164.

17. Ebel 1997, pp. 40, 71, 125, 150.

18. Jonathan Stern, 'Oil and Gas in the Former Soviet Union: The Changing Foreign Investment Agenda', in *Investment Opportunities in Russia and*

the CIS, ed. David Dyker (London: Royal Institute of International Affairs, 1995), p. 23.
19. 'World Oil and Gas Production', *Petroleum Economist*, 64, no. 7, July 1997, p. 52.
20. *Ibid*; Stern, p. 30.

Chapter 3

1. Cesare P. R. Romano, 'La Caspienne: Un Flou Juridique, Source de Conflits', *CEMOTI*, no. 23, January–June 1997, pp. 41–4; Rodman R. Bundy, 'The Caspian – Sea or Lake?, Consequences in International Law', *Labyrinth: Central Asia Quarterly*, 2, no. 3, Summer 1995, p. 28.
2. Bundy, p. 28.
3. Henn-Jüri Uibopuu, 'The Caspian: A Tangle of Legal Problems', *The World Today*, 51, no. 6, June 1995, p. 120; 'Validity of Treaties at Heart of Legal Disputes over Caspian Sea Rights', *Oil and Gas Journal*, 94, no. 1, 1 January 1996, p. 29.
4. David Allonsius, *Le Régime Juridique de la Mer Caspienne: Problèmes Actuels de Droit International Public* (Paris: L.G.D.J., 1997), pp. 32–33.
5. *Ibid*, pp. 39–47.
6. Sergei Vinogradov and Patricia Wouters, 'The Caspian Sea: Current Legal Problems', *Zeitschrift für Ausländisches Recht und Völkerrecht*, 55, no. 2, pp. 612–13; Martin Pratt and Clive Schofield, 'International Boundaries, Resources and Environmental Security in the Caspian Sea', in *International Boundaries and Environmental Security: Frameworks for Regional Cooperation*, Gerald Blake et al. (eds.), (London/The Hague/Boston: Kluwer Law International, 1997), pp. 86–7.
7. Dilip Hiro, 'Troubled Waters: The Legal Status of the Caspian Sea', *Middle East International*, no. 574, 8 May 1998, p. 19.
8. Allonsius, p. 50.
9. Uibopuu, pp. 121–2; Allonsius, pp.78–84.
10. An International Law Commission is currently preparing a convention on the non-navigational uses of international watercourses. See Bernard H. Oxman, 'Caspian Sea or Lake: What Difference Does It Make?', *Caspian Crossroads*, 1, no. 4, Winter 1995–96, pp. 3–4.
11. Allonsius, pp. 75–8.
12. Vinogradov and Wouters, p. 615.
13. Vyacheslav Gizzatov, 'The Legal Status of the Caspian', *Labyrinth: Central Asia Quarterly*, 2, no. 3, Summer 1995, pp. 34, 36; Uibopuu, pp. 119–20.
14. Romano, p. 45.
15. Ebel 1997, pp. 16–18; 'Turkmenistan Starts New Caspian Wrangle', *Labyrinth: Central Asia Quarterly*, 4, no. 1, Winter 1997, p. 35.

16. 'Country Report: Kazakhstan', *Economist Intelligence Unit (EIU)*, 2nd quarter 1997, p. 35.
17. Ron Synovitz, 'Russia/Kazakhstan: Yeltsin, Nazarbayev Ink Accord On Caspian Oil Rights', *RFE/RL Weekly Magazine*, 6 July 1998.
18. 'Russia Proposes Joint Development of Disputed Caspian Oilfields', *AFP*, 14 July 2000.
19. Henry, pp. 46, 59, 103.
20. George S. Golitsyn, 'Overview: History and Causes of Caspian Sea Level Change', in *Scientific, Environmental, and Political Issues in the Circum-Caspian Region*, Michael H. Glantz and Igor S. Zonn (eds), (Dordrecht/Boston/London: Kluwer Academic Publishers/NATO Advanced Science Institutes Series, 1997), p. 18.
21. Türker Altan, 'An Exhausted Environmental Legacy: Environmental Problems in the Central Asia Beyond Borders, and Destruction of Natural Resources', *Eurasian Studies*, 2, no. 1, Spring 1995, p. 43.
22. Jean-Robert Raviot, 'Environnement contre Géopolitique: Les Enjeux Ecologiques dans la Région Caspienne', *CEMOTI*, no. 23, January–June 1997, pp. 69–72.
23. Ze'ev Wolfson and Zia Daniell, 'Azerbaijan', in *Environmental Resources and Constraints in the Former Soviet Republics*, ed. Philip R. Pryde (Boulder, CO: Westview Press, 1995), pp. 242–3.
24. Wolfson and Daniell, p. 239; Raviot, p. 69.
25. Ruben A. Mnatsakanian, *Environmental Legacy of the Former Soviet Republics* (Edinburgh: Centre for Human Ecology, 1992) pp. 75–6,111.
26. David R. Smith, 'Kazakhstan', in *Environmental Resources and Constraints*, p. 264.
27. Tatyana A. Saiko, 'Environmental Problems of the Caspian Sea Region and the Conflict of National Priorities', in *Circum-Caspian*, p. 43.
28. Arif Sh. Mekhtiev and A. K. Gul, 'Ecological Problems of the Caspian Sea and Perspectives on Possible Solutions', in *Circum-Caspian*, p. 91.
29. Yuriy S. Chuikov, 'Problems of Ecological Safety of the Astrakhan Region due to the Rise of the Caspian Sea', in *Circum-Caspian*, p. 126; Saiko, p. 44.
30. Igor S. Zonn, 'Assessment of the State of the Caspian Sea', in *Circum-Caspian*, p. 27.
31. 'World: Forum Places Sturgeon Fish on Endangered List', *RFE/RL Weekday Magazine*, 19 June 1997.
32. Don Hill, 'Kazakhstan: Caspian Sea Rise Threatens Cities, Industries, Oil Fields', *RFE/RL Online*, 18 July, 1997; Jalal Shayegan and Amir Badakhshan, 'Iranian Research on Caspian Sea Level Rise', in *Circum-Caspian*, p. 72.
33. Genady N. Golubev, 'Environmental Policy-Making for Sustainable

Development of the Caspian Sea Area', in *Central Eurasian Water Crisis: Caspian, Aral, and Dead Seas*, Iwao Kobori and Michael H. Glantz (eds), (Tokyo/New York/Paris: United Nations University Press, 1998), p. 100.
34. Raviot, p. 72.
35. *Ibid*, p. 79; Douglas W. Blum, 'Domestic Politics and Russia's Caspian Policy', *Post-Soviet Affairs*, 14, no. 2, April-June 1998, 142n.
36. Zonn, pp. 34-6.
37. Golitsyn, p. 20.
38. Zonn, p. 32.
39. Philip Micklin, 'Turkmenistan', in *Environmental Resources and Constraints*, p. 285.
40. Raviot, pp. 74-7.
41. Saiko, p. 49; Denis J. B. Shaw and Jonathan Oldfield, 'The Natural Environment of the CIS in the Transition from Communism', *Post-Soviet Geography and Economics*, 39, no. 3, March 1998, pp. 171-74.
42. Terry Macalister, 'Oil's New Frontier', *The Guardian*, 15 November 2000, p. 28.
43. 'The Bergedorf Forum on the Caspian', *International Affairs (Moscow)*, 45, no. 3, 1999, pp. 177-78 and 181.

Chapter 4
1. Julia Nanay, 'The Industry's Race for Caspian Oil Reserves', in *Caspian Energy Resources: Implications for the Arab Gulf* (Abu Dhabi: Emirates Center for Strategic Studies and Research, 2000), pp. 111-12.
2. Natalia A. Feduschak, 'Kazakhstan's Oil Estimates Spark Rush to Risky Region', *The Wall Street Journal*, 17 June 1993, p. A7.
3. Rosemarie Forsythe, *The Politics of Oil in the Caucasus and Central Asia: Prospects for Oil Exploitation and Export in the Caspian Basin*, Adelphi Papers no. 300 (Oxford: Oxford University Press, 1996), p. 11; John Roberts, *Caspian Pipelines* (London: Royal Institute of International Affairs, 1996), p. 2.
4. Sagers 1994a, pp. 269-70; Charles Fenyvesi, 'Caspian Sea: U.S. Experts Say Oil Reserves Are Huge', *RFE/RL Weekday Magazine*, 5 May 1998.
5. Anthony Hyman, 'Kuwait by the Caspian', *The Middle East*, no. 238, October 1994b; Laurie Laird, 'Is Kazakhstan the New Kuwait?', *Europe*, no. 341, November 1994; Hans Nijenhuis: 'Azerbaijan: Kuwait of the Caucasus', *World Press Review*, 42, no. 1, January 1995; Chris Kutschera, 'Azerbaijan: The Kuwait of the Caucasus?', *The Middle East*, no. 254, March 1996.
6. Sagers 1994a, pp. 268n., 270.

7. *Ibid.*, pp. 270–1.
8. 'Key Issue: Control of Central Asia Oil Reserves', *Oil and Gas Journal*, 94, no. 11, 11 March 1996, p. 104.
9. Josh Martin, 'Afghanistan: Pipeline Wrangle Continues', *The Middle East*, no. 267, May 1997, p. 24.
10. Thomas Land, 'Caspian Neighbours Seek Accord on Offshore Deals', *The Middle East*, no. 265, March 1997, p. 22; Alain Giroux, 'Le Kazakhstan entre Russie et Caspienne', *CEMOTI*, no. 23, January–June 1997, p. 173.
11. Charles Clover and Robert Corzine, 'Treasure Under the Sea: The Caspian's Oil Reserves Could be Enormous but There are Disputes to Overcome', *Financial Times*, 30 April 1997, p. 25.
12. Marat Gurt, 'Turkmens Detail Riches of Tendered Caspian Oil, Gas', *Reuters*, 2 September 1997 p. 25.
13. Dominique Pianelli, 'L'Enjeu Pétrolier dans le Caucase', in *Arménie–Azerbaïjan–Géorgie: L'An V des Indépendances; La Russie: 1995–1996. International Ex-URSS Edition 1996*, Roberte Berton Hogge and Marie-Agnès Crosnier (eds), (Paris: Les Etudes de la Documentation Française, 1996), p. 70.
14. Hugh Pope, 'Caspian Oil Deposits Might Be Twice as Large as Expected', *Wall Street Journal*, 30 April 1997, p. A10.
15. Dilip Hiro, 'Why is the US Inflating Caspian Oil Reserves?', *Middle East International*, no. 558, 12 September 1997a, p. 18.
16. Pope.
17. 'Country Report: Kazakhstan', *EIU*, 4th quarter 1997, p. 35; 'Le Deuxième Gisement Mondial', *Le Monde*, 12 November 1997, p. 2.
18. International Institute for Strategic Studies, 'Caspian Oil: Not the Great Game Revisited', *Strategic Survey 1997/98*, April 1998, pp. 22–9; Manik Talwani, Andrei Belopolsky, and Dianne L. Berry, 'Geology and Petroleum Potential of the Caspian Sea Region', *Unlocking the Assets: Energy and the Future of Oil from Central Asia and the Caucasus* (Houston, TX: Center for International Political Economy and the James A. Baker III Institute for Public Policy of Rice University, April 1998).
19. Carlotta Gall, 'Consortium Quits Azerbaijan', *Financial Times*, 22 January 1999, p. 4.
20. 'Azerbaijan's North Apsheron Oil Project Confirmed Unviable', *BBC Worldwide Monitoring*, 2 April 1999.
21. 'As a Third Caspian Consortium Faces Liquidation', *RFE/RL Newsline*, 16 March 1999.
22. 'Azeri Test Well Could Bump up Shakh Deniz Reserves', *Reuters*, 10 September 1999.

REFERENCES

23. 'Azerbaijan Plays Down Poor Results in Caspian Oil Exploration', *AFP*, 13 July 2000.
24. Aida Sultanova, 'Azerbaijan AIOC Strikes High-Sulfur Gas', *Dow Jones International News*, 14 July 2000.
25. 'State Oil Chief Boasts of Huge Oil Reserves', *BBC Summary of World Broadcasts (SWB)*, SU/W0666/S1, 17 November 2000.
26. Christopher Cooper and Hugh Pope, 'Dry Wells Hope for Big Caspian Reserves – Bad Luck, Low Oil Prices Lead Some to Reassess, Put Clinton Plan at Risk', *Wall Street Journal*, 12 October 1998, p. A13.
27. 'Energie: Un Premier Sondage Décevant: Elf Abandonne son Forage Kazakh', *Les Echos*, 16 August 1994, p. 7.
28. Dmitry Zhdannikov, 'Russian Lukoil Makes Major Caspian Oil Find', *Reuters*, 23 March 2000; Steve LeVine, 'Consortium Finds Oil in Big Caspian Field', *New York Times*, 6 May 2000, p. C2; Sujata Rao, 'OKIOC Says Speculation on Kazakh Oil Find Premature', *Reuters*, 19 May 2000; Murat Budekbayev, 'Kazakhoil Says Caspian Oilfield Has Up to 50 bln bls', *Reuters*, 4 July 2000; Matthew Jones, 'Doubts Over Caspian Oil Find', *FT.com*, 4 July 2000; Hugh Pope, 'New Caspian Well Yields Substantial Oil and Gas', *Wall Street Journal*, 25 July 2000, p. A17.
29. 'Iran's Caspian Oil Finds Will Require Deep Drilling', *Middle East Economic Digest*, 1 September 2000, p. 10; Vahe Petrossian, 'Raising the Stakes', *Middle East Economic Digest*, 8 September 2000, p. 8.
30. Figures provided by Wood Mackenzie, Edinburgh, Scotland.
31. BP–Amoco, *Statistical Review of World Energy*, available online at http://www.bp.com/worldenergy/index.htm
32. 'Worldwide Look at Reserves and Production', *Oil and Gas Journal*, 97, no. 51, 20 December 1999, pp. 92–3. The BP and *Oil and Gas Journal* statistics do not take into account the discoveries made in 2000 in the Russian and Kazakh sectors of the Caspian.
33. Figures provided by Wood Mackenzie, Edinburgh, Scotland; Terry Macalister, 'Baku to the Future: Will BP-Amoco's Natural Gas Discovery put the Boom back into the Caspian Sea Oil Capital?', *The Guardian*, 14 July 1999; 'Azeri Test Well could Bump up Shakh Deniz Reserves', *Reuters*, 10 September 1999; Sevindzh Abdullayeva and Viktor Shulman, 'Azerbaijani–Georgian Group Meets to Discuss Gas Supply', *Itar-Tass*, 28 November 1999.
34. BP–Amoco, *Statistical Review of World Energy*, available online at http://www.bp.com/worldenergy/index.htm
35. 'Worldwide Look at Reserves and Production', *Oil and Gas Journal*, 97, no. 51, 20 December 1999, pp. 92–3.
36. Roberts, pp. 3–4; Joseph P. Riva, Jr., *Petroleum in the Muslim Republics of*

the Commonwealth of Independent States: More Oil for OPEC? (Bethesda, Maryland: Congressional Information Service, 1992), p. 6.
37. 'Bergedorf Forum on the Caspian', pp. 171–2.
38. *Ibid.*, p. 159.
39. *Ibid.*, Carlotta Gall, 'Consortium Quits Azerbaijan', *Financial Times*, 22 January 1999, p. 4.
40. Robert Corzine, 'The Oil Industry Takes a Gamble: The Promise of Untold Wealth has Drawn Big Companies into a Difficult Project', *Financial Times*, 1 July 1999, p. S3; Robert Corzine, 'Cash is Gone, Please Find a Lot of Oil: The Hopes of the World's Largest Petroleum Companies and the US Government Rest on a Drilling Venture in Kazakhstan', *Financial Times*, 10 November 1999, p. 27.
41. 'Exxon Venture May Delay Caspian Sea Project', *New York Times*, 29 November 2000, p. C4; David Stern, 'International Group Hails Big Oil Discovery in Kazakhstan', *Financial Times*, 6 October 2000, p. 12.
42. International Energy Agency, *Caspian Oil and Gas: The Supply Potential of Central Asia and Transcaucasia* (Paris: OECD Publications, 1998), pp. 47–9; Katherina Dittmann, Hella Engerer, Christian von Hirschhausen, 'Much Ado About ... Little? Disenchantment in the Kazakh and Caspian Oil and Gas Sector', *Kazakhstan Economic Trends*, July–September 1998, pp. 38–9.
43. Liz Fuller, '1998 in Review: Delays and Disappointment in the Caspian', *RFE/RL Weekday Magazine*, 21 December 1998.
44. Saule Omarova, 'Oil, Pipelines, and the 'Scramble for the Caspian': Contextualizing the Politics of Oil in Post-Soviet Kazakhstan and Azerbaijan', in *Space and Transport in the World-System*, Paul S. Ciccantell and Stephen G. Bunker (eds), (Westport, CT: Greenwood Press, 1998), pp. 179–80.
45. Roberts, pp. 3–12; Forsythe, pp. 44–54.; Kemp and Harkavy, pp. 137–53; Ebel 1997, pp. 6–8; George Lenczowski, 'The Caspian Oil and Gas Basin: A New Source of Wealth', *Middle East Policy*, 5, no. 1, January 1997, pp. 114–19.
46. 'A New Way out for Turkmen Gas?', *Jamestown Foundation Monitor*, 12 June 1995; 'Eastward', *Jamestown Foundation Monitor*, 11 September 1995; Michael Kaser and Santosh Mehrotra, 'The Central Asian Economies after Independence', in *Challenges for the Former Soviet South* ed. Roy Allison (London: Royal Institute of International Affairs, 1996), pp. 236–8; Ebel 1997, pp. 137–9; 'Uzbekistan Pipeline Developments', *Labyrinth: Central Asia Quarterly*, 4, no. 1, 1997, p. 37.
47. Forsythe, pp. 49–52; Roberts, pp. 24–32; Ebel 1997, pp. 102–13.
48. 'Country Report: Kazakhstan', *EIU*, 3rd quarter 1999, p. 29.

REFERENCES

49. Isabel Gorst, 'Russia Dithers over Transit Role', *Petroleum Economist*, 64, no. 1, January 1997, p. 36.
50. 'Chine/Kazakhstan: Un Accord Pétrolier', *Le Monde*, 27 September 1997, p. 5; 'Kazakhstan: China to Prise Open Export Path', *Petroleum Economist*, 64, no. 10, October 1997, p. 55.
51. Michael Lelyveld, 'Kazakhstan: Pipeline Projects to China Become Pipe Dreams', *RFE/RL. Weekday Magazine*, 8 July 1999.
52. Ebel 1997, pp. 51–6; Forsythe, pp. 45–7; Roberts, pp. 35–9.
53. 'First Azeri Oil Pumped along Baku–Novorossiisk Pipeline', *BBC Summary of World Broadcasts (SWB)*, Weekly Economic Report, Part 1, Former USSR, SUW/0510 WF/1, 31 October 1997; Vahe Petrossian, 'Iran ready to Play Caspian Oil Game', *MEED*, 41, no. 45, 7 November 1997, p. 5.
54. 'West-Bound Caspian Oil Pipeline Inaugurated', *Jamestown Foundation Monitor*, 19 April 1999. 'Geo-political Wishful Thinking vs. Economic Reality', *RFE/RL Caucasus Report*, 5 May 1998.
55. 'Baku–Ceyhan Oil and Gas Agreements Signed', *Jamestown Foundation Monitor*, 29 November 1999.
56. James P. Dorian, Ian Sheffield Rosi and S. Tony Indriyanto, 'Central Asia's Oil and Gas Pipeline Network: Current and Future Flows', *Post-Soviet Geography*, 35, no. 7, September 1994, p. 425.
57. Roberts, pp. 62–7; 'Turkmenistan Greets US Decision not to Block Iran Pipeline', *SWB*, SU/2988 G/3, 4 August 1997; 'Les Etats-Unis ne vont pas s'opposer à un Gazoduc Transiranien', *Le Monde*, 29 July 1997, p. 3.
58. 'Enron Submits Feasibility Study for Trans-Caspian Gas Pipeline', *The Jamestown Monitor*, 5, no. 19, 28 January 1999; 'Turkmenistan–Turkey Pipeline Contract Signed', *The Jamestown Monitor*, 5, no. 37, 23 February 1999.
59. An excellent presentation of the pipeline projects through Afghanistan is provided in Paul F. Hueper, 'Afghanistan: Risk and Reward between the Front Lines', *Gas in the CIS and Eastern Europe (Annual Supplement of the Petroleum Economist)*, September 1997, pp. 37–40.
60. Martin, pp. 24–5; Thomas Land, 'Pipelines and Politics', *The Middle East*, no. 252, January 1996, pp. 25–6; Roberts, pp. 69–71; Ebel, pp. 132–4; 'Country Report: Kyrgyz Republic, Tajikistan, Turkmenistan', *EIU*, 2nd quarter 1997, pp. 47–48; 'Gas pipeline Agreement Signed with Pakistan', *SWB*, SUW/0497 WE/3, 1 August 1997.
61. 'Turkménistan: Un Consortium International', *Le Monde*, 28 October 1997, p. 4.
62. Michael Lelyveld, 'Russia: Ruble, Oil Prices Change Caspian Oil

Scene', *RFE/RL Weekday Magazine,* 26 August 1998; 'UNOCAL Pulls out of Turkmen Projects', *RFE/RL Newsline,* 8 December 1998.
63. Ebel 1997, pp. 137–9; Roberts, pp. 62 and 71–4.
64. 'Turkmenistan: Country Report', *EIU,* 3rd quarter 1998, pp. 24–5; Thomas R. Stauffer, 'The Iranian Connection': The Geo-economics of Exporting Central Asian Energy Via Iran', *International Research Center for Energy and Economic Development Occasional Papers* no. 29 (Boulder, CO: International Research Center for Energy and Economic Development, 1997).
65. David Stern, 'Pipeline Contenders Eye Kazakh Oil Prospect', *Financial Times,* 9 May 2000, p. 15.

Chapter 5
1. Philip Hanson and Michael J. Bradshaw, 'The Territories and the Federation: An Economic Perspective', in *The Territories of the Russian Federation* (London: Europa Publications, 1999), p. 6.
2. James P. Dorian, *Oil and Gas in Russia and the Former Soviet Union* (London: Financial Times Energy Publishing, 1997), p. 21.
3. 'Country Report: Russia', *EIU,* June 2000, p. 35.
4. 'Country Report: Russia', *EIU,* 4th quarter 1999, p. 45.
5. 'Country Report: Russia', *EIU,* June 2000, p. 39.
6. Dorian 1997, pp. 22–3.
7. Andrew Higgins, 'BP Seeks to Shield Russian Oil Holding Through Last-Ditch Pact with Moscow', *Wall Street Journal,* 8 September 1999, p. A21; Jeanne Whalen and Bhushan Bahree, 'How Siberian Oil Field Turned Into a Minefield', *Wall Street Journal,* 9 February 2000, p. A21; 'Country Report: Russia', *EIU,* 1st quarter 2000, p. 36.
8. 'Country Report: Iran', *EIU,* June 2000, p. 6.
9. 'Country Report: Iran', *EIU,* 4th quarter 1999, pp. 22–4.
10. International Energy Agency, *Caspian Oil and Gas: The Supply Potential of Central Asia and Transcaucasia* (Paris: OECD Publications, 1998), pp. 114–15.
11. Martha Brill Olcott, 'Democratization and the Growth of Political Participation in Kazakstan', in *Conflict, Cleavage, and Change in Central Asia and the Caucasus,* Karen Dawisha and Bruce Parrott (eds), (Cambridge: Cambridge University Press, 1997), pp. 209–29.
12. John Anderson, *The International Politics of Central Asia* (Manchester: Manchester University Press, 1997), p. 84.
13. Olcott 1997, p. 215.
14. Alexei Agureyev, 'Nazarbayev Proposes Fund for Protecting Russian', *Itar-Tass,* 19 June 2000.
15. 'Kazakhstan's Presidential Campaign Found Grossly Unfair', *Human*

REFERENCES

Rights Watch Online, 5 January 1999 [http://www.hrw.org/hrw/press/1999/jan/kaza0105.htm]

16. Mike Collett-White, 'Kazakh Leader Brushes Off Poll Criticism', *Reuters*, 15 January 1999.
17. 'Country Report: Kazakhstan', *EIU*, 4th quarter 1998, pp. 10–11.
18. Roland Eggleston, 'Kazakhstan: OSCE Report Cites Breaches of Standards during Elections', *RFE/RL Weekday Magazine*, 19 October 1999; Bruce Pannier, 'Kazakhstan: Second Election Round Resembles First', *RFE/RL Weekday Magazine*, 26 October 1999.
19. Bruce Pannier, 'Kazakhstan: Early Elections put Opposition at Disadvantage', *RFE/RL Weekday Magazine*, 8 July 1999.
20. Nurbulat E. Masanov, 'The Role of Clans in Kazakhstan Today', *Jamestown Foundation Prism*, 4, no. 3, February 6, 1998, p. 10.
21. 'Country Report: Kazakhstan', *EIU*, 4th quarter 1998, p. 5; Olcott 1997, p. 217; Alain Giroux, 'Kazakhstan 1997: L'Espoir Renaît avec la Croissance', *Le Courrier des Pays de l'Est*, nos. 428–9, March–April–May 1998, pp. 64–5.
22. 'Country Report: Kazakhstan', *EIU*, April 2000, p. 11.
23. Gregory Gleason and Sergey Sologub, 'Asian Flu and Russian Roulette: Kazakhstan amid the Storms', *Analysis of Current Events*, 10, nos. 9–10, September–October 1998, p. 8.
24. Steve LeVine and John Tagliabue, 'Swiss Freeze Bank Account Linked to Kazakh President', *New York Times*, 16 October 1999, p. A6; Steve LeVine and Bill Powell, 'A President and His Counselor', *Newsweek*, 10 July 2000, pp. 40–1; John Tagliabue, 'Kazakhstan Is Suspected of Oil Bribes in the Millions', *New York Times*, 28 July 2000, p. A5.
25. Anthony Hyman, 'The Feeble Breath of Democracy', *Transitions*, 5, no. 9, September 1998, p. 81.
26. 'If the Worms Turn', *The Economist*, 22–8 July 2000, pp. 41–2; Sergei Duvanov, 'Nazarbayev Granted Lifetime Powers', *IWPR Reporting Central Asia*, no. 9, 30 June 2000.
27. Audrey L. Altstadt, *The Azerbaijani Turks: Power and Identity under Russian Rule* (Stanford, CA: Hoover Institution Press, 1992).
28. Shireen T. Hunter, *The Transcaucasus in Transition: Nation-Building and Conflict* (Washington, DC: Center for Strategic and International Studies, 1994), p. 15.
29. Hunter, p. 75.
30. 'Country Profile Azerbaijan, 1997–98', *EIU*, 15 August 1997, p. 5.
31. The Talysh are an ethnic group living on both sides of the Azerbaijani–Iranian border who speak an Iranian-related language. Estimates as to their numbers vary, but at least 200,000 live in Azerbaijan.
32. Laura Le Cornu, 'Azerbaijan's September Crisis: An Analysis of the

Causes and Implications', *Royal Institute of International Affairs Former Soviet South Briefing Papers*, no. 1, 1995.
33. Michael Ochs, 'Azerbaijan: Oil, Domestic Stability and Geopolitics in the Caucasus', in *The Caucasus and The Caspian Seminar Series, Strengthening Democratic Institutions Project Working Paper*, (Cambridge: MA: John F. Kennedy School of Government, Harvard University, 4 March 1996), pp. 36–46.
34. Zardusht Ali-Zade, 'Independence without Freedom', *War Report*, no. 56, November 1997, p. 32.
35. 'Azerbaijan What Next?', *The Economist*, 11–17 November 2000, p. 63.
36. Ochs, p. 44.
37. *Ibid.*
38. Elmar Gusseinov, 'The Nakhichevan Factor', *IWPR Caucasus Reporting Service*, no. 7, 19 November 1999.
39. Joseph A. Kechichian and Theodore W. Karasik, 'The Crisis in Azerbaijan: How Clans Influence the Politics of an Emerging Republic', *Middle East Policy*, 4, nos 1–2, September 1995, p. 60.
40. Jean Radvanyi (ed.), *De l'U.R.S.S. à la C.E.I.: 12 Etats en Quête d'Identité* (Paris: Langues'O/Ellipses, 1997), p. 117.
41. 'Political Parties of Azerbaijan', *Soros Foundation Central Eurasia Program Online*, consulted on 8 January, 1999. [http://www.soros.org/cen_eurasia/elections/azparties.html]
42. Hunter, p. 69.
43. 'Political Parties of Azerbaijan'
44. 'Why Musavat?', *RFE/RL Caucasus Report*, 11 February 2000.
45. Tom Warner, 'Azerbaijan's Oil Man Steps Out of Line', *Transition*, 2, no. 22, 1 November 1996, p. 59; 'New Political Alignment Emerges in Azerbaijan', *RFE/RL Caucasus Report*, 31 March 2000; Rasul Gouliev, *Path to Democracy* (New York: Liberty Publishing House), 1997.
46. *Ibid.*, pp. 136, and 148.
47. Audrey L. Altstadt, 'Azerbaijan's Struggle toward Democracy', in *Conflict, Cleavage, and Change in Central Asia and the Caucasus*, Karen Dawisha and Bruce Parrott (eds), (Cambridge: Cambridge University Press, 1997), p. 136.
48. 'Notes from along the Way: South Caucasus and Central Asia', *Transitions*, 5, no. 12, December 1998, p. 5.
49. For a biography of Aliyev and an analysis of the system he set up in Soviet Azerbaijan, see John P. Willerton, *Patronage and Politics in the USSR* (Cambridge: Cambridge University Press, 1992), pp. 191–222.
50. Dilip Hiro, 'The Emergence of Multi-Party Politics in the Southern Caucasus: Azerbaijan', *Perspectives on Central Asia*, 2, no. 11, February 1998, p. 4.

51. Jonathan Aves, 'Politics, Parties and Presidents in Transcaucasia', *Caucasian Regional Studies*, 1, no. 1, 1996.
52. 'Country Report: Azerbaijan', *EIU*, 2nd quarter 2000, p. 5.
53. 'Azerbaijan Looks beyond Oil for Developments in 1999', *Reuters*, 15 January 1999.
54. *Caspian Oil and Gas*, p. 159.
55. *Ibid.*, p. 156.
56. *Ibid.*, p. 174.
57. Leila Aliyeva, 'Political Leadership Strategies in Azerbaijan', *Graduate Training and Research Program on the Contemporary Caucasus*, 1, no. 1, Spring 1995, p. 15.
58. Jolyon Naegele, 'Azerbaijan: Censorship Illegal but still Restricting the Press', *RFE/RL Weekday Magazine*, 12 March 1998.
59. Michael Ochs, 'Turkmenistan: The Quest for Stability and Control', in *Conflict, Cleavage, and Change in Central Asia and the Caucasus*, Karen Dawisha and Bruce Parrott (eds), (Cambridge: Cambridge University Press, 1997), pp. 322–3.
60. 'Turkmenistan', *Human Rights Watch Online, World Report 1999*.
61. John Anderson, 'Authoritarian Political Development in Central Asia: The Case of Turkmenistan', *Central Asian Survey*, 14, no. 4, 1995, pp. 512–13.
62. Dilip Hiro, 'Turkmenistan: President in Washington', *Middle East International*, 5 June 1998, p. 15.
63. Ochs, pp. 316–17.
64. Country Report: Turkmenistan', *EIU*, June 2000, p. 20.
65. 'Country Report Turkmenistan', *EIU*, 4th quarter 1998; Stuart Parrott, 'Turkmenistan: First Positive Growth Expected in Six Years Says EBRD', *RFE/RL Weekday Magazine*, 16 April 1997.
66. *Caspian Oil and Gas*, pp. 248–9.
67. *Ibid.*, pp. 250–5.

Chapter 6
1. Bruce D. Porter and Carol R. Saivetz, 'The Once and Future Empire: Russia and the "Near Abroad"', *The Washington Quarterly*, 17, no. 3, Summer 1994, p. 77.
2. Mark Webber, *CIS Integration Trends: Russia and the Former South* (London: Royal Institute of International Affairs, 1997), pp. 8–16; Porter and Saivetz, pp. 76–7.
3. The following articles are representative of Western concerns about Russian activities in the former Soviet South: Paul A. Goble, 'Russia and its Neighbors', *Foreign Policy*, no. 90, Spring 1993; Thomas Goltz, 'Letter From Eurasia: The Hidden Russian Hand', *Foreign Policy*, no.

92, Fall 1993; Stephen Page, 'The Creation of a Sphere of Influence: Russia and Central Asia', *International Journal*, 159, no. 4, Autumn 1994; Stephen Blank, 'Russia's Real Drive to the South', *Orbis*, 39, no. 3, Summer 1995; Rajan Menon, 'In the Shadow of the Bear: Security in Post-Soviet Central Asia', *International Security*, 20, no. 1, Summer 1995; Fred Halliday, 'The Empires Strike Back? Russia, Iran and the New Republics', *The World Today*, 51, no. 11, November 1995; David E. Mark, 'Eurasia Letter: Russia and the New Transcaucasus', *Foreign Policy*, no. 105, Winter 1996–97.
4. Pavel Baev, *Russia's Policies in the Caucasus* (London: Royal Institute of International Affairs, 1997), p. 30; Irina Zviagelskaia, *The Russian Policy Debate on Central Asia* (London: Royal Institute of International Affairs, 1995), pp. 26–8.
5. Igor Khripunov and Mary M. Matthews, 'Russia's Oil and Gas Interest Group and its Foreign Policy Agenda', *Problems of Post-Communism*, 43, no. 3, May–June 1996, pp. 38–9; Vicken Cheterian, 'Sea or Lake, A Major Issue for Russia', *CEMOTI*, no. 23, January–June 1997, pp. 105–9; V. V. Razuvaev, 'The Oil Companies in Russia Politics', *Russian Politics and Law*, 34, no. 2, March–April 1996, p. 72.
6. Yuri Fedorov, 'Russia's Policies toward Caspian Region Oil: Neo-Imperial or Pragmatic?' *Perspectives on Central Asia*, 1, no. 7, October 1996, pp. 1–4.
7. 'Country Report: Kazakhstan', *EIU*, 2nd quarter 1999, p. 29.
8. Charles Clover, Andrew Jack, and David Stern, 'Putin Calls for Bigger Russian Oil in Caspian', *Financial Times*, 22 April 2000, p. 6; Andrei Baturin, 'Putin Appoints Kalyuzhny His Envoy to Russia's Caspian Region', *Itar-Tass*, 25 May 2000; Catherine Belton, 'Gazprom, Oil Giants Unite in Caspian', *Moscow Times*, 26 May 2000; Charles Clover 'Russian Trio Join Forces to Exploit Caspian Oil', *Financial Times* 26 July 2000, p. 3.
9. For an excellent analysis of Iranian policy in the Caucasus and Central Asia, see Edmund Herzig, *Iran and the Former Soviet South* (London: Royal Institute of International Affairs, 1995).
10. For some of these points, see Mohammad-Reza Djalali, 'Mer Caspienne: Perspectives Iraniennes', *CEMOTI*, no. 23, January–June 1997, pp. 133–6.
11. Herzig, pp. 8–10.
12. Djalali, pp. 127–30.
13. Adam Tarock, 'Iran's Policy in Central Asia', *Central Asia Survey*, 16, no. 2, June 1997, p. 192.
14. Halliday, p. 221; Herzig, p. 8.
15. Roland Dannreuther, 'Russia, Central Asia and the Persian Gulf',

REFERENCES

Survival, 35, no. 4, Winter 1993-94, pp. 106-7; Herzig, pp. 9-10; Stephen Blank, 'Russia's Return to Mideast Diplomacy', *Orbis*, 40, no. 4, Fall 1996, pp. 530-1.

16. Shireen Hunter, *Central Asia since Independence* (Washington, D.C.: The Center for Strategic and International Studies, 1996), p. 132.
17. Tarock, pp. 190-1; Hunter 1996, pp. 132-3; Herzig, p. 31.
18. Alexandre Toumarkine, 'Ambitions Nationales et Désenclavement Régional: Les Politiques Turque et Iranienne en Transcaucasie', in *Arménie-Azerbaïjan-Géorgie: L'An V des Indépendances; La Russie: 1995-1996. International Ex-URSS Edition 1996*, p. 58.
19. Blank 1996, p. 530; Hunter 1996, p. 134.
20. Darius Bazargan, 'Iran: From Russia with Love', *The Middle East*, no. 266, April 1997, p. 9.
21. Tarock, p. 196; Hanna Yousif Freij, 'State Interests vs. the Umma: Iranian Policy in Central Asia', *Middle East Journal*, 50, no. 1, Winter 1996, pp. 77-8.
22. Herzig, p. 17.
23. Dominique Gallois, 'La Bataille pour le Partage du Pétrole de la Caspienne est Ouverte', and Mouna Naïm, 'L'Iran Insiste sur la Nécessité d'un Consensus entre Riverains', *Le Monde*, 11 July 1998, p. 2.
24. Michael Lelyveld, 'Azerbaijan: Officials Reach Agreement with Iran over Caspian', *RFE/RL Weekday Magazine*, 1 August 2000.
25. Michael Lelyveld, 'Russia: Iran Maintains Strained Relations', *RFE/RL Weekday Magazine*, 3 December 1999.
26. Blank 1996, p. 530.
27. Herzig, p. 20.
28. Djalali, p. 135.
29. Vicken Cheterian, 'Sous la Menace de la Crise Afghane: Les Ambitions Contrariées de l'Ouzbékistan', *Le Monde Diplomatique*, 44, no. 520, July 1997a, p. 21.
30. Hunter 1996, p. 133; 'Iran and Kazakhstan', *Gulf States Newsletter*, 22, no. 566, 28 July 1997, p. 10.
31. 'Nazarbayev Gives Conflicting Signals over Iran Pipeline', *RFE/RL Newsline*, 21 November 1997.
32. Herzig, pp. 32-45; Tarock, p. 195.
33. 'Spying Incident may Affect Kazakh-Iranian Economic Cooperation', *Labyrinth: Central Asia Quarterly*, 5, no. 1, 1998, p. 22.
34. 'New Agreements with Central Asian States', *RFE/RL Iran Report Online*, 1 November 1999; 'Kazakhstan's President Wraps up Iran Visit', *RFE/RL Newsline*, 11 October 1999.
35. David Stern, 'Pipeline Contenders Eye Kazakh Oil Prospect', *Financial Times*, 9 May 2000, p. 15.

36. 'Kazakh FM Hails Iran's Stance on Caspian Status', *Interfax*, 6 November 1999; Kianouche Dorranie, 'Geste de l'Iran envers ses Voisins Riverains de la Caspienne', *AFP*, 10 June 2000.
37. Dilip Hiro, 'Turkmenistan and Iran: US Advice Ignored', *Middle East International*, no. 551, May 30, 1997, pp. 19–20.
38. Witold Raczka, 'La Mer Caspienne et le Turkmenistan', *CEMOTI*, no. 23, January–June 1997, pp. 199–202.
39. 'Turkmenistan to Discuss Caspian Status Only If Iran is Included', *RFE/RL Turkmen Report*, 24 July 2000.
40. 'New Agreements with Central Asian States', *RFE/RL Iran Report*, 1 November 1999.
41. Michael Lelyveld, 'Iran: Dispute Over Gas Endangers Turkmenistan's Plans', *RFE/RL Weekday Magazine*, 12 May 2000; Michael Lelyveld, 'Turkmenistan: Ashgabat Backs Tehran in Caspian Dispute', *RFE/RL Weekday Magazine*, 29 November 2000.
42. 'Iran Seeks Cooperation with other Gas Exporters', *IRNA*, 31 May 2000.
43. Herzig, p. 26.
44. Freij, pp. 72–7.
45. Vaner, pp. 161–2.
46. Daniel Southerland, 'Azerbaijan Picks Exxon Over Iran for Oil Deal', *Washington Post*, 11 April 1995, p. A5.
47. Michael Lelyveld, 'Azerbaijan; Officials Reach Agreement with Iran Over Caspian', *RFE/RL Weekday Magazine*, 1 August 2000.
48. 'Ethnic Azeris Say 17 Injured in Iran Demonstrations', *Reuters*, 7 January 2000.
49. K. P. Foley, 'Azerbaijan: Minister Says Iran on Verge of Big Changes', *RFE/RL Weekday Magazine*, 2 May 2000.
50. Michael Lelyveld, 'Azerbaijan: Dispute With Tehran Surfaces', *RFE/RL Weekday Magazine*, 2 November 2000; 'Iran Closes Consulate in Azerbaijan After Attack', *AFP*, 10 November 2000.
51. Eugene B. Rumer, 'Russia and Central Asia after the Soviet Collapse', in *After Empire: The Emerging Geopolitics of Central Asia*, ed. Jed C. Snyder (Washington, DC: National Defense University Press, 1995), pp. 58–9; Webber, p. 18.
52. Alexandra Viktorovna Dokuchayeva et al., 'Protecting Russia's Interests in Kazakhstan', *The Current Digest of the Post-Soviet Press*, 49, no. 27, 6 August 1997, p. 2.
53. Dannreuther, pp. 102–3; Martha Brill Olcott, 'The Asian Interior: The Myth of "Tsentral'naia Aziia"', *Orbis*, 38, no. 4, Fall 1994b, pp. 558–61; Martha Brill Olcott, "Sovereignty and the Near Abroad", *Orbis*, 39, no. 3, Summer 1995, 359–61; Paul Kubicek, 'Regionalism,

Nationalism and Realpolitik in Central Asia', *Europe–Asia Studies*, 49, no. 4, June 1997, pp. 648–9; Olivier Roy, 'Les Evolutions de l'Asie Centrale', *Hérodote*, no. 84, Spring 1997, pp. 52–3.

54. Robert Lucca, 'Russia–Kazakh Relations Remain Rocky Despite Strategic Alliance', *Jane's Intelligence Review*, 12, no. 9, September 2000, pp. 25–8.
55. Page, p. 808; Mehdi Mozaffari, 'CIS' Southern Belt: Regional Cooperation and Integration', in *Security Politics in the Commonwealth of Independent States: The Southern Belt*, ed. Mehdi Mozaffari (London: Macmillan Press, 1997a), p. 180.
56. Webber, pp. 29–31 and 55; Hunter 1996, pp. 114–15; Olcott 1995, p. 360; Daniel Balland, 'Diviser l'Indivisible: Les Frontières Introuvables des Etats Centrasiatiques', *Hérodote*, no. 84, Spring 1997, p. 86.
57. 'Exit CIS Customs Union, Enter Eurasian Economic Community?' *Jamestown Foundation Monitor*, 10 October 2000; 'Political Implications of the Eurasian Economic Union Treaty', *Jamestown Foundation Monitor*, 11 October 2000; 'Eurasian Economic Community Supercedes Customs Union', *RFE/RL Kazakh Report*, 13 October 2000.
58. Vyacheslav Gizzatov, 'The Legal Status of the Caspian Sea', *Labyrinth: Central Asia Quarterly*, 2, no. 3, Summer 1995, pp. 33–6; Giroux 1997, pp. 173–7; Robert Corzine, 'China a Counter-Weight to Russia's Influence: Proposed Oil Pipelines "Go to the Heart of the Issue of Territorial Integrity"', *Financial Times*, 23 July 1997, Survey Kazakhstan, p. VI; 'Country Report: Kazakhstan', *EIU*, 1st quarter 1997, pp. 36–7/2nd quarter 1997, p. 35.
59. 'Kazakhstan Concerned about Russia's Caspian Tender', *RFE/RL Newsline*, 28 August 1997.
60. 'Iranian Official Warns of Oil Threat to Caspian Sturgeon', *SWB*, SUW/0510 WF/3, 31 October 1997.
61. Cheterian 1997, p. 111; Hunter 1996, p. 118; Giroux 1997, pp. 175–7; Forsythe, pp. 38–42; Valera Belousova and Isabel Gorst, 'Pipeline Problems Block Oil Sector Development', *Petroleum Economist*, 63, no. 4, April 1996, pp. 10–11.
62. Danielle Robinson, 'Chevron: Tengiz is Coming Good', *Petroleum Economist*, 64, no. 6, June 1997, p. 39.
63. 'Country Report: Kazakhstan', *EIU*, 4th quarter 1997, p. 36.
64. 'Country Report: Kazakhstan', *EIU*, 2nd quarter 1999, p. 29. and April 2000, p. 28; 'Thorny Problems in Kazakh–Russian Economic Relations', *The Jamestown Foundation Monitor*, 14 June 1999; 'Russia Increases Kazakh Oil Quota', *Interfax*, 19 April 2000; 'Nazarbayev Urges Russia, China to Open Routes for Kashagan Oil', *SWB*, SU/D 3887/G, 8 July 2000.

65. 'Russian Community in Kazakhstan Appeals on Behalf of "Separatist"...', *RFE/RL Newsline*, 14 January 2000; Liz Fuller, 'Trial of "Separatists" Highlights Plight of Kazakhstan's Russians', *RFE/RL Newsline Endnote*, 15 May 2000; Bruce Pannier, 'Kazakhstan: Convictions of Russian "Separatists" Upset Relations', *RFE/RL Weekday Magazine*, 15 June 2000.
66. Slujan Ismailova, 'Russian Kazakhs Push for Autonomy', *IWPR Research on Central Asia*, no. 11, 14 July 2000; 'Will Moscow Demand Territorial Autonomy for Russians in Kazakhstan?', *RFE/RL Newsline*, 8 June 2000.
67. Merhat Sharipzhan, 'Kazakhstan: Chechens Receive no Welcome', *RFE/RL Weekday Magazine*, 13 December 1999.
68. Mohiaddin Mesbahi, 'Russia and the Geopolitics of the Muslim South', in *Central Asia and the Caucasus after the Soviet Union: Domestic and International Dynamics*, ed. Mohiaddin Mesbahi (Gainesville, FL: University Press of Florida, 1994a), p. 291.
69. R. Freitag-Wirminghaus, 'Turkmenistan's Place in Central Asia and the World', in *Security Politics in the Commonwealth of Independent States*, pp. 74–6 and 84n; Raczka, p. 193.
70. The details of the treaty are given in Mesbahi 1994a, pp. 289–90, and Susan Clark, 'The Central Asian States: Defining Security Priorities and Developing Military Forces', in *Central Asia and the World* ed. Michael Mandelbaum (New York: Council on Foreign Relations Press, 1994), pp. 192–195.
71. Freitag-Wirminghaus, p. 73.
72. Alvin Z. Rubinstein, 'The Asian Interior: The Geopolitical Pull on Russia', *Orbis*, 38, no. 4, Fall 1994, p. 574.
73. Lena Jonson, *Russia and Central Asia: A New Web of Relations* (London: Royal Institute of International Affairs, 1998), p. 35; 'Turkmenistan Terminates Border Protection Treaty with Russia', *Jamestown Foundation Monitor*, 26 May 1999.
74. Freitag-Wirminghaus, p. 73; 'Gazprom Eyes Turkmen Export Markets after Joint Venture is Closed', *SWB*, SUW/0498 WF/1, 8 August 1997; 'Russian, Turkmen Presidents Agree on Caspian Sea Issues', *SWB*, SU/2993 B/7, 9 August 1997; 'Country Report: Kyrgyz Republic, Tajikistan, Turkmenistan', *EIU*, 4th quarter 1997, pp. 49–50.
75. 'Country Report: Turkmenistan', *EIU*, 1st quarter 2000, p. 19. There was a brief resumption of exports to Ukraine in early 1999, soon to be halted due to Ukraine's inability to pay for the supplies.
76. Hugh Pope, 'Moscow Lures back Central Asia', *Wall Street Journal*, 22 May 2000, p. A29; James M. Dorsey, 'Turkmenistan Deal May Kill

REFERENCES

Pipeline Backed by the US', *Wall Street Journal*, 14 November 2000, p. A22.
77. 'Russia, Turkmenistan Fail to Reach Gas-Export Agreement', *SWB*, SU/2993 B/7, 9 August 1997.
78. 'Caspian Sea Status: Moscow Reaches Back to Soviet Treaties', *Jamestown Foundation Monitor*, 23 September 1999.
79. 'Caspian Waters Muddied by New Diplomatic Moves', *Labyrinth: Central Asian Quarterly*, 4, no. 2, Spring 1997, pp. 19–20; 'Country Report: Kyrgyz Republic, Tajikistan, Turkmenistan', *EIU*, 1st quarter 1997, p. 45; 2nd quarter 1997, pp. 39–40/4th quarter 1997, pp. 34–5.
80. 'Russian President's Envoy Suggests Joint Exploitation of Disputed Caspian Field', *SWB*, SU/D3895/F, 18 July 2000; 'Talks with Turkmen Leader on Caspian Sea Constructive But Difficult', *Interfax*, 19 July 2000.
81. Baev, pp. 16–18; Shireen T. Hunter, *The Transcaucasus in Transition: Nation-Building and Conflict* (Washington, DC: Center for Strategic and International Studies, 1994), pp. 66–88.
82. 'Aliyev against One Country Dominating CIS', *SWB*, SU/3058 F/1, 24 October 1994.
83. Baev, p. 20.
84. Sanjian, p. 17; Blank 1995, pp. 369–72; Forsythe, p. 15; Baev, p. 32.
85. Thomas Goltz, 'Oil and Civil Society Don't Mix', *War Report*, no. 45, September 1996, p. 42; Baev, p. 33; Forsythe, p. 15; Barylski, pp. 223–4; Roberts, p. 16. According to Baev and Roberts, Aliyev organized the coup himself to get rid of opponents.
86. Sanjian, p. 20; 'Country Report: Azerbaijan', *EIU*, 3rd quarter 1997, p. 12.
87. 'Guluzade Proposes Western Military Base in Azerbaijan', *Jamestown Foundation Monitor*, 19 January 1999.
88. 'Country Report: Azerbaijan', *EIU*, 2nd quarter 2000, p. 24; Michael Lelyveld, 'Azerbaijan: Russians Exert New Pressure', *RFE/RL Weekday Magazine*, 12 July 2000; 'Russia Demands Azerbaijan Pay 29 Mln Dollar Fine Over Oil Exports', *AFP*, 12 July 2000.
89. Martha Brill Olcott, 'Kazakhstan', in *Central Asia and the Caucasus after the Soviet Union*, p. 127.
90. *Ibid.*, p. 122.
91. On a comparison between Azerbaijan and Kazakhstan, see Aleksandr Akimov, 'Oil and Gas in the Caspian Sea Region: An Overview of Cooperation and Conflict', *Perspectives on Central Asia*, 1, no. 6, June 1996, p. 4; Richard R. Dion, 'How Oil and Gas Investment Prospects Compare for Azerbaijan, Kazakhstan', *Oil and Gas Journal*, 95, no. 30, 28 July 1997, pp. 25–31.

92. 'Kazakh–Azerbaijani Memorandum', *Oil and Gas Journal*, 95, no. 24, 16 June 1997, pp. 35–6; 'Country Report: Kazakhstan', *EIU*, 3rd quarter 1997, p. 34.
93. 'Baku Port Expanding to Handle Central Asia Oil', *SWB*, SUW/0510 WF/3, 31 October 1997.
94. Giroux 1997, pp. 176–7; 'Country Report: Kazakhstan', *EIU*, 1st quarter 1997, p. 36.
95. 'Kazakhstan, Azerbaijan Want Diversity of Oil Pipelines', *Interfax*, 22 October 1999.
96. Mike Collett-White, 'Kazakh Oil Supplies for Azeri Pipeline Unclear – President', *Reuters*, 23 November 1999.
97. 'Niyazov Seeks Export Options for Oil and Gas', *Labyrinth: Central Asia Quarterly*, 4, no. 2, Winter 1997, p. 21.
98. Andrei G. Nedvetsky, 'Turkmenistan', in *Central Asia and the Caucasus after the Soviet Union*, p. 199.
99. Constantin Yablonsky, 'L'Asie Centrale et ses Voisins: Une Intégration à Plusieurs Variables', *Le Courrier des Pays de l'Est*, no. 406, January–February 1996, pp. 40–1; Alain Giroux, 'Les Etats d'Asie Centrale face à l'Indépendance: Ouzbékistan, République Kirghize, Tadjikistan, Turkménistan', *Le Courrier des Pays de l'Est*, no. 388, April 1994, p. 30.
100. 'Country Report: Turkmenistan', *EIU*, 4th quarter 1999, p. 11.
101. 'Country Report: Kazakhstan', *EIU*, 1st quarter 1997, pp. 36–7; 2nd quarter 1997, p. 35; 'Country Report: Kyrgyz Republic, Tajikistan, Turkmenistan', *EIU*, 1st quarter 1997, p. 45; 2nd quarter 1997, pp. 39–40; 'Russian–Turkmen Communique Hails "Strategic Partnership"', *SWB*, SU/2993 B/6, 9 August 1997.
103. Nedvetsky, p. 202; Raczka, p. 197.
104. 'Country Profile: Georgia, Armenia, Azerbaijan', *EIU*, 1996–97, p. 56; 'Azerbaijan: Imports Rise as West Foregoes Gas Exploration', *Petroleum Economist*, 64, no. 5, May 1997, p. 119; 'Gas Famine to Last Another Five Years', *SWB*, SUW/0494 WD/1, 11 July 1997.
105. Robert Corzine, 'Turkmenistan Lays Claim to Disputed Caspian Oil', *Financial Times*, 22 January 1997, p. 4.
106. Sanjian, p. 35.
107. 'Caspian Waters Muddied by New Diplomatic Moves', p. 19; 'Turkmenistan Starts New Caspian Wrangle', *Labyrinth: Central Asian quarterly*, 4, no. 1, 1997, pp. 35–6; 'Country Report: Kyrgyz Republic, Tajikistan, Turkmenistan', *EIU*, 2nd quarter 1997, pp. 39–41.
108. Uibopuu, p. 122; Sonni Efron, 'Western Oil Firms Sign Deal for Drilling in Caspian Sea', *Los Angeles Times*, 21 September 1994, p. D2; Roberts, pp. 52–3; Raczka, p. 202.

109. 'Caspian Waters Muddied by New Diplomatic Moves', p. 19.
110. Sanjian, p. 19.
111. Forsythe, p. 31.
112. 'Country Report: Kyrgyz Republic, Tajikistan, Turkmenistan', *EIU*, 4th quarter 1997, pp. 39–40; 'Turkmenistan Disputes Russian and Azeri Rights to Caspian Oilfield', *SWB*, SUW/0494 WF/3, 11 July 1997; 'Turkmen–Azeri Oilfield Dispute Remains Unresolved', *SWB*, SUW/0498 WF/2, 8 August 1997; Sanjian, pp. 51–3.
113. 'Tukmenistan Now Firmly on the Side of International Law in Caspian Sea', *Jamestown Foundation Monitor*, 6 February 1998.
114. Marat Gurt, 'Turkmen Leader Sees Trans-Caspian Gas Link Delayed', *Reuters*, 17 May 2000; Michael Lelyveld, 'Turkmenistan: Ties to West May be Worsening', *RFE/RL Weekday Magazine*, 2 May 2000.

Chapter 7

1. Anthony Hyman, 'Afghanistan and Central Asia', in *Security Politics in the Commonwealth of Independent States*, pp. 122–32.
2. Olivier Roy, 'Rivalités Ethniques et Religieuses, Jeu des Puissances en Afghanistan: Avec les Talibans, la Charia plus le Gazoduc', *Le Monde Diplomatique*, 43, no. 512, November 1996, pp. 6–7.
3. 'Country Report: Kyrgyz Republic, Tajikistan, Turkmenistan', *EIU*, 2nd quarter 1997, p. 48.
4. 'Afghan Taliban Unhappy about Turkmen Gas Pipeline Project', *SWB*, SU/3063 G/3, 30 October 1997.
5. *Reuters*, 4 January 1998.
6. Laurent Zecchini, 'Les Féministes Américaines Contrarient un Projet Pétrolier avec les Talibans', *Le Monde*, 18–19 January 1998, p. 3.
7. 'L'Américain Unocal Suspend son Projet de Gazoduc', *Le Monde*, 26 August 1998, p. 3.
8. 'Afghan Official Discusses Resumption of Peace Talks in Turkmenistan ... and Pipeline Project', *RFE/RL Newsline*, 10 May 1999.
9. 'Musharraf Discusses Pipeline with Niyazov', *RFE/RL Turkmen Report*, 15 May 2000.
10. 'Russia: Moscow May Target Training Camps in Afghanistan', *RFE/RL Weekday Magazine*, 22 May 2000.
11. Hunter 1996, pp. 91–101. In recent months links between the Tajiks and Uzbek governments have somewhat deteriorated. See Cheterian 1997a, p. 21.
12. Ironically, not only was Tamerlane not an ethnic Uzbek, but his descendants were expelled from Central Asia by the Uzbeks.
13. Kubicek, p. 646; Martha Brill Olcott, 'Ceremony and Substance: The

Illusion of Unity in Central Asia', in *Central Asia and the World*, 1994, p. 41.
14. Kubicek, p. 638.
15. On Central Asian regional cooperation and integration attempts, see Olcott, 1994b, pp. 567–83; Hunter 1996, pp. 101–6; Mozaffari 1997a, pp. 151–88; Kubicek, pp. 637–55.
16. 'Country Report: Kazakhstan', *EIU*, 3rd quarter 1997, p. 13.
17. Ahmed Rashid, 'A New "Great Game" – for Fuel', *World Press Review*, 44, no. 6, June 1997, p. 33.
18. Hugh Pope, 'Moscow Lures back Central Asia', *Wall Street Journal*, 22 May 2000, p. A29.
19. 'Karimov Lashes Out at Moscow's Policy in Central Asia', *Jamestown Foundation Monitor*, 26 September 2000; Vladimir Socor, 'East of the Oder: Another Russian Christmas in Afghanistan?', *Wall Street Journal Europe*, 24 November 2000, p. 7.
20. 'Country Report: Kazakhstan', *EIU*, 1st quarter 2000, pp. 39–40; Andrew Chebotarev, 'Kazakstan Courts Moscow', *IWPR Reporting Central Asia*, no. 28, 3 November 2000.
21. 'Le Grand Jeu Iranien en Asie Centrale', *Nouvelles d'Arménie Magazine*, no. 7, October 2000, p. 8.
22. Suha Bolukbasi, 'Ankara's Baku-Centered Transcaucasia Policy: Has it Failed?', *Middle East Journal*, 51, no. 1, Winter 1997, pp. 84–5.
23. For an analysis of Armenian foreign policy, see Rouben Paul Adalian, 'Armenia's Foreign Policy: Defining Priorities and Coping with Conflict', in *The Making of Foreign Policy in Russia and the New States of Eurasia*, Adeed Dawisha and Karen Dawisha (eds), (Armonk, NY: M. E. Sharpe, 1995), pp. 309–39.
24. David B. Ottaway and Dan Morgan, 'Ex-Top Aides Seek Caspian Gusher', *Washington Post*, 6 July 1997, p. A1.
25. 'A Billion Dollar Mistake', *Wall Street Journal*, 11 April 1997, p. A14; Sanjian, pp. 43–4.
26. Caspar Weinberger and Peter Schweizer, 'Russia's Oil Grab', *New York Times*, 9 May 1997, p. A23; S. Rob Sobhani, 'The "Great Game" in Play in Azerbaijan', *Washington Times*, 20 February 1997.
27. The construction of the gas pipeline was announced in May 1995. See Beniamine Kéchichian, 'Energie: L'Arménie Sort de l'Impasse', *Nouvelles d'Arménie Magazine*, no. 4, June 1995, p. 14; and 'Iran and Armenia Agree on Construction of Gas Pipeline', *Deutsche Presse-Agentur*, 3 February 1997, by way of ANN/Groong.
28. Adalian, pp. 315–16.
29. Alexei Vassiliev, 'Turkey and Iran in Transcaucasia and Central Asia', in *From the Gulf to Central Asia: Players in the New Great Game*, ed. Anoush-

iravan Ehteshami (Exeter: University of Exeter Press, 1994), pp. 140-2.
30. Robin Bhatty and Rachel Bronson, 'NATO's Mixed Signals in the Caucasus and Central Asia, *Survival*, 42, no. 3, Autumn 2000, pp. 134-5.
31. Bolukbasi, p. 85; Toumarkine, pp. 58, 62-3; Cheterian, p. 22; Stéphane Yerasimos, 'Transcaucasie: Le Retour de la Russie', *Hérodote*, no. 81, April-June 1996a, p. 206.
32. Matthew Der Manuelian and Nerses Mkrtchian, 'Managing the Turkish Threat', *War Report*, no. 52, June-July 1997, pp. 44-5.
33. 'La Carotte', *Nouvelles d'Arménie Magazine*, July 1995, p. 20; Roberts, p. 18; Yerasimos, 1996a, p. 120; Sanjian, p. 32.
34. 'Oil Official Rules out Export Route via Armenia', *SWB*, SU/3098 F/3, 10 December 1997.
35. 'Statement by the Ministry of Foreign Affairs of the Republic of Armenia', *Armenpress*, 1 March 1997; 'Ministry Accuses Azerbaijan of Breaching CFE Treaty', *SWB*, SU/2988 F/2, 4 August 1997; Svante E. Cornell, 'The Unruly Caucasus', *Current History*, 96, no. 612, October 1997a, p. 343.
36. 'Operation Pipeline', *Index on Censorship*, 26, no. 4, July-August 1997, pp. 76-7.
37. 'Country Report: Azerbaijan', *EIU*, 3rd quarter 1997, p. 14.
38. Richard R. Dion, 'Turkmenistan Emerging as Key Player in Central Asian FSU', *Oil and Gas Journal*, 95, no. 30, 28 July 1997, p. 26; Gordon Feller, 'Central Asia's Growing Links Improve Economy', *Washington Report on the Middle East*, 16, no. 1, June-July 1997, p. 47; Raczka, pp. 191-2.
39. Personal meeting of one of the authors with Ambassador Carey Cavanaugh, 31 July 2000.
40. Gareth M. Winrow, *Turkey in Post-Soviet Central Asia* (London: Royal Institute of International Affairs, 1995); Bolukbasi, pp. 80-94.
41. Hélène Carrère d'Encausse, *Islam and the Russian Empire: Reform and Revolution in Central Asia* (London: I. B. Tauris, 1988), p. 66. For a description of the role of Turkey in Central Asia and the Caucasus since independence, in addition to Winrow and Bolukbasi, see Anoushiravan Ehteshami and Emma C. Murphy, 'The Non-Arab Middle East States and the Caucasian/Central Asian Republics: Turkey', *International Relations*, 11, no. 6, December 1993: 513-31; Patricia M. Carley, 'Turkey and Central Asia: Reality Comes Calling', in *Regional Power Rivalries in the New Eurasia: Russia, Turkey, and Iran*, Alvin Z. Rubinstein and Oles M. Smolansky (eds), (Armonk, NY: M. E. Sharpe, 1995), pp. 169-97; Hunter 1994, pp. 161-70; Hunter 1996,

pp. 136–9; Kemal H. Karpat, 'Turkish Foreign Policy: Some Introductory Remarks', in *Turkish Foreign Policy: Recent Developments*, ed. Kemal H. Karpat (Madison: University of Wisconsin Press, 1996a), pp. 5–10; Kemal H. Karpat, 'The Foreign Policy of the Central Asian States, Turkey, and Iran', in *Turkish Foreign Policy*, pp. 101–18; Daniel Pipes, 'The Event of Our Era: Former Soviet Muslim Republics Change the Middle East', in *Central Asia and the World*, pp. 47–93; Toumarkine, pp. 55–65; Vassiliev, pp. 129–45.
42. Anthony Hyman, 'Turkey: Eastern Approaches', *The Middle East*, no. 242, February 1995, pp. 32–4; Nur Dolay, 'Comment les Hommes d'Affaires Turcs ont Conquis l'Asie Centrale', *Les Cahiers de l'Orient*, no. 42, Spring 1996, pp. 71–84.
43. Karpat, 1996a, p. 8.
44. Yusuf Kanli, 'Aliev Visit Highlights Ankara Losing a Key Ally', *Turkish Daily News*, 8 May 1997.
45. Ehteshami and Murphy 1993, p. 526.
46. A recent report indicated BP involvement in Elchibey's overthrow. See details in chapter 10.
47. Bolukbasi, pp. 88–9; Mehmet Öğütçü, 'Eurasian Energy Prospects and Politics: Need for a Longer-Term Western Strategy', *Futures*, 27, no. 1, January–February 1995, p. 55.
48. John Barham, 'Turkey Presses Case for Pipeline', *Financial Times*, 5 September 1997, p. 1; 'Blood: Thicker than Water, about as Thick as Oil', *Briefing*, no. 1159, 15 September 1997, pp. 12–13; Leyla Boulton and Robert Corzine, 'Turkey Set to Boycott BP and Amoco over Pipeline Opposition', *Financial Times*, 20 November 1998, p. 26; 'Turks Launch Petroleum Boycott; Government Refiner Ordered to Limit Purchases from BP, Amoco', *Houston Chronicle*, 21 November 1998, p. B2.
49. Saadat Oruc, 'Turkey, Israel to Enhance Strategic Ties with Georgia and Azerbaijan', *Turkish Daily News*, 16 March 1998.
50. Robert Olson, 'The Kurdish Question and Chechnya: Turkish and Russian Foreign Policies since the Gulf War', *Middle East Policy*, 4, no. 3, March 1996, pp. 106–18; David Nissman, 'Kurds, Russians, and the Pipeline', *Eurasian Studies*, 2, no. 1, Spring 1995, pp. 30–5.
51. Amberin Zaman, 'Turkey: Historic Rivals Find some Common Grounds', *The Middle East*, no. 249, October 1995, pp. 14–15; Cheterian 1997b, p. 22.
52. 'Turquie/Russie', *Le Monde*, 17 December 1997, p. 3.
53. Saadet Oruc, 'Debate on Turkmen Gas Intensifies, Criticisms against ANAP Continue', *Turkish Daily News*, 14 October 1999; Bruce Pannier, 'Turkmenistan: Gas Industry Seeks Export Routes', *RFE/RL Weekday Magazine*, 15 October 1999.

54. Sanjian, pp. 28-9; David Gamsemelidze, 'Back on the Great Silk Road', *War Report*, no. 50, April 1997, p. 37.
55. Hunter 1994, pp. 119-35.
56. For details of Russian interference in Georgia, see Goltz 1993; Goble 1993; Mark; Michael P. Croissant, 'Oil and Russian Imperialism in the Transcaucasus', *Eurasian Studies*, 3, no. 1, Spring 1996, pp. 16-26.
57. George Tarkhan-Mouravi, 'The Road from Moscow', *War Report*, no. 51, May 1997, p. 15; 'GUAM Alliance Aimed at Restraining Russia's "Urge towards Unification"', *SWB*, SU/3090 F/5, 1 December 1997; Elizabeth Fuller, 'Introducing the Other GUAM', *RFE/RL Newsline*, 1, no. 169, 1 December 1997.
58. 'Uzbekistan Joins GUAM', *RFE/RL Newsline*, 26 April 1999.
59. Lawrence Sheets, 'Ukraine, Georgia and Azerbaijan Pledge Closer Ties', *Reuters*, 22 January 1999; 'Tripartite Force Planned for Pipeline Protection', *Jamestown Foundation Monitor*, 19 March 1999; 'Rump GUUAM Actively Considers Joint Battalion', *Jamestown Foundation Monitor*, 22 March 2000.
60. 'Turkish Chief of Staff in Baku and Tbilisi', *RFE/RL Newsline*, 16 April 1998.
61. Toumarkine, p. 56.
62. 'Cracks Emerge in Georgian-Turkish Partnership', *RFE/RL Caucasus Report*, 14 April 1998.
63. Leonid Gankin and Gennady Sysoyev, 'Aliyev and Shevardnadze Try to Trade Moscow for Washington', *The Current Digest of the Post-Soviet Press*, 49, no. 31, 3 September 1997, pp. 27-8.
64. 'President Shevardnadze Says Russia's Treatment of Georgia Unjust', *SWB*, SU/3056 F/2, 22 October 1997.
65. 'President Shevardnadze Attacks Russian PM for Declaring End to Abkhaz Blockade', *SWB*, SU/3080 F/1, 19 November 1997.
66. 'Russia Agrees to Begin Removal of Troops and Equipment', *Jamestown Foundation Monitor*, 2 May 2000.

Chapter 8
1. 'Country Report: Kazakhstan', *EIU*, 3rd quarter 1997, p. 33; 4th quarter 1997, p. 37; 'News in Brief', *Petroleum Economist*, 64, no. 7, July 1997, p. 46; no. 8, August 1997, p. 33; no. 9, September 1997, p. 123; 'China to Build Pipeline from Kazakhstan', *SWB*, SUW/0490 WE/1, 13 June, 1997; 'China Wins Oil Deposit Tender', *SWB*, SUW/0498 WE/1, 8 August 1997; Anthony Davis, 'The Big Oil Shock: How China Beat the West in Central Asia and Helped Secure its Future', *Asiaweek*, 9 October 1997.

2. Michael Lelyveld, 'Iran: Energy Ties to China Puzzling', *RFE/RL Weekday Magazine*, 20 September 1999; Michael Lelyveld, 'Iran: Oil Deal with China May Have Hit a Snag', *RFE/RL Weekday Magazine*, 22 June 2000.
3. 'Export of Kazakh Oil through China Can Grow', *Labyrinth: Central Asia Quarterly*, 5, no. 1, 1998, p. 33.
4. Ho See Lin, 'China Approves Construction of Its Biggest Natural Gas Pipeline', *Financial Times*, 1 March 2000, p. 6.
5. On the situation in Xinjiang, see Elisabeth Allès, 'Stratégies Chinoises en Asie Centrale et Nationalisme Minoritaire au Xinjiang', *Hérodote*, no. 84, Spring 1997, pp. 201–16; Claude Collin-Delavaud, 'Le Xinjiang', *Hérodote*, no. 84, Spring 1997, pp. 177–200; Michael Dillon, 'Central Asia: The View from Beijing, Urumqi and Kashghar', in *Security Politics in the Commonwealth of Independent States*, pp. 133–48; Felix K. Chang, 'China's Central Asian Power and Problems', *Orbis*, 41, no. 3, Summer 1997, pp. 401–25; Vincent Fourniau, 'Un Conflit Latent en Asie Centrale: Pékin face au Mouvement National Ouïgour', *Le Monde Diplomatique*, 44, no. 522, September 1997, pp. 10–11.
6. Ross H. Munro, 'The Asian Interior: China's Waxing Spheres of Influence', *Orbis*, 38, no. 4, Fall 1994, pp. 599–600.
7. Dillon, p. 135.
8. Thierry Kellner, 'La Chine et les Républiques d'Asie Centrale: De la Défiance au Partenariat', *CEMOTI*, no. 22, July–December 1996, pp. 298–304; Munro 1994, p. 601; Yablonski, pp. 41–6.
9. 'La Chine et le Kazakhstan s'Accordent sur leur Frontière', *Le Monde*, 7 July 1998, p. 4.
10. Munro 1994, p. 604; Fourniau, pp. 10–11; Hunter 1996, pp. 126–8; Kellner, pp. 306–10; Allès, pp. 209–11.
11. 'Kazakhstan–China Pipeline Provides Opportunities for Russia', *SWB*, SUW/0510 WF/1, 31 October 1997.
12. 'Kazakhstan: China to Prise Open Export Path', *Petroleum Economist*, 64, no. 10, October 1997, p. 55; Munro, pp. 604–5.
13. Mike Collett-White, 'China, Russia Key for Central Asia Future', *Reuters*, 23 August 1999.
14. Tyler Marshall, 'Anti-NATO Axis Could Pose Threat, Experts Say', *Los Angeles Times*, 27 September 1999, pp. A1, A12.
15. Anthony Hyman, 'Central Asia's Relations with Afghanistan and South Asia', in *The New Central Asia and its Neighbours*, ed. Peter Ferdinand (London: Pinter Publishers, 1994), pp. 86–93.
16. Michael Collins Dunn, 'Great Games and Small: Afghanistan, Tajikistan and the New Geopolitics of Southwest Asia', *Middle East Policy*, 5, no. 2, May 1997, pp. 146–7.

REFERENCES

17. 'Pakistan is Prepared to Help Azerbaijan Return Nagorno-Karabakh', *Kommersant*, 14 June 2000, p. 11.
18. Hyman 1994, p. 82.
19. *Ibid.*, p. 85; Madan Mohan Puri, 'Central Asian Geopolitics: The Indian View', *Central Asian Survey*, 16, no. 2, June 1997, p. 254. This excellent article is, to the authors' knowledge, the most comprehensive one written to date on Indian–Central Asian relations.
20. 'India Lukewarm on Turkmenistan's Cross-Country Gas Pipeline Project', *AFP*, 6 April 2000; Hueper, p. 38; Puri, p. 251.
21. Puri, p. 244.
22. Hunter 1996, pp. 140–1.
23. Acil Tabbara, 'Gulf States Prepare to Meet Threat of Caspian Oil', *AFP*, 27 October 1998.
24. Ludmila Polonskaya and Alexei Malashenko, *Islam in Central Asia* (Reading, England: Ithaca, 1994), p. 117.
25. 'Kazakhstan Said to Face Upsurge in Islamic Propaganda', *Jamestown Foundation Monitor*, 13 May 1999.
26. 'Arab Countries Deny Kazakh Media Claims They Support Islamic Extremism', *RFE/RL Newsline*, 31 May 2000.
27. Anoushiravan Ehteshami, 'New Frontiers: Iran, the GCC and the CCARs', in *From the Gulf to Central Asia*, p. 96.
28. 'Nazarbayev Strengthens Relations with Gulf States', *Jamestown Foundation Monitor*, 4 June 1998; 'Saudi Arabia Interested in Increasing Trade Turnover with Kazakhstan', *Interfax-Kazakhstan News Agency*, 13 October 1999.
29. Pamela Ann Smith, 'Gulf States Expand Caspian Activities', *The Middle East*, no. 279, June 1998, pp. 22–3.
30. 'UAE Oil Company to Invest 35 Million Dollars in Turkmen Offshore Development This Year', *BBC Monitoring Service*, 6 June 2000.
31. David Ignatius, 'Where the Oil Is', *Washington Post*, 7 February 1999, p. B07.
32. 'Yamani Urges Gulf to Open Up Oil Sector', *Middle East Economic Digest*, 6 November 1998, p. 21.
33. Anoushiravan Ehteshami and Emma C. Murphy, 'The Non-Arab Middle East States and the Caucasian/Central Asian Republics: Iran and Israel', *International Relations*, 12, no. 1, April 1994, p. 98.
34. Hunter 1996, p. 143.
35. Jane Hunter, 'Israel and Turkey: Arms for Azerbaijan?', *Middle East International*, no. 23, October 1992, p. 12; Ehteshami and Murphy, p. 99; Hunter 1994, p. 177; Bülent Aras, 'Post-Cold War Realities: Israel's Strategy in Azerbaijan and Central Asia', *Middle East Policy*, 5, no. 4, January 1998, p. 73.

36. 'Azerbaijan–Iran Ambivalence', *Jamestown Foundation Monitor*, 29 August 1996; R. Hrair Dekmejian and Angelos Themelis, *Ethnic Lobbies in US Foreign Policy: A Comparative Study of the Jewish, Greek, Armenian & Turkish Studies*, Occasional Research Paper no. 13 (Athens: Institute of International Relations/Panteion University of Social and Political Sciences, 1997).
37. Yasemin Dobra-Manco, 'Jewish–American Coalition Recognizes Turkey's Vital Importance in the Region', *Turkish Daily News*, 29 July 1999.
38. 'Netanyahu Shops for Oil during Azeri Stopover', *Reuters*, 29 August 1997; Aras, p. 74.
39. For an Arab point of view, see 'Syrian Paper Warns Against "Zionist Penetration" of Central Asia', *BBC Worldwide Monitoring*, 13 January 1998.
40. 'OIC Summit Adopts Resolution on Nagorno-Karabakh', *RFE/RL Armenia Report*, 12 December 1997.
41. 'Shevardnadze Receives Democracy Prize in Israel', *Jamestown Foundation Monitor*, 16 January 1998; 'Georgia, Israel Strengthen Ties', *Jamestown Foundation Monitor*, 24 March 1999.
42. David B. Ottaway and Dan Morgan, 'Jewish–Armenian Split Spreads on the Hill', *Washington Post*, 9 February 1999, p. A15.
43. 'Armenian Genocide Should go on Israeli School Programme: Education Minister', *Agence France Press*, 24 April 1999; 'Turkey Awaits Israeli Answer', *Turkish Daily News*, 28 April 2000.
44. 'Progress on Trans-Caspian Gas Pipeline and Turkmen–Turkish Relations', *Jamestown Foundation Monitor*, 14 April 1999.
45. 'Turkmenistan Offers Its Gas to Israel', *Jamestown Foundation Monitor*, 21 March 1997.
46. Ehteshami and Murphy, p. 89; Hunter 1996, pp. 143–4.
47. Aras, pp. 76–7.
48. Emil Danielyan, 'Armenia: Officials Endorse Trilateral Economic Cooperation', *RFE/RL Weekday Magazine*, 9 September 1999.
49. 'Armenian–Greek Military Ties Develop', *Jamestown Foundation Monitor*, 24 June 1997.
50. 'Timeo Danaos et Dona Ferentes (Je Crains les Grecs, Même Quand Ils Font des Offrandes)', *Nouvelles d'Arménie Magazine*, no. 23, May 1997, p. 27.
51. Minas Analytis, 'Le Projet d' Oléoduc Bourgas-Alexandroupolis: Un Enjeu Géostratégique', *Le Courrier des Pays de l'Est*, no. 411, August 1996, pp. 50–2; Michael L. Myrianthis, *Oleaginous Geopolitics in SW Asia and the Burgas-Alexandroupolis Oil Pipeline*, Occasional Paper no. 10 (Athens: Institute of International Relations/Panteion University of Social and Political Sciences, 1996).

REFERENCES

52. 'Russia Promotes Greek, Novorossiisk Oil Pipelines', *RFE/RL Newsline*, 21 May 1999; 'Greece's Caspian Export Alternative Bypasses Bosphorus Straits', *Oil and Gas Journal*, 98, no. 13, 27 March 2000, p. 28.
53. Petko Bocharov, 'Bulgaria/Kazakhstan: Partners Agree on Oil Transport', *RFE/RL Weekday Magazine*, 17 March 1998; 'Trans-Balkan Pipeline for Kazakhstani Oil Considered', *Jamestown Foundation Monitor*, 22 June 1999; 'Balkan Route Rival for Baku-Ceyhan', *Turkish Daily News*, 18 June 1999.
54. Yasemin Dobra-Manco, 'Baku-Ceyhan on the Verge of Death', *Turkish Daily News*, 15 June 1999; Paul Michael Wihbey, 'Looking at Balkans Route for Caspian Crude', *UPI*, 23 June 1999.
55. Andrei Naryshkin, 'Bulgaria's Stoianov Leaves for Caucasus to Talk Fuel Issues', *Itar-Tass*, 1 December 1999; 'Bulgaria Wants to be Caspian Oil Transit to Europe', *Reuters*, 2 December 1999.
56. Giuliano Caroli, 'Il Petrolio del Caucaso e il "Crocevio" Romeno', *Rivista di Studi Politici Internazionali*, 66, no. 2, April–June 1999, pp. 245–9. To the knowledge of the authors, this article is the most comprehensive source on Romanian involvement in the Caspian. Another excellent synopsis on Romania is by Derek Brower, 'A New Oil Corridor', *Petroleum Economist*, 65, no. 9, September 1998, pp. 34–5.
57. 'Petrom to Start Crude Oil Extraction in Kazakhstan', *Rompres/FBIS*, 16 November 1999, by way of ANN/Groong.
58. Ron Synovitz, 'Romania: Port Constanta Could Alter Black Sea Trade Patterns', *RFE/RL Weekday Magazine*, 29 September 1998.
59. Stefan Korshak, 'Ukraine: Russia's Gazprom Boss to Join Foreign Investment Council', *RFE/RL Weekday Magazine*, 15 May 1998; 'Kuchma comes to Terms with Putin on Partial Takeover of Gas System', *Jamestown Foundation Monitor*, 18 October 2000.
60. Michael Lelyveld, 'Ukraine: Russia Intensifies Energy Squabble', *RFE/RL Weekday Magazine*, 16 December 1999; 'Russia Routing Gas Exports via Belarus', *Jamestown Foundation Monitor*, 24 September 1999.
61. 'Turkmen–Ukrainian Gas Deal Collapses', *Jamestown Foundation Monitor*, 23 April 1999.
62. 'Turkmenistan, Ukraine Sign Gas Deal', *RFE/RL Turkmen Report*, 4 October 2000; 'Kuchma Succeeds in Signing Gas Supply Agreement with Turkmenistan', *Jamestown Foundation Monitor*, 5 October 2000.
63. 'Ukraine Offers to Provide Transit Route for Caspian Oil', *Jamestown Foundation Prism*, 10 June 1998, pp. 3–4; 'Poland, Ukraine's Anchor to Europe', *Jamestown Foundation Monitor*, 29 June 1999.
64. 'Ukrainian Reformers Encouraged during Albright Visit', *Jamestown Foundation Monitor*, 19 April 2000.
65. *Ibid.*, p. 4.

66. 'Kuchma in Georgia and Azerbaijan', *Jamestown Foundation Monitor*, 20 March 2000.

Chapter 9
1. Jim Nichol, *Central Asia's New States: Political Developments and Implications for U.S. Interests* (Bethesda, MD: Library of Congress/Congressional Research Service, 1994); Jim Nichol, *Transcaucasus Newly Independent States: Political Developments and Implications for U.S. Interests* (Bethesda, MD: Library of Congress/Congressional Research Service, 1995).
2. Paul A. Goble, 'The 50 Million Muslim Misunderstanding: The West and Central Asia Today', in *From the Gulf to Central Asia*, pp. 1–5.
3. Porter and Saivetz, p. 89; Hunter 1996, p. 20.
4. Abdul Shakoor, 'Central Asia: The US Interest-Perception and Its Security Policies', *Eurasian Studies*, 2, no. 2, Summer 1995, p. 20; Zbigniew Brzezinski, 'The Premature Partnership', *Foreign Affairs*, 73, no. 2, March–April 1994, p. 70.
5. Nur Dolay, 'L'Incertaine Recomposition de l'Espace Soviétique: Grandes Manoeuvres Pétrolières dans le Caucase', *Le Monde Diplomatique*, 42, no. 496, July 1995, p. 15.
6. Hunter 1994, p. 92; Martha Brill Olcott, *Central Asia's New States: Independence, Foreign Policy, and Regional Security* (Washington, DC: United States Institute of Peace, 1996), p. 132; Nichol 1994, pp. 16–17.
7. Nichol 1994, p. 5.
8. Nichol 1995, p. 3.
9. Hunter 1996, p. 160.
10. Cheterian 1997a, p. 21; S. Frederick Starr, 'Making Eurasia Stable', *Foreign Affairs*, 75, no. 1, January–February 1996, pp. 80–92; Hunter 1996, p. 163; 'Country Profile: Uzbekistan', *EIU*, 1997–98, p. 8; 'Country Report: Kyrgyz Republic, Tajikistan, Turkmenistan', *EIU*, 2nd quarter 1997, p. 42; Igor Rotar, 'Moscow and Tashkent Battle for Supremacy in Central Asia', *Jamestown Foundation Prism*, 5, no. 4, 26 February 1999, p. 7.
11. Roy 1996, p. 6.
12. Dilip Hiro, 'Why is the US Inflating Caspian Oil Reserves?', *Middle East International*, no. 558, 12 September 1997a, p. 19.
13. Daniel Southerland, 'Azerbaijan Picks Exxon Over Iran for Oil Deal', *Washington Post*, 11 April 1995, p. A5; Bhushan Bahree and Anne Reifenberg, 'Russia Wins the First Round in Battle to Control Oil Flowing from Caspian', *Wall Street Journal*, 9 October 1995, p. A8; Richard Boudreaux, 'Caspian Connection: Oil Companies Agree to Export Oil Through Georgia', *Los Angeles Times*, 10 October 1995; Roberts, pp. 35–6; Sanjian, p. 24.

REFERENCES

14. Cynthia M. Croissant and Michael P. Croissant, 'The Caspian Sea Status Dispute: Context and Implications', *Eurasian Studies*, 3, no. 3, Winter 1996-97, p. 36.
15. Georgi-Ann Oshagan, 'Clinton Wants a Quick End to Karabakh Conflict, Says Presel', *Asbarez-On-Line*, 15 November 1996.
16. David B. Ottaway and Dan Morgan, 'Ex-Top Aides Seek Caspian Gusher', *Washington Post*, 6 July 1997, p. A1.
17. Too many articles appeared on the issue to be quoted here, in such newspapers as The *New York Times*, *Wall Street Journal*, *Washington Post*, and *Washington Times*. Some of these articles are quoted in the Armenia section of this paper.
18. S. Frederick Starr, 'Power Failure: American Policy in the Caspian', *The National Interest*, no. 47, Spring 1997, pp. 20-31; Zbigniew Brzezinski, Brent Scowcroft, and Richard Murphy, 'Differentiated Containment', *Foreign Affairs*, 76, no. 3, May-June 1997, pp. 20-30.
19. Starr, p. 25; Thomas Goltz, 'Catch-907 in the Caucasus', *The National Interest*, no. 48, Summer 1997, pp. 37-45.
20. Sonia Winter, 'Central Asia: U.S. Says Resolving Conflicts a Top Priority', *RFE/RL Weekday Magazine*, 22 July 1997; the full text of Talbott's address is available online at http://www.state.gov/www/regions/nis/970721talbott.html
21. Dan Morgan and David Ottaway, 'Drilling for Influence in Russia's Back Yard', *Washington Post*, 22 September 1997, p. A1.
22. Paul Goble, 'Central Asia: Analysis from Washington – A Jump Too Far?', *RFE/RL Weekday Magazine*, 2 September 1997.
23. See Chapter IV, endnote 17.
24. Charles Fenyvesi, 'Caspian Sea: US Experts Say Oil Reserves are Large', *RFE/RL Weekday Magazine*, 5 May 1998.
25. David Swanson, 'Turkey: Delegates to Conference Discuss over 65 Energy Projects', *RFE/RL Weekday Magazine*, 29 May 1998; Michael Lelyveld, 'Caucasus: Deadline Nears on Oil Transit Routes', *RFE/RL Weekday Magazine*, 16 June 1998.
26. Brian Humphrey, 'Washington Splashes Out on Caspian Dreams', *Moscow Times*, 15 June 1999.
27. Tamara Pataraia, 'South Caucasus Security: Cooperation or Rivalry?' *The Army and Society in Georgia*, November 1998, by way of Turkestan Newsletter, 7 January 1999.
28. Sonia Winter, 'Turkmenistan: President Receives Low-Key Welcome at White House', *RFE/RL Weekday Magazine*, 23 April 1998.
29. Lowell Bezanis, 'Turkmenistan: Niyazov Talks of Democratization and Pipelines', *RFE/RL Weekday Magazine*, 22 April 1998; Michael

Lelyveld, 'Turkmenistan: President Refuses to Sign Oil Pipeline Agreement', *RFE/RL Weekday Magazine*, 4 November 1998.
30. 'US Promises Financial Support for Turkmen Pipelines', *RFE/RL Newsline*, 18 December 1998.
31. Michael Lelyveld, 'Turkmenistan: President Refuses to Sign Oil Pipeline Agreement', *RFE/RL Weekday Magazine*, 4 November 1998; Michael Lelyveld, 'Iran: Energy Ties to China Puzzling', *RFE/RL Weekday Magazine*, 20 September 1999.
32. Davit Berdzenishvili, 'Caucasus: Oil Companies Make Ultimate Pipeline Route Decisions', *RFE/RL Weekday Magazine*, 12 November 1998.
33. Philip Kurata, 'US Promotes Energy Development of Caspian Basin', *US Information Agency Press Release*, by way of ANN/Groong, 8 April 1999.
34. 'Ex-US Secretary of State Henry Kissinger Gives Preference to Caspian Oil Transit along Baku-Ceyhan Route', *AssA-Irada*, 11 January 1999.
35. Richard C. Longworth, 'Destitute Plum of Caspian Has Many Suitors', *Chicago Tribune*, 9 February 1998.
36. Richard Sokolsky and Tanya Charlick-Paley, *NATO and Caspian Security: A Mission Too Far?* (Santa Monica, CA: Rand Corporation, 1999).
37. 'Baku-Ceyhan Oil and Gas Agreements Signed', *Jamestown Foundation Monitor*, 29 November 1999.
38. Graham E. Fuller, *Central Asia: The New Geopolitics* (Santa Monica: Rand Corporation, 1992), p. 77.
39. 'Statement of Martha Brill Olcott, Senior Associate, Carnegie Endowment for International Peace, Washington, DC', in *Implementation of US Policy on Caspian Sea Oil Exports: Hearing Before Subcommittee on International Economic Policy, Export, and Trade Promotion of the Committee on Foreign Relations United States Senate, One Hundred Fifth Congress, Second Session, July 8th 1998* (Washington, DC: US Government Printing Office, 1998), pp. 35–49.
40. Paul Goble, 'The New Geopolitics of Oil', *RFE/RL Weekday Magazine*, 23 July 1997.
41. Boris Yunanov, 'Clinton Crosses the Caucasus Range', *The Current Digest of the Post-Soviet Press*, 49, no. 35, October 1997, p. 22; Paul Taylor, 'Analysis – New Caucasus Order Shaped Despite Russia', *Reuters*, 19 November 1999.
42. 'USA Seeks to Dominate Caspian Region, Iranian Newspaper Says', *SWB*, SU/3085 G/4, 25 November 1997.
43. Elaine Sciolino, 'It's a Sea! It's a Lake! No. It's a Pool of Oil', *New York Times*, 21 June 1998, p. 16.

44. For details, see chapter 10.
45. René Leray, 'European Union Policy and Action Toward Central Asia and the Caspian Sea Countries', in *A Great Game No More: Oil, Gas and Stability in the Caspian Sea Region*, ed. Dieter Dettke (Washington, DC: Friedrich-Ebert-Stiftung, 1999), p. 60.
46. Leray, pp. 58–61; Michael C. Evans, 'Europe's Strategic Role in the Caucasus and the Black Sea', *Strategic Review*, 27, no. 2, Spring 1999, pp. 4–10.
47. Stuart Parrott, 'Central Asia: EU Aids Fight Against Drug Smugglers with New Routes', *RFE/RL Weekday Magazine*, 13 February 1998.
48. Jeremy Brantsen, 'Azerbaijan: "Silk Road" Conference Paves Way for Transport Corridor', *RFE/RL Weekday Magazine*, 4 September 1998.
49. 'Historic TRACECA Agreement Signed: Russia and Iran Dissent', *Jamestown Foundation Monitor*, 9 September 1998.
50. Jeremy Bransten, 'Central Asia/Caucasus: Silk Road Conference Agrees on Eurasian Corridor', *RFE/RL Weekday Magazine*, 9 September 1998.
51. 'EU/NIS: INOGATE Summit Opens Energy Umbrella Agreement over NIS', *European Report*, 24 July 1999; 'EU/Ex-USSR: New TACIS Programme Approved', *European Report*, 7 January 2000.
52. 'EU Commission Adopts Global Plan for Southern Caucasus Humanitarian Aid', *European Report*, 17 April 1999; 'EU–Caucasus: EU Gives Conditional Support to the Region', *European Report*, 23 June 1999; 'Foreign Ministry Says Cooperation with Armenia Impossible on EU Terms', *SWB*, SU/D3668/F, 18 October 1999.
53. 'EU/NIS: INOGATE Summit Opens Energy Umbrella Agreement over NIS', *European Report*, 24 July 1999; A. Pivovarov, N. Babichev and A. Ryabov, 'A Joint-Stock Company, Called the Commonwealth of Independent States', *Kommersant-Vlast*, nos. 16–17, May 1998, pp. 24–5; Stanislav Cherniavskii, 'The West Steps Up Activity in the Transcaucasus', *International Affairs*, 44, no. 4, 1998, pp. 45–53.
54. Eka Mekhuzla, 'Georgia, Ukraine Launch New Ferry Service', *Itar-Tass*, 17 April 1999; 'EU to Back Revitalization of Romanian Port', *SWB*, EE/W0557/WB, 1 October 1998; 'Romania Presses Case as Caspian Oil Transit Route', *SWB*, EE/W0557/WB, 1 October 1998.
55. Simon Henderson, 'Crowding around the Caspian', *Jerusalem Post*, 19 November 1999, p. 6B.
56. 'The Bergedorf Forum on the Caspian', *International Affairs*, 45, no. 3, 1999, p. 134.
57. Pataraia.
58. Bhatty and Bronson, p. 141.

59. 'United States/European Union Statement on Caspian Energy', *Weekly Compilation of Presidential Documents*, 34, no. 21, 25 May 1998, pp. 922–3.
60. William Echikson, 'EU Rethinks Its Funding to East', *RFE/RL Newsline*, 4 September 1997.
61. 'Britain and Azerbaijan Sign Joint Declaration', *Itar-Tass*, 28 September 1992.
62. 'Aliyev in Britain; Meets Major; Baku Ready to Sign Agreement with BP', *SWB*, SU/1932/F, 26 February 1994.
63. 'Aliyev in Britain', *Jamestown Foundation Monitor*, 24 July 1998.
64. Michael Dynes, 'Caspian Pipe Dreams could be the Making of Monument', *The Times*, 19 May 1998.
65. 'Nazarbayev's Visit to London', *SWB*, SU/1218/A1/1, 1 November 1991.
66. 'Britain Invested about $100 million in Kazakhstan in 1999', *Interfax*, 16 March 2000.
67. David Stern, 'Aliyev Opens Major Oil, Gas conference amid Franco–US Sparring on Iran', *AFP*, 2 June 1998.
68. Igor Shchegolev, 'Azeri President Calls His French Visit Useful', *Itar-Tass*, 23 December 1993.
69. Sophie Shihab, 'La France Promet de Construire une Europe Allant "de Brest à Bakou"', *Le Monde*, 15 October 1996, p. 6; Jacques Amalric, 'La Diplomatie Française Renoue avec le Caucase', *Libération*, 14 October 1996, p. 9; Hervé de Charette, 'Le Caucase est une Zone Stratégique pour la France', *Le Figaro*, 14 October 1996, p. 5.
70. 'Azerbaijani–French Summit Yields Big Oil Contract', *Jamestown Foundation Monitor*, 15 January 1997; 'Azerbaijan Thwarts Special Role for France in Karabakh Negotiations', *Jamestown Foundation Monitor*, 17 January 1997. In response to Azeri opposition to France's co-chairmanship with Russia, it was agreed to include the United States as a third co-chair.
71. 'Azeri President Calls for French Assistance', *Turan*, 24 April 1998.
72. Sergei Kozlov, 'Alma-Ata Signs Oil Agreements. Russia and Azerbaijan Remain at Sidelines', *Nezavisimaya Gazeta*, p. 3, 4 December 1993.
73. 'Kazakh Oil Giant, French Firm to Develop Oil Fields', *BBC Monitoring International Reports*, 30 June 2000; 'Kazakh President Hails Results of European Tour', *Interfax*, 29 June 2000.
74. 'French Resources Down the Straits?', *Jamestown Foundation Monitor*, 4 August 1998.
75. Michael Schmunk, 'German Policy Towards the Caspian Sea Region', in *A Great Game No More*, pp. 72–3.
76. *Ibid.*

REFERENCES

77. Gernot Erler and Friedemann Müller, 'Region of the Future: The Caspian Sea. German Interests and European Politics in the Transcaucasian and Central Asian Republics. Policy Paper of the SPD Parliamentary Group in the German Bundestag', in *A Great Game No More*, p. 94.
78. *Ibid.*, pp. 74–5.
79. 'Germany's Schroeder Arrives in Georgia', *Reuters*, 31 March 2000; 'Foreign Statemen Show Support for Shevardnadze', *Jamestown Foundation Monitor*, 3 April 2000.
80. Bhatty and Bronson, p. 136.
81. 'Kazakh Leadership Wants to Expand Economic Cooperation with Germany, Japan', *RFE/RL Newsline*, 4 November 1999.
82. 'Turkmen Oil-Refining Complex Undergoes Modernization', *Jamestown Foundation Monitor*, 30 August 1996; 'German Project in Turkmenistan to Increase Gas Export', *Jamestown Foundation Monitor*, 15 February 1999.
83. 'Italian–Kazakh Deals Not Hurt by Russia's Crisis', *Capital Markets Russia*, 24 September 1998; 'ENI Begins Exploration in Azerbaijan's Kurdashi Offshore', *AFX European Focus*, 26 April 2000.
84. 'Putin Welcomes Partnership Between Italy's Eni Concern and Gazprom', *RFE/RL Turkmen Report*, 4–10 June 2000.
85. Hugh Pope, 'Russian–Italian Pipeline to Turkey Wins Support – ABN–Amro Backs Plan in Blow to US', *Wall Street Journal*, 25 February 1999, p. A10. 'Turkmenistan–Turkey Pipeline Contract Signed', *Jamestown Foundation Monitor*, 23 February 1999; 'Gazprom Throws Gauntlet to US-Backed Trans-Caspian Pipeline', *Jamestown Foundation Monitor*, 19 March 1999.
86. 'Belgium PM Calls for Increased Cooperation with Azerbaijan', *AFP*, 13 April 1998; 'Belgium and Kazakhstan Consolidate Economic Relations', *Jamestown Foundation Monitor*, 24 April 1998. Tractebel's involvement in Kazakhstan ended amid a scandal in 1999.
87. 'Japan Joins Azerbaijan's "Deal of the Century"', *Jamestown Foundation Monitor*, 3 April 1996.
88. 'Azerbaijan Ratifies Another Big Oil Contract', *Jamestown Foundation Monitor*, 26 February 1997; 'Japan Entering Caspian Oil Business in Force', *Jamestown Foundation Monitor*, 20 June 1997; 'Yanan Tava, Atashgah and Mugan Daniz', *Azerbaijan International Magazine*, 6, no. 4, Winter 1998, p. 85.
89. 'Aliyev Brings Home Oil Contracts and Credit Agreements from Japan', *Jamestown Foundation Monitor*, 2 March 1998; 'Kurdashi, Araz and Kirgan Daniz', *Azerbaijan International Magazine*, 6, no. 3, Autumn 1998, p. 85.

90. 'Azerbaijan, Japan Sign a Number of Important Agreements', *Tass*, 3 May 1999.
91. 'A New Way Out for Turkmen Gas?', *Jamestown Foundation Monitor*, 12 June 1995.
92. 'Turkmen Oil-Refining Complex Undergoes Modernization', *Jamestown Foundation Monitor*, 30 August 1996.
93. 'Eastward', *Jamestown Foundation Monitor*, 11 September 1995.
94. 'Turkmenistan Modernizes Oil Refining', *Jamestown Foundation Monitor*, 28 February 1996.
95. 'Turkmenistan to Add Japanese-Built Plant to Turkmenbashi Complex', *Jamestown Foundation Monitor*, 7 October 1998.
96. 'Japanese Lending in the Region', *Jamestown Foundation Monitor*, 7 September 1995.
97. 'Japan Boosts Economic Presence in Kazakhstan', *Jamestown Foundation Monitor*, 15 September 1998; 'Japan to Rebuild Oil Refinery in Kazakhstan', *RFE/RL Newsline*, 4 February 2000; 'Japan Secures 7% Stake in Huge Kazakh Oil Field', *Yomiuri Shimbun/Daily Yomiuri*, 4 July 2000.
98. 'Japan Expands Lending to Uzbekistan', *Jamestown Foundation Monitor*, 20 September 1995; 'Japanese Lending Targets Infrastructure Programs', *Jamestown Foundation Monitor*, 31 October 1996.
99. 'Japan to Build Oil Refineries in Kyrgyzstan, Georgia', *RFE/RL Newsline*, 17 September 1997; 'Japan to Build Oil Refinery in Georgia', *RFE/RL Newsline*, 12 January 1998.
100. On the Japanese role in Central Asia and the Caucasus, see Michael Robert Hickok, 'The Other End of the Silk Road: Japan's Eurasian Initiative', *Central Asian Survey*, 19, no. 1, March 2000, pp. 17–39.
101. 'East Asian Economic Powers Assisting Uzbekistan's Modernization', *Jamestown Foundation Monitor*, 8 October 1999; 'South Korea's Ambassador Still Bullish on Kazakhstan', *Financial Times Asia Intelligence Wire*, 1 December 1998; Kim Ji-Ho, 'Kazakhstan Invites Kim to 30-Nation "Eurasia Economic Summit"', *Korea Herald*, 13 January 2000.
102. 'Central Asia Petroleum Ltd Wins Contract on Kazakh Oil Fields', *Interfax*, 11 January 1998.
103. 'Turkmen President Meets with Malaysian Tycoon', *Interfax*, 18 March 1998; 'Malaysian Firm Strikes Oil in Turkmenistan', *BBC Monitoring Service*, 20 March 1999.

Chapter 10

1. Eric Gujer, 'Caspian Oil and Chechen Instability', *Swiss Review of World Affairs*, no. 2, February 1997, pp. 11–14.
2. Yuri Akbashev, 'Rebellion Simmers in Daghestan', *Institute for War and Peace Reporting Caucasus Reporting Service*, no. 40, 14 July 2000.

REFERENCES

3. 'Lezgin Irredentism Aired in Russian Duma, Disavowed by Ambassador in Baku', *Jamestown Foundation Monitor*, 13 June 1997; the most comprehensive source on the Lezgins is the article by Anna Matveeva and Clem McCartney, 'Policy Responses to an Ethnic Community Division: Lezgins in Azerbaijan', *International Journal on Minority and Group Rights*, 5, no. 3, 1997–98, pp. 213–52.
4. Alexander Voronin, 'Ossetians Turn Back Ingush Refugees', *IWPR Caucasus Reporting Service*, no. 37, 23 June 2000.
5. 'How Unstable is Western Georgia?', *RFE/RL Caucasus Report*, 13 July 2000.
6. Voitsekh Guretski, 'The Question of Javakheti', *Caucasian Regional Studies*, 3, no. 1, 1998.
7. Ugur Akinci, 'Javakhetia: The Bottle-Neck of the Baku-Ceyhan Pipeline', *Silk Road: A Journal of West Asian Studies*, 1, no. 2, December 1997, pp. 26–9.
8. 'Rebel Kurds Damage Oil Pipeline in Turkey', *Los Angeles Times*, 27 November 1998, p. A24; 'PKK Wields Pipeline Leverage', *Stratfor*, 23 November 1999.
9. Maya Bitokova, 'Wahhabis Unsettle Nalchik Regime', *IWPR Caucasus Reporting Service*, no. 37, 23 June 2000.
10. Irada Husseinova, 'Azerbaijani Muslims Lose Faith', *IWPR Caucasus Reporting Service*, no. 27, 14 April 2000.
11. 'Fundamentalist Ideas Spread in Kazakhstan by Foreigners', *Itar-Tass*, 11 May 1999; 'Kazakhstan Said to Face Upsurge in Islamic Propaganda', *Jamestown Foundation Monitor*, 13 May 1999.
12. On the ideology and origins of this group, see R. Hrair Dekmejian, *Islam in Revolution* (Syracuse, NY: Syracuse University Press, 2nd edn, 1995), pp. 84–91.
13. 'Russia, Allies to Set Up Joint Force', *The Hindu*, 12 October 2000; Michael Lelyveld, 'Central Asia: Summits Link Security, Economics', *RFE/RL Weekday Magazine*, 17 October 2000; Vladimir Radyhin, 'Closing Ranks', *The Hindu*, 22 October 2000.
14. Camille Verleuw, *Trafics et Crimes en Asie Centrale et au Caucase* (Paris: Presses Universitaires de France, 1999), pp. 39–47; Kadir Alimov, 'Central Asian Big Business: The Mafia's Drug Trade', *Jamestown Foundation Prism*, 1, no. 23, 3 November 1995.
15. Tamara Makarenko, 'Kyrgystan and the Global Narcotics Trade', *Central Eurasia Project Eurasia Insight*, 6 December 1999; see also Mark Galeotti, 'Crime in Central Asia: A Regional Problem with Global Implications', *Boundary and Security Bulletin*, 3, no. 4, Winter 1995–96, pp. 68–74.
16. Kendal Nezan, 'La Turquie, Plaque Tournante du Trafic de Drogue',

Le Monde Diplomatique, 45, no. 532, juillet 1998, p. 13; Toktobai Mulkubatov, 'Kyrgyz General Blames Fighting on Drug Barons', *IWPR Reporting on Central Asia*, 24 March 2000; Verleuw, p. 78.

17. 'Uzbekistan: Conference on Drugs Opens in Tashkent', *RFE/RL Weekday Magazine*, 19 October 2000; Douglas Frantz, 'Afghan Opium Crop Declines, But Central Asians Still Worry', *New York Times*, 20 October 2000, p. A5.

18. Sophie Shihab, 'Mafias et Groupes Intégristes Signent les Rapts dans le Caucase', *Le Monde*, 15 December 1998, p. 3.

19. 'Caspian Pipeline Battle Reaches Endgame', *Labyrinth: Central Asian Quarterly*, 3, no. 1, 1996, p. 35; Craig Mellow, 'Big Oil's Pipe Dream', *Fortune*, 137, no. 4, 2 March 1998, pp. 158–64.

20. Steve LeVine and Bill Powell, 'A President and His Counselor', *Newsweek*, 10 July 2000, pp. 40–1.

21. James M. Dorsey, 'Israeli Is Subtle Player in Central Asia Oil', *Wall Street Journal*, 7 April 1999, p. A19; 'Progress On Trans-Caspian Gas Pipeline and Turkmen–Turkish Relations', *Jamestown Foundation Monitor*, 14 April 1999.

22. Dan Morgan and David B. Ottaway, 'Multinationals' Aims, Ties Cloudy in Race for Caspian Reserves', *Washington Post*, 31 May 1998, p. A14.

23. David Hoffman, 'Itera: Mystery Player in Russia's Natural Gas Market', *Washington Post*, 21 May 2000, p. H1.

24. Steve LeVine, 'Investor Is Accused of Fraud Over Azerbaijan Venture', *New York Times*, 22 December 1999, p. 4; Peter Elkind, 'The Incredible Half-Billion-Dollar Azerbaijani Oil Swindle', *Fortune*, 141, no. 5, 6 March 2000, pp. 106–26; Peter Elkind, 'Kozeny to Investors: Let's Sue the Azeris', *Fortune*, 141, no. 7, 3 April 2000, p. 56.

25. Zina Moukheiber, 'Mr. Five Percent?', *Forbes*, 154, no. 1, 4 July 1994, p. 74; 'Azeri Pipeline Gets Dollars 2bn Funding', *Lloyd's List*, 1 December 1995; 'Oil Capital Looks for New Turkmen Opportunities', *Middle East News Items*, 25 September 1997; Guy Gugliotta, 'Senate Campaign Probes Release Findings', *Washington Post*, 6 March 1998, p. A6; David Ignatius, 'Moscow Money Trail', *Washington Post*, 12 April 2000, p. A27; James Risen, 'New Evidence in a Fund-Raising Inquiry', *New York Times*, 24 June 2000, p. 10.

26. 'Amerada Hess Increases Stake in Caspian Sea Oil Project', *AFP*, 17 July 2000.

27. Paul Klebnikov, 'The Quietly Determined American', *Forbes*, 154, no. 10, 24 October 1994, p. 48; Anne Kessler, 'Trailblazer in Pursuit of Oil: The Reopening of Azerbaijan to the West', *Azerbaijan International Magazine*, 2, no. 4, Autumn 1994, pp. 34–5 and 69; Sanjian, pp. 9–10;

REFERENCES

'Ramco Energy Comments on the Future of the Caspian Region at the International Institute of Petroleum Conference', *Two-Ten News Network*, 18 February 1999; Gregor Paul, 'Ramco Hopes to Turn Corner as Losses Grow', *The Scotsman*, 19 April 2000, p. 24.

28. Peter Nulty, 'The Black Gold Rush in Russia', *Fortune*, 125, no. 12, 15 June 1992, p. 126.
29. 'Caspian Route Is Not Seen as Viable', *New York Times*, 23 October 1998; Paul Sampson, 'Lubricating the Caspian: Disputes Over an Azerbaijan Oil Pipeline Are Causing a Geopolitical Stampede', *Transitions*, 6, no. 2, February 1999, p. 26.
30. 'BP-Amoco Backs Baku-Ceyhan Oil Pipeline', *Reuters*, 20 October 1999; Selina Williams, 'Baku-Ceyhan Oil Pipeline Lacks Key Volumes', *Reuters*, 21 October 1999.
31. 'US Intruding in Caspian', *Oil and Gas Journal*, 97, no. 39, 27 September 1999, p. 23.
32. Lena Jonson, *Russia and Central Asia: A New Web of Relations* (London: Royal Institute of International Affairs, 1998), pp. 64 and 73; it must be noted that Russian oil companies have complained as well from heavy-handed treatment at the hands of Gazprom, which has prevented them from using its pipeline network to export their gas output. See Andrew Jack, 'Gazprom Chief Warns of Break-Up', *Financial Times*, 29–30 January 2000, p. 10.
33. 'Deal Between Russia's Gazprom and Bulgaria Agreed', *SWB*, EE/W0553/WB, 3 September 1998.
34. David Leppard, Paul Nuki, and Gareth Walsh, 'BP Accused of Backing "Arms for Oil" Coup', *Sunday Times*, 26 March 2000. All parties concerned have denied this report.
35. S. Neil MacFarlane and Oliver Thränert, *Balancing Hegemony: The OSCE in the CIS* (Kingston, Ont.: Queen's University Centre for International Relations, 1997); S. Neil MacFarlane, *Western Engagement in the Caucasus and Central Asia* (London: Royal Institute of International Affairs, 1999).
36. 'EBRD Grants 200 Million Dollars to Azeri Consortium', *AFP*, 18 February 1999; John Kenyon, 'Caspian Oil Group Gets $400 M Boost', *Moscow Times*, 19 February 1999; 'EBRD Ready to Aid Foreign Caspian Investors', *Interfax*, 13 October 1999; 'Dragon Oil Unit Signs 60 Mln USD Loan from EBRD; *AFX.Com*, 20 December 1999; Isabel Gorst, 'Lukoil: Worth Another Look', *Petroleum Economist*, 67, no. 6, June 2000, p. 66.
37. Philip Bowring, 'Asian Bank Takes a Westward Leap', *The Guardian*, 10 June 1993, p. 14; 'Islamic Development Bank to Loan 30m Dollars', *SWB*, SU/W0615/WD, 19 November 1999; 'Islamic Bank to Lend Kazakhstan $20 Million', *Interfax*, 26 January 2000.

38. Neil MacFarlane, *Western Engagement in the Caucasus and Central Asia* (London: Royal Institute of International Affairs, 1999), pp. 25–6.
39. Mark I. Karpyuk and Vasiliy V. Shavandin, 'Astrakhaners on the Caspian Sea', *International Affairs*, 42, no. 1, January–February 1996, pp. 141–7; Douglas W. Blum, 'Domestic Politics and Russia's Caspian Policy', *Post-Soviet Affairs*, 14, no. 2, April–June 1998, pp. 154–5.
40. *Ibid.*, p. 153 and p. 155n.
41. 'Iranian Companies to Build Caspian Seaport', *SWB*, SU/W0648/WC1, 14 July 2000.
42. Hooshang Amirahmadi, 'Does Iran Have a Future in Central Asia? Tehran's Policy Could Lead to Growth – Or Conflict', *Middle East Insight*, 10, no. 1, November–December 1993, p. 42; Herzig, pp. 35–6; Mohammad-Reza Djalali, 'Mer Caspienne: Perspectives Iraniennes', *CEMOTI*, January–June 1997, pp. 135–6; Karpyuk and Shavandin, p. 146; 'Iran in "Struggle For Influence" With Turkey and Saudi Arabia in Central Asia', *SWB*, SU/1273/A4/1, 9 January 1992; 'Kazakh and Iranian Caspian Coast Regions Strengthen Ties', *SWB*, SU/2033/G, 28 June 1994; 'Iran Supplies Additional Power to Border Town', *SWB*, SU/W062/S1, 11 February 2000.

Chapter 11
1. Recent discoveries in Kazakhstan's offshore Kashagan sector may significantly add to this estimate.
2. For various methods of political risk analysis, see Wenlee Ting, *Multinational Risk Assessment and Management: Strategies for Investment and Marketing Decisions* (New York: Quorum Books, 1988), pp. 1–37.

Bibliography

Abazov, R., 'The Disintegration of the Economy of Central Asia in the Post-Soviet Period', *Russian Politics and Law*, 35, no. 1, January–February 1997, pp. 83–94.

Achdjian, Giraïr, 'La Transcaucasie, Un Pont Stratégique entre Deux Mers et Deux Mondes', *Le Courrier des Pays de l'Est*, no. 423, October 1997, pp. 34–59.

Adalian, Rouben Paul, 'Armenia's Foreign Policy: Defining Priorities and Coping with Conflict', in *The Making of Foreign Policy in Russia and the New States of Eurasia*, Adeed Dawisha and Karen Dawisha (eds), (Armonk, New York: M. E. Sharpe, 1995).

Adams, Jan S., 'The Dynamics of Integration: Russia and the Near Abroad', *Demokratizatsiya*, 6, no. 1, Winter 1998, pp. 50–64.

———, 'Pipelines and Pipedreams: Can Russia Continue to Dominate Caspian Energy?' *Problems of Post-Communism*, 45, no. 5, September–October 1998, pp. 26–36.

———, 'The US–Russian Face-Off in the Caspian Basin', *Problems of Post-Communism*, 47, no. 1, January–February 2000, pp. 49–58.

Adams, Terry, 'Oil and Geopolitical Strategy in the Caucasus', *Asian Affairs*, 30, no. 1, February 1999, pp. 11–20.

Adelman, Morris Albert, *The Genie out of the Bottle: World Oil since 1970*. (Cambridge, Massachusetts: MIT Press, 1995).

Afanasyev, Yuri N., 'A New Russian Imperialism', *Perspective*, 4, no. 3, February–March 1994, pp. 1 and 7–10.

———, 'Russian Reform is Dead', *Foreign Affairs*, 73, no. 2, March–April 1994, pp. 21–6.

Ahmar, Moonis, 'Management of Water Resources in Central Asia: Lessons for the South Asian Countries', *Eurasian Studies*, no. 15, Summer 1999, pp. 97–120.

Ahrari, M. E. and James Beal, 'The New Great Game in Muslim Central Asia', *McNair Paper*, no. 47. (Washington, DC: Institute for National Strategic Studies/National Defense University, January 1996).

Akbarzadeh, Shahram, 'The Political Shape of Central Asia', *Central Asian Survey*, 16, no. 4, December 1997, pp. 517–42.

Akimov, Aleksandr, 'Oil and Gas in the Caspian Sea Region: An Overview of Cooperation and Conflict', *Perspectives on Central Asia*, 1, no. 5, June 1996, pp. 1–4.

Akinci, Ugur, 'Javakhetia: The Bottle-Neck of the Baku–Ceyhan Pipeline', *Silk Road*, 1, no. 2, December 1997, pp. 26–9.

Akiner, Shirin, 'Conflict, Stability and Development in Central Asia', in *Between Development and Destruction: An Enquiry into the Causes of Conflict in Post-Colonial States*, Luc van de Goor, Kumar Rupesinghe, and Paul Sciarone (eds), (London: MacMillan Press, 1996).

———, 'Ethnicity, Nationality and Citizenship as Expressions of Self-Determination in Central Asia', in *Self-Determination: International Perspectives*, Donald Clark and Robert Williamson (eds), (London: Macmillan Press, 1996).

———, 'Melting Pot, Salad Bowl–Cauldron? Manipulation and Mobilization of Ethnic and Religious Identities in Central Asia', *Ethnic and Racial Studies*, 20, no. 2, April 1997, pp. 362–98.

Aleksandrov, Valentin, 'Ecological Problems of the Black Sea', *International Affairs*, 43, no. 2, 1997, pp. 87–99.

———, 'Caspian Oil: Blessing or Curse?' *International Affairs*, 43, no. 6, 1997, pp. 74–82.

Aliev, Ilham, 'Azerbaijan: The New Source of Energy of the 21st Century', *Caucasus and the Caspian Seminar Series, Strengthening Democratic Institutions Project Working Paper* (Cambridge, MA: John F. Kennedy School of Government, Harvard University, 21 November 1997).

Aliriza, Bulent, 'Overview of the Turkish Pipeline Route Alternative', *Caspian Crossroads*, 1, no. 1, Winter 1995, pp. 7–8.

Aliyev, Heydar, *Azerbaycan Oil In the World Policy* (Baku: 'Azerbaijan' Publishing House, 1997).

Allès, Elisabeth, 'Stratégies Chinoises en Asie Centrale et Nationalisme Minoritaire au Xinjiang', *Hérodote: Revue de Géographie et de Géopolitique*, no. 84, Spring 1997, pp. 201–16.

Allonsius, David, *Le Régime Juridique de la Mer Caspienne: Problèmes Actuels de Droit International Public* (Paris: Université Panthéon-Assas [Paris II], L.G.D.J., E.J.A., 1997).

Altan, Türker, 'An Exhausted Environmental Legacy: Environmental Problems in the Central Asia beyond Borders, and Destruction of Natural Resources', *Eurasian Studies*, 2, no. 1, Spring 1995, pp. 36–51.

Altstadt, Audrey L, 'From White Oil to Black Caviar: Baku Commerce through the Ages', *Caspian Crossroads*, 1, no. 2, Spring 1995, pp. 3–6.

Amirahmadi, Hooshang, 'Does Iran Have a Future in Central Asia? Tehran's

Policy Could Lead to Growth – or Conflict', *Middle East Insight*, 10, no. 1, November–December 1993, pp. 41–4.

———, *Oil at the Turn of the Twenty-First Century: Interplay of Market Forces and Politics* (Abu Dhabi: The Emirates Center for Strategic Studies and Research, 1996).

Analytis, Minas, 'Le Projet d'Oléoduc Bourgas-Alexandroupolis: Un Enjeu Géostratégique', *Le Courrier des Pays de l'Est*, no. 411, August 1996, pp. 45–54.

Anderson, John, *The International Politics of Central Asia*. Manchester: Manchester University Press, 1997.

Andrianopoulos, Andreas, 'The Long Arm of Oil Interests: Cyprus and Central Asian Oil', *Transitions*, 4, no. 1, June 1997, pp. 36–37.

Arapov, Aleksei and Iakov Umanskii, 'Asianism: The External and Internal Manifestation of Ethnopolitics in Central Asia', *Russian Politics and Law*, 32, no. 3, May–June 1994, pp. 29–44.

Aras, Bülent, 'Post-Cold War Realities: Israel's Strategy in Azerbaijan and Central Asia', *Middle East Policy*, 5, no. 4, January 1998, pp. 68–81.

Arbatov, Alexei G., 'Russia's Foreign Policy Alternatives', *International Security*, 18, no. 2, Fall 1993, pp. 5–43.

———, 'Russian National Interests', in *Damage Limitation or Crisis? Russia and the Outside World*, Robert D. Blackwill and Sergei A. Karaganov (eds), (Washington, DC: Brassey's, 1994).

Ardebili, Hossein Kazempour, 'The Caspian Sea, Its Resources, Its Legal Status and Its Future'. *OPEC Bulletin*, 28, no. 3, March 1997, pp. 8–11.

Arik, Umut, 'The New Independent States and Turkish Foreign Policy', in *Turkish Foreign Policy: Recent Developments*, ed. Kemal H. Karpat (Madison: University of Wisconsin Press, 1996).

Auty, Richard, 'Does Kazakhstan Oil Wealth Help or Hinder the Transition?' *Development Discussion Papers*, no. 615 (Cambridge, Massachusetts: Harvard Institute of Development, Harvard University, December 1997).

Aydin, Mustafa, 'Turkey and Central Asia: Challenges of Change', *Central Asian Survey*, 15, no. 2, June 1996, pp. 157–77.

Aydinli, Ersel, 'Russia's "Kurdish Card" in Turkish–Russian Rivalry', *Caspian Crossroads*, 2, no. 3, Winter 1997, pp. 9–13.

Baev, Pavel, *Russia's Policies in the Caucasus* (London: Royal Institute of International Affairs, 1997).

———, 'Russia's Departure from Empire: Self-Assertiveness and a New Retreat', in *Geopolitics in Post-Wall Europe: Security, Territory and Identity* ed. Ola Tunander, Pavel Baev, and Victoria Ingrid Einagel. London: Sage Publications / Oslo: International Peace Research Institute, 1997.

Bagirov, Sabit, 'Azerbaijani Oil: Glimpses of a Long History', *Perceptions*, 1, no. 2, June–August 1996, pp. 22–52.

Bahgat, Gawdat, 'Beyond Containment: US–Iranian Relations at a Crossroads', *Security Dialogue*, 28, no. 4, December 1997, pp. 453–64.

———, 'Oil Security in the New Millenium: Geo-Economy vs. Geo-Strategy', *Strategic Review*, 26, no. 4, Fall 1998, pp. 22–30.

———, 'The Caspian Sea Geopolitical Game: Prospects for the New Millenium', *OPEC Review*, 23, no. 3, September 1999, pp. 197–211.

Baker Institute, 'Executive Summary Report', *Unlocking the Assets: Energy and the Future of Oil from Central Asia and the Caucasus* (Houston, TX: The Center for International Political Economy and the James A. Baker III Institute for Public Policy of Rice University, April 1998).

Baker, James, 'The State of Affairs of the Transcaucasus', interview by Jayhum Mollazade, *Caspian Crossroads*, 1, no. 2, Spring 1995, pp. 28–9.

Balland, Daniel, 'Diviser l'Indivisible: Les Frontières Introuvables des Etats Centrasiatiques', *Hérodote: Revue de Géographie et de Géopolitique*, no. 84, Spring 1997: 77–123.

Baranovsky, Vladimir (ed.), *Russia and Europe: The Emerging Security Agenda* (Oxford: Oxford University Press/Solna, Sweden: Stockholm International Peace Research Institute, 1997).

Barnes, Joe, 'US Interests in the Caspian Basin: Getting Beyond the Hype', *Unlocking the Assets: Energy and the Future of Oil from Central Asia and the Caucasus* (Houston, TX: The Center for International Political Economy and the James A. Baker III Institute for Public Policy of Rice University, April 1998).

Barry, Michael, 'Washington–Téhéran: De l'Endiguement à l'Enlisement? *Politique Internationale*, no. 76, Summer 1997, pp. 193–219.

Barylski, Robert V., 'The Russian Federation and Eurasia's Islamic Crescent', *Europe–Asia Studies*, 46, no. 3, 1994, pp. 389–416.

———, 'Russia, the West, and the Caspian Energy Hub', *Middle East Journal*, 49, no. 2, Spring 1995, pp. 217–232.

———, 'The Caspian Oil Regime: Military Dimensions', *Caspian Crossroads*, 1, no. 2, Spring 1995a, pp. 7–10.

———, 'Russian Domestic Politics, Military Power, and the Eurasian State System', in *The Roles of the United States, Russia, and China in the New World Order*, ed. Hafeez Malik (New York: St Martin's Press, 1996).

Batur-VanderLippe, Pinar and Stephen Simmons, 'Oil and Regional Relations in the Caucasus and Central Asia in the Post-Soviet Period', in *Oil in the New World Order*, Kate Gillespie and Clement Moore Henry (eds), (Gainesville, FL: University Press of Florida, 1995).

Bayulgen, Oksan, 'External Capital and Political Structures: The Case of Azerbaijan', *Anthropology of East Europe Review*, 17, no. 2, Autumn 1999, pp. 15–23.

Bazargan, Darius, 'Iran: From Russia with Love', *The Middle East*, no. 266, April 1997, p. 9.

Becker, Abraham S., 'Russia and Economic Integration in the CIS', *Survival*, 38, no. 4, Winter 1996–97, pp. 117–136.

Bell, Jonathan, 'Troubled Caspian Waters', *Project and Trade Finance*, no. 173, September 1997, p. 36.

Belokrenitski, Viacheslav, 'La Russie Contemporaine et la Région de l'Asie Centrale', *Lettre d'Asie Centrale*, no. 4, Winter 1995, pp. 3–4.

Belousova, Valera and Isabel Gorst, 'Pipeline Problems Block Oil Sector Development', *Petroleum Economist*, 63, no. 6, June 1997, pp. 10–12.

Béraud, Philippe, 'Des Economies à la Recherche d'une Transition', *Les Cahiers de l'Orient*, no. 41, Winter 1996, pp. 81–101.

Bernstein, Richard and Ross H. Munro, 'The Coming Conflict with America', *Foreign Affairs*, 76, no. 2, March–April 1997, pp. 18–32.

Bezanis, Lowell, 'China Strikes at Uighur "Splittists"', *Transition*, 2, no. 17, August 23, 1996, pp. 34–35, 64.

Bhatty, Robin and Rachel Bronson, 'NATO's Mixed Signals in the Caucasus and Central Asia', *Survival*, 42, no. 3, Autumn 2000, pp. 129–45.

Billingsley, Dodge, 'Confederates of the Caucasus', *Jane's Intelligence Review*, 9, no. 2, February 1997, pp. 65–8.

———, 'Truce Means Nothing in Western Georgia', *Jane's Intelligence Review*, 10, no. 6, June 1998, pp. 13–17.

Birol, Fatih and Nadir Guerer, 'Long-Term Oil Outlook of Eight CIS Members', *Revue de l'Energie*, 47, no. 474, January 1996, pp. 16–24.

Blacher, Philippe S., 'Turkménistan: Une Politique d'Ouverture et de Coopération Culturelle Internationale', *Lettre d'Asie Centrale*, no. 5, Summer 1996, pp. 14–16.

Blacker, Coit, 'The Challenge of Statehood: Independence and Cooperation in the Caucasus', *AGBU News*, 7, no. 3, September 1997, pp. 24–5.

Blackwill, Robert D. and Sergei A. Karaganov (eds), *Damage Limitation or Crisis? Russia and the Outside World* (Washington, D.C.: Brassey's, 1994).

Blank, Stephen, 'Russia's Real Drive to the South', *Orbis*, 39, no. 3, Summer 1995, pp. 369–86.

———, 'Energy, Economics and Security in Central Asia: Russia and Its Rivals', *Central Asian Survey*, 14, no. 3, 1995, pp. 373–406.

———, 'Energy and Security in Transcaucasia', *Journal of Muslim Minority Affairs*, 16, no. 2, July 1996, pp. 241–56.

———, 'Russia's Return to Mideast Diplomacy', *Orbis*, 40, no. 4, Fall 1996, pp. 517–35.

———, and Alvin Z. Rubinstein, 'Is Russia still a Power in Asia?' *Problems of Post-Communism*, 44, no. 2, March–April 1997, pp. 37–46.

———, 'Instability in the Caucasus: New Trends, Old Traits-Part One', *Jane's Intelligence Review*, 10, no. 4, April 1998, pp. 14–17.
———, 'Instability in the Caucasus: New Trends, Old Traits-Part Two', *Jane's Intelligence Review*, 10, no. 5, May 1998, pp. 18–21.
———, 'American Grand Strategy and the Transcaspian Region', *World Affairs*, 163, no. 2, Fall 2000, pp. 65–79.
'Blood: Thicker than Water, about as Thick as Oil', *Briefing*, no. 1159, September 15, 1997, pp. 12–13.
'Bloodshed in the Caucasus: Indiscriminate Bombing and Shelling by Azerbaijani Forces in Nagorno-Karabakh', *Human Rights Watch/Helsinki*, 5, no. 10, July 1993.
Blum, Douglas W., 'Domestic Politics and Russia's Caspian Policy', *Post-Soviet Affairs*, 14, no. 2, April–June 1998, pp. 137–64.
Bobrovnikov, Vladimir, 'Ethnic Migrations and Problems of Security in the Republic of Dagestan', *Caucasian Regional Studies*, 1, no. 1, 1997. No pagination, available only on website, http://poli.vub.ac.be/publi/crs/0201-03.htm
Bolukbasi, Suha, 'Ankara's Baku-Centered Transcaucasia Policy: Has it Failed?' *Middle East Journal*, 51, no. 1, Winter 1997, pp. 80–94.
———, 'The Controversy over the Caspian Sea Mineral Resources', *Europe–Asia Studies*, 50, no. 3, May 1998, pp. 397–414.
Borko, Yuriy, 'Possible Scenarios for Geopolitical Shifts in Russian–European Relations', in *Geopolitics in Post-Wall Europe: Security, Territory and Identity*, Ola Tunander, Pavel Baev, and Victoria Ingrid Einagel (eds), (London: Sage Publications/Oslo: International Peace Research Institute, 1997).
Bremmer, Ian, 'Rethinking US Policy in the Caucasus', *Analysis of Current Events*, 9, no. 10, October 1997, pp. 7–8.
———, 'Oil Politics: America and the Riches of the Caspian', *World Politics*, 15, no. 1, Spring 1998, pp. 27–35.
Bronson, Rachel, 'NATO's Expanding Presence in the Caucasus and Central Asia', in *NATO After Enlargement: New Challenges, New Missions, New Forces*, Stephen J. Blank (Carlisle, Pennsylvania: Strategic Studies Institute, 1998).
Brown, Bess A., 'Security Concerns of the Central Asian States', in *After Empire: The Emerging Geopolitics of Central Asia*, ed. Jed C. Snyder (Washington, D.C.: National Defense University Press, 1995).
Brownback, Sam, 'U.S. Economic and Strategic Interests in the Caspian Sea Region: Policies and Implications', *Caspian Crossroads*, 3, no. 2, Fall 1997, pp. 2–5.
Brzezinski, Zbigniew, 'The Premature Partnership', *Foreign Affairs*, 73, no. 2, March–April 1994, pp. 67–82.

——, 'Recent Memoirs: An Interview with Former National Security Adviser Zbigniew Brzesinski', interview by Jayhun Mollazade, *Caspian Crossroads*, 1, no. 3, Summer–Fall 1995, pp. 29–31.
——, Brent Scowcroft and Richard Murphy, 'Differentiated Containment', *Foreign Affairs*, 76, no. 3, May–June 1997, pp. 20–30.
——, 'A Geostrategy for Eurasia', *Foreign Affairs*, 76, no. 5, September–October 1997a, pp. 50–64.
——, 'The Grand Chessboard: US Geostrategy for Eurasia', *Harvard International Review*, 20, no. 1, Winter 1997–98, pp. 48–53.
——, 'Geopolitics and the National Interest: Iran, Central Asia and the Middle East', *Middle East Insight*, 13, no. 5, September–October 1998, pp. 21–3.
Brunot, Patrick, 'Actualité Géopolitique du Caucase', *Défense Nationale*, 50, March 1994, pp. 141–51.
Brusstar, James H., 'Russian Vital Interests and Western Security', *Orbis*, 38, no. 4, Fall 1994, pp. 607–19.
Bundy, Rodman R., 'The Caspian – Sea or Lake? Consequences in International Law', *Labyrinth: Central Asian Quarterly*, 2, no. 3, Summer 1995, pp. 26–9.
Burrows, Mathew and Carter Page, 'Waiting for the Flow: The Value of Patience in the Caspian', *National Security Studies Quarterly*, 5, no. 4, Autumn 1999, pp. 77–84.
Caccamo, Domenico, 'Panslavismo, Eurasismo, Guerra in Cecenia', *Rivista di Studi Politici Internazionali*, 62, no. 3, July–September 1995, pp. 337–51.
Calder, Kent E., 'Asia's Empty Tank', *Foreign Affairs*, 75, no. 2, March–April 1996, pp. 55–69.
Caponnetto, Fabrizio, 'Possible Gas Transportation Options from the Russian Federation and Central Asia', *Rivista di Studi Politici Internazionali*, 67, no. 3, July–September 2000, pp. 417–26.
Carley, Patricia M., 'Turkey and Central Asia: Reality Comes Calling', in *Regional Power Rivalries in the New Eurasia: Russia, Turkey, and Iran*, Alvin Z. Rubinstein and Oles M. Smolansky (eds), (Armonk, NY: M. E. Sharpe, 1995).
Carlton, David, Paul Ingram and Giancarlo Tenaglia (eds), *Rising Tension in Eastern Europe and the Former Soviet Union* (Aldershot, England: Dartmouth Publishing, 1996).
Caroli, Giuliano, 'Il Petrolio del Caucaso e il "Crocevia" Romeno', *Rivista di Studi Politici Internazionali*, 66, no. 2, April–June 1999, pp. 245–49.
Carrère d'Encausse, Hélène, *Islam and the Russian Empire: Reform and Revolution in Central Asia* (London: I. B. Tauris & Co., 1988).
Carter, Jack, 'The Great Game: The Struggle for Caspian Oil', *Caucasus*

and Caspian Seminar Series, Strengthening Democratic Institutions Project Working Paper (Cambridge, MA: John F. Kennedy School of Government, Harvard University, March 13, 1996).

Carver, Jeremy P. and Greg Englefield, 'Oil and Gas Pipelines from Central Asia: A New Approach', *The World Today*, 50, no. 6, June 1994, pp. 119–21.

Chang, Felix K., 'China's Central Asian Power and Problems', *Orbis*, 41, no. 3, Summer 1997, pp. 401–25.

Chatelus, Michel, 'La Méditerranée Orientale, la Mer Noire et la Géopolitique du Transit des Hydrocarbures', *La Revue Internationale et Stratégique*, no. 29, Spring 1998, pp. 120–28.

Chatterjee, Pratap, 'Scramble for the Caspian: Big Oil Looks to Divvy Up Caspian Sea Oil Riches', *Multinational Monitor*, 19, no. 9, September 1998, pp. 16–20.

Cherniavskii, Stanislav, 'The West Steps Up Activity in the Transcaucasus', *International Affairs*, 44, no. 4, 1998, pp. 45–53.

Cheterian, Vicken, 'Intégration Régionale Incertaine en Asie Centrale', *Le Monde Diplomatique*, 43, no. 513, December 1996, p. 14.

——, 'Sea or Lake, a Major Issue for Russia', *Cahiers d'Etudes sur la Méditerranée Orientale et le Monde Turco-Iranien (CEMOTI)*, no. 23, January–June 1997, pp. 103–25.

——, 'Sous la Menace de la Crise Afghane: Les Ambitions Contrariées de l'Ouzbékistan', *Le Monde Diplomatique*, 44, no. 520, July 1997a, p. 21.

——, 'Face-à-Face Américano–Russe autour de la Caspienne: "Grand Jeu" Pétrolier en Transcaucasie', *Le Monde Diplomatique*, 44, no. 523, October 1997b, pp. 22–3.

Chkuaseli, Mikhail, 'From Stability to Growth: Georgia's 26-year-old Finance Minister's Hopes', interview by Anne Nivat. *Transitions*, 4, no. 4, September 1997, pp. 55–7.

Chufrin, Gennady I. and Harold H. Saunders, 'The Politics of Conflict Prevention in Russia and the Near Abroad', *Washington Quarterly*, 20, no. 4, Autumn 1997, pp. 35–54.

Chylinski, Ewa A., 'De la Souveraineté à l'Indépendance: Les Contraintes Economiques Régionales de l'Asie Centrale', *Lettre d'Asie Centrale*, no. 4, Winter 1995, pp. 5–7.

Ciller, Tansu, 'The Role of Turkey in "The New World"', *Strategic Review*, 22, no. 1, Winter 1994, pp. 7–11.

Clagett, Brice M., 'Ownership of Seabed and Subsoil Resources in the Caspian Sea Under the Rules of International Law', *Caspian Crossroads*, 1, no. 3, Summer–Fall 1995, pp. 3–12.

Clark, Susan, 'The Central Asian States: Defining Security Priorities and

Developing Military Forces', in *Central Asia and the World: Kazakhstan, Uzbekistan, Tajikistan, Kyrgyzstan, Turkmenistan*, ed. Michael Mandelbaum (New York: Council on Foreign Relations Press, 1994).

Clawson, Patrick, 'The Former Soviet South and the Muslim World', in *After Empire: The Emerging Geopolitics of Central Asia*, ed. Jed C. Snyder (Washington, DC: National Defense University Press, 1995).

———, 'Iran and Caspian Basin Oil and Gas', *Perceptions*, 2, no. 4, December 1997–February 1998, pp. 17–27.

Cohen, Ariel, 'The "New Great Game": Pipeline Politics in Eurasia', *Eurasian Studies*, 3, no. 1, Spring 1996, pp. 2–15.

———, 'The "New Great Game": Pipeline Politics in Eurasia', *Caspian Crossroads*, 2, no. 1, Spring–Summer 1996a, pp. 14–21.

———, 'The Ethnic Threats to the Caucasian Pipelines', *Caspian Crossroads*, 2, no. 4, Spring 1997, pp. 7–11.

———, 'Toward a Theory of Post-Imperial Space: The Case of Central Asia', *Demokratizatsiya*, 7, no. 2, Spring 1999, pp. 253–263.

Collett, Naomi, 'Land of Black Gold', *The Middle East*, no. 265, March 1997, pp. 26–27.

Collin-Delavaud, Claude, 'Le Xinjiang', *Hérodote: Revue de Géographie et de Géopolitique*, no. 84, Spring 1997, pp. 177–200.

Coppieters, Bruno (ed.), *Contested Borders in the Caucasus* (Brussels: VUB University Press, 1996).

———, 'The Relationship between Internal Cohesion and External Sovereignty in Central Asia and the Caucasus', *Perspectives on Central Asia*, 2, no. 2, May 1997, pp. 1–4.

Cordier, Bruno de, 'The Economic Cooperation Organization: Towards a New Silk Road on the Ruins of the Cold War?' *Central Asian Survey*, 15, no. 1, March 1996, pp. 47–57.

Cornell, Svante E., 'A Chechen State?' *Central Asian Survey*, 16, no. 2, June 1997, pp. 201–13.

———, 'Iran and the Caucasus', *Middle East Policy*, 5, no. 4, January 1998, pp. 51–67.

Coville, Thierry, 'Les Relations Economiques entre l'Iran et les Nouvelles Républiques d'Asie Centrale', *Lettre d'Asie Centrale*, no. 3, Spring 1995, pp. 5–6.

———, 'The Unruly Caucasus', *Current History*, 96, no. 612, October 1997a, pp. 341–47.

Croissant, Cynthia M. and Michael P. Croissant, 'The Caspian Sea Status Dispute: Context and Implications', *Eurasian Studies*, 3, no. 4, Winter 1996–97, pp. 23–40.

Croissant, Michael P., 'Oil and Russian Imperialism in the Transcaucasus', *Eurasian Studies*, 3, no. 1, Spring 1996, pp. 16–26.

———, 'Tensions Renewed in Nagorno-Karabakh', *Jane's Intelligence Review*, 9, no. 7, July 1997, pp. 308–11.

———, 'U.S. Interests in the Caspian Sea Basin', *Comparative Strategy*, 16, no. 4, 1997, pp. 353–67.

———, and Cynthia M. Croissant, 'The Caspian Sea Status Dispute: Azerbaijani Perspectives', *Caucasian Regional Studies*, 3, no. 1, 1998.

———, 'Armenian President Quits As Line Hardens Over Nagorno-Karabakh', *Jane's Intelligence Review*, 10, no. 4, April 1998, pp. 18–20.

Cummings, Sally N., 'Russian Foreign Policy in the "Near Abroad"', in *New Studies in Post-Cold War Security*, ed. Ken R. Dark (Aldershot, England: Dartmouth Publishing, 1996).

Curran, Diane, Fiona Hill, and Elena Kostritsyna (eds), 'The Search for Peace in Chechnya: A Sourcebook 1994–1996', *Strengthening Democratic Institutions Project Working Paper* (Cambridge, MA: John F. Kennedy School of Government, Harvard University, March 1997).

Curtis, William Eleroy, *Around the Black Sea: Asia Minor, Armenia, Caucasus, Circassia, Daghestan, The Crimea, Roumania* (New York: Hodder & Stoughton, 1911).

Cutler, Robert, 'Towards Cooperative Energy Security in the South Caucasus', *Caucasian Regional Studies*, 1, no. 1, 1996.

———, 'A Strategy for Cooperative Energy Security in the Caucasus', *Caspian Crossroads*, 3, no. 1, Summer 1997, pp. 23–9.

———, 'Cooperative Energy Security in the Caspian Region: A New Paradigm for Sustainable Development?' *Global Governance*, 5, no. 2, April–June 1999, pp. 251–71.

Dadwal, Shebonti Ray, 'Iran and the US: In the Shadow of Containment', *Strategic Analysis*, 21, no. 4, July 1997, pp. 599–610.

———, 'Iran – Total Deal: Beginning of the End of ILSA?' *Strategic Analysis*, 21, no. 9, December 1997, pp. 1277–86.

Daly, John, 'Oil, Guns, and Empire: Russia, Turkey, Caspian "New Oil" and the Montreux Convention', *Caspian Crossroads*, 3, no. 2, Fall 1997, pp. 20–32.

Danielyan, Emil, 'No War, no Peace in Nagorno–Karabakh: Even Oil Politics Won't Heal the Armenian–Azerbaijani Conflict', *Transitions*, 4, no. 3, August 1997, pp. 44–9.

Dannreuther, Roland, 'Russia, Central Asia and the Persian Gulf', *Survival*, 35, no. 4, Winter 1993–94, pp. 92–112.

Darchiashvili, David, 'Georgia – The Search for State Security', *Caucasus Working Papers* (Stanford, CA: Center for International Security and Arms Control, December 1997).

Dark, Ken R. (ed.), *New Studies in Post-Cold War Security* (Aldershot, England: Dartmouth Publishing, 1996).

Davitashvili, Zurab, 'The Ethnopolitical Situation in the Caucasus and the Problem of Oil Transportation', *Caspian Crossroads*, 2, no. 2, Fall 1996, pp. 21-4.

Dekmejian, R. Hrair, and Angelos Themelis, *Ethnic Lobbies in U.S. Foreign Policy: A Comparative Analysis of the Jewish, Greek, Armenian & Turkish Lobbies* (Athens: Institute of International Relations, Panteion University of Social and Political Sciences, 1997).

Dieter, Heribert, 'Regional Integration in Central Asia: Current Economic Position and Prospects', *Central Asian Survey*, 15, nos. 3-4, December 1996, pp. 369-86.

Dietl, Gulshan, 'Quest for Influence in Central Asia: India and Pakistan', *International Studies*, 34, no. 2, April-June 1997, pp. 111-43.

Dion, Richard R., 'How Oil and Gas Investment Prospects Compare for Azerbaijan, Kazakhstan', *Oil and Gas Journal*, 95, no. 30, 28 July, 1997, pp. 25-31.

———, 'Turkmenistan Emerging as Key Player in Central Asian FSU', *Oil and Gas Journal*, 95, no. 30, 28 July, 1997, pp. 26-7.

———, 'Cutting Up the Caspian', *The World Today*, 54, no. 3, March 1998, pp. 80-2.

Dillon, Michael, 'Central Asia: The View from Beijing, Urumqi and Kashghar', in *Security Politics in the Commonwealth of Independent States: The Southern Belt*, ed. Mehdi Mozaffari. (London: Macmillan Press, 1997).

Dixit, J. N., 'India and Central Asia', in *Indian Foreign Policy: Agenda for the 21st Century*, Lalit Mansingh and others (eds), vol. 2 (New Delhi: Foreign Service Institute/Konark Publishers, 1998).

Djalali, Mohammad-Reza (ed.), 'Iran: Vers un Nouveau Rôle Régional', *Problèmes Politiques et Sociaux*, no. 720, January 1994.

——— (ed.), *Le Caucase Postsoviétique: La Transition dans le Conflit* (Brussels: Bruylant, 1995).

———, 'La Mer Caspienne: Jeu d'Echecs autour d'un Nouvel Enjeu International', *Lettre d'Asie Centrale*, no. 6, Spring 1997, p. 1.

———, 'Mer Caspienne: Perspectives Iraniennes', *Cahiers d'Etudes sur la Méditerranée Orientale et le Monde Turco-Iranien (CEMOTI)*, no. 23, January-June 1997, pp. 127-41.

———, 'La Redécouverte de l'Asie Centrale par la Communauté Internationale: Du Discours aux Réalités', in *Les Pays de la CEI Edition 1997*, Roberte Berton-Hogge and Marie-Agnès Crosnier (eds), (Paris: Les Etudes de la Documentation Française, 1997).

———, and Thierry Kellner, 'Pétrole et Gaz de la Mer Caspienne: Entre Mythe et Réalité', *Transitions*, 39, no. 2, 1998, pp. 119-58.

Doherty, Carroll J., 'Armenia's Special Relationship with U.S. is Showing

Strain', *Congressional Quarterly Weekly Report*, 55, no. 22, May 31, 1997, pp. 1270–71.

Dokuchayeva, Aleksandra Viktorovna, Andrei Valentinovich Grozin, and Konstantin Fyodorovich Zatulin, 'Protecting Russia's Interests in Kazakhstan', *Current Digest of the Post-Soviet Press*, 49, no. 27, August 6, 1997, pp. 1–5.

Dolay, Nur, 'L'Incertaine Recomposition de l'Espace Soviétique: Grandes Manoeuvres Pétrolières dans le Caucase', *Le Monde Diplomatique*, 42, no. 496, pp. 14–15.

———, 'Comment les Hommes d'Affaires Turcs ont Conquis l'Asie Centrale', *Les Cahiers de l'Orient*, no. 41, Winter 1996, pp. 145–9.

———, and Radiy Fish, 'Politique et Pétrole: L'Imbroglio du Caucase', *Les Cahiers de l'Orient*, no. 42, Spring 1996, pp. 71–84.

Dorian, James P., Ian Sheffield Rosi and S. Tony Indriyanto, 'Central Asia's Oil and Gas Pipeline Network: Current and Future Flows', *Post-Soviet Geography*, 35, no. 7, September 1994, pp. 412–30.

———, Brett Wigdortz and Dru Gladney, 'Central Asia and Xinjiang, China: Emerging Energy, Economic and Ethnic Relations', *Central Asian Survey*, 16, no. 4, December 1997, pp. 461–86.

Dorsey, James M., 'Oil Companies Rejecting US-Turkish Plans to Bypass Iran for Pipeline to Transport Caspian Oil', *Washington Report on Middle East Affairs*, 17, no. 8, January–February 1999, pp. 49, 91.

Dougherty, James E. and Robert L. Pfaltzgraff, Jr, *Contending Theories of International Relations: A Comprehensive Survey* 3rd edn. (New York: Harper Collins Publishers, 1990).

Dragadze, Tamara, 'Caucasian Views', *War Report*, no. 50, April 1997, pp. 19–20.

Dunn, Michael Collins, 'Great Games and Small: Afghanistan, Tajikistan and the New Geopolitics of Southwest Asia', *Middle East Policy*, 5, no. 2, May 1997, pp. 142–9.

Ebel, Robert E., 'The History and Politics of Chechen Oil', *Caspian Crossroads*, 1, no. 1, Winter 1995, pp. 9–11.

———, *Energy Choices in the Near Abroad: The Haves and Have-Nots Face the Future* (Washington, DC: The Center for Strategic and International Studies, 1997).

———, 'Geopolitics and Pipelines', *Analysis of Current Events*, 9, no. 2, February 1997, pp. 1–3.

———, 'The Political and Economic Implications of Transcaucasus Oil', *AGBU News*, 7, no. 3, September 1997, pp. 22–3.

Ebneyousef, Hossein, 'Caspian Oil and Gas Development', *Silk Road*, 1, no. 1, October 1997, pp. 10–13.

'Economy: Lights On, Lights Off', *Briefing*, no. 1156, 25 August, 1997, pp. 13–14.

Ehteshami, Anoushiravan, and Emma C. Murphy, 'The Non-Arab Middle East States and the Caucasian/Central Asian Republics: Turkey', *International Relations*, 11, no. 6, December 1993, pp. 513-31.

———, and ———, 'The Non-Arab Middle East States and the Caucasian/Central Asian Republics: Iran and Israel', *International Relations*, 12, no. 1, April 1994, pp. 81-107.

———, 'New Frontiers: Iran, the GCC and the CCARs', in *From the Gulf to Central Asia: Players in the New Great Game* ed. Anoushiravan Ehteshami (Exeter: University of Exeter Press, 1994).

———, 'Iran and Central Asia: Responding to Regional Change', in *Security Politics in the Commonwealth of Independent States: The Southern Belt*, ed. Mehdi Mozaffari (London: Macmillan Press, 1997).

Ellison, Herbert J. and Bruce A. Acker, 'Azerbaijan: U.S. Policy Options', *National Bureau of Asian Research (NBR) Briefing*, no. 2, June 1997, pp. 1-10.

Endo, Masao, 'Caspian Energy Resources and the Gulf States', *JIME Review*, 11, no. 42, Winter 1998, pp. 43-51.

'Energy and Geostrategy in the Caspian Region: Actors, Interests, Conflict Potentials. The 113th Conference of the Bergedorf Forum, Baku, Azerbaijan, 1998' *International Affairs*, 45, no. 3, 1999, pp. 113-211.

Englefield, Greg, 'Oil and Gas Pipeline in Central Asia', *Boundary and Security Bulletin*, 1, no. 4, January 1994, pp. 53-6.

———, 'A Spider's Web: Jurisdictional Problems in the Caspian Sea', *Boundary and Security Bulletin*, 3, no. 3, Autumn 1995, pp. 30-3.

Evans, Michael C., 'Europe's Strategic Role in the Caucasus and the Black Sea', *Strategic Review*, 27, no. 2, Spring 1999, pp. 4-10.

Fedorov, Yuri, 'Russia's Policies toward Caspian Region Oil: Neo-Imperial or Pragmatic?' *Perspectives on Central Asia*, 1, no. 6, September 1996, pp. 1-4.

———, 'Russia's Policies toward Caspian Region Oil: Neo-Imperial or Pragmatic? Part II' *Perspectives on Central Asia*, 1, no. 7, October 1996, pp. 1-4.

Feller, Gordon, 'Oil and Gas in the Caspian Sea Region', *The Washington Report on Middle East Affairs*, 15, no. 5, November-December 1996, pp. 39 and 115-16.

———, 'Central Asia's Growing Links Improve Economy', *The Washington Report on Middle East Affairs*, 16, no. 1, June-July 1997, pp. 47 and 90-1.

———, 'Turkey's New Government Looking Again to the Caucasus and Central Asia', *Washington Report on Middle East Affairs*, 16, no. 4, December 1997, pp. 26, 132.

———, 'With Billions of Petrodollars at Stake, Russia Offers Compromise on Whether Caspian is Sea or Lake', *Washington Report on Middle East Affairs*, 17, no. 4, May-June 1998, p. 57.

———, 'Central Asian states Find Neither Privatization Nor Political Reforms Correlate Exactly With Economic Growth', *Washington Report on Middle East Affairs*, 17, no. 7, October–December 1998, pp. 57–8.

Fischer, Louis, *Oil Imperialism: The International Struggle for Petroleum* (London: George Allen & Unwin, 1926).

Fontanges, E., 'Les Echanges entre la Chine et le Kazakhstan: La Fin de l'Enthousiasme', *Lettre d'Asie Centrale*, no. 3, Spring 1995, p. 8.

Forsythe, Rosemarie, *The Politics of Oil in the Caucasus and Central Asia: Prospects for Oil Exploitation and Export in the Caspian Basin; Adelphi Papers* no. 300 (Oxford: Oxford University Press, 1996).

Fourniau, Vincent, 'L'Asie Centrale et la Russie', *Lettre d'Asie Centrale*, no. 4, Winter 1995, pp. 1–3.

———, 'Un Conflit Latent en Asie Centrale: Pékin face au Mouvement National Ouïgour', *Le Monde Diplomatique*, 44, no. 522, September 1997, pp. 10–11.

———, 'La Transition depuis 1992: Politique et Institutions des Etats', in *Les Pays de la CEI Edition 1997* ed. Roberte Berton-Hogge and Marie-Agnès Crosnier (eds), (Paris: Les Etudes de la Documentation Française, 1997).

Foye, Stephen, 'Russia and the Near Abroad'', *Post-Soviet Prospects*, 3, no. 12, December 1995, pp. 1–4.

Freedman, Robert O., 'Russian Foreign Policy in the Middle East: The Kozyrev Legacy', *Caspian Crossroads*, 1, no. 4, Winter 1995–96, pp. 18–20.

———, 'Russian Policy Making and Caspian Sea Oil', *Analysis of Current Events*, 9, no. 2, February 1997, pp. 6–7.

———, 'Russia and Azerbaijan: Are Relations Beginning to Improve?' *Caspian Crossroads*, 2, no. 4, Spring 1997a, pp. 2–6.

Freij, Hanna Yousif, 'State Interests vs. the Umma: Iranian Policy in Central Asia', *Middle East Journal*, 50, no. 1, Winter 1996, pp. 71–83.

Freitag-Wirminghaus, R., 'Turkmenistan's Place in Central Asia and the World', in *Security Politics in the Commonwealth of Independent States: The Southern Belt*, ed. Mehdi Mozaffari (London: Macmillan Press, 1997).

Fuller, Elizabeth, 'The Tussle for Influence in Central Asia and the Caucasus', *Transition*, 2, no. 12, June 14, 1996, pp. 11–15.

———, 'Transcaucasus: Doomed to Strategic Partnership', *Transition*, 2, no. 23, November 15, 1996, pp. 29–31.

Fuller, Graham E., 'Russia and Central Asia: Federation or Fault Line?' in *Central Asia and the World: Kazakhstan, Uzbekistan, Tajikistan, Kyrgyzstan, Turkmenistan* ed. Michael Mandelbaum (New York: Council on Foreign Relations Press, 1994).

———, 'Central Asia's Geopolitical Future', *Post-Soviet Prospects*, 2, no. 8, October 1994, pp. 1–2.

———, 'A New World Order in Eurasia? Ideology and Geopolitics', in *The Roles of the United States, Russia, and China in the New World Order*, ed. Hafeez Malik (New York: St Martin's Press, 1996).
———, and John Arquilla, 'The Intractable Problem of Regional Powers', *Orbis*, 40, no. 4, Fall 1996, pp. 609–21.
———, 'Central Asia and Transcaucasia after the Cold War: Conflict Unleashed', in *New Studies in Post-Cold War Security*, ed. Ken R. Dark (Aldershot, England: Dartmouth Publishing, 1997).
———, 'Geopolitical Dynamics of the Caspian Region', *Caspian Crossroads*, 3, no. 2, Fall 1997a, pp. 6–9.
Funabahi, Yoichi, 'Bridging Asia's Economics-Security Gap', *Survival*, 38, no. 4, Winter 1996–97, pp. 101–16.
Galeotti, Mark, 'The Cossacks: A Cross-Border Complication to Post-Soviet Eurasia', *Boundary and Security Bulletin*, 3, no. 2, Summer 1995, pp. 55–60.
———, 'Crime in Central Asia: A Regional Problem with Global Implications', *Boundary and Security Bulletin*, 3, no. 4, Winter 1995–96, pp. 68–74.
Gamsemelidze, David, 'Back on the Great Silk Road', *War Report*, nc. 50, April 1997, p. 37.
Gankin, Leonid and Gennady Sysoyev, 'Aliyev and Shevarnadze Try to Trade Moscow for Washington', *The Current Digest of the Post-Soviet Press*, 49, no. 31, September 3, 1997, pp. 27–28.
Garcelon, Marc et al. (eds), 'Institutions, Identity, and Ethnic Conflict: International Experience and Its Implications for the Caucasus. May 2–3, 1997, Conference Report', *Berkeley Program in Soviet and Post-Soviet Studies Working Paper Series* (Berkeley, CA: Berkeley Program in Soviet and Post-Soviet Studies, 1997).
Garnett, Sherman, 'Russia's Illusory Ambitions', *Foreign Affairs*, 76, no. 2, March–April 1997, pp. 61–76.
Garthoff, Raymond L., 'The United States and the New Russia: The First Five Years', *Current History*, 96, no. 612, October 1997, pp. 305–12.
George, D., 'Caspian Equal to Mideast Gulf', *Offshore*, 56, no. 3, March 1996, p. 34.
Ghanem, Shokri, 'The Future Relationship Between OPEC and the Countries of the Former Soviet Union', *OPEC Bulletin*, 26, no. 2, February 1995, pp. 4–8.
Ghazi, Siavoch, 'Le Pétrole en Azerbaïdjan', *Lettre d'Asie Centrale*, no. 2, Fall 1994, pp. 12–13.
Giroux, Alain, 'Les Etats d'Asie Centrale face à l'Indépendance: Ouzbékistan, République Kirghize, Tadjikistan, Turkménistan', *Le Courrier des Pays de l'Est*, no. 388, April 1994, pp. 3–43.
———, 'Le Kazakhstan: Un Géant Fragile', *Lettre d'Asie Centrale*, no. 3, Spring 1995, p. 9.

———, 'La Position des Autres Etats Riverains sur le Statut de la Caspienne', *Le Courrier des Pays de l'Est*, no. 411, August 1996, pp. 58–9.

———, 'Le Kazakhstan entre Russie et Caspienne', *Cahiers d'Etudes sur la Méditerranée Orientale et le Monde Turco-Iranien (CEMOTI)*, no. 23, January–June 1997, pp. 167–81.

———, 'La Caspienne: Un Gâteau Pétrolier à Partager', *Le Courrier des Pays de l'Est*, no. 423, October 1997, pp. 5–15.

Gizzatov, Vyacheslav, 'The Legal Status of the Caspian Sea', *Labyrinth: Central Asia Quarterly*, 2, no. 3, Summer 1995, pp. 33–6.

Gladney, Dru C., 'Ethnicity and Separatism in China: Rumblings from Xinjiang's Uyghurs', *Analysis of Current Events*, 9, no. 4, April 1997, pp. 7, 11.

Gleason, Gregory, *The Central Asian States: Discovering Independence* (Boulder, CO: Westview Press, 1997).

———, 'Independence and Decolonization in Central Asia', *Asian Perspective*, 21, no. 2, Fall 1997, pp. 223–46.

———, 'Impact of the Global Financial Crisis on Political Dynamics in Central Asia', *Demokratizatsiya*, 7, no. 2, Spring 1999, pp. 241–52.

Goble, Paul A., 'Russia and its Neighbors', *Foreign Policy*, no. 90, Spring 1993, pp. 79–88.

———, 'The 50 Million Muslim Misunderstanding: The West and Central Asia Today', in *From the Gulf to Central Asia: Players in the New Great Game*, ed. Anoushiravan Ehteshami (Exeter: University of Exeter Press, 1994).

———, 'Pipeline and Pipedreams: The Geopolitics of the Transcaucasus', *Caspian Crossroads*, 1, no. 1, Winter 1995, pp. 3–6.

———, 'From Myths to Maps: American Interests in the Countries of Central Asia and the Caucasus', *Caspian Crossroads*, 3, no. 1, Summer 1997, pp. 30–32.

Goetz, Roland, 'Political Spheres of Interest in the Southern Caucasus and in Central Asia', *Aussen Politik*, 48, no. 3, 1997, pp. 257–66.

Gol, Ayla, 'Turkey: A Bridge Too Far', *War Report*, no. 50, April 1997, pp. 27–8.

Goltz, Thomas, 'Letter From Eurasia: The Hidden Russian Hand', *Foreign Policy*, no. 92, Fall 1993, pp. 92–116.

———, 'Oil and Civil Society Don't Mix', *War Report*, no. 45, September 1996, pp. 41–3.

———, 'A Contrarian View on the Caspian Oil Sweepstakes', *War Report*, no. 50, April 1997, pp. 21–2.

———, 'Catch-907 in the Caucasus', *The National Interest*, no. 48, Summer 1997a, pp. 37–45.

———, 'The Caspian Oil Sweepstakes', *The Nation*, 265, no. 16, November 17, 1997, pp. 18–21.

——, 'Aliyev's Finest Hour', *War Report*, no. 57, December–January 1997–98, p. 19.

Gorst, Isabel, 'Russia Dithers over Transit Role', *Petroleum Economist*, 64, no. 1, January 1997, pp. 35–6.

——, and Nina Poussenkova, 'Petroleum Ambassadors of Russia: State Versus Corporate Policy in the Caspian Sea Region', *Unlocking the Assets: Energy and the Future of Oil from Central Asia and the Caucasus* (Houston, TX: The Center for International Political Economy and the James A. Baker III Institute for Public Policy of Rice University, April 1998).

Gorvett, Jon, 'Pipeline Wrangle Continues', *The Middle East*, no. 287, February 1999, pp. 19–20.

——, 'How Safe is the Bosphorus?' *The Middle East*, no. 289, April 1999, pp. 31–2.

Gözen, Ramazan, 'Between Europe and Asia: Security Dimensions of Turkey's Role in the Middle East', in *New Studies in Post-Cold War Security*, ed. Ken R. Dark (Aldershot, England: Dartmouth Publishing, 1996).

Graham, Gael, 'Sorting Out the Caspian', *Financial Times East European Business Law*, no. 9, September 1996, pp. 5–6.

Granmayeh, Ali, 'The Caspian Sea in Iranian History and Politics', *Labyrinth: Central Asia Quarterly*, 2, no. 3, Summer 1995, pp. 36–40.

Grare, Frédéric, 'Les Ambitions Economiques du Pakistan en Asie Centrale: Chronique d'une Désillusion Annoncée', *Lettre d'Asie Centrale*, no. 3, Spring 1995, pp. 6–8.

——, 'La Nouvelle Donne Energétique autour de la Mer Caspienne: Une Perspective Géopolitique'. *Cahiers d'Etudes sur la Méditerranée Orientale et le Monde Turco-Iranien (CEMOTI)*, no. 23, January–June 1997, pp. 15–38.

——, 'Les Relations entre la Turquie et les Pays Riverains de la Caspienne à la Lumière des Enjeux Energétiques', *Lettre d'Asie Centrale*, no. 6, Spring 1997, pp. 16–18.

Gray, Colin S., *The Geopolitics of the Nuclear Era: Heartland, Rimland and the Technological Revolution* (New York: Crane and Russak, 1997).

Griffith, Brent, 'Back Yard Politics: Russia's Foreign Policy Toward the Caspian Basin', *Demokratizatsiya*, 6, no. 2, Spring 1998, pp. 426–41.

Grigoriev, Sergei, 'The China Card and Russia Roulette', *Perspective*, 6, no. 2, November–December 1995, pp. 1, 7.

Guerer, Nadir and Fatih Birol, 'Assessing Future Oil Export Potential in Transcaucasia and Central Asia', *OPEC Bulletin*, 26, no. 8, September 1995, pp. 8–15.

Gujer, Eric, 'Caspian Oil and Chechen Instability', *Swiss Review of World Affairs*, no. 2, February 1997, pp. 11–14.

Gulbenkian, Calouste, 'La Péninsule d'Apchéron et le Pétrole Russe', *Revue des Deux Mondes*, 61, no. 3 (105), May–June 1891, pp. 356–97.

Guliev, Hasan, 'Oil in Troubled Waters', *War Report*, no. 50, April 1997, pp. 17–18.
Guliev, Zafar, 'Great Expectations', *War Report*, no. 50, April 1997, pp. 30–2.
Gültekin, N. Bülent and Ayíe Mumcu, 'Black Sea Economic Cooperation', in *Turkey Between East and West: New Challenges for a Rising Regional Power*, ed. Vojtech Mastny and R. Craig Nation (eds) (Boulder, CO: Westview Press, 1996).
Gumpel, Werner, 'Die Schwarzmeer-Wirtschaftskooperation: Strukturen einer Neuen Staatengemeinschaft', *Europäische Rundschau*, 21, 1993, pp. 125–32.
———, 'Determinanten der Türkischen Aussenpolitik in der Schwarzmeerregion und in Mittelasien', *Südosteuropa Mitteilungen*, 38, no. 1, 1998, pp. 23–32.
Gungor, Ali and Ersel Aydlnll, 'The Dual Pipeline: Cooperation Versus Competition', *Caspian Crossroads*, 2, no. 1, Spring–Summer 1996, pp. 22–5.
Gurdon, Charles and Sarah Lloyd (eds), *Oil and Caviar in the Caspian* (London: Menas Associates, 1995).
Guseinov, Elmar and Gennady Charodeyev, 'Stakes are Greater than Oil', *The Current Digest of the Post-Soviet Press*, 47, no. 24, July 12, 1995, pp. 22–3.
Hadji-Zadeh, Hikmet, 'Russia in the Transcaucasus or Democracy in a State of Emergency', *Caspian Crossroads*, 2, no. 2, Fall 1996, pp. 5–10.
———, 'Democracy in a State of Emergency', *Transition*, 3, no. 4, March 7, 1997, pp. 42–5.
———, 'War Blockades Everyone', *War Report*, no. 50, April 1997, p. 32.
Hafiz-Khodja, Mohamed, 'Re-Igniting Oil Production in the CIS: Some Key Issues During the Transition', *OPEC Bulletin*, 24, no. 1, January 1993, pp. 7–11.
Halbach, Uwe, 'The Caucasus as a Region of Conflict', *Aussen Politik*, 48, no. 4, 1997, pp. 358–67.
Hale, William and Eberhard Kienle (eds), *After the Cold War: Security and Democracy in Africa and Asia* (London: I.B. Tauris, 1997).
Halliday, Fred, 'The Empires Strike Back? Russia, Iran and the New Republics', *The World Today*, 51, no. 11, November 1995, pp. 220–22.
Hanks, Reuel R., 'Directions in the Ethnic Politics of Kazakhstan: Concession, Compromise, or Catastrophe?' *Journal of Third World Studies*, 15, no. 1, Spring 1998, pp. 143–62.
Haquani, Zalmaï, 'La Crise Afghane: Une Menace pour l'Asie Centrale', *Le Courrier des Pays de l'Est*, no. 423, October 1997, pp. 30–3.
Harary, Frank and Harold Miller, 'A Graph-Theoretic Approach to the

Analysis of International Relations', *Journal of Conflict Resolution*, 14, no. 1, March 1970, pp. 57–63.

Hardt, John P., James Voorhees and Phillip Kaiser, *Beyond Chechnya: Some Options for Russia and the West* (Bethesda, MD: Library of Congress/Congressional Research Service, 1995).

Harris, Andrew, 'The Azerbaijan–Turkmenistan Dispute in the Caspian Sea', *Boundary and Security Bulletin*, 5, no. 4, Winter 1997–8, pp. 56–62.

Harris, George S., 'The Russian Federation and Turkey', in *Regional Power Rivalries in the New Eurasia: Russia, Turkey, and Iran*, Alvin Z. Rubinstein and Oles M. Smolansky (eds), (Armonk, NY: M. E. Sharpe, 1995).

Hasanov, Hasan, 'Oil is our Destiny: Azerbaijan Wields a New Political Weapon', Interview by Anne Nivat. *Transitions*, 4, no. 4, September 1997, pp. 63–5.

Hassan-Yari, Houchang, 'Organisation de la Coopération Economique – Un Pont Stratégique entre le Moyen-Orient et l'Asie Centrale', *Etudes Internationales*, 28, no. 1, March 1997, pp. 47–71.

Hauner, Milan, *What is Asia to Us? Russia's Asian Heartland Yesterday and Today* (London: Routledge, 1992).

Hays, F. Wallace, 'US Congress and the Caspian', *Caspian Crossroads*, 3, no. 3, Winter 1998, pp. 8–11.

Hekimyan, Vedi, 'Echanges et Coopération entre les Etats-Unis et Douze Etats Issus de l'URSS', *Le Courrier des Pays de l'Est*, no. 407, March 1996, pp. 53–81.

Henley, John S. and George B. Assaf, 'Re-Integrating the Central Asian Republics into the World Economy', *Intereconomics*, 30, no. 5, September–October 1995, pp. 235–46.

Henry, J. D., *Baku: An Eventful History* (London: Archibald Constable & Co., 1905).

Henze, Paul, 'Russia and the Caucasus', *Perceptions*, 1, no. 2, June–August 1996, pp. 53–71.

———, and Enders Winbush, 'American Middle East Policy: The Need for New Thinking'. *Caspian Crossroads*, 2, no. 3, Winter 1997, pp. 2–8.

———, 'Boundaries and Ethnic Groups in Central Asia and the Caucasus: Cause of Conflict and Change?' *Caspian Crossroads*, 3, no. 1, Summer 1997, pp. 6–17.

Herzig, Edmund, *Iran and the Former Soviet South* (London: Royal Institute of International Affairs, 1995).

Heslin, Sheila, 'Key Constraints to Caspian Energy Development: Status, Significance, and Outlook', *Unlocking the Assets: Energy and the Future of Oil from Central Asia and the Caucasus* (Houston, TX: The Center for International Political Economy and the James A. Baker III Institute for Public Policy of Rice University, April 1998).

Hewins, Ralph, *Mr Five Per Cent: The Story of Calouste Gulbenkian* (New York: Rinehart & Co., 1958).

Hill, Fiona and Pamela Jewett, 'Report on Ethnic Conflict in the Russian Federation and Transcaucasia', *Strengthening Democratic Institutions Project Working Paper* (Cambridge, MA: John F. Kennedy School of Government, Harvard University, July 1993).

——, ——, Sergei Grigoriev and Elena Kostritsyna, 'Back in the USSR: Russia's Intervention in the Internal Affairs of the Former Soviet Republics and the Implications for United States Policy Toward Russia', *Strengthening Democratic Institutions Project Working Paper* (Cambridge, MA: John F. Kennedy School of Government, Harvard University, January 1994).

——, 'Russia's Tinderbox: Conflict in the North Caucasus and its Implications for the Future of the Russian Federation', *Strengthening Democratic Institutions Project Working Paper* (Cambridge, MA: John F. Kennedy School of Government, Harvard University, September 1995).

——, 'Pipeline Politics, Russo–Turkish Competition and Geopolitics in the Eastern Mediterranean', *Cyprus Review*, 8, no. 1, Spring 1996, pp. 83–100.

——, 'Pipeline Dreams in the Caucasus', *Caucasus and Caspian Seminar Series, Strengthening Democratic Institutions Project Working Paper* (Cambridge, MA: John F. Kennedy School of Government, Harvard University, September 1996).

——, 'Russian Policy in the Caspian, Black Sea and the Eastern Mediterranean', *Cyprus Review*, 9, no. 1, Spring 1997, pp. 22–43.

Hiro, Dilip, 'Turkmenistan and Iran: US Advice Ignored', *Middle East International*, no. 551, 30 May, 1997, pp. 19–20.

——, 'Why is the US Inflating Caspian Oil Reserves?' *Middle East International*, no. 558, 12 September, 1997a, pp. 18–19.

——, 'Kazakhstan Turns East', *Middle East International*, no. 560, 10 October, 1997b, pp. 19–20.

——, 'Oil and Gas in the Caspian Basin', *Middle East International*, no. 563, 21 November, 1997c, pp. 16–17.

——, 'Troubled Waters: The Legal Status of the Caspian', *Middle East International*, no. 574, 8 May, 1998, pp. 19–20.

Hirschhausen, Christian von and Hella Engerer, 'Energy in the Caspian Sea Region in the late 1990s: The End of the Boom?' *OPEC Review*, 23, no. 4, December 1999, pp. 273–91.

Hitchens, Christopher, 'In the Pipeline', *The Nation*, 265, no. 11, 13 October, 1997, p. 9.

Hollis, Rosemary, 'Western Security Strategy in South West Asia', in *From the Gulf to Central Asia: Players in the New Great Game*, ed. Anoushiravan Ehteshami (Exeter: University of Exeter Press, 1994).

Holoboff, Elaine M., 'Oil and the Burning of Groznyy', *Jane's Intelligence Review*, 7, no. 6, June 1995, pp. 253–7.

———, 'Russia: Oil, Guns, and Pipes', *War Report*, no. 50, April 1997, pp. 25–6.

Hovannisian, Raffi K., 'Les Perspectives de Paix et de Sécurité dans le Caucase', *Politique Etrangère*, 61, no. 4, Winter 1996–97, pp. 881–6.

Howard, Glen E., 'NATO and the Caucasus: The Caspian Axis', in *NATO After Enlargement: New Challenges, New Missions, New Forces*, ed. Stephen J. Blank (Carlisle, PA: Strategic Studies Institute, 1998).

Hueper, Paul H., 'Afghanistan: Risk and Reward between the Front Lines', *Gas in the CIS and Eastern Europe (Annual Supplement of the Petroleum Economist)*, September 1997, pp. 37–40.

Hulings, Joseph, 'Is there a Future for Reform in the Caspian Basin?' *Caspian Crossroads*, 2, no. 3, Winter 1997, pp. 14–17.

Hunter, Richard and David Riley, 'Caspian Energy: "The Oil is not Enough"', *Fitch IBCA Corporates* (London: Fitch IBCA, June 2000).

Hunter, Shireen T., *The Transcaucasus in Transition: Nation-Building and Conflict* (Washington, DC: The Center for Strategic and International Studies, 1994).

———, *Central Asia since Independence* (Washington, DC: The Center for Strategic and International Studies, 1996).

Huntington, Samuel P., *The Clash of Civilizations and the Remaking of World Order* (New York: Simon and Schuster, 1996).

Hutchings, Raymond, *Japan's Economic Involvement in Eastern Europe and Eurasia* (Houndmills, Basingstoke, Hampshire: Macmillan Press, 1999).

Huttenbach, Henry R., 'Chaos in Post-Soviet Caucasia, Crossroads of Empires: in Search of a U.S. Foreign Policy', in *The Successor States to the USSR*, ed. John W. Blaney (Washington, DC: Congressional Quarterly, 1995).

Hyman, Anthony, 'Central Asia's Relations with Afghanistan and South Asia', in *The New Central Asia and its Neighbours*, ed. Peter Ferdinand (London: Pinter Publishers, 1994).

———, 'Central Asia and the Middle East: The Emerging Links', in *Central Asia and the Caucasus after the Soviet Union: Domestic and International Dynamics*, ed. Mohiaddin Mesbahi (Gainesville, FL: University Press of Florida, 1994a).

———, 'Kuwait by the Caspian', *The Middle East*, no. 238, October 1994b, p. 32.

———, 'Turkey: Eastern Approaches', *The Middle East*, no. 242, February 1995, pp. 32–4.

———, 'Afghanistan and the Middle East', in *Security Politics in the Commonwealth of Independent States: The Southern Belt*, ed. Mehdi Mozaffari (London: Macmillan Press, 1997).

Ibrahimov, Mahir and Erjan Kurbanov, 'Getting it Wrong in the Caucasus', *Middle East Quarterly*, 1, no. 1, December 1994, pp. 65–70.

International Institute for Strategic Studies. 'Caspian Oil: Not the Great Game Revisited', *Strategic Survey 1997/98*, April 1998, pp. 22–9.

Isa-Zade, Azad, 'Who Gets the Oil?' *War Report*, no. 42, June 1996, pp. 40–1.

———, 'Armeniagate', *War Report*, no. 51, May 1997, pp. 16–17.

Ivanov, Alexander, 'Inter-Ethnic Conflicts of the New Generation': A Russian View', in *Rising Tension in Eastern Europe and the Former Soviet Union*, David Carlton, Paul Ingram and Giancarlo Tenaglia (eds), (Aldershot, England: Dartmouth Publishing, 1996).

Jaffe, Amy Myers and George Marcus (eds), 'Social, Cultural, and Religious Factors That Affect the Supply of Oil from Central Asia and the Caucasus', *Unlocking the Assets: Energy and the Future of Oil from Central Asia and the Caucasus* (Houston, TX: The Center for International Political Economy and the James A. Baker III Institute for Public Policy of Rice University, April 1998).

———, 'The Gulf and the Basin: Stability, Development and Falling Prices', *Middle East Insight*, 13, no. 6, November–December 1998, pp. 17–18, 52–3.

Jean, François, 'Tchétchénie: Guerre Totale et Complaisance Internationale', *Relations Internationales et Stratégiques*, no. 23, Fall 1996, pp. 24–33.

Jones, Stephen F., 'Georgia: The Caucasian Context', *Caspian Crossroads*, 1, no. 2, Spring 1995, pp. 11–13.

Jonson, Lena and Clive Archer (eds), *Peacekeeping and the Role of Russia in Eurasia* (Boulder, Colorado: Westview Press, 1996).

Joseph, Ira, 'Caspian Gas Exports: Stranded Reserves in a Unique Predicament', *Unlocking the Assets: Energy and the Future of Oil from Central Asia and the Caucasus* (Houston, TX: The Center for International Political Economy and the James A. Baker III Institute for Public Policy of Rice University, April 1998).

Kachia, Janri, 'Caucase: Le Vrai-Faux Contrat du Siècle', ' *Politique Internationale*, no. 70, Winter 1995–96, pp. 39–51.

Kalicki, Jan H., 'US Policy in the Caspian: Pipelines, Partnership and Prosperity', *Middle East Policy*, 6, no. 2, October 1998, pp. 145–49.

Kalugin, Oleg D., 'At the Crossroads', *Caspian Crossroads*, 2, no. 4, Spring 1997, pp. 18–20.

Kangas, Roger D., 'Uzbekistan: Taking the Lead in Central Asian Security', *Transition*, 2, no. 9, 3 May, 1996, pp. 52–5.

Karapetian, Suren, 'The Economics of Isolation', *War Report*, no. 50, April 1997, pp. 35–6.

Karpat, Kemal H., 'The Sociopolitical Environment Conditioning the Foreign Policy of the Central Asian States', in *The Making of Foreign Policy in Russia and the New States of Eurasia*, Adeed Dawisha and Karen Dawisha (eds), (Armonk, NY: M. E. Sharpe, 1995).

———, 'The Ottoman Rule in Europe from the Perspective of 1994', in *Turkey Between East and West: New Challenges for a Rising Regional Power*, Vojtech Mastny and R. Craig Nation (eds), (Boulder, CO: Westview Press, 1996).

———, 'Turkish Foreign Policy: Some Introductory Remarks', in *Turkish Foreign Policy: Recent Developments*, ed. Kemal H. Karpat (Madison: University of Wisconsin Press, 1996a).

———, 'The Foreign Policy of the Central Asian States, Turkey, and Iran', in *Turkish Foreign Policy: Recent Developments*, ed. Kemal H. Karpat (Madison: University of Wisconsin Press, 1996b).

Karpyuk, Mark Ivanovich and Vasiliy Valentinovich Shavandin, 'Astrakhaners on the Caspian Sea', *International Affairs*, 42, no. 1, January–February, pp. 141–7.

Kaser, Michael and Santosh Mehotra, 'The Central Asian Economies after Independence', in *Challenges for the Former Soviet South*, ed. Roy Allison (London: The Royal Institute of International Affairs, 1996).

Kaser, Michael, *The Economies of Kazakstan and Uzbekistan* (London: Royal Institute of International Affairs, 1997).

Kasimov, S. M., 'Uzbekistan's Place in the World Economy', in *Security Politics in the Commonwealth of Independent States: The Southern Belt*, ed. Mehdi Mozaffari (London: Macmillan Press, 1997).

Katz, Mark N., 'Emerging Patterns in the International Relations of Central Asia', in *The Making of Foreign Policy in Russia and the New States of Eurasia*, Adeed Dawisha and Karen Dawisha (eds), (Armonk, NY: M. E. Sharpe, 1995).

———, 'An Emerging Russian–Iranian Alliance?' *Caspian Crossroads*, 1, no. 4, Winter 1995–96, pp. 21–4.

———, 'Central Asian Stability: Under Threat?' *SAIS Review*, 17, no. 1, Winter–Spring 1997, pp. 31–46.

———, 'Tajikistan and Russia: Sources of Instability in Central Asia', *Caspian Crossroads*, 2, no. 4, Spring 1997, pp. 12–17.

Katzman, Kenneth, 'Iran, Russia, and the New Muslim States', *Caspian Crossroads*, 1, no. 2, Spring 1995, pp. 14–16.

Kellner, Thierry, 'La Chine et les Républiques d'Asie Centrale: De la Défiance au Partenariat', *Cahiers d'Etudes sur la Méditerranée Orientale et le Monde Turco-Iranien (CEMOTI)*, no. 22, July–December 1996, pp. 277–313.

Kemp, Geoffrey and Robert E. Harkavy, *Strategic Geography and the Changing Middle East* (Washington, DC: Carnegie Endowment for International Peace, 1997).

Keohane, Robert O. (ed.), *Neorealism and its Critics* (New York: Columbia University Press, 1986).

———, and Joseph Nye, *Power and Interdependence: World Politics in Transition* (Boston: Little, Brown, 1977).

Kepbanov, Yolbars A., 'The New Legal Status of the Caspian Sea is Basis of Regional Cooperation and Stability', *Perceptions*, 2, no. 4, December 1997–February 1998, pp. 8–16.

Khachatrian, Haroutiun, 'Is Armenia Blockaded?' *War Report*, no. 50, April 1997, pp. 33–4.

Khan, Shahid S. and Clyde Mark, *Islamic Movements in Selected Asian Countries: U.S. Interests and Policy Options* (Bethesda, MD: Library of Congress/Congressional Research Service, 1995).

Khavand, Fereydoun A., 'L'Organisation de Coopération Economique: Un Regroupement Incertain', *Le Courrier des Pays de l'Est*, no. 423, October 1997, pp. 16–23.

Khodakov, Alexander, 'The Legal Framework for Regional Cooperation in the Caspian Sea Region', *Labyrinth: Central Asia Quarterly*, 2, no. 3, Summer 1995, pp. 30–3.

Khripunov, Igor and Mary M. Matthews, 'Russia's Oil and Gas Interest Group and Its Foreign Agenda', *Problems of Post-Communism*, 43, no. 3, May–June 1996, pp. 38–48.

Khutsishvili, George, 'Intervention in Transcaucasus', *Perspective*, 4, no. 3, February–March 1994, pp. 2–3, 6.

Kielmas, Maria, 'Caspian Energy: Politics vs. Economics', *Middle East International*, no. 593, 12 February 1999, pp. 18–19.

Kirimli, Meryem, 'Uzbekistan in the New World Order', *Central Asian Survey*, 16, no. 1, March 1997, pp. 53–64.

Kissinger, Henry A., *A World Restored – Europe After Napoleon: The Politics of Conservatism in a Revolutionary State* (New York: Grosset and Dunlap, 1964).

Klid, Bohdan, 'Ukraine as a Transportation Corridor for Caspian Sea Oil to Europe', *Caspian Crossroads*, 3, no. 1, Summer 1997, pp. 18–22.

Kolchin, Sergei, 'Foreign Investment in Kazakhstan's Oil and Gas Complex', *Jamestown Foundation Prism*, 3, no. 17, 24 October, 1997, pp. 8–10.

Kopanski, Ataullah Bogdan, 'Burden of the Third Rome: The Threat of Russian Orthodox Fundamentalism and Muslim Eurasia', *Islam and Christian–Muslim Relations*, 9, no. 2, July 1998, pp. 193–216.

Kortunov, Andrei, 'Russia and Central Asia: Evolution of Mutual Perceptions, Policies, Interdependence', *Unlocking the Assets: Energy and the Future of Oil from Central Asia and the Caucasus* (Houston, TX: The Center for International Political Economy and the James A. Baker III Institute for Public Policy of Rice University, April 1998).

Kovalev, Sergei, 'The Anti-NATO Coterie', *Perspective*, 7, no. 4, March–April 1997, pp. 2–4.

Kramer, Heinz and Friedemann Müller, 'Relations with Turkey and the Caspian Basin Countries', in *Allies Divided: Transatlantic Policies for the Greater Middle East*, Robert D. Blackwill and Michael Stürmer (eds), (Cambridge, MA: MIT Press, 1997).

Kremeniuk, Victor, *Conflicts In and Around Russia: Nation-Building in Difficult Times* (Westport, CT: Greenwood Press, 1994).

———, 'Post-Soviet Conflicts: New Security Concerns', in *Russia and Europe: The Emerging Security Agenda* ed. Vladimir Baranovsky (Oxford: Oxford University Press/Solna, Sweden: Stockholm International Peace Research Institute, 1997).

Krikorian, Robert, 'Odd Bedfellows: Armenia and Caspian Oil', *Analysis of Current Events*, 9, no. 2, February 1997, pp. 10–11.

Krikorian, Van Z., ' "Sisyphus" Oil: Pipelines and Politics in the Caspian Basin', *CIS Law Notes*, December 1995, pp. 1–7.

———, 'Turkmenistan's Petroleum Law', *CIS Law Notes*, September 1997, pp. 14–22.

Krylov, N. A., A. A. Bokserman and E. R. Stavrovsky (eds), *The Oil Industry of the Former Soviet Union* (Amsterdam: Gordon and Breach Science Publishers, 1998).

Kubicek, Paul, 'Regionalism, Nationalism and Realpolitik in Central Asia', *Europe–Asia Studies*, 49, no. 4, June 1997, pp. 637–55.

Kunilholm, Bruce, 'The Geopolitics of the Caspian Basin', *Midddle East Journal*, 54, no. 4, Autumn 2000, pp. 546–71.

Kunzweiler, William R., 'The New Central Asian Great Game', *Strategic Review*, 26, no. 3, Summer 1998, pp. 24–33.

Kupchan, Charles, A., 'NATO Maneuvers on Russia', *The Nation*, 265, no. 20, 15 December, 1997, pp. 24–6.

Kurbanov, Erjan, 'Azerbaijan Security Concerns: Conflict with Armenia over Nagorno-Karabakh and Potentials for Other Internal Discords', *Eurasian Studies*, 3, no. 4, Winter 1996–97, pp. 2–22.

———, 'Oil, Ethnic Relations, and Azerbaijani Security', *Analysis of Current Events*, 9, no. 10, October 1997, pp. 6, 9.

Kutschera, Chris, 'Azerbaijan: The Kuwait of the Caucasus?' *The Middle East*, no. 254, March 1996, pp. 6–9.

La Casse, Chantale, 'On the Renewal of Concern for the Security of Oil Supply', *The Energy Journal*, 16, no. 2, 1995, pp. 1–21.

Laird, Laurie, 'Is Kazakhstan the New Kuwait?' *Europe*, no. 341, November 1994, pp. 18–19.

Laitin, David D. and Ronald Grigor Suny, 'Armenia and Azerbaijan: Thinking a Way Out of Karabakh', *Middle East Policy*, 7, no. 1, October 1999, pp. 145–76.

Land, Thomas, 'Regional: Pipelines and Politics', *The Middle East*, no. 252, January 1996, pp. 25–6.

———, 'Caspian Neighbours Seek Accord on Offshore Deals', *The Middle East*, no. 265, March 1997, pp. 22–3.

Lange, Keely, 'Nationals, Citizens, Countrymen: A New Analysis of Identities with a Focus on Central Asia', *Journal of Third World Studies*, 12, no. 2, Fall 1995, pp. 174–99.

Lanskoy, Miriam, 'Georgia: "A Far-Off Country..."?' *Perspective*, 7, no. 3, January–February 1997, pp. 3, 9–10.

Larrabee, F. Stephen, 'U.S. and European Policy toward Turkey and the Caspian Basin', in *Allies Divided: Transatlantic Policies for the Greater Middle East*, Robert D. Blackwill and Michael Stürmer (eds), (Cambridge, MA: MIT Press, 1997).

Legault, Albert and Isabelle Desmartis, 'Le Cancer Tchétchéne', *Relations Internationales et Stratégiques*, no. 17, Spring 1995, pp. 39–46.

Lehman, Susan Goodrich, 'Islam and Ethnicity in the Republics of Russia', *Post-Soviet Affairs*, 13, no. 1, January–March 1997, pp. 78–103.

Lenczowski, George, 'Caspian Oil and Gas: A New Source of Wealth?' *Middle East Policy*, 5, no. 1, January 1997, pp. 111–19.

Lepingwell, John W.R., 'The Russian Military and Security Policy in the Near Abroad", *Survival*, 36, no. 3, Autumn 1994, pp. 70–92.

Lepor, Keith Philip, 'Pipelines, Pragmatism and Geopolitics', *Middle East Insight*, 13, no. 4, May–June 1998, pp. 11–12, 59–60.

Lester, Toby, 'New-Alphabet Disease?' *The Atlantic Monthly*, 280, no. 1, July 1997, pp. 20–27.

Libaridian, Gerard J., 'The Politics of Promises', *AGBU News*, 7, no. 3, September 1997, pp. 19–21.

Liscia, Claude, 'Au Kazakhstan, la Nostalgie des Réfugiés', *Le Monde Diplomatique*, 44, no. 522, September 1997, pp. 10–11.

Lloyd, Sarah J., 'Pipelines to Prosperity?' *The International Spectator*, 32, no. 1, January–March 1997, pp. 53–70.

———, 'Land-Locked Central Asia: Implications for the Future', *Geopolitics and International Boundaries*, 2, no. 1, Summer 1997, pp. 97–133.

Locatelli, Catherine, 'Le Secteur des Hydrocarbures Russes: Entre Economie de Marché et Economie Planifiée', *Revue de L'Energie*, 47, no. 474, January 1996, pp. 25–38.

———, 'Les Enjeux Caspienne-Russie dans l'Approvisionnement Gazier Asiatique', *Revue de L'Energie*, 49, no. 501, November 1998, pp. 568–78.

Longworth, Richard C., 'Boomtown Baku', *The Bulletin of Atomic Scientists*, 54, no. 3, May–June 1998, pp. 34–8.

Love, Patrick, 'The Changing Face of Energy Geopolitics', *OECD Observer*, nos. 217–18, Summer 1999, pp. 48–50.

Lucca, Robert, 'Russia–Kazakh Relations Remain Rocky Despite Strategic Alliance', *Jane's Intelligence Review*, 12, no. 9, September 2000, pp. 25–8.

Luong, Pauline Jones, 'Energy and International Relations in Central Asia', *Analysis of Current Events*, 9, no. 11, November 1997, pp. 6–8.

MacDougall, Jim, 'Russian Policy in the Transcaucasian Near Abroad': The Case of Azerbaijan', *Demokratizatsiya*, 5, no. 1, Winter 1997, pp. 89–101.

MacFarlane, S. Neil, 'The Structure of Instability in the Caucasus', *Internationale Politik und Gesellschaft*, no. 4, 1995, pp. 380–93.

———, 'The UN, the OSCE, and the Southern Caucasus', *Caspian Crossroads*, 2, no. 3, Winter 1997, pp. 18–23.

———, 'Democratization, Nationalism and Regional Security in the Southern Caucasus', *Government and Opposition*, 32, no. 3, Summer 1997, pp. 399–420.

Mackinder, Halford, *Democratic Ideals and Reality* (New York: Norton, 1962).

Mahmood, Tehmina, 'Pakistan and Central Asia', *Eurasian Studies*, 3, no. 4, Winter 1996–97, pp. 79–94.

Makarenko, Tamara, 'Crime and Terrorism in Central Asia', *Jane's Intelligence Review*, 12, no. 7, July 2000, pp. 16–17.

———, 'Central Asia Commits to Military Reform', *Jane's Intelligence Review*, 12, no. 9, September 2000, pp. 29–32.

Makarychev, Andrey S., 'Russian Regions as International Actors', *Demokratizatsiya*, 7, no. 4, Fall 1999, pp. 501–26.

Malashenko, Aleksei, 'The Taliban's Success in Afghanistan: Causes and Possible Consequences', *Prism (Jamestown Foundation)*, 3, no. 1, January 1997, pp. 1, 12–13, 18.

———, 'What Will Chechnya Do with Its Sovereignty?' *Prism (Jamestown Foundation)*, 3, no. 5, April 18, 1997, pp. 5, 10–11.

Malcolm, Neil, Alex Pravda, Roy Allison and Margot Light (eds), *Internal Factors in Russian Foreign Policy* (London: Royal Institute of International Affairs/Oxford: Oxford University Press, 1996).

Malik, Hafeez (ed.), *The Roles of the United States, Russia, and China in the New World Order* (New York: St Martin's Press, 1996).

Manafi, Kambiz, 'Refining, Oil Balances and Trade in the Black Sea, Transcaucasian and Central Asian Republics', *OPEC Bulletin*, 24, no. 8, September 1993, pp. 9–11.

Mandelbaum, Michael, 'Westernizing Russia and China', *Foreign Affairs*, 76, no. 3, May–June 1997, pp. 80–96.

Mango, Andrew J. A., 'Testing Time in Turkey', *The Washington Quarterly*, 20, no. 1, Winter 1997, pp. 3–20.

Mardin, Serif, 'Culture in Geopolitics', *Caspian Crossroads*, 1, no. 2, Spring 1995, pp. 17–19.

Maresca, John J., 'A 'Peace Pipeline' to end the Nagorno–Karabakh Conflict', *Caspian Crossroads*, 1, no. 1, Winter 1995, pp. 17–18.

Mark, David E., 'Eurasia Letter: Russia and the New Transcaucasus', *Foreign Policy*, no. 105, Winter 1996–97, pp. 141–159.

Markov, Sergei, 'In Defense of Moscow's Anti-Western Tilt', *Perspective*, 6, no. 2, November–December 1995, pp. 2–3 and 8.

Martin, Josh, 'Afghanistan: Pipeline Wrangle Continues', *The Middle East*, no. 267, May 1997, pp. 24–25.

———, 'Arabs Cast Wary Eye on Caspian Oil', *The Middle East*, no. 289, April 1999, pp. 35–36.

———, 'Pipeline to Profits', *Management Review*, April 1999, pp. 45–50.

Masih, Joseph R. and Michael P. Croissant, 'Pipeline Politics in the Transcaucasus', *National Security Studies Quarterly*, 3, no. 1, Winter 1997, pp. 61–74.

Matejka, Harriet, 'Mer Caspienne: Questions de Coopération Economique', *Cahiers d'Etudes sur la Méditerranée Orientale et le Monde Turco–Iranien (CEMOTI)*, no. 23, January–June 1997, pp. 89–100.

Matveev, Alexandre, 'Le Statut de la Mer Caspienne: Le Point de Vue Russe', *Le Courrier des Pays de l'Est*, no. 411, August 1996, pp. 55–61.

Mayer, Alfred Thayan, *The Influence of Sea Power upon History, 1660–1783* (Boston: Little, Brown, 1897).

McCallin, Jessica, 'The Race is On', *Project Finance*, no. 186, October 1998, pp. 18–23.

McCauley, Martin (ed.), *Investing in the Caspian Sea Region: Opportunity and Risk* (London: Catermill Publishing, 1996).

McCarthy, John, 'The Geo-Politics of Caspian Oil', *Jane's Intelligence Review*, 12, no. 7, July 2000, pp. 20–5.

McDonald, Paul, 'Finding An Exit from Central Asia: Can the Region's Oil Be Exported?' *JIME Review*, 11, no. 41, Autumn 1998, pp. 5–17.

McDonell, Gavan, 'The Euro-Asian Corridor', in *Challenges for the Former Soviet South*, ed. Roy Allison (London: The Royal Institute of International Affairs, 1996).

McFaul, Michael, 'Russia's Many Foreign Policies', *Demokratizatsiya*, 7, no. 3, Summer 1999, pp. 393–412.

McGuinn, Bradford, 'From the Caspian to the Gulf: The Assertion of U.S. Power', *Middle East Insight*, 13, no. 1, November–December 1997, pp. 10–15.

———, 'NATO's Prize: The Euro-Atlantic Security System and the Caspian Sea Region', *Silk Road*, 1, no. 2, December 1997, pp. 8–17.

———, 'The Caspian Region: Capitalism's New Comrades', *Middle East Insight*, 13, no. 5, September–October 1998, pp. 18–20.

Mehden, Fred R. von der, 'Islam and Energy Security in Central Asia', *Unlocking the Assets: Energy and the Future of Oil from Central Asia and the Caucasus* (Houston, TX: The Center for International Political Economy and the James A. Baker III Institute for Public Policy of Rice University, April 1998).

Mendras, Marie (ed.), 'Russie: Le Débat sur l'Intérêt National', *Problèmes Politiques et Sociaux*, no. 694, December 1992.

Menon, Rajan, 'In the Shadow of the Bear: Security in post-Soviet Central Asia', *International Security*, 20, no. 1, Summer 1995, pp. 149–81.

———, 'Central Asia's Foreign Policy and Security Challenges: Implications for the United States', *National Bureau of Asian Research (NBR) Analysis*, 6, no. 4, December 1995, pp. 5–15.

———, 'The Strategic Convergence Between Russia and China', *Survival*, 39, no. 2, Summer 1997, pp. 101–25.

———, 'Treacherous Terrain: The Political and Security Dimensions of Energy Developments in the Caspian Sea Zone', *NBR Analysis*, 9, no. 1, February 1998, pp. 7–44.

Merzliakov, Iu, 'Legal Status of the Caspian Sea', *International Affairs*, 45, no. 1, 1999, pp. 33–9.

Mesbahi, Mohiaddin, 'Introduction: The Emerging Muslim' States of Central Asia and the Caucasus', in *Central Asia and the Caucasus after the Soviet Union: Domestic and International Dynamics*, ed. Mohiaddin Mesbahi (Gainesville, FL: University Press of Florida, 1994).

———, 'Russia and the Geopolitics of the Muslim South', in *Central Asia and the Caucasus after the Soviet Union: Domestic and International Dynamics*, ed. Mohiaddin Mesbahi (Gainesville, FL: University Press of Florida, 1994a).

———, 'Russia and Its Central Asian Near-Abroad': Towards a Doctrine for the Periphery', in *The Roles of the United States, Russia, and China in the New World Order*, ed. Hafeez Malik (New York: St Martin's Press, 1996).

———, 'Tajikistan, Iran, and the International Politics of the "Islamic Factors"', *Central Asian Survey*, 16, no. 2, June 1997, pp. 141–58.

Miles, Carolyn, 'The Caspian Pipeline Debate Continues: Why Not Iran?' *Journal of International Affairs*, 53, no. 1, Fall 1999, pp. 325–46.

Milivojevic, Marko, 'Transcaucasia's Godot', *War Report*, no. 50, April 1997, pp. 23–4.

Miller, Steven E., 'Russian National Interests', in *Damage Limitation or Crisis? Russia and the Outside World*, Robert D. Blackwill and Sergei A. Karaganov (eds), (Washington, DC: Brassey's, 1994).

Mitchell, John V., Peter Beck and Michal Grubb, *The New Geopolitics of Energy* (London: Royal Institute of International Affairs, 1996).

Miyamoto, Akira, *Natural Gas in Central Asia: Industries, Markets and Export Options of Kazakhstan, Turkmenistan and Uzbekistan* (London: Royal Institute of International Affairs, 1997).

Mkrttchian, Nerses, 'European Security and Conflict Resolution in the Transcaucasus', *Caucasus Working Papers* (Stanford, CA: Center for International Security and Arms Control, December 1997).

Mobekk, Eiren, 'Nationalism and Inter-Ethnic Conflict: The Case of Armenia and Azerbaijan', in *New Studies in Post-Cold War Security*, ed. Ken R. Dark (Aldershot, England: Dartmouth Publishing, 1996).

Mohsenin, Mehrdad, 'Iran's Relations with Central Asia and the Caucasus', *Iranian Journal of International Affairs*, 7, no. 4, Winter 1996, pp. 834–53.

——, 'Pipeline Options for Exporting Oil and Gas from the Caspian Basin', *Relazioni Internazionali*, no. 47, November–December 1998, pp. 63–5.

Molla-Zade, Jayhun, 'Azerbaijan and the Caspian Basin: Pipelines and Geopolitics', *Caucasus and Caspian Seminar Series, Strengthening Democratic Institutions Project Working Paper* (Cambridge, MA: John F. Kennedy School of Government, Harvard University, April 4, 1996).

——, 'Azerbaijan and the Caspian Basin: Pipelines and Geopolitics', *Demokratizatsiya*, 6, no. 1, Winter 1998, pp. 28–34.

Momtaz, Djamchid, 'Le Statut Juridique de la Mer Caspienne', *Espaces et Ressources Maritimes*, no. 5, 1991, pp. 149–55.

——, 'Quel Régime pour la Mer Caspienne?' *Espaces et Ressources Maritimes*, no. 10, 1996, pp. 83–93.

Morningstar, Richard L., 'Coordinating US Caspian Policy: Interview with Ambassador Richard L. Morningstar', *Middle East Insight*, 13, no. 6, November–December 1998, p. 19.

Mouradian, Claire (ed.), 'Le Caucase des Indépendances: La Nouvelle Donne', *Problèmes Politiques et Sociaux*, no. 718, December 1993.

——, 'La CEI: Un Nouvel Acteur sur la Scène Internationale', *Problèmes Politiques et Sociaux*, no. 760, January 1996.

Mozaffari, Mehdi, 'The CIS' Southern Belt: A New Security System', in *Security Politics in the Commonwealth of Independent States: The Southern Belt*, ed. Mehdi Mozaffari (London: Macmillan Press, 1997).

——, 'CIS' Southern Belt: Regional Cooperation and Integration', in *Security Politics in the Commonwealth of Independent States: The Southern Belt*, ed. Mehdi Mozaffari (London: Macmillan Press, 1997a).

Müftüler, Meltem, 'Turkey's New Vocation', *Journal of South Asian and Middle Eastern Studies*, 22, no. 3, Spring 1999, pp. 1–15.

Munro, Ross H., 'The Asian Interior: China's Waxing Spheres of Influence', *Orbis*, 38, no. 4, Fall 1994, pp. 585–605.

———, 'China, India and Central Asia', in *After Empire: The Emerging Geopolitics of Central Asia*, ed. Jed C. Snyder (Washington, DC: National Defense University Press, 1995).

Myrianthis, Michael L., *Oleaginous Geopolitics in SW Asia and the Burgas-Alexandroupolis Oil Pipeline* (Athens: Institute of International Relations, Panteion University of Social and Political Sciences, 1996).

Naby, Eden, 'Turkestan or Xinjiang? Inducements and Constraints for Political Action', in *The Roles of the United States, Russia, and China in the New World Order*, ed. Hafeez Malik (New York: St Martin's Press, 1996).

Nanay, Julia, 'The US in the Caspian: The Divergence of Political and Commercial Interests', *Middle East Policy*, 6, no. 2, October 1998, pp. 150–7.

———, 'The Industry's Race For Caspian Oil Reserves', in *Caspian Energy Resources: Implications For the Arab Gulf* (Abu Dhabi: Emirates Center For Strategic Studies and Research, 2000).

Nasibli, Nasib, 'The Azeri Question in Iran: A Crucial Issue for Iran's Future', *Caspian Crossroads*, 3, no. 3, Winter 1998, pp. 12–14.

Nation, R. Craig, 'The Turkic and Other Muslim Peoples of Central Asia, the Caucasus, and the Balkans', in *Turkey Between East and West: New Challenges for a Rising Regional Power*, Vojtech Mastny and R. Craig Nation (eds), (Boulder, CO: Westview Press, 1996).

Naumkin, Vitaly V., 'The Political and Security Linkages Between the Gulf and the Muslim States of CATR', in *From the Gulf to Central Asia: Players in the New Great Game*, ed. Anoushiravan Ehteshami (Exeter: University of Exeter Press, 1994).

———, 'Russia and the States of Central Asia and the Transcaucasus', in *Damage Limitation or Crisis? Russia and the Outside World*, Robert D. Blackwill and Sergei A. Karaganov (eds), (Washington, DC: Brassey's, 1994).

———, 'Russia and Transcaucasia', *AGBU News*, 7, no. 3, September 1997, pp. 26–7.

Nedvetsky, Andrei G., 'Turkmenistan', in *Central Asia and the Caucasus after the Soviet Union: Domestic and International Dynamics*, ed. Mohiaddin Mesbahi (Gainesville, FL: University Press of Florida, 1994).

Nei, Hisanori and Geoffrey J. Aultman, 'Asian Interests in the Caspian', *Unlocking the Assets: Energy and the Future of Oil from Central Asia and the Caucasus* (Houston, TX: The Center for International Political Economy and the James A. Baker III Institute for Public Policy of Rice University, April 1998).

Nichol, Jim, *Central Asia's New States: Political Developments and Implications for U.S. Interests* (Bethesda, MD: Library of Congress/Congressional Research Service, 1994).

———, *Transcaucasus Newly Independent States: Political Developments and*

Implications for U.S. Interests (Bethesda, MD: Library of Congress/Congressional Research Service, 1995).

———, *Chechnya Conflict: Recent Developments and Implications for U.S. Interests* (Bethesda, MD: Library of Congress/Congressional Research Service, 1996).

Nijenhuis, Hans, 'Azerbaijan: Kuwait of the Caucasus', *World Press Review*, 42, no. 1, January 1995, p. 34.

Nikitin, Alexander I., 'Peace Support Operations on the Territory of the Former Soviet Union', in *Rising Tension in Eastern Europe and the Former Soviet Union*, David Carlton, Paul Ingram and Giancarlo Tenaglia (eds), (Aldershot, England: Dartmouth Publishing, 1996).

Nissman, David, 'Competition for Pipeline Route Heats Up', *Caspian Crossroads*, 1, no. 1, Winter 1995, pp. 19–20.

———, 'Kurds, Russians, and the Pipeline', *Eurasian Studies*, 2, no. 1, Spring 1995, pp. 30–5.

———, 'The Two Azerbaijans: A Common Past and a Common Future', *Caspian Crossroads*, 1, no. 2, Spring 1995a, pp. 20–4.

———, 'Russia and the Caucasus: Maintaining the Imbalance of Power', *Perceptions*, 1, no. 2, June–August 1996, pp. 72–81.

———, 'Iran and the Transcaucasus', *Caspian Crossroads*, 2, no. 2, Fall 1996, pp. 11–14.

———, 'Nuclear Tests, Oil, and Justice in East Turkestan', *Analysis of Current Events*, 9, no. 4, April 1997, pp. 6, 8.

———, 'Japan's Caspian Direction and the Caucasus', *Caspian Crossroads*, 3, no. 3, Winter 1998, pp. 30–2.

Nodia, Ghia, 'Ethnic Conflicts and Oil Politics in the Caucasus', *Analysis of Current Events*, 9, no. 2, February 1997, pp. 8–9.

Noreng, Øystein, *Oil and Islam: Social and Economic Issues* (Chichester, England: John Wiley & Sons for the Research Council of Norway, 1997).

Nugman, Gulnar, 'The Legal Status of the Caspian Sea', *Eurasian Studies*, no. 13, Spring 1998, pp. 80–92.

Ochs, Michael, 'Turkmenistan: Pipeline Dreams II', *Caspian Crossroads*, 1, no. 1, Winter 1995, pp. 23–5.

———, 'Azerbaijan: Oil, Domestic Stability and Geopolitics in the Caucasus', *Caucasus and Caspian Seminar Series, Strengthening Democratic Institutions Project Working Paper* (Cambridge, MA: John F. Kennedy School of Government, Harvard University, March 4, 1996).

Odell, Peter R., *Oil and World Power*. New York: Penguin Books, 1983.

Odom, William E. and Robert Dujarric, *Commonwealth or Empire? Russia, Central Asia, and the Transcaucasus* (Indianapolis, IN: Hudson Institute, 1995).

———, 'US Policy toward Central Asia and the Transcaucasus', *Caspian Crossroads*, 3, no. 1, Summer 1997, pp. 2–5.

———, 'The Caspian Sea Littoral States: The Object of a New Great Game?' *Caspian Crossroads*, 3, no. 3, Winter 1998, pp. 4–7.

Öğütçü, Mehmet, 'Eurasian Energy Prospects and Politics: Need for a Longer-Term Western Strategy', *Futures*, 27, no. 1, January–February: 1995, pp. 37–63.

———, 'Eurasian Energy Prospects and Politics: Need for a Fresh Perspective', *Cahiers d'Etudes sur la Méditerranée Orientale et le Monde Turco-Iranien (CEMOTI)*, no. 19, January–June 1995a, pp. 365–413.

Olcott, Martha Brill, 'Kazakhstan', in *Central Asia and the Caucasus after the Soviet Union: Domestic and International Dynamics*, ed. Mohiaddin Mesbahi (Gainesville, FL: University Press of Florida, 1994).

———, 'Ceremony and Substance: The Illusion of Unity in Central Asia', in *Central Asia and the World: Kazakhstan, Uzbekistan, Tajikistan, Kyrgyzstan, Turkmenistan*, ed. Michael Mandelbaum (New York: Council on Foreign Relations Press, 1994a).

———, 'The Asian Interior: The Myth of "Tsentral'naia Aziia"', *Orbis*, 38, no. 4, Fall 1994b, pp. 567–83.

———, 'Oil and Politics in Kazakhstan', *Caspian Crossroads*, 1, no. 1, Winter 1995, pp. 21–2.

———, 'Kazakhstan's Political Crisis', *Caspian Crossroads*, 1, no. 2, Spring 1995a, pp. 25–7.

———, 'Sovereignty and the Near Abroad", *Orbis*, 39, no. 3, Summer 1995b, pp. 353–367.

———, *Central Asia's New States: Independence, Foreign Policy, and Regional Security* (Washington, DC: United States Institute of Peace Press, 1996).

———, 'Central Asia: Confronting Independence', *Unlocking the Assets: Energy and the Future of Oil from Central Asia and the Caucasus* (Houston, TX: The Center for International Political Economy and the James A. Baker III Institute for Public Policy of Rice University, April 1998).

———, 'Pipelines and Pipe Dreams: Energy Development and Caspian Society', *Journal of International Affairs*, 53, no. 1, Fall 1999, pp. 305–23.

Olson, Robert, 'The Kurdish Question and Chechnya: Turkish and Russian Foreign Policies since the Gulf War', *Middle East Policy*, 4, no. 3, March 1996, pp. 106–18.

Omarova, Saule, 'Oil, Pipelines, and the Scramble for the Caspian': Contextualizing the Politics of Oil in Post-Soviet Kazakhstan and Azerbaijan', in *Space and Transport in the World-System*, Paul S. Ciccantell and Stephen G. Bunker (eds), (Westport, CT: Greenwood Press, 1998).

Öniş, Ziya, 'Turkey in the Post-Cold War Era: In Search of Identity', *Middle East Journal*, 49, no. 1, Winter 1995, pp. 48–68.

Oskanian, Vartan, 'A New Security Agenda for Armenia: What It Will Take to Befriend the Neighbors', *Transitions*, 4, no. 4, September 1997, pp. 58–62.

O'Sullivan, Diarmid, 'Pipe Dreams Come Closer to Reality', *Middle East Economic Digest*, March 28, 1997, pp. 2–3.

O'Sullivan, Patrick, *Geopolitics* (New York: St Martin's Press, 1986).

Ottoman, Ali, 'Le Désenclavement de l'Asie Centrale et du Caucase: Rôle Inédit pour une Ere Nouvelle', *Cahiers d'Etudes sur la Méditerranée Orientale et le Monde Turco-Iranien (CEMOTI)*, no. 18, July–December 1994, pp. 201–31.

Oxman, Bernard H., 'Caspian Sea or Lake: What Difference Does it Make?' *Caspian Crossroads*, 1, no. 4, Winter 1995–96, pp. 1–12.

Page, Stephen, 'The Creation of a Sphere of Influence: Russia and Central Asia', *International Journal*, 159, no. 4, Autumn 1994, pp. 788–813.

Pahlavan, Tschanguiz, 'Iran: New Policies for New Times', *War Report*, no. 50, April 1997, p. 29.

Palacín, José, 'Oil and Politics in the Caspian', *Daiwa Economic & Political Research* (London: Daiwa Institute of Research Europe, 26 January 1999).

Pannier, Bruce and Peter Rutland, 'Central Asia's Uneasy Partnership with Russia', *Transition*, 2, no. 23, November 15, 1996, pp. 26–8.

———, 'The Gordian Knot of Energy', *Transition*, 3, no. 3, 21 February, 1997, pp. 36–9.

———, 'Same Game, Second Round', *Transitions*, 4, no. 1, June 1997, pp. 20–5.

Pasha, S. A. M., 'Turkey and the Republics of Central Asia: Emerging Relations and Dilemmas', *International Studies*, 34, no. 3, July–September 1997, pp. 343–57.

Pavilionis, Peter, 'Iran: Elections, Oil, and Foreign Policy', *Analysis of Current Events*, 9, no. 6, June 1997, pp. 6, 8.

Pavlov, Stefan, 'Bulgaria in a Vise', *The Bulletin of Atomic Scientists*, 54, no. 1, January–February 1998, pp. 28–31.

Pelletreau, Robert H., 'An Interview with Robert H. Pelletreau', interview by Kurt D. Volkan. *Silk Road*, 1, no. 1, October 1997, pp. 4–9.

Petrossian, Vahe, 'Iran Ready to Play Caspian Oil Game', *Middle East Economic Digest (MEED)*, 41, no. 45, November 7, 1997, pp. 4–5.

Peuch, Jean-Christophe, 'Caspian Sea Oil: The Role of Private Corporations', *The Fletcher Forum of World Affairs*, 22, no. 2, Summer–Fall 1998, pp. 27–41.

Piacentini, Valeria F., 'Islam: Iranian and Saudi Arabian Religious and Geopolitical Competition in Central Asia', in *From the Gulf to Central Asia: Players in the New Great Game*, ed. Anoushiravan Ehteshami (Exeter: University of Exeter Press, 1994).

Pianelli, Dominique, 'L'Enjeu Pétrolier dans le Caucase', in *Arménie-Azerbaïjan-Géorgie: L'An V des Indépendances; La Russie: 1995-1996. Ex-URSS Edition 1996*, Roberte Berton-Hogge and Marie-Agnès Crosnier (eds), (Paris: Les Etudes de la Documentation Française, 1996).

Pipes, Daniel and Patrick Clawson, 'Ambitious Iran, Troubled Neighbors', *Foreign Affairs*, 72, no. 1, January-February 1993, pp. 124-41.

———, 'The Politics of the "Rip Van Winkle" States: The Borders of the Middle East Move North', *Middle East Insight*, 10, no. 1, November-December 1993, pp. 30-40.

———, 'The Event of Our Era: Former Soviet Muslim Republics Change the Middle East', in *Central Asia and the World: Kazakhstan, Uzbekistan, Tajikistan, Kyrgyzstan, Turkmenistan*, ed. Michael Mandelbaum (New York: Council on Foreign Relations Press, 1994).

———, 'A New Axis: The Emerging Turkish-Israeli Entente', *The National Interest*, no. 50, Winter 1997-98, pp. 31-8.

Pipes, Richard, 'Is Russia Still an Enemy?' *Foreign Affairs*, 76, no. 5, September-October 1997, pp. 65-78.

Polukhov, Elkhan, 'Contract of the Century (The Problem in an Historical Perspective)', *Caucasian Regional Studies*, 1, no. 1, 1997. No pagination, available only on website, http://poli.vub.ac.be/publi/crs/0201-05.htm

Pomfret, Richard, 'The Economic Cooperation Organization: Regional Forum or Irrelevant Talking Shop?' *Caspian Crossroads*, 2, no. 4, Spring 1997, pp. 21-6.

Porter, Bruce D. and Carol R. Saivetz, 'The Once and Future Empire: Russia and the "Near Abroad"', *The Washington Quarterly*, 17, no. 3, Summer 1994, pp. 75-90.

Poujol, Catherine, 'Cosaques contre Kazakhs: Nationalismes, Identités et Territoire au Kazakhstan', *Hérodote: Revue de Géographie et de Géopolitique*, no. 84, Spring 1997, pp. 124-44.

Presel, Joseph, 'Nagorno-Karabakh and United States Policy in the Caucasus', *Caucasus and Caspian Seminar Series, Strengthening Democratic Institutions Project Working Paper* (Cambridge, MA: John F. Kennedy School of Government, Harvard University, May 20, 1996).

Protonotarios, Nicolas, 'Russia and Western Access to Caspian Oil', in *Southeast Europe Factbook & Survey, 1996-1997*, Thanos M. Verenis and Nicolas Protonotarios (eds), (Athens/Cambridge, MA: Hellenic Foundation for European and Foreign Policy/Hellenic Resources Institute, 1996).

Pryde, Philip R. (ed.), *Environmental Resources and Constraints in the Former Soviet Republics* (Boulder, CO: Westview Press, 1995).

Puri, Madan Mohan, 'Central Asian Geopolitics: The Indian View', *Central Asian Survey*, 16, no. 2, June 1997, pp. 237-68.

Putnam, Tonya L., 'The States of Central Asia and the Transcaucasus and Russia', in *Damage Limitation or Crisis? Russia and the Outside World*, Robert D. Blackwill and Sergei A. Karaganov (eds), (Washington, DC: Brassey's, 1994).

Ra'anan, Uri and Kate Martin (eds), *Russia: A Return to Imperialism?* (New York: St Martin's Press, 1996).

Racine, Jean-Luc, 'Le Cercle de Samarcande: Géopolitique de l'Asie Centrale', *Hérodote: Revue de Géographie et de Géopolitique*, no. 84, Spring 1997, pp. 6–43.

Raczka, Witold, 'Le Turkménistan: Futur Koweït de la Caspienne?' *Cahiers d'Etudes sur la Méditerranée Orientale et le Monde Turco-Iranien (CEMOTI)*, no. 23, January–June 1997, pp. 183–206.

——, 'Le Turkménistan peut-il Devenir le Carrefour de l'Asie Centrale?' *Lettre d'Asie Centrale*, Spring 1997, pp. 2–3.

Rase, Glen, 'A Washington Perspective on Caspian Oil and the Pipeline Options', in *Oil and Caviar in the Caspian*, Charles Gurdon and Sarah Lloyd (eds), (London: Menas Associates, 1995).

——, 'Interview with Glen Rase', interview by Terry Manzi. *Caspian Crossroads*, 1, no. 1, Winter 1995, pp. 29–30.

Rashid, Ahmed, 'The New Great Game: Battle for Central Asia's Oil', *World Press Review*, 44, no. 6, 1997, pp. 32–3.

Rasizade, Alec, 'Azerbaijan and the Oil Trade: Prospects and Pitfalls', *Brown Journal of World Affairs*, 4, no. 2, Summer–Fall 1997, pp. 277–94.

——, 'Azerbaijan, the US, and Oil Prospects on the Caspian Sea', *Journal of Third World Studies*, 16, no. 1, Spring 1999, pp. 29–48.

Raviot, Jean-Robert, 'Environnement contre Géopolitique: Les Enjeux Ecologiques dans la Région Caspienne', *Cahiers d'Etudes sur la Méditerranée Orientale et le Monde Turco-Iranien (CEMOTI)*, no. 23, January–June 1997, pp. 65–87.

Razuvaev, V. V., 'The Oil Companies in Russian Politics', *Russian Politics and Law*, 34, no. 2, March–April 1996, pp. 71–81.

Retondo, Charles, 'A Groundhog's View of Baku: An Inside View of the US Oil Industry in Azerbaijan', *Caucasus and Caspian Seminar Series, Strengthening Democratic Institutions Project Working Paper* (Cambridge, MA: John F. Kennedy School of Government, Harvard University, December 9, 1996).

Reynolds, Douglas R., 'Oil Exploration in Transitional Economies: The Present Status of Kazakhstan's Onshore Proven Oil Reserves', *OPEC Review*, 22, no. 1, March 1998, pp. 31–40.

Rich, Greg, 'Interview with Greg Rich', interview by Terry Manzi. *Caspian Crossroads*, 1, no. 1, Winter 1995, p. 31.

——, 'Interview with Greg Rich of Azerbaijan International Oil

Company (AIOC)', interview by Jayhun Mollazade. *Caspian Crossroads*, 2, no. 3, Winter 1997, pp. 30-1.
Richter, Anthony, 'Frozen Hostility', *War Report*, no. 45, September 1996, pp. 49-50.
Rizhinashvili, Constantine, 'Poor Prospects for Regional Integration: Dissecting the CIS', *CIS Law Notes*, September 1997, pp. 7-13, 36.
Roberts, John, *Caspian Pipelines* (London: Royal Institute of International Affairs, 1996).
Robins, Philip, 'Between Sentiment and Self-Interest: Turkey's Policy toward Azerbaijan and the Central Asian States', *Middle East Journal*, 47, no. 4, Autumn 1993, pp. 593-610.
Robinson, Danielle, 'Chevron: Tengiz is Coming Good', *Petroleum Economist*, 64, no. 6, June 1997, pp. 38-9.
Roeder, Philip G., 'From Hierarchy to Hegemony: The Post-Soviet Security Complex', in *Regional Orders: Building Security in a New World*, David A. Lake and Patrick M. Morgan (eds), (University Park, PA: Pennsylvania State University Press, 1997).
Romano, Cesare, 'La Caspienne: Un Flou Juridique, Source de Conflits', *Cahiers d'Etudes sur la Méditerranée Orientale et le Monde Turco-Iranien (CEMOTI)*, no. 23, January-June 1997, pp. 39-63.
Rondeli, Alexander, 'Security Threats in the Caucasus: Georgia's View', *Perceptions*, 3, no. 2, June-August 1998, pp. 43-53.
Rose, Richard, 'Teddy Bears', *National Review*, 49, no. 16, 1 September, 1997, pp. 42-43, 56.
Rosenberger, Chandler, 'Moscow's Multipolar Mission', *Perspective*, 8, no. 2, November-December 1997, pp. 2-6.
Rotar, Igor, 'Will Caspian Oil Flow along the Northern Variant'?' *Prism (Jamestown Foundation)*, 3, no. 12, 25 July, 1997, pp. 8-9.
———, 'State of Disunion', *Perspective*, 8, no. 2, November-December 1997, pp. 1, 7-8.
———, 'Grozny Lobbies for a Caucasus Common Market', *Prism (Jamestown Foundation)*, 3, no. 20, 5 December, 1997, pp. 6-7, 14.
Roy, Olivier, 'Rivalités Ethniques et Religieuses, Jeu des Puissances en Afghanistan: Avec les Talibans, la Charia plus le Gazoduc', *Le Monde Diplomatique*, 43, no. 512, November 1996, pp. 6-7.
———, 'Les Evolutions de l'Asie Centrale', *Hérodote: Revue de Géographie et de Géopolitique*, no. 84, Spring 1997, pp. 44-56.
———, 'Le Nœud Caspien', *Politique Internationale*, no. 76, Summer 1997, pp. 221-33.
———, 'Crude Manoeuvres', *Index on Censorship*, 26, no. 4, July-August 1997a, pp. 144-52.
Royen, Christoph, 'Conflicts in the CIS and their Implications for Europe',

in *Russia and Europe: The Emerging Security Agenda*, ed. Vladimir Baranovsky (Oxford: Oxford University Press/Solna, Sweden: Stockholm International Peace Research Institute, 1997).

Ruban, Larisa, 'Growing Instability in the North Caucasus: A Major Threat to Russian Regional Security', *Caspian Crossroads*, 3, no. 2, Fall 1997, pp. 15–19.

Rubinstein, Alvin Z., 'The Asian Interior: The Geopolitical Pull on Russia', *Orbis*, 38, no. 4, Fall 1994, pp. 567–83.

Rumer, Eugene B., 'Russia and Central Asia after the Soviet Collapse', in *After Empire: The Emerging Geopolitics of Central Asia*, ed. Jed C. Snyder (Washington, DC: National Defense University Press, 1995).

Ruseckas, Laurent, 'Which Way Will Azerbaijan's Oil Flow? The Pipeline Debate Continues', *Caspian Crossroads*, 1, no. 3, Summer–Fall 1995, pp. 26–8.

——, 'Caspian Oil: Getting Beyond the 'Great Game', *Analysis of Current Events*, 9, no. 2, February 1997, pp. 44–5.

——, 'Caspian Oil Transportation: Insights from a Commercial Perspective', *Caspian Crossroads*, 3, no. 2, Fall 1997a, pp. 10–14.

Rusi, Alpo M., *Dangerous Peace: New Rivalry in World Politics* (Boulder, CO: Westview Press, 1997).

Rutland, Peter, 'Lost Opportunities: Energy and Politics in Russia', *National Bureau of Asian Research (NBR) Analysis*, 8, no. 5, December 1997, pp. 5–30.

Rywkin, Michael, 'From Silk Route to Oil Route: The Caspian Sea Basin', *American Foreign Policy Interests*, 19, no. 2, April 1997, pp. 8–15.

——, 'The Politics of the Caspian Sea Basin', *American Foreign Policy Interests*, 20, no. 5, October 1998, pp. 1–8.

Saakashvili, Mikheil, 'Growing Attraction of the Georgian Alternative', *Caspian Crossroads*, 1, no. 1, Winter 1995, pp. 15–16.

Sadri, Houman A., 'Integration in Central Asia: From Theory to Policy', *Central Asian Survey*, 16, no. 4, December 1997, pp. 573–86.

Sagers, Matthew J., 'Long-Term Plans for Oil and Gas Sector in Kazakhstan', *Post-Soviet Geography*, 34, no. 1, January 1993, pp. 66–9.

——, 'The Energy Industries of the Former USSR: A Mid-Year Survey', *Post-Soviet Geography*, 34, no. 6, June 1993a, pp. 341–420.

——, 'Long-Term Program for Turkmenistan's Oil and Gas Sector', *Post-Soviet Geography*, 35, no. 1, January 1994, pp. 50–6.

——, 'The Oil Industry in the Southern-Tier Former Soviet Republics', *Post-Soviet Geography*, 35, no. 5, May 1994a, pp. 267–98.

——, 'Turkmenistan's Gas Trade: The Case of Exports to Ukraine', *Post-Soviet Geography and Economics*, 40, no. 2, March 1999, pp. 142–49.

Sajjadpour, Seyed Kazem, 'The Caspian Sea Region: Iranian Policy Positions', *Analysis of Current Events*, 9, no. 6, June 1997, pp. 7, 11.

Salameh, Mamdouh G., 'The Soviet Oil Industry in mid-1991', *OPEC Review*, 15, no. 4, Winter 1991, pp. 379–88.

———, 'China, Oil and the Risk of Regional Conflict', *Survival*, 37, no. 4, Winter 1995–96, pp. 133–46.

Salmin, Aleksei M., 'Russia's Emerging Statehood in the National Security Context', in *Russia and Europe: The Emerging Security Agenda*, ed. Vladimir Baranovsky (Oxford: Oxford University Press/Solna, Sweden: Stockholm International Peace Research Institute, 1997).

Sander, Oral, 'Turkey and the Organization for Black Sea Economic Cooperation', in *Turkish Foreign Policy: Recent Developments*, ed. Kemal H. Karpat (Madison: University of Wisconsin Press, 1996).

Sanguineti, Vittorio, 'La Geopolitica delle Vie del Petrolio tra Caucaso, Caspio e Golfo', *Rivista di Studi Politici Internazionali*, 65, no. 2, April–June 1998, pp. 235–46.

Sanjian, Ara, *The Negotiation of the 'Contract of the Century' and the Background to the Revival of Azerbaijan's Oil Industry* (Yerevan: The Armenian Center for National and International Studies, 1997).

Savran, Sungur, 'From the Balkans to Central Asia: Kosovo as Harbinger', *Socialism and Democracy*, 13, no. 2, Fall–Winter 1999, pp. 111–32.

Seek, Andrew, Safa Mirzoyev, Vagif Nasibov and Fatima Mamedova, 'Azerbaijan: Rediscovering its Oil Potential? A Legal Perspective', *Journal of Energy and Natural Resources Law*, 13, no. 3, August 1995, pp. 147–52.

Sezer, Duygu Bazolu, 'Turkey in the New Security Environment in the Balkan and Black Sea Region', in *Turkey Between East and West: New Challenges for a Rising Regional Power*, Vojtech Mastny and R. Craig Nation (eds), (Boulder, CO: Westview Press, 1996).

———, 'From Hegemony to Pluralism: The Changing Politics of the Black Sea', *SAIS Review*, 17, no. 1, Winter–Spring 1997, pp. 1–30.

Shams-Ud-Din, 'The New Great Game in Central Asia', *International Studies*, 34, no. 3, July–September 1997, pp. 329–41.

Shashenkov, Maxim, 'Russia in Central Asia: Emerging Security Links', in *From the Gulf to Central Asia: Players in the New Great Game*, ed. Anoushiravan Ehteshami (Exeter: University of Exeter Press, 1994).

———, 'Russian Peacekeeping in the Near Abroad'', *Survival*, 36, no. 3, Autumn 1994, pp. 46–69.

———, 'Central Asia: Emerging Military-Strategic Issues', in *After Empire: The Emerging Geopolitics of Central Asia*, ed. Jed C. Snyder (Washington, DC: National Defense University Press, 1995).

———, 'Russia in the Caucasus: Interests, Threats and Policy Options', in *Russia and Europe: The Emerging Security Agenda*, ed. Vladimir Baranovsky (Oxford: Oxford University Press/Solna, Sweden: Stockholm International Peace Research Institute, 1997).

Shepherd, Monika, 'Intervention in Central Asia', *Perspective*, 7, no. 3, January–February 1997, pp. 1, 6–8.

Shermukhamedov, Abbas, 'All Rails Lead to Turkmenistan: The Development of Rail Lines in Central Asia', *Caspian Crossroads*, 2, no. 2, Fall 1996, pp. 15–17.

Shorokhov, Vladislav, 'Energy Resources of Azerbaijan: Political Stability and Regional Relations', *Caucasian Regional Studies*, 1, no. 1, 1996. No pagination, available only on website, http://poli.vub.ac.be/publi/crs/0101-04.htm

Shoumikhin, Andrei, 'Economics and Politics of Developing Caspian Oil Resources', *Perspectives on Central Asia*, 1, no. 8, November 1996, pp. 1–4.

———, 'New Developments Related to Caspian Oil', *Perspectives on Central Asia*, 1, no. 9, December 1996, pp. 1–4.

———, 'Developing Caspian Oil: Between Conflict and Cooperation', *Comparative Strategy*, 16, no. 4, 1997, pp. 337–51.

Sickles, Robin C., Patrick T. Hultberg and Lily Fu, 'Convergent Economies: Implications for World Energy Use', *Unlocking the Assets: Energy and the Future of Oil from Central Asia and the Caucasus* (Houston, TX: The Center for International Political Economy and the James A. Baker III Institute for Public Policy of Rice University, April 1998).

Skagen, Ottar, *Caspian Gas* (London: Royal Institute of International Affairs, 1997).

Smith, David R., 'Environmental Security and Shared Water Resources in Post-Soviet Central Asia', *Post-Soviet Geography*, 36, no. 6, June 1995, pp. 351–70.

Smith, Dianne L., 'Central Asia: A New Great Game', *Asian Affairs*, 23, no. 3, Fall 1996, pp. 147–75.

———, 'Central Asian Militaries: Breaking away from the Bear', *Post-Soviet Prospects*, 5, no. 7, December 1997, pp. 1–4.

———, *Breaking Away from the Bear* (Carlisle, PA: Strategic Studies Institute, 1998).

Smith, Pamela Ann, 'Gulf States Expand Caspian Activities', *The Middle East*, no. 279, June 1998, pp. 22–3.

———, 'Pipeline Poker', *The Middle East*, no. 281, August 1998, pp. 40–1.

Sobhani, S. Rob, 'President Clinton's Iran Option', *Caspian Crossroads*, 1, no. 1, Winter 1995, pp. 12–14.

———, 'US, Iran, Russia and Turkey: The Struggle for Azerbaijan', *Caucasus and Caspian Seminar Series, Strengthening Democratic Institutions Project Working Paper* (Cambridge, MA: John F. Kennedy School of Government, Harvard University, 11 March, 1997).

———, 'The United States, Iran, Russia, and Turkey: The Struggle for Azerbaijan', *Demokratizatsiya*, 6, no. 1, Winter 1998, pp. 35–40.

Soligo, Ronald and Amy Jaffe, 'The Economics of Pipeline Routes: The Conundrum of Oil Exports from the Caspian Basin', *Unlocking the Assets: Energy and the Future of Oil from Central Asia and the Caucasus* (Houston, TX: The Center for International Political Economy and the James A. Baker III Institute for Public Policy of Rice University, April 1998).

Spechler, Martin C., 'Regional Economic Cooperation in Central Asia: The Middle Road', *Analysis of Current Events*, 9, no. 12, December 1997, pp. 1, 3–4.

Speckhard, Daniel, 'The Politics of Caspian Oil', *Caucasus and Caspian Seminar Series, Strengthening Democratic Institutions Project Working Paper* (Cambridge, MA: John F. Kennedy School of Government, Harvard University, 22 May, 1996).

Sreedhar, 'Pakistan's Afghan Policy at the Crossroads', *Strategic Analysis*, 21, no. 8, November 1997, pp. 1175–85.

Starr, S. Frederick, 'United States Policy and National Development in the Post-Soviet States', in *The Successor States to the USSR*, ed. John W. Blaney (Washington, DC: Congressional Quarterly, 1995).

———, 'Making Eurasia Stable', *Foreign Affairs*, 75, no. 1, January–February 1996, pp. 80–92.

———, 'Power Failure: American Policy in the Caspian', *The National Interest*, no. 47, Spring 1997, pp. 20–31.

———, Thomas R. Stauffer and Julia Nanay, 'Symposium – Caspian Oil: Pipelines and Politics', *Middle East Policy*, 5, no. 4, January 1998, pp. 27–49.

Stauffer, Thomas R., 'Exporting Energy via Iran', *Silk Road*, 1, no. 1, October 1997, pp. 14–15.

———, 'The Iranian Connection': The Geo-Economics of Exporting Central Asian Energy Via Iran', *International Research Center for Energy and Economic Development Occasional Papers* no. 29 (Boulder, CO: International Research Center for Energy and Economic Development, 1997).

Stern, Jonathan, 'Oil and Gas in the Former Soviet Union: The Changing Foreign Investment Agenda', in *Investment Opportunities in Russia and the CIS*, ed. David A. Dyker (London: Royal Institute of International Affairs, 1995).

Stevens, Paul, 'Pipelines or Pipe Dreams? Lessons From the History of Arab Transit Pipelines', *Middle East Journal*, 54, no. 2, Winter 2000, pp. 224–41.

Stobdan, P., 'Mongolia and Asian Security', *Strategic Analysis*, 21, no. 8, November 1997, pp. 1187–98.

'Storm in the Caspian?' *Energy Economist*, no. 141, July 1993, pp. 3–6.

'Succession and Long-Term Stability in the Caspian Region'.*Caspian Studies Program Experts Conference Report, Strengthening Democratic Institutions Project*

Working Paper (Cambridge, MA: John F. Kennedy School of Government, Harvard University, October 1999).

Suny, Ronald Grigor, 'Living with the Other: Conflict and Cooperation among the Transcaucasian Peoples', *AGBU News*, 7, no. 3, September 1997, pp. 27–9.

Surtsukov, Mikhail, 'The Oil Crisis in the Commonwealth of Independent States', in *The Russian Economy: From Rags to Riches*, ed. Andrei Sizov (Commack, NY: Nova Science Publishers, 1995).

Talwani, Manik, Andrei Belopolsky and Dianne L. Berry, 'Geology and Petroleum Potential of the Caspian Sea Region', *Unlocking the Assets: Energy and the Future of Oil from Central Asia and the Caucasus* (Houston, TX: The Center for International Political Economy and the James A. Baker III Institute for Public Policy of Rice University, April 1998).

Tarkhan-Mouravi, George, 'The Road from Moscow', *War Report*, no. 51, May 1997, p. 15.

Tarock, Adam, 'Iran's Policy in Central Asia', *Central Asian Survey*, 16, no. 2, June 1997, pp. 185–200.

———, 'Iran and Russia in Strategic Alliance'', *Third World Quarterly*, 18, no. 2, June 1997, pp. 207–23.

———, 'The Politics of the Pipeline: The Iran and Afghanistan Conflict', *Third World Quarterly*, 20, no. 4, August 1999, pp. 801–20.

Tchihatchef, P. de, 'Le Pétrole aux Etats-Unis et en Russie', *Revue des Deux Mondes*, 58, no. 3 (89), September–October 1888, pp. 632–52.

Teimourian, Hazhir, 'Caspian Oil: First Moves in a Long-Term Game', *Pointer (Supplement to Jane's Intelligence Review)*, 2, no. 12, December 1995, pp. 2–3.

Thomas, Paul, 'The Caspian – Nitty Gritty, Nuts and Bolts', *Energy Economist*, no. 182, December 1996, pp. 2–7.

Tinguy, Anne de and Mohammad-Reza Djalili, 'La Caspienne, Terrain d'Entente, de Rivalité ou de Conflit?' *Cahiers d'Etudes sur la Méditerranée Orientale et le Monde Turco–Iranien (CEMOTI)*, no. 23, January–June 1997, pp. 7–10.

Tinguy, Anne de, 'Les Nouveaux Etats Indépendants et la Caspienne: L'Apprentissage d'une Nouvelle Vie Internationale', *Cahiers d'Etudes sur la Méditerranée Orientale et le Monde Turco-Iranien (CEMOTI)*, no. 23, January–June 1997, pp. 207–28.

Tonchev, Plamen, 'Rising Asian Oil Demand and Caspian Reserves', *Caspian Crossroads*, 3, no. 3, Winter 1998, pp. 24–9.

Toumarkine, Alexandre, 'Ambitions Nationales et Désenclavement Régional: Les Politiques Turque et Iranienne en Transcaucasie', in *Arménie – Azerbaïjan – Géorgie: L'An V des Indépendances; La Russie: 1995–1996. Ex-URSS Edition 1996*, Roberte Berton-Hogge and Marie-Agnès Crosnier (eds), (Paris: Les Etudes de la Documentation Française, 1996).

Trofimenko, Henry, '"New World Order" and Russian–American Relations', in *The Roles of the United States, Russia, and China in the New World Order*, ed. Hafeez Malik (New York: St Martin's Press, 1996).

Truscott, Peter, *Russia First: Breaking with the West*. London: I.B. Tauris, 1997.

Tunander, Ola, Pavel Baev and Victoria Ingrid Einagel (eds), *Geopolitics in Post-Wall Europe: Security, Territory and Identity* (London: Sage Publications/ Oslo: International Peace Research Institute, 1997).

Ugur, Halil, 'Turkmenistan: Political, Economic, and International Developments in the Wake of Soviet Imperialism', *Journal of Third World Studies*, 13, no. 1, Spring 1996, pp. 15–23.

Uibopuu, Henn-Jüri, 'The Caspian Sea: A Tangle of Legal Problems', *The World Today*, 51, no. 6, June 1995, pp. 119–23.

Vaner, Semih, 'La Caspienne: Enjeu pour l'Azerbaïdjan et l'Azerbaïdjan comme Enjeu', *Cahiers d'Etudes sur la Méditerranée Orientale et le Monde Turco-Iranien (CEMOTI)*, no. 23, January–June 1997, pp. 143–66.

———, 'La Zone de Coopération Economique de la Mer Noire', *Le Courrier des Pays de l'Est*, no. 423, October 1997, pp. 24–9.

Vassiliev, Alexei, 'Turkey and Iran in Transcaucasia and Central Asia', in *From the Gulf to Central Asia: Players in the New Great Game*, ed. Anoushiravan Ehteshami (Exeter: University of Exeter Press, 1994).

———, 'Russia and Central Asia', in *Rising Tension in Eastern Europe and the Former Soviet Union*, David Carlton, Paul Ingram and Giancarlo Tenaglia (eds), (Aldershot, England: Dartmouth Publishing, 1996).

Vinogradov, Sergei and Patricia Wouters, 'The Caspian Sea: Current Legal Problems', *Zeitschrift für Ausländisches Recht und Völkerrecht*, 55, no. 2, 1995, pp. 604–23.

———, and ———, 'The Caspian Sea: Quest for a New Legal Régime', *Leiden Journal of International Law*, 9, 1996, pp. 87–98.

———, 'Transboundary Water Resources in the Former Soviet Union: Between Conflict and Cooperation', *Natural Resources Journal*, 36, no. 2, Spring 1996, pp. 393–415.

Wacker, Gudrun, 'China Builds Ties, Trade across Its Western Border', *Transition*, 2, no. 17, 23 August, 1996, pp. 30–3.

Waelde, Thomas, Sergei Vinogradov and Armando Zamora, 'The Caspian: Prosperity or Conflict?' *OPEC Bulletin*, 30, no. 10, October 1999, pp. 12–15, 54.

Wallander, Celeste A (ed.), *The Sources of Russian Foreign Policy after the Cold War* (Boulder, CO: Westview Press, 1996).

Waller, J. Michael, 'Who is Making Foreign Policy?' *Perspective*, 5, no. 3, January–February 1995, pp. 2–5, 10.

———, 'Primakov's Imperial Line', *Perspective*, 7, no. 3, January–February 1997, pp. 2, 4–6.

Walsh, J. Richard, 'China and the New Geopolitics of Central Asia', *Asian Survey*, 33, no. 3, March 1993, pp. 272–85.

Waltz, Kenneth M., *Theory of International Politics* (Reading, MA: Addison-Wesley Publishing, 1979).

Webber, Mark, 'Coping with Anarchy: Ethnic Conflict and International Organizations in the Former Soviet Union', *International Relations*, 13, no. 1, April 1996, pp. 1–27.

———, *CIS Integration Trends: Russia and the Former Soviet South* (London: Royal Institute of International Affairs, 1997).

Wiarda, Howard J. (ed.), *U.S. Foreign and Strategic Policy in the Post-Cold War Era: A Geopolitical Perspective* (Westport, CT: Greenwood Press, 1996).

Winrow, Gareth M., *Turkey in Post-Soviet Central Asia*. London: Royal Institute of International Affairs, 1995.

———, 'Turkey's Role in Asian Pipeline Politics', *Jane's Intelligence Review*, 9, no. 2, February 1997, pp. 74–7.

———, 'Turkish Policy in Central Asia', in *Security Politics in the Commonwealth of Independent States: The Southern Belt*, ed. Mehdi Mozaffari (London: Macmillan Press, 1997).

———, 'Turkey and Caspian Energy', *The Emirates Occasional Papers*, no. 37 (Abu Dhabi, United Arab Emirates: The Emirates Center for Strategic Studies and Research, 1999).

Witte, Pol de, 'Fostering Stability and Security in the Southern Caucasus', *NATO Review*, 47, no. 1, Spring 1999, pp. 14–15.

Woodard, Colin, 'Reviving the Black Sea', *Transition*, 3, no. 4, 7 March, 1997, pp. 50–51, 56.

Wyatt, Christopher, 'The Problems of Russian Security in Central Asia: Late Cold War Experiences in the Post-Cold War World', in *New Studies in Post-Cold War Security*, ed. Ken R. Dark (Aldershot, England: Dartmouth Publishing, 1996).

Xu, Xiaojie, 'The Oil and Gas Linkage Between Central Asia and China: A Geopolitical Perspective', *Unlocking the Assets: Energy and the Future of Oil from Central Asia and the Caucasus* (Houston, TX: The Center for International Political Economy and the James A. Baker III Institute for Public Policy of Rice University, April 1998).

———, 'The Oil and Gas Links Between Central Asia and China: A Geopolitical Perspective', *OPEC Review*, 23, no. 1, March 1999, pp. 33–54.

Yablonski, Constantin, 'L'Asie Centrale et ses Voisins: Une Intégration à Plusieurs Variables', *Le Courrier des Pays de l'Est*, no. 406, January–February 1996, pp. 32–50.

Yamani, Mai, 'Saudi Arabia and Central Asia: The Islamic Connection', in *From the Gulf to Central Asia: Players in the New Great Game*, ed. Anoushiravan Ehteshami (Exeter: University of Exeter Press, 1994).

Yerasimos, Stéphane, 'Des Histoires de Tuyaux et de Pétrole', *Hérodote: Revue de Géographie et de Géopolitique*, no. 81, April–June 1996, pp. 106–25.

———, 'Transcaucasie: Le Retour de la Russie', *Hérodote: Revue de Géographie et de Géopolitique*, no. 81, April–June 1996a, pp. 179–213.

Yergin, Daniel, *The Prize: The Epic Quest for Oil, Money, and Power* (New York: Touchstone/Simon & Schuster, 1992).

Young, Steven, 'US Interests in the Caucasus', *Caucasus and Caspian Seminar Series, Strengthening Democratic Institutions Project Working Paper* (Cambridge, MA: John F. Kennedy School of Government, Harvard University, 28 October, 1996).

Yunanov, Boris, 'Clinton Crosses the Caucasus Range', *The Current Digest of the Post-Soviet Press*, 49, no. 35, 1 October, 1997, pp. 22–3.

Yusifzade, Khoshbakht B., 'Oil in the Caspian Basin: The Oil Industry in Azerbaijan', *Geotimes*, 45, February 2000, pp. 18–20.

Zaman, Amberin, 'Turkey: Historic Rivals Find Some Common Ground', *The Middle East*, no. 249, October 1995, pp. 14–15.

Zhukov, Stanislav V. and Oksana B. Reznikova, 'Central Asia in World Politics and Economics', *Problems of Economic Transition*, 38, no. 8, December 1995, pp. 59–81.

Zilanov, Vyacheslav Konstantinovich, 'Will Oil Destroy Caspian's Unique Ecosystem?' *The Current Digest of the Post-Soviet Press*, 49, no. 35, 1 October, 1997, pp. 8–9.

Ziring, Lawrence, 'The Caucasus and Central Asia: Historic and Contemporary Linkages', *Archivum Ottomanicum*, 13, 1993–94, pp. 347–68.

Zoppo, Ciro E., 'Turkey and the Independent States of Central Asia', in *Rising Tension in Eastern Europe and the Former Soviet Union*, David Carlton, Paul Ingram and Giancarlo Tenaglia (eds), (Aldershot, England: Dartmouth Publishing, 1996).

Zviagelskaia, Irina, *The Russian Policy Debate on Central Asia*. London: Royal Institute of International Affairs, 1995.

The Caspian region is covered in numerous news broadcast services, newspapers and magazines, including:
AIM (Armenian International Magazine) (Glendale, CA).
Azerbaijan International Magazine (Sherman Oaks, CA).
BBC Summary of World Broadcasts
Central Asia Newsfile (London).
The Economist
The Economist Intelligence Unit (London).
Financial Times
Groong-Armenian News Network
Jamestown Foundation

Labyrinth: Central Asia Quarterly (London).
Le Monde
New York Times
Oil and Gas Journal (Houston, TX).
Petroleum Economist (London)
RFE/RL Newsline
Transcaucasus: A Chronology (Washington, DC).
Wall Street Journal
Washington Post
Washington Times

Index

Abashidze, Aslan, 153
Abazas, 152
Abdallah, Crown Prince, 169
Abildin, Serikbolsyn, 55
Abkhazia / Abkhazians, 112, 113, 114, 134, 138, 139, 141, 152, 153, 164, 170
Adygea, 152
Afghanistan, 9, 36, 38, 78, 88, 99–101, 103, 119, 121, 122, 131, 134, 141, 147, 155, 156, 157; Northern Alliance, 101
Ajaria / Ajars, 112, 113, 153
Akaev, Askar, 102, 109, 135
Akhtuba River, 22, 23
Albania, 128
Albright, Madeleine, 130
Aliyev, Haidar, 60–67, 74, 82, 89, 90, 91, 106, 110, 120, 125, 133, 134, 136, 137, 143, 144, 146, 159
Aliyev, Ilham, 62, 66, 106
Aliyev, Natiq, 31
Alizadeh, Zardusht, 64
Allonsius, David, 21
Almaty (former Alma-Ata), 23, 44, 54, 56, 91, 117
Amerada Hess, 160
Amnesty International, 165
Anglo-Iranian Oil Company (AIOC), 15
Ankara Declaration, 136
Apsheron Peninsula, 15, 16, 24, 25, 137
Arabs, 10, 48, 122, 123, 124, 125, 127, 138
Arak, 39
Aral Sea, 21, 26, 27
Argentina, 104
Armenia, 9, 12, 35, 61, 62, 82, 87, 89, 90, 99, 103–107, 111, 112, 121, 125, 126, 127, 128, 132, 133, 135, 141, 142, 144, 153, 154, 159, 164
Armenian massacres; genocide in Ottoman Turkey, 105, 106, 107, 109, 121, 126; in Baku, 16, 60; in Sumgait, 61
Armenians, 11, 12, 15, 16, 48, 61, 64, 82, 104, 105, 108, 121, 139, 153, 154
Ashghabad, 23, 119
Asian Development Bank, 165
Assyrians, 48
Astana (former Akmola, Tselinograd), 54, 91, 148
Astrakhan, 10, 20, 25, 165, 166
Atyrau, 17, 27, 59, 86, 144, 156
Azerbaijan, 3, 9, 12, 13, 14, 17, 18, 33, 34, 35, 36, 37, 38, 43, 48, 72, 75, 78, 81, 84, 116, 121, 123, 127, 128, 129, 153, 154, 155, 156, 157, 159, 160, 162, 163, 164, 166, 168, 170; and Caspian environmental issues, 24, 25, 26, 27; energy sector, 29, 30, 31, 32, 33, 66–67; foreign policy determinants, 74; Lezgin minority, 151–152; political and economic system, 60–66; position on Caspian legal status, 20, 21, 23, 82, 83, 84, 89, 90, 91, 93–94, 95; relations with Armenia, 103–107; European countries, 141–146; Georgia, 112–113; Israel, 125–126; Kazakhstan, 90–91; Iran, 82–83; Pakistan, 119–120; relations Russia, 88–90; Turkey, 108–112; Turkmenistan, 92–95; Ukraine, 129–130; United States, 133–139
Azerbaijan International Oil Company (AIOC), 31, 37, 143, 144, 146, 160

INDEX

Azerbaijan Popular Front (APF), 60, 61, 63, 64, 65, 82
Azeris / Azerbaijanis, 11, 14, 16, 48, 60, 63, 77, 82, 90, 92, 104, 105, 106, 107, 110, 111, 112, 113, 123, 125, 126, 130, 133, 134, 137, 139, 142, 143, 144, 145, 146, 147, 151, 152, 154, 157, 159, 160, 162; minority in Georgia, 153–154; minority in Iran, 83, 154

Baha'is, 48
Baker Institute, 30, 135
Baker, James, 30, 135
Baku, 11, 12, 13, 14, 15, 16, 17, 24, 27, 34, 36, 38, 61, 63, 66, 82, 89, 90, 92, 93, 94, 106, 110, 119, 124, 125, 130, 135, 141, 144, 159; pogroms of Armenians in, 16, 60
Baku Commune, 12
Baku-Ceyhan pipeline, 31, 37, 78, 91, 106, 109, 110, 111, 113, 124, 125, 128, 136, 137, 139, 142, 143, 144, 153, 154, 159, 160, 161, 162, 170, 172
balance of power, 5, 6–7, 79, 131, 171
Balgimbayev, Nurlan, 59
Balkans, 35, 37, 108, 128
Baltic republics, 132
Baltic Sea, 21
Baluch, 48
Bamyan, 101
Basmachi movement, 12
Batumi, 16, 91, 153
Beilin, Yossi, 126
Belarus, 44, 84, 129
Belgium, 146
Bin Laden, Usama, 100, 101
Bishkek, 156
Black Sea, 16, 21, 35, 36, 37, 108, 113, 128, 129, 141, 142, 147, 153, 170
Black Sea Economic Cooperation (BSEC), 108
Bolsheviks, 12, 14
Bonyad-e Mostazafin, 50
Bosphorus / Dardanelles, 35, 110

Bouygues, 144
BP–Amoco, 48, 110, 143, 162, 163, 164
BP–Amoco *Statistical Review of World Energy*, 32
Bridas, 72
Burgas, 128
Brzezinski, Zbigniew, 135, 137
Bukhara, 11, 12, 109
Bulgaria, 9, 35, 128, 141
Bush, George H. W., 161
Bush, George W., vi

Canada, 104, 163
Caspian energy resources; estimates, 28–33, 167–168; production costs, 3, 33–35, 39, 168, 172
Caspian Finance Centre, 136
Caspian International Petroleum Company (CIPCO), 31, 34
Caspian Pipeline Consortium (CPC), 86, 123, 137, 145, 158
Caspian region, 9, 30, 32, 67, 76, 110, 115, 118, 124, 131, 135, 137, 138, 142, 146, 154, 157, 163, 164, 169, 171, 173; history, 10–18; under Soviet rule, 10, 13, 14, 17, 18, 20, 21, 24, 25, 27, 28, 29
Caspian Sea, 10, 16, 17, 18, 19, 24, 26, 29, 43, 84, 90, 95, 140, 156; energy resources, 6, 7, 8, 17, 28–33, 48, 67, 74, 77, 90, 107, 111, 118, 131, 140, 167–168, 170; environmental issues, 19, 24–27; legal status, 19–24, 76, 77, 79, 80, 81, 82, 83, 84, 85, 88, 89, 90, 91, 92, 93, 94, 95, 134; physical characteristics, 19; riparian states, 3, 6, 7, 9, 19–27, 43–95, 74, 77, 80, 81, 90, 99
Caspian Sea Cooperation Organization, 90
Caucasus region, 3, 4, 10, 11, 12, 13, 16, 17, 18, 60, 75, 78, 79, 88, 89, 90, 92, 99, 114, 119, 120, 122, 124, 125, 155, 157, 170; and European countries, 140–145; and Turkey, 107–112; and United States,

INDEX

132–138; conflicts in, 150–154
caviar, 24, 25–26
Cavanaugh, Carey, 107
Central Asia / Central Asian states, 3, 4, 5, 10, 12, 13, 19, 23, 24, 36, 51, 52, 54, 60, 64, 75, 78, 79, 80, 83, 86, 87, 88, 89, 90, 92, 102, 103, 106, 119, 120, 129, 150, 152, 154, 156, 157, 164, 165; and Afghanistan, 99–101; Arab states, 121–124; China, 115–118; East Asian states, 148–149; European countries, 139–146; India, 119–121; Israel, 124–127; Japan, 146–148; Pakistan, 118–119; Turkey, 107–111; United States, 131–139
Central Asia Institute, 135
Central Asia Petroleum, 148
Central Intelligence Agency (CIA), 134, 160
Ceyhan, Gulf of, 35, 37, 90, 106, 110, 124, 136
Charette, Hervé de, 144
Chechens, 45, 89, 101, 111, 139, 150–151, 157
Chechnya / Chechen wars, 37, 44, 45, 48, 78, 79, 85, 86, 89, 90, 101, 114, 123, 134, 138, 150, 151, 152, 154, 155, 157, 170
Cheney, Richard, vi, 135
Chernomyrdin, Viktor, 47, 76
Chevron, 36, 85, 158, 164
Chile, 161
China, 6, 9, 36, 37, 38, 53, 74, 84, 107, 115–118, 120, 138, 141, 147, 156, 168, 172
China National Petroleum Corporation (CNPC), 36, 116
Chisinau Summit, 85
clash of civilizations, 7
Clinton, Hillary, 135
Clinton, William Jefferson, 82, 132, 133, 134, 135, 136, 138, 160, 161, 162
Cold War, 3, 4, 6, 14, 107, 125, 171
Commonwealth of Independent States (CIS), 44, 52, 53, 71, 75, 81, 84, 85, 86, 87, 89, 90, 92, 101, 103, 113, 114, 129, 142, 156, 158, 164
Collective Security Treaty, 103, 114, 156
Communist Party (USSR), 43, 57, 65, 68, 70
Constanza, 129, 142
Contract of the Century, 20, 29, 31, 82, 89, 116, 134, 143, 146, 160, 162
Convention on International Trade in Endangered Species (CITES), 25–26
Convention on the Law of the Sea (UNCLOS), 21, 22
Cooperman, Leon, 159
Cossacks, 56, 152
Council of Europe, 140, 142, 144, 164
Crimean Tatars, 13
Cyprus, 107, 109, 127

Daghestan, 20, 45, 101, 151, 152, 155, 165, 170
Dead Sea, 21
Dehaene, Jean-Luc, 146
Delta Nimir, 38, 123
Denikin, Anton, 11
Deuss, Johann, 158
Dostum, General, 100, 103
Dudayev, Dzhokhar, 151
Dunn, Michael, 119

Economic Cooperation Organization (ECO), 90, 119
Effimoff, Igor, 33
Egypt, 104, 123
Elchibey, Abulfez, 61, 63, 65, 66, 32, 89, 108, 110, 133, 163
Elf Aquitaine, 31, 144, 161
Eni (Agip), 31, 145, 146, 164
Enver Pasha, 12
Erbakan, Necmettin, 109
Erzerum, 38
Escudero, Stanley, 133
Eurasia Foundation, 165
Eurasian Corridor, 112, 141, 152, 154
Eurasian Economic Community (former

263

INDEX

Customs Union), 84
Eurasian Union, 84
Europe / European countries, 4, 6, 11, 37, 54, 87, 108, 112, 113, 118, 131, 139–146, 160, 172
European Bank for Reconstruction and Development (EBRD), 141, 142, 164
European Union, vi, 9, 84, 107, 139, 140, 141, 142, 145, 146; European Energy Charter and Treaty, 140; Interstate Oil and Gas Transport to Europe (INOGATE), 140, 141, 142; Partnership and Cooperation Agreements (PCA), 140; Technical Assistance Programs (TACIS), 140, 141; Transport Corridor Europe Caucasus Asia (TRACECA), 112, 141, 142
Export-Import Bank, 136, 147
Exxon-Mobil, 164

Ferghana, 17, 147, 156
First World War, 12, 14
France, 104, 144, 147
Freedom Support Act, Section 907, 135, 137
Fuller, Graham, 138

Gambar, Isa, 63, 64
Gamsakhurdia, Zviad, 153
Ganja (Kirovabad), 61, 63
Gapurov, Muhammednazar, 68
Gazprom, 48, 71, 76, 85, 87, 88, 146, 159, 162
Gdansk, 130
geopolitics, 3, 4, 5–6, 37–39, 43, 74, 94, 99, 101, 107, 131, 143, 150, 164, 165, 171, 174;
Great Game, 3, 6, 10, 15, 127, 128, 135, 138, 158, 167, 171, 172;
Heartland theory, 5–6, 11
Georgia, 9, 12, 16, 35, 36, 37, 75, 77, 87, 89, 91, 99, 104, 105, 106, 110, 111, 112–114, 126, 130, 147, 157, 159, 160, 164, 170; ethnic conflicts in, 105, 152–154; relations with European countries, 141–145; United States, 132–139
Georgians, 11, 12, 112, 113, 152, 157
Germans, 150
Germany, 5, 6, 12, 13, 14, 49, 145, 147, 163
Giffen, James, 158
Gilan, 13, 14, 77, 166
glasnost, 43
globalization, 4, 5, 131, 150, 165, 167, 171, 172
Gorbachev, Mikhail, 43, 44, 52, 65, 68, 77, 119, 122, 152, 158
Gouliev, Rasul, 63, 64
Great Game, 3, 6, 10, 15, 127, 128, 135, 138, 158, 167, 171, 172
Great Britain, 3, 5, 6, 10, 12, 14, 15, 16, 49, 89, 139, 143, 163, 172
Greece, 9, 104, 112, 127–128
Grey Wolf, 64
Grozny, 16, 37
Gulbenkian, Calouste, 16, 157–158
Gulf Arab states, 9, 121–124, 169
Gulf Cooperation Council (GCC), 121, 122, 123, 124
Guliev, Velayat, 83
Guluzade, Vafa, 90
GUUAM (former GUAM), 113, 129

Halk Maskhalaty, 68, 69
Hamidov, Iskendar, 64
Hashimoto, Ryutaro, 148
Hassanov, Hassan, 125
Hazar (Cheleken), 124
Hazaras, 101
Heartland theory, 5–6, 11
Henry, J. D., 24, 137
Heslin, Sheila, 135
Himmatov, Akram, 61, 63
Hizb al-Tahrir, 156
Human Rights Watch, 54, 165
Hunter, Shireen, 78
Huntington, Samuel, 7
Husseinov, Surat, 61, 62, 63

Idrisov, Erlan, 80

India / Indians, 6, 10, 38, 115, 118, 119, 120–121, 168
Indian Ocean, 36, 119
Indonesia, 148, 168
Indonesian Petroleum Ltd., 147
Ingush / Ingushetia, 152, 155
Inpex Nord, 34, 147
International Institute of Strategic Studies (IISS), 30
international law, 19–24
International Monetary Fund (IMF), 57, 164
international relations theories, 3–8; balance of power / neorealism, 5, 6–7, 79, 102, 131, 140, 151, 171, 172; clash of civilizations, 7; geopolitics, 3, 4, 5–6, 37–39, 43, 74, 79, 94, 99, 101, 107, 131, 143, 150, 164, 165, 171, 174; globalization, 4, 5, 131; levels of analysis, 8, 9; neoliberalism, 7, 131, 171
Iran, vi, 3, 9, 13, 14, 15, 26, 34, 35, 36, 37, 38, 39, 43, 60, 74, 75, 86, 88, 90, 94, 101, 102, 103, 105, 107, 108, 110, 112, 121, 122, 123, 149, 156, 157, 158, 161, 162, 163, 165, 166, 168, 169, 171, 172; Azerbaijan provinces / Azeri minority, 48, 60, 83, 154, 166; energy sector, 30, 31, 50–51; foreign policy determinants, 76–77; Iran-Iraq war, 50; Islamic Republic of, 15, 48–50, 77, 105; minority groups, 48; political and economic system, 48–50; position on Caspian legal status, 20, 21, 23, 77, 79, 80, 81, 82, 83, 84; relations with Azerbaijan, 82–83; European countries, 141–145; Iran, 116–117; Israel, 124–127; Kazakhstan, 79–80; Russia, 77–79; Turkmenistan, 80–82; Israel, 124–127; United States, 131–139
Iraq, 34, 49, 50, 76, 107, 123, 127, 169
irredentism, 7, 117
Isfahan, 39
Islam / Islamic, 7, 10, 11, 15, 48, 49, 50, 51, 63, 77, 79, 102, 103, 105, 118, 119, 120, 122, 123, 125, 139, 148, 155, 156, 165
Islamic Bank of Development, 165
Islamism / Islamists, 11, 45, 50, 63, 81, 86, 88, 99, 101, 103, 109, 116, 117, 121, 122–123, 124, 125, 126, 132, 134, 138, 151, 155, 156, 157, 171
Ismailov, Madel, 56
Israel, 9, 76, 81, 82, 105, 111, 115, 123, 124–127, 132, 133, 158
Italy, 145–146
Itera, 158, 159
Itochu, 146, 147

Jadidism, 11
Japan, 4, 9, 6, 36, 37, 118, 131, 146–148, 163
Japan National Oil Corporation, 147
Japan Petroleum Exploitation Co., 147
Javadov, Rovshan, 62
Javakhk / Javakheti, 105, 112, 153
Jews, 48
Jucker, Vittorio, 142

Kabardino-Balkaria, 152, 155
Kabul, 87, 100
Kalmykia, 20, 165, 166
Kalyuzhny, Viktor, 76, 79, 88
Kara–Bogaz–Gol Bay, 26
Karachaevo–Cherkessia, 152
Karasik, Theodore W., 63
Karimov, Islam, 102, 103, 106, 109, 133
Kazakhs, 11, 12, 51, 52, 53, 56, 79, 84, 85, 86, 91, 117, 127, 133
Kazakhstan, 3, 9, 16, 17, 18, 33, 34, 35, 36, 43, 51, 72, 76, 94, 102, 103, 112, 120, 122, 126, 127, 128, 130, 148, 154, 156, 157, 163, 164, 168; and Caspian environmental issues, 24, 25, 26, 27; economic system, 57–59; energy sector, 29, 30, 31, 32, 33, 59–60; foreign policy determinants, 74–75; Hordes / clans, 56–57; Kazakhization policy,

INDEX

53, 84; political system, 51–55;
position on Caspian legal status, 20,
21, 22, 23, 80, 84, 85, 91, 92;
relations with Azerbaijan, 90–91;
China, 116–118; European
countries, 141–146; Iran, 79–80;
Japan, 146–147; Russia, 83–86;
Turkmenistan, 91–92; United States,
132–137; Russian / Slavic
minorities, 52, 53, 54, 56, 84, 85
Kazakoil, 59
Kazan, 10
Kazhegeldin, Akezhan, 54, 56, 59
Kechichian, Joseph A., 63
Kelbajar, 61
KGB, 45, 55, 65
Khamenei, Ali, 49, 51, 83, 139
Khatami, Muhammad, 49, 50, 51, 80, 154, 169
Khiva, 11, 12
Khojaly, 61
Khoja-Mukhamedov, Durdymurat, 70
Khomeini, Ruhallah, 15, 48, 49, 77
Khorasan, 13, 166
Khrushchev, Nikita S., 13, 54, 150
King Fahd, 122
Kipling, Rudyard, 10
Kiriyenko, Sergei, 46
Kissinger, Henry, 137
Kjellen, Rudolf, 5
Kocharian, Robert, 126
Komura, Masahiko, 147
Kozeny, Viktor, 158, 159
Kozyrev, Andrei, 75, 78
Kuchma, Leonid, 130
Kultur Kampf, 7
Kunaev, Dinmukhamed, 56
Kura River, 24
Kurds, 14, 48, 77, 107, 111, 121, 139, 154, 170
Kuwait, 29, 34, 71, 107, 124, 169
Kyrgyzstan, 51, 79, 84, 102, 109, 117, 118, 133, 135, 136, 141, 156, 157

Lasmo, 143
Latvia, 136

Lebanon, 104, 159
Lezgins, 139, 151–152
Libya, 123, 127
Li Peng, 117
Lukarco, 31
Lukoil, 47, 48, 76, 94, 162, 164
Lurs, 48
Luzhkov, Yuri, 46

Macedonia, 128
Mackinder, Sir Halford, 5, 6, 11
mafia / mafiosi, 151, 156
Mahabad Republic, 14
Mahan, Admiral Alfred Thayer, 5
Maiman, Yossi, 126, 158
Makarov, Igor, 158, 159
Makhachkala, 36
Malaysia, 148–149
Mamedov, Etibar, 63, 64
Mangyshlak, 26, 92
Mangistau, 144, 148, 166
Mannesmann, 145
Marneuli, 112, 153
Marubeni, 147
Masanov, Nurbulat, 57
Maskhadov, Aslan, 151
Mazanderan, 13, 166
Mazar-i-Sharif, 101
McDermott, 146
Meghri, 107
Mercator Corp, 158
Meskhetian Turks / Meskhetians, 13, 153
Mihranian, Andranik, 78
Mingrelians, 112, 153
Mitchell, George, 159
Mitsubishi, 103, 147
Mitterrand, François, 161
Mnatsakanian, Ruben, 25
Moldova, 113, 141, 159
Mongolia, 53
Monument Oil and Gas, 143
Morningstar, Richard, 137
Moscow, 13, 46, 62, 68, 70, 79, 86, 88, 89, 93, 110, 111, 113, 133, 151, 154, 164, 165

INDEX

Muehlemann, Ernst, 142
Muhammad Reza Shah Pahlavi, 14, 15, 50
Mullah Omar, 101
Musaddiq, Muhammad, 15
Musavat party, 60, 63, 64, 65
Musavat regime, 12
Mutalibov, Ayaz, 61
Musharraf, General Parvez, 101, 119, 120

Nagorno-Karabakh conflict, 60, 61, 64, 65, 66, 67, 74, 82, 89, 90, 104, 106, 107, 119, 120, 125, 127, 128, 134, 138, 139, 141, 142, 143, 144, 145, 146, 154, 164, 170
Nakhichevan, 61, 62, 63, 83, 106, 166
National Iranian Oil Company (NIOC), 50
NATO, 6, 82, 90, 107, 118, 129, 134, 137, 139, 140, 142
Nazarbayev, Nursultan, 52–59, 72, 80, 84, 85, 90, 91, 92, 102, 103, 127, 132, 143, 144, 154, 158
Neka, 39, 116
neoliberalism, 7, 131, 171
neorealism, 5, 6–7, 79, 102, 171
Netanyahu, Binyamin, 125, 126
Niyazov, Saparmurad (Turkmenbashi), 67–73, 80, 81, 86, 87, 88, 91, 92, 93, 94, 100, 101, 102, 103, 106, 111, 119, 126, 136, 158
Nobel brothers, 16, 157
non-state actors, 9, 150; criminal gangs, 9, 156–157; ethnonationalists, 9, 117, 150–155; international organizations, 9, 164–165; maverick entrepreneurs, 9, 157–160; multinational companies (MNCs), 7, 8, 160–164
non-governmental organizations (NGOs), 9, 165–166; religious activists, 9, 45, 155–156; state interests vs. company interests, 28, 126
North Apsheron Operating Company (NAOC), 31

North Caucasian confederation, 11
North Sea, 28, 34, 160, 169
Norway, 146
Novorossiisk, 34, 35, 36, 37, 86, 110, 128, 137, 144, 151, 158
Novy-Uzen riots, 90
Nurmyradov, Shiraly, 70

Ocalan, Abdullah, 154
Odessa, 130
Offshore Kazakhstan International Operating Company (OKIOC), 29–30, 59, 144, 146, 147
Oguz Turks, 92
oil and gas fields; Ashrafi, 31, 146; Azeri (former 26 Baku Commissars), 31, 93; Burun, 143; Cheleken, 17, 124; Chirag (former Kaverochkin), 93; Dan Ulduzu, 31, 146; Dossor, 16; Karabakh, 31; Karachaganak, 85, 145; Kashagan, 31, 34, 39, 80, 158; Kenkayak, 116; Kurdashi, 31, 146; Kyapaz / Serdar (former October Revolution), 88, 94; Makat, 16; Neft Dashlary (Neftyaniye Kamni), 17; Severny, 31; Shah Deniz (former Shakhovo More), 31, 32; Tasbulat, 129; Tengiz, 30, 34, 36, 85, 158; Uzen, 116; Yalama, 31; Zhanazhol, 116
Oil and Gas Journal, 32, 162
Oil and Gas producing regions, Aktyubinsk, 31, 116; Emba, 17; Ferghana valley, 17, 156; Grozny, 16, 37; Kuban, 16; Mangistau, 144, 148; Telavi, 16; Terek, 16, 19; Urals–Volga, 17
Oman, 123, 124, 158
Omarova, Saule, 34
Open Society Institute, 165
Ordubad, 63
Orenburg, 86
Organization of the Islamic Conference (OIC), 125
Organization for Security and Cooperation in Europe (OSCE), 37,

54, 55, 62, 91, 107, 137, 140, 144, 154, 157, 164
Organization of Petroleum Exporting Countries (OPEC), 50, 82, 168
Oryx Energy, 31
Ossetia (North), 152; Prigorodny Raion, 152
Ossetia (South), 112, 113, 114, 139, 141, 152, 164, 170
Ottoman Empire, 10, 11, 12, 14, 108, 109
Overseas Private Investment Corporation (OPIC), 136, 159

Pakistan, 9, 36, 38, 78, 81, 99, 100, 101, 115, 118–120, 121, 132, 155, 156
Palestine, 123, 125
Pan-Islamism, 11
Pan-Turkism, 11, 12, 56, 63, 65, 108, 109, 117
parameters of competitiveness, 167–171; global demand, 168; Gulf states policies, 169; magnitude of reserves, 167–168; new discoveries, 169; political risk, 170–171; productions costs, 168; transport issues, 168
Pavlodar, 59
Pax Americana, 138
Peña, Federico, 135, 136
Peres, Shimon, 126
perestroika, 43, 70
Persia / Persian Empire, 10, 13, 14, 20, 108; and the Caspian region, 30, 32, 67, 76, 110, 115, 118, 124, 131, 135, 137, 138, 142, 146, 154, 157, 163, 164, 169, 171, 173
Persian Gulf, 28, 29, 30, 35, 36, 39, 71, 76, 78, 124, 168, 169, 172
Peter the Great, 10
Petronas, 148, 149
Phillips Petroleum, 34, 147
Pierret, Christian, 144
Pipelines, 28, 34–39; Baku–Ceyhan, 31, 37, 78, 91, 106, 109, 110, 111, 113, 124, 125, 128, 136, 137, 139, 142, 143, 144, 153, 154, 159, 160, 161, 162, 170, 172; Baku–Novorossiisk, 36, 37, 89, 90, 137, 151; Baku–Supsa, 34, 37, 130, 142, 153; Blue Stream, 111, 113, 139, 146; Burgas–Alexandroupolis, 128, 162; Tengiz–Novorossiisk, 34, 36, 85, 86; trans–Afghan, 29, 38, 81, 100, 101, 119, 121, 123, 124, 147; trans–Asian, 36, 37, 38, 103, 116, 147; trans–Caspian (or sub–Caspian), 35, 38, 78, 81, 91, 92, 94, 111, 137, 139, 158; trans–Iranian, 38–39, 78, 80, 81, 82, 136
PKK (Kurdistan Workers' Party), 154
Poland, 130
political risk analysis, 4, 137, 170–71
Poti, 142
Powell, Colin, vi
Pratt, Martin, 21
Primakov, Yevgeny, 46
Production Sharing Agreements (PSA), 67, 146, 148, 162
provincial entities, 9, 165
Putin, Vladimir, 45, 46, 48, 53, 76, 86, 87, 90, 103, 138, 139, 156, 163

Qajar dynasty, 14
Qatar, 51, 124, 169

Rafsanjani, Ali Akbar, 49
Ramco Energy Plc., 143, 160
Ratzel, Friedrich, 5
Remp, Stephen, 158, 160
Reza Shah Pahlavi, 14, 48
Rice, Condoleezza, vi
Richardson, Bill, 136
riparian states: interstate relations, 77–95; foreign policy determinants, 74–77; Azerbaijan and Iran, 82–83; Azerbaijan and Kazakhstan, 90–91; Azerbaijan and Russia, 88–90; Azerbaijan and Turkmenistan, 92–95; Iran and Kazakhstan, 79–82; Iran and Russia, 77–79; Iran and Turkmenistan, 80–82; Kazakhstan

and Russia, 83–86; Kazakhstan and Turkmenistan, 91–92; Russia and Turkmenistan, 86–88
riparian states: politics and interests, 43–73; Azerbaijan, 60–67; Kazakhstan, 51–60; Iran, 48–51; Russia, 43–48; Turkmenistan, 67–73
Roberts, John, 33, 38
Romania, 9, 35, 128–129, 141, 142
Rosneft, 47, 94
Rothschilds, 16
Royal Dutch Shell, 164
Russia / Russian Federation, vi, 3, 4, 5, 6, 9, 10–13, 14, 15, 16, 17, 28, 34, 35, 36, 43, 51, 52, 53, 59, 62, 71, 74, 81, 82, 91, 92, 93, 94, 100, 101, 122, 123, 127, 128, 152, 153, 154, 155, 156, 157, 158, 161, 162, 164, 165, 168, 171, 172; and Caspian environmental issues, 25, 26, 27; Communist Party, 44–45, 46; Duma, 44, 45, 46; energy sector, 30, 31, 47–48; ethnic conflicts in, 150–152; foreign policy determinants, 75–76; political and economic system, 44–47; position on Caspian legal status, 20, 21, 22, 23, 76, 79, 82, 83, 84, 85, 88, 89, 90; relations with Armenia, 104–107; Azerbaijan, 88–90; China, 115, 118; European countries, 141–146; Georgia, 113–114; India, 121; Iran, 77–79; Kazakhstan, 83–86; Turkey, 108–112; Turkmenistan, 86–88; Ukraine, 129–30; United States, 131–139; Uzbekistan, 102–103
Russian Empire 10–11, 13–14, 20; and the Caspian region, 10–11, 13–14, 17, 18, 20, 30, 32, 67, 76, 110, 115, 118, 124, 131, 135, 137, 138, 142, 146, 154, 157, 163, 164, 169, 171, 173
Russian Revolution, 11, 14, 17, 20

Sagers, Matthew, 29
Samtskhe-Javakhetia (Meskhet-Javakhetia), 105, 112, 153

Saratov, 86
Sarid, Yossi, 126
Sari-Shaghan Radar Site, 83
Saudi / Saudis, 38, 49, 99, 115, 121, 122, 123, 124, 155, 168, 169, 172
Saudi Arabia, 9, 34, 49, 115, 121–124, 155, 168, 169, 172
Schofield, Clive, 21
Schroeder, Gerhard, 145
Second World War, 6, 13, 14, 146
Shanghai Five, 118
Shevardnadze, Eduard, 105, 113, 114, 126, 132, 136, 145
Shi'ite / Shi'tes, 10, 11, 48, 49, 60, 82, 101, 108, 122, 156
Shimkent, 59
Shusha / Shushi, 61
Sidanco, 47
Siemens, 145
Silk Road, 112, 125, 129, 141, 147
Silk Road Strategy Act, 125
SNP Petrom, 129
South Korea, 36, 37, 148
Soviet Union, 3, 4, 6, 12, 13, 14, 19, 20, 21, 22, 28, 43, 44, 46, 51, 52, 55, 56, 57, 58, 59, 60, 61, 63, 64, 65, 66, 67, 68, 69, 70, 71, 72, 75, 76, 77, 78, 79, 104, 107, 112, 116, 118, 120, 126, 133, 156, 158; and Caspian environmental issues, 24, 25; Caspian legal status, 19, 20, 21, 22; oil production, 17–18, 29
Soviet South (Caucasus / Central Asia), 78, 99, 107, 108, 111, 116, 119, 121, 122, 123, 125, 132, 135, 140, 143, 148, 155
Spykman, Nicholas, 6
Stalin, Josef Vissarionovich, 13, 56, 61, 104, 145, 148, 150, 152, 153
State Oil Corporation of the Azerbaijan Republic (SOCAR), 31, 62, 67, 94, 106, 159
Statoil, 146
Stoyanov, Peter, 128
Sufi movements, 11, 155
Suleimanov, Nizami, 64

INDEX

Sultan Qabus, 158
Sultanov, Utkur, 136
Sumgait, 25, 26, 61; pogroms of Armenians in, 61
Sunni / Sunnites, 10, 11, 51, 101, 103, 121, 122, 156
Sununu, John, 135
Supsa, 37, 130, 147, 153
Surgutneftegas, 47
Switzerland, 59
Syria, 104, 126

Tabriz, 83
Tajikistan / Tajiks, 75, 77, 84, 99, 102, 117, 118, 141, 156, 157
Talbott, Strobe, 30, 133, 134, 135
Taliban, 38, 76, 78, 81, 87, 99, 100, 101, 103, 119, 121, 122, 134, 139, 156
Talysh, 62, 63
Talysh-Mughan Republic, 62
Tamraz, Roger, 158, 159, 160
Tashkent, 99, 103, 109, 120, 157
Tatars (present-day Azeris), 16
Tatarstan, 44
Tbilisi, 126
Tehran, 13, 39, 78, 80, 82, 83, 103, 116, 119, 125, 139
Terek river, 16, 19
Texaco, 164
Tikhoretsk, 37
Totalfina, 144, 164
Tractebel, 146
Trade Development Agency (TDA), 136
Transcaucasia, 10, 12, 75, 78, 88, 92, 125, 132
Transcaucasus, 107, 108, 145, 151
Transneft, 48, 90
Treaty of Gulistan (1813), 20
Treaty of Rasht (1729), 20
Treaty of Turkmenchai (1828), 20
Trieste, 129
Tudeh party, 15
Turkestan, 11, 99, 116
Turkey, 6, 9, 12, 35, 37, 38, 65, 66, 76, 78, 81, 82, 88, 89, 90, 94, 99, 103, 104, 105, 106, 107–112, 113, 117, 118, 121, 125, 126, 127, 128, 141, 142, 143, 145, 146, 147, 153, 154, 157, 161, 162, 170; and United States, 132–139
Turkic peoples, 11, 64, 92, 107, 119
Turkmenbashi (former Krasnovodsk), 26, 69, 91, 92, 126, 145, 147, 158
Turkmengaz, 72
Turkmenistan, 3, 9, 17, 18, 33, 35, 36, 37, 38, 39, 43, 51, 59, 74, 77, 100, 101, 112, 123, 126, 154, 156, 157, 158, 159, 162, 163, 168; and Caspian environmental issues, 26, 27; economic system, 71–72; energy sector, 29, 30, 32, 33, 72–73; foreign policy determinants, 74; political system, 67–71; and position on Caspian legal status, 20, 21, 23, 81, 88, 92, 93–94, 95; relations with Armenia, 106–107; Azerbaijan, 92–94; East Asian states, 148–149; with European countries, 141–145; Iran, 80–82, 107; Japan, 146–147; Kazakhstan, 91–92; Russia, 86–88; relations with United States, 133–137; relations with Uzbekistan, 102–103; tribes, 71
Turkmenneft, 72
Turkmenneftegaz, 72
Turkmenneftegazstroi, 72
Turkmenrosgaz, 87
Turkmens, 12, 48, 69, 70, 71, 72, 87, 88, 92, 94, 99, 147
Tyumenoil, 48

Ukraine, 35, 44, 87, 106, 113, 115, 129–130, 132, 141, 142, 159
United Arab Emirates, 124, 169
United Nations, 86, 93, 157, 164
United States, 3, 4, 5, 9, 14, 15, 27, 59, 64, 67, 70, 76, 78, 79, 81, 82, 89, 90, 94, 99, 100, 111, 118, 122, 127, 131–139, 142, 143, 144, 148, 149, 154, 171, 172; and Caspian policy, vi, 36, 37, 38, 49, 50, 74, 75, 76, 78, 82, 83, 90, 102, 104, 106, 107, 108,

109, 111–112, 113, 116, 124, 125, 127, 128, 129, 130, 144, 162, 163, 171, 172, 173; national interests in Caspian region, 43, 77, 94, 115, 139, 148, 158, 161, 173
Unocal, 38, 101
Ural River, 19, 24
USSR, 6, 15, 19, 43, 77
Ust-Kamenogorsk, 85
Uyghurs, 116, 117
Uzbeks, 81, 92, 99, 100, 101, 102, 103, 109, 116, 120, 133, 134, 136, 154
Uzbekistan, 9, 17, 18, 51, 59, 74, 75, 77, 80, 84, 92, 99, 100, 101–103, 109, 113, 117, 120, 129, 133, 135, 136, 141, 144, 146, 147, 148, 155, 156, 157, 168
energy reserves, 29, 30, 32, 33

vali-e faqih, 48
Venezuela, 34
Vienna Convention on Succession of States, 21
Vinogradov, Sergei, 21
Volga-Baltic canal, 23
Volga-Don canal, 23
Volga River, 10, 19, 22, 23, 24, 25, 26

Wahhabis (Muwahhidun), 122, 155, 156
Welfare Party (Refah), 109
Western influences, 28, 51, 65, 67, 75, 107, 110, 112, 118, 125, 131, 137, 163, 171, 172, 173; east–west strategy, 171; economic interests, 5, 29, 67, 88, 118, 119, 129, 141, 142, 145, 161, 171
White Sea, 21
Wood Mackenzie, 30, 32, 33
World Bank, 164
Wouters, Patricia, 21

Xinjiang (Eastern Turkestan), 116, 117

Yamani, Ahmad Zaki al-, 124
Yandarbiev, Zelimkhan, 101
Yavlinsky, Gregory, 46
Yellow Sea, 37
Yeltsin, Boris, 44, 45, 46, 76, 78, 86, 94, 114, 132, 138, 160
Yerazeris (Yerevan Azeris), 63
Yerevan, 63
Yukos, 47, 76
Yumurtalik, 35, 110

Zhirinovsky, Vladimir, 46, 133
Zionists, 126
Zoroastrians, 10, 48
Zyuganov, Gennady, 45, 46